# THE
# CAVALRY
# MAIDEN

"Cornet Aleksandrov," Nadezhda Andreevna Durova, in the uniform of the Mariupol' Hussars. From oil portrait, c. 1810.

# Nadezhda Durova

# THE

# CAVALRY

# MAIDEN

Journals of a Russian Officer
in the Napoleonic Wars

Translation, Introduction, and Notes by
Mary Fleming Zirin

INDIANA UNIVERSITY PRESS
BLOOMINGTON AND INDIANAPOLIS

First Midland Book edition 1989

This book was brought to publication with the assistance of a grant from the Andrew W. Mellon Foundation to the Russian and East European Institute, Indiana University, and the Center for Russian and East European Studies, University of Michigan.

Manufactured in the United States of America

**Library of Congress Cataloging-in-Publication Data**

Durova, N. A. (Nadezhda Andreevna), 1783–1866.
The cavalry maiden.

(Indiana–Michigan series in Russian and
East European studies)
Translation of: Zapiski kavalerist-devitsy.
Bibliography: p.
Includes index.
1. Durova, N.A. (Nadezhda Andreevna), 1783–1866.
2. Russia. Armiia. Kavaleriia—Biography.   3. Soldiers
—Soviet Union—Biography.   4. Napoleonic Wars, 1800–
1814—Personal narratives, Russian.   5. Authors,
Russian—Biography. I. Zirin, Mary Fleming. II. Title.
DK190.6D8A3   1988      940.2′7      87-45395
ISBN 0-253-31372-4 cl.
ISBN 0-253-20549-2 pbk.
3  4  5  6  7  98  97  96  95  94

# CONTENTS

# Nadezhda Durova, Russia's "Cavalry Maiden"

In 1806 Russia's beloved young Emperor Alexander I was facing the greatest challenge of his five-year reign. The attempt of a combined Austro-Russian army to counter Napoleon's continental ambitions had ended in crushing defeat at Austerlitz in late 1805, and the Austrians signed a separate peace. Now France threatened Prussia, and Russia was arming once more to check Napoleon, this time near her own western borders.

In September of that year Nadezhda Durova (1783–1866), disguised as a boy, ran away from her home in the foothills of the Ural mountains and joined the Russian cavalry. That she could do so is not surprising: women throughout history have been swept up in war. Durova, however, is exceptional among them in her determination to escape what she later described as the "sphere prescribed by nature and custom to the female sex," in her dedication to the military vocation and, above all, in her gift to posterity of a lengthy account of the nine years of service during which she saw combat in the 1807 and 1812–1814 wars against Napoleon.

Durova embarked upon an equally remarkable, even briefer, literary career in the late 1830s. She published a series of autobiographical and fictional works drawn largely from the adventures and settings of the military years. Her dated fiction is still of interest to scholars of the late romantic period, but it is her edited journals, *The Cavalry Maiden* (1836), and to a lesser extent *The Notes of Aleksandrov (Durova)* (1839), that merit a secure place they have yet to win in Russian literature, the universal annals of women's experience, and the cultural history of the Russian Empire.[1]

For the present-day English-reading audience *The Cavalry Maiden,* one of the first autobiographical works of any kind to be published in Russia, is a "period piece" in the best sense of the phrase: an idiosyncratic portrait of the times as Durova witnessed them. With family and friends in mind as eventual audience, she kept sporadic journals, noting amusing and significant anecdotes and recording her adventures and reactions to events that ranged from earthshaking (the French invasion of Russia in June 1812) to trivial (a visit to a Jesuit monastery; a major's courtship).

Her pages reflect the fervor, idealism, and disillusion that swept Russia during the Napoleonic era. Today *The Cavalry Maiden* stands also as a unique record of the outlook and emotions of one of the rare Russian women of her time who managed to create an autonomous life outside the patriarchal confines of home and family.

*The Cavalry Maiden* consists of an introductory memoir, "My Child-hood Years" (1783–1801), and Durova's selection of excerpts from the journals of the military years (1806–1816). In this introduction I discuss some of the characteristics of *The Cavalry Maiden*, what we know or can guess about the text, the missing years of Durova's life (1799–1806), her other published writings, her long life in retirement, and the vicissitudes of her posthumous reputation. The introduction, annotation, appended documents, and bibliography will appeal variously to different readers. They are meant to supplement *The Cavalry Maiden* rather than supplant it, and some readers may prefer to skip lightly over them and concentrate on Durova's own words.

## ALEXANDER PUSHKIN AND DUROVA'S LITERARY CAREER

It was Russia's revered poet Alexander Pushkin who, through seren-dipity, discovered the existence of *The Cavalry Maiden* and, in mid-1836, first published a long excerpt from it. In 1829 Pushkin had made the acquaintance of Durova's eccentric brother, Vasily, and offered him a ride in his carriage back to Moscow from the Caucasus, where Durov was "recuperating from some kind of surprising illness, a sort of catalepsy, and gambling from morning to night." Pushkin later recalled that Durov spent the journey discussing bizarre ways to secure the one hundred thousand rubles he considered indispensable to his future "peace of mind and prosperity."[2] This good deed bore unexpected fruit six years later, when Pushkin became the editor-publisher of his own magazine, *The Contemporary.* In 1835 Durov wrote to him and offered him his sister's military journals. Publication was delayed by mischance: the first man-uscript, which Durova sent by post (part 1 of *The Cavalry Maiden*, or chaps. 1–6 below), never reached Pushkin. It was eventually returned to her at home in Elabuga, and she carried it personally to him in Peterburg in May 1836.

Durova was well aware that the aplomb Pushkin displayed at their first meeting concealed amusement. In retirement years she kept to the man's clothing and masculine speech forms that marked her independence, and her amiable account shows that she was accustomed to reactions to her appearance varying from curiosity to consternation:

> He took my manuscript . . . and, after finishing his obliging speech, kissed my hand. I hastily snatched [*vykhvatila*, in which the -a marks

feminine gender] it away, blushed, and said, I don't in the least know why, "Oh, my God! I got out of that habit long ago!" [Ja tak davno otvyk (masculine consonantal ending) ot etogo!] Not even the shadow of an ironic smile appeared on Aleksandr Sergeevich's face, but I dare say that at home he did not restrain himself and, as he related the circumstances of our first meeting to his family, undoubtedly laughed wholeheartedly over this exclamation. (From *A Year of Life in Peterburg*, Durova's account of her disillusioning experiences of literary lionization in 1836–1837)[3]

Durova had offered Pushkin her manuscript as raw material for his pen, but he convinced her that it needed no revision from him and rushed into print Durova's account of the 1812 campaign from part 2 (chaps. 7–13), the first to reach him by post. "Charming! Vivid, original, beautiful style. Their success is undoubted," he wrote to her brother on March 27, 1836.[4] Pushkin had trouble persuading the distressed author to accept the use of her own name in the title ("Notes of N. A. Durova") when she would have preferred her longtime military pseudonym, "Aleksandr Andreevich Aleksandrov": "Be daring—step into your literary career as courageously as into that which made you famous."[5] Pushkin further offered to see the entire manuscript into print, but, burdened as he was with other affairs, he could not work fast enough to suit the impetuous Durova, and his friends persuaded her that to ask him to undertake the edition at all was an imposition he could ill afford. Tsarist censorship forbade any direct mention of the duel which cost Pushkin his life in January 1837, but the bitterness that Durova expresses against Peterburg society in *A Year of Life in Peterburg* undoubtedly reflects the tragedy that deprived Russia of its greatest poet and Durova of an enthusiastic sponsor.

Durova turned to her cousin, the writer and doctor Ivan Butovsky, to edit the two volumes of *The Cavalry Maiden*. He made no effort to help her sell the books when they came from the printer in late 1836, and her room in Peterburg remained stacked with copies until she managed to place them with booksellers. From the shops they filtered slowly into a literary community shocked by Pushkin's untimely death. This first selection from her journals, Durova's finest work, received only one condescending review, but as her further writings brought the "cavalry maiden" enthusiastic notices from Russian critics, *The Cavalry Maiden* sold out.

Durova afterward attributed her ensuing literary career to her need to compensate for Butovsky's feckless mishandling. From 1837 to 1840 Durova, hoping to profit from the popularity of *The Cavalry Maiden* and curiosity about its author, brought out a spate of "tales, describing now the legends, now the traditions [*pover'ja*], now one or another of the stories of the inhabitants of the area where I was quartered while I was still serving."[6] In 1839 she added one last volume of *Notes* gleaned from the military journals to the autobiographical corpus (*The Cavalry Maiden*, *Year*, "A Few Traits from Childhood Years," and several fictional tales that have authorial frame narration). Writing was not a viable profession in Russia in the 1830s. Even Pushkin struggled to make a living from his pen, and later in the century many hopeful authors still led the rough life of the dispossessed in Peterburg and Moscow garrets. In 1840 Durova abandoned literature as abruptly as she had the cavalry and returned to the obscurity of Elabuga. Her works, never reprinted, soon became bibliographic rarities.

## DUROVA AND THE RUSSIAN AUTOBIOGRAPHICAL TRADITION

Chronologically, the Russian tradition of autobiography stretches from the moving life story of the seventeenth-century Old Believer martyr, Archpriest Avvakum, to a flood of works reflecting the Soviet experience. By the mid-eighteenth century, members of the newly westernized Russian nobility had begun keeping diaries and writing reminiscences for their heirs. (Pushkin used the convention of the family memoir to frame his 1836 historical novel *The Captain's Daughter*: Petr Grinev records his youthful experiences during the Pugachev rebellion for the edification of his grandson.) We would expect and, indeed, we find that Russian women as well as men left personal records of the unmatched epoch during which four empresses, including Catherine the Great, occupied the throne for nearly seventy years. In the 1830s, however, this respectable collection of autobiographical literature was largely a mass of manuscripts moldering in family cupboards and government archives. Russia was still struggling to recover the broad outlines of her history, and individual experience had not yet become an established part of historiography. Few of these early memoirs saw print before the late nineteenth century, when the proliferation of popular historical magazines led descendants and scholars to ferret them out.

*The Cavalry Maiden* was the first major Russian autobiography to be published during the author's lifetime. Perhaps the fact that so many pages of the journals of this essentially private woman are devoted to depicting the life of "Aleksandrov," a somewhat distanced *male* persona, made it possible for her to consider publication at all. We may deplore Durova's failures of candor, but we have to respect her courage in deciding to share as much of her remarkable life as she did with a Russian public not yet used to seeing authors exposing their private experience to print.[7]

Two specialized offshoots of autobiography did begin to find their way into print in Russia by the early years of the nineteenth century: the subjective travel journal that was the Russian reflex of Laurence Sterne's

*Sentimental Journey* (discussed in the next section); and the military memoir. The approaching twenty-fifth anniversary of the War of 1812 gave impetus to the idea of recording the national epos, and the publication of other eyewitness accounts of the Napoleonic campaigns probably played a role in prompting Durova to dig out her scattered notes.[8] *The Cavalry Maiden* fits formally into the category of military memoir; Durova authenticates her unlikely story with the names of her commanders and fellow officers (many of them still alive in 1836), the dates and places of her service, and inimitable details of army life. Overall, however, *Maiden's* relationship to the genre is marked more by contrast than by influence; the diaries of a woman cavalry officer are by definition *sui generis*.

It was taken for granted that the cavalry was a desirable career for a man, but Durova had to justify her decision to infiltrate the bastion of male privilege. *The Cavalry Maiden* differs from male reminiscences in starting from a narrative of the childhood experiences that led Durova to take up her martial vocation. The authors of military reminiscences were for the most part noblemen of prominent families who moved easily in the rarefied atmosphere of Peterburg and elite guards regiments. Many of them could expect to reach high rank in the army. Although the unlikely realization of Durova's dream of a cavalry commission led her to hope for further miracles, realistically she could expect no future beyond duty in a line regiment. A good part of the charm and value of *The Cavalry Maiden* as military memoir lies in its depiction of the life of the junior officer; there are few military autobiographies in any literature so completely focused on the day-to-day life of the squadron and platoon. Durova served in regiments stationed far from Russia's two capitals. Much of her time was spent on the western borders in lands acquired when Russia, Austria, and Prussia dismembered Poland in the late eighteenth century. Two of her three regiments were Polish/Lithuanian, and there were Polish officers and soldiers in the third as well. *The Cavalry Maiden* appeared soon after the Polish rebellion of 1830–1831, but Durova expresses a great affection for Poland and her peoples—tinged, however, with that unwitting sense of superiority to other nationalities within the state that marks Russian attitudes even today. Her comments on the mores of the border regions offer a rare glimpse of everyday life in Polish territory during the first years of Russian rule. Her account echoes Adam Mickiewicz's depiction of the Lithuania of 1811 in *Pan Tadeusz*, as an epoch when Poles could still feel that:

> . . . if at times we saw a Russian helm,
> The Muscovite left but a memory warm
> Behind him of a glittering uniform—
> We knew the serpent only by his skin.[9]

The military men usually wrote retrospectively, reviewing strategy and battlefield movements with the confidence born of education in elite academies. The untutored Durova records only her immediate impressions and limits herself to bewildered comments about tactics which seem odd to her. The men tend to treat peace mainly as preparation for campaigns to come. Durova covers her experiences in the Napoleonic wars of 1807 and 1812–1814 lightly; approximately two-thirds of the pages of The Cavalry Maiden are devoted to the routine of peacetime service, and, of the wartime chapters, only chapters 2 and 8 describe actual combat. Durova deals extensively with the life that Tolstoy described as the state of prelapsarian "obligatory and blameless idleness which has been and will continue to be the main attraction of military service."[10] Those idle days are not dwelt on because they gave Durova more leisure to write her journal; they also afforded her the minor "adventures" that could best test her adaptation to masculine liberties. As the hussar poet Denis Davydov remarked, there was no time on the battlefield to worry about niceties like gender (see Appendix B). Durova seeks her adventures in quieter times and in the freedoms denied her sex: roaming where she pleases, exploring the communities where she is quartered, and meeting the wide world alone and on her own terms.

Military memoirists generally concentrated on the public experience and left the expression of private emotion to Davydov and his followers. The poems in which Davydov defined the light cavalry ethos were known, quoted, and taken as a model by his fellow officers throughout the first decades of the nineteenth century.[11] Durova shares her feelings about her new life with lyric verve, uninhibitedly, and at times clumsily. She speculates on her fearlessness almost as a phenomenon independent of her volition. The closest cognate portrayal of army life viewed by an outsider comes a century later in Isaak Babel's Red Cavalry cycle, masterfully honed sketches of the experiences of a bespectacled Jewish propaganda officer among rough Cossacks during the Soviet Civil War.

## DUROVA'S LITERARY ANTECEDENTS

In the first quarter of the nineteenth century Russian writers were still eagerly absorbing foreign models in the search for a national literary identity. Durova's works display a mixed set of values stemming from voracious reading of whatever texts came to hand in Russian or French. She refers often to figures from classic mythology and expects her readers to grasp the passing allusion. She quotes Racine and La Fontaine's fables and mentions Voltaire and Corneille. Her fiction shows that she had absorbed the works of Mrs. Radcliffe and other Gothic novelists in translation. She knew late eighteenth-century Russian poetry and drama. References to Polish and Lithuanian history and literature inform her accounts of life in Russia's newly acquired western borderlands; Conrad

Wallenrod, Queen Bona Sforza, and the legendary King Popel are all mentioned in her pages.

In the *Notes* Durova tells how embarrassed she was by a proposal that she read aloud to a lady landowner a racy passage from Sterne's *Sentimental Journey* (in French or the 1793 Russian translation). She undoubtedly knew the *Letters of a Russian Traveller* (1801) by the "Russian Sterne" Nikolaj Karamzin. The influence of Sterne in military circles is attested by Fedor Glinka's *Letters of a Russian Officer* (1808, 1815–1816). Durova's journals are closer in spirit than Glinka's letters to Pastor Yorick's humorous, somewhat deprecating self-analysis. Whereas Russian male Sterneans tended to look for the socially or politically significant in their travels, the influence of Sterne on *The Cavalry Maiden* is most evident in Durova's descriptions of her rambles on foot, usually alone and often by night, which are emblematic of the broader freedoms she gained in the military life.[12]

Durova's profound religious sense appears to stem as much from the deism of the Enlightenment as from Orthodox Christianity. Her belief in the rational is at the heart of her courage and enables her to face and overcome unknown terrors. She expresses her sense of the godhead in figures ranging from the personal, protective deity invoked by her grandmother to a more generalized sense of a nature that set her potentialities and a providence that guides her destiny. Durova occasionally pays homage to contemporary civic ideals of duty to the state and filial loyalty both to her own father and to Russia's "little father," the tsar. She addresses these ideals in the exaggerated rhetoric of neoclassicism, as if to emphasize that she has not only taken on masculine status, but is determined to exemplify patriarchal values writ large.

Although Durova's rhetoric, literary terms of reference, and philosophical outlook stem largely from classic and sentimental models, her thirsting spirit responds directly to the nascent romanticism that was to peak in Russia in the 1830s. She catches the spirit of Davydov's hussar lyrics in their glorification of cavalry dash and splendor, while necessarily remaining only a spectator of the warriors' exploits in salons, bedrooms, and taverns, which were the other facet of the life sung by Davydov. Much of *The Cavalry Maiden* would be mere literary cliché, if it were not for Durova's feisty, original voice which transcends eclectic elements. One critic, in a review of the 1839 *Notes*, resorted to the words "free rein," "sweep," "expansiveness" [*razgul, razmakh, razdol'e*] to characterize the tone of her journals.[13]

## DUROVA AND THE LIFE OF HER SEX

Durova's attitudes toward the female sex and her own sexuality can be read in and between the lines of *The Cavalry Maiden*. She saw women as a primary audience and urged Pushkin to buy her notes because: "Your beautiful pen can make of them something quite absorbing for our female compatriots [sootechestvenits]. [14] Her introductory memoir, "My Childhood Years," makes it clear that her rebellion was not against her sex *per se*, but against the restrictions that hemmed in women and limited their possibilities.

The Russia of Durova's time was a divinely ordained autocracy in which everyone's situation was rigidly defined. Men were bound by their duty to God and the tsar He had set to rule over them; women were subordinated to men. Noblewomen, unlike their peers in West Europe, were entitled to own and dispose of property, but the right was meaningless in a society where they were bound legally to their father's tutelage and, if they married, to a husband chosen or approved by him. They could not live or travel separately without the male guardian's sanction. Divorce was limited and frowned on by church and society; widowhood or retreat to a situation as patron in a nunnery offered women of property the best chance to exercise at least some degree of personal autonomy. Despite the brilliant example set by Catherine the Great and her immediate circle in the latter half of the eighteenth century, the only respectable career open to women was teaching in the rigidly supervised setting of one of the rare girls' boarding schools. Ladies in Peterburg or Moscow might dabble in literature (primarily translation or poetry), music, art, or amateur theatricals and circulate freely in educated society, but in the more conservative provinces even these innocent activities were suspect. Girls in Russia as elsewhere could flourish in loving and stable families, but there must have been many who, like Durova, chafed under parental caprice and social restriction. [15]

The confines of Durova's family home in Sarapul could not contain her restless energy and self-reliant spirit. She was driven to seek freedom outside it, but it is clear from *The Cavalry Maiden* that she continued to identify with her own sex. Durova differs from male military writers yet again in noticing and sketching women of various classes and nationalities. Her attitudes toward their lives hint at a buried ambivalence: they range from broad tolerance and affection for more conventional members of her sex to suppressed hostility and support for the patriarchal mores she defied as a woman and subscribed to as an honorary male. Durova avoids suggesting that her rebellion should be considered in any way exemplary, but the mere fact that she portrays her adaptation to a military career with such joy speaks for itself. *The Cavalry Maiden* emphasizes the benefits of her decision, the autonomy she gained, rather than the emotional dislocation she must have suffered in adopting a transsexual disguise.

As we have seen, to publish writings about the self was still a novelty in Russia of the 1830s. Durova could not have discussed her sexuality more openly than she does in "My Childhood Years," but she makes it clear that the option of marrying her first admirer was foreclosed for her and not by her own wish. (For what we can guess about Durova's brief unhappy marriage, see " 'Truth' and Fiction . . ." below.) When she ran away to the cavalry, Durova was acting on her father's repeated insistence that she had the qualities of a "good son"; from January 1808, she was constrained by the tsar's mandate to serve as a *chevalier pur et sans reproche* (chap. 3). She played the traditional role of the woman—in particular, the nun and the amazon of legend and history—who sacrifices her sexuality in order to attain honorary male status. From our modern perspective, this renunciation seems nearly tragic, but the gallantry and good faith with which Durova kept her draconian bargain are admirable.

Few women have left us written records of rebellion against the patriarchy. *The Cavalry Maiden* speaks for those who, throughout the world and throughout history, have chosen or been forced into a life of action beyond the limits of the stereotyped figures of "wife, mother, mistress, muse." Marina Warner's description of Joan of Arc's historical significance applies equally well to Durova:

> Joan of Arc . . . is anomalous in our culture, a woman renowned for doing something on her own, not by birthright. She has extended the taxonomy of female types; she makes evident the dimension of women's dynamism. It is urgent that this taxonomy be expanded further and that the multifarious duties that women have historically undertaken be recognized, researched and named.[16]

One finds legends, rumors, and substantiated instances of female warriors throughout the ages. The Russians took particular pride in the Amazons whose legendary homeland was the south Russian steppes. A few of the Russian epic songs [*byliny*] featured distant echoes of the Amazons, fierce maidens who, after challenging their men in single combat, became meek and dutiful wives.[17] The legend of the *"divci valka"* [the maidens' war] has been preserved in Czech folklore. Camilla, the virgin warrior of the *Aeneid,* and the tale of Zenobia, Queen of Palmyra, testify to the Romans' fascination with women who took up arms. Maxime Hong Kingston's expressionistic portrait of Fa Mu Lan in *Woman Warrior* (Vintage, 1977), extends the taxonomy to the Orient. Historical women soldiers were for the most part unlettered and, until the twentieth century, their stories were preserved only in scattered eyewitness reports and a few oral memoirs.[18] Joan of Arc was urged by her "voices" to save France. Durova was apparently not prepared to go so far as actually to kill (chap. 7), but her journals show a rare sense of vocation for the profession of arms. She is, moreover, already our contemporary, a product of the romantic epoch, and her rebellion against women's fate is more readily comprehensible than Joan's mystic call.

## *The Cavalry Maiden:* THE TEXT

Faced with this vital hybrid, critics worried uneasily whether Alexander Pushkin might not have played a more substantial role in the appearance of *The Cavalry Maiden* than that to which he admitted. After all, Pushkin's *Tales of Belkin* (1830) featured as putative author a domestically educated, retired military officer from the provincial nobility who patterned his tales on the popular genres of the time. Vissarion Belinskij speculated that Durova herself might be another such product of Pushkin's pen:

> If this is mystification, then we admit that it is a masterful one; if these are genuine journal notes, they are diverting and absorbing to an unbelievable degree. It is only strange that in 1812 one could write in such good language, and who besides? A woman. But perhaps they have been recently corrected by the author.[19]

During Durova's years in the cavalry she covered "a great number of sheets of paper with writing" and carried them about in her valise.[20] By 1835, mired in the boredom of retirement, and perhaps egged on by her eccentric brother to put her unique experience to some monetary profit, Durova records that

> I took a notion to look over and read the various fragments of my *Notes* which had survived my not always quiet life. This occupation, which revived my past in my memory and soul, gave me the idea of collecting these fragments, assembling them into some sort of whole, and publishing them.[21]

The degree to which Durova revised *The Cavalry Maiden* in the 1830s will probably never be known for sure. The manuscripts were scattered and lost; her one servant in Elabuga evidently gave them away to his friends, much as Belkin's housekeeper used his writings "for various domestic needs." However, some educated guesses are possible about the degree to which Durova rewrote and revised the journals for publication.

Some of Durova's anecdotes show signs of polishing and artistic conflation of events, and much of the dialogue bears the stamp of literary reconstruction. She obviously edited her journals with the slapdash haste and enthusiasm that marked her approach to life in general. Were there really two commission-agents with the initial P. who told anecdotes of the "Amazon"? Durova may be exercising poetic license when she portrays herself as jotting down notes on horseback during fatiguing marches, but the passages carry the force of immediate experience. A few anachronisms have crept in of the sort that come naturally to a text assembled from loose pages after a lapse of twenty years.[22] Overall, however, Durova's language and general culture are consistent with those of the first decade of the nineteenth century and reinforce her insistence that *The Cavalry Maiden* and *Notes* were drawn directly from the journals of her cavalry years. For example, it is only in *A Year of Life in Peterburg*— Durova's one work set (and thus entirely written) in the late 1830s—that we find references to works published after 1810 (i.e., Sir Walter Scott's *The Heart of Midlothian* [1818]).

*The Cavalry Maiden* was Durova's first cut at selecting materials from her journals and organizing them into a coherent whole. It combines the retrospective quality of the autobiography and the immediacy of the diary. She chose passages that give *The Cavalry Maiden* a novelesque quality in its depiction of her adaptation over time to her new role and her development from fiery young warrior intoxicated with her freedoms to bored veteran mired (literally) in backwoods Poland and Russia. In Durova's selection, the text abounds in ironies, both intentional (an amused account of her change in attitude toward the wagon-train between 1807 and 1812, chap. 8) and inadvertent (the deaths of her warhorse and a stray pup, chaps. 3 and 13). More pervasively, I am sure that Durova was aware of the tension she creates by relating her male persona's adventures from her own authentic female viewpoint. I am equally sure that she was unconscious of the disjunction between the lip service she pays to paternal authority and the near-maternal indulgence she shows for her weak, spoiled father's whims. The tight thematic organization of *The Cavalry Maiden* becomes more apparent when it is contrasted with the scrappy, unfocused 1839 *Notes*. In both works, Durova adapted some of her anecdotes to a point the twentieth-century, genre-conscious reader would label fiction, but the *Notes* have been more blatantly reworked. In the extended narrative "Love," for example, Durova describes in detail scenes from which she was absent, a liberty she did not take in the earlier selection. Originally I thought of combining materials from both journals, but I found no way to amalgamate the two texts without disrupting the integrity of *The Cavalry Maiden*.

## "Truth" and Fiction in "My Childhood Years"

Durova always insisted on the authenticity of her journals: "I assure you on my word of honor of the truth of everything I wrote, and I hope you will not believe all the gossip and condemnations made hit or miss by scandal-mongers."[23] There is one "truth," however, that Durova fails to tell, and this failure of candor badly mars our reading of the journals. In "My Childhood Years" Durova describes herself as running away from home at age sixteen. In reality, as the Russian *Military Encyclopedia* primly noted, "the sobriquet of 'cavalry-maiden' does not correspond to the truth."[24] In 1806 Nadezhda Durova was twenty-three years old. In

October 1801 she married, and she gave birth to a son in January 1803. It is tempting to see her tale "Elena, the Beauty of T." (described in the next section) as a partial reflection of horrors Durova herself experienced with a dissolute husband, but she never discussed the marriage and we have no way of knowing what actually happened. The legend was still alive in Sarapul late in the nineteenth century that she ran away to the cavalry to escape "family dissension" over a romance with a Cossack captain.[25] No evidence of such an affair has ever come to light. The one extant version of a comrade's boast that she left home for love of him is clearly an inept invention, and her own description of a day spent riding with this "lover" is detached and sardonic.[26] It is more likely that the dissension in the Durov family was over Nadezhda's anomalous position as a rebellious wife seeking refuge with her parents.

We do not know why Durova eliminated all mention of her marriage from "My Childhood Years," to the point of consistently lopping seven years off her own age, her mother's, and even that of her faithful steed Alcides. She had not deceived her protector. Alexander I knew that Durova was married: the official document by which he ordered the affair of the female soldier investigated describes her as "by marriage Chernova."[27] Nicholas I's Victorian censors could have compelled her to eliminate the passages; or self-censorship might have been at work—a conviction that the Russian reader would be too shocked by the confession of a runaway wife and mother to value the daring of her exploit. Whatever the case, the authenticity of *The Cavalry Maiden* is reinforced when Durova's real age and sexual experience are kept in mind: the poise with which she settles into her unique situation comes more believably from a woman in her twenties than from a sixteen-year-old girl.

## DUROVA'S FICTION

The fictional works that Durova published in a burst of literary activity from 1837 to 1840 belong chiefly to the "hyperromantic" school of Russian prose. Her novels and tales at their best are original in subject and move from romanticism toward a grim naturalism. Most of them have what the modern reader would consider an outlandish plot, and all suffer from the clumsiness of structure typical of much early Russian fiction by half-educated authors who learned their craft on the streets of the capitals or, like Durova, in provincial isolation.[28]

The officer led an existence that was externally a fiction, and the author chose to portray that life in works in which fact and invention mingle. *The Cavalry Maiden* and Durova's tale "Nurmeka" both carry the word "occurrence" [proisshestvie] in their subtitles to suggest their factual basis, and "Elena" is emphatically described as a "true [istinnoe] occurrence." In several stories Durova testifies to their origin in the experience of her military years by using a wandering female officer as frame narrator. Parts of three of her stories ("Count Mauritius," "The Pavilion," and "Elena") first appeared in Durova's autobiographical works. "Count Mauritius" is an expansion of the anecdote about Count Ossoliński and his two wives from *The Cavalry Maiden* (chap. 4). The fictional story addresses the riddle of the count's desertion of a charming and suitably noble wife for a poor Cossack's daughter, here called Józefa. The version that appeared in Osip Senkovsky's magazine *Library for Reading* in 1838 bears all the hallmarks of a society tale by "Baron Brambeus" (Senkovsky's literary pseudonym), and the frivolous ending, in which the narrator says that the count's second marriage also ended in divorce, is clearly his. It was typical of Durova's fiery character that she defended her conception of her stories by reprinting the original versions of those she felt had been distorted by heavy editing. Durova included in the 1839 *Notes* her variant of the scene where the count first encounters his charming Cossack and a brief summary of the premature death of Józefa and her son. She did not, however, repeat the rumor recorded in *The Cavalry Maiden* that their death was unnatural.

Some of Durova's tales express directly the chance her masculine guise afforded her to explore an unfamiliar town, talk to its inhabitants, and ferret out its secrets. A good half of "The Pavilion" is devoted to the female officer's frame narrative. Describing her move into new quarters in a Polish village, she alternates brief passages about her duties with "adventures": rescuing a grief-stricken old priest from a graveyard at night; getting to know her landlord, the retired National Cavalry Sergeant Rudzikowski; and prying out of him a secret that, as she proudly announces, until then had been strictly guarded by the sergeant and the priest's housekeeper. The confidence she extracts from Rudzikowski is a romantic horror story of the ill-fated love of a Catholic priest for a ward he raised and educated in secret. Rudzikowski, in turn, introduces subnarrators who sprout like mushrooms with improbably omniscient accounts of portions of the story. As was the case with "Count Mauritius," Durova was unhappy with the cuts made by A. A. Kraevsky when the tale came out in his magazine *Notes of the Fatherland*. She reprinted "The Pavilion" in two parts. The frame tale (to which she restored passages describing her activities as platoon leader and a lengthy sketch of Rudzikowski's character and past) was included in the 1839 *Notes* as part of her own autobiography. The central plot of the priest and his ward appeared in her *Short Fiction* as "Ljudgarda."[29]

In the *Notes* Durova describes how the officers of her squadron decided to relieve the monotony of peacetime service in the Russian provinces by composing literary works to read aloud to one another (a contest which began and ended with Durova's own contribution). Dipping into the store of scribbled papers in her valise, she found "one of the occurrences of our wild forested land, that of the ill-fated Elena G. (. . .) I saw her; she appeared in all her permutations: child, maiden, young woman; beauty, frightful monstrosity, and at last a frigid corpse covered in rags!"[30] First printed in Senkovsky's magazine as "Elena, the Beauty of T." in 1837, the tale was republished with only minor changes under the title of "Plaything of Fate, or Illicit Love: A True Occurrence in the Author's Native Land," in Durova's *Short Fiction* (1839). As frame narrator, Durova testifies to her childhood acquaintance with Elena and follows Elena's subsequent fate on journeys home to Sarapul on leave. The clinical observation of the tale's harsh final scenes confirms the kernel of "truth" that Durova stressed in her subtitle: she witnesses Elena's decline and death from syphilis contracted from the dissolute husband to whom her well-meaning but foolish parents married her at thirteen.[31]

All three stories are linked by plots about young girls who become objects of the obsessive passion of older, experienced men. As in almost all of Durova's tales, women function as the voice of society, a chorus that gossips, speculates, and comments with varied degrees of sympathy or malice on situations whose real significance they fail to grasp. They are generally portrayed as passive and unable or unwilling to influence the events they witness.

Durova's other fiction has a broad diversity of theme and setting. *The Nook* is a Peterburg society tale of a young aristocrat who manages to keep a merchant-class wife and growing family secreted in a wing of the family mansion away from the notice of his snobbish mother. Several stories reflect the life and legends of the Ural region Durova knew best. "The Sulphur Spring," like "The Tatar's Tale" in *The Cavalry Maiden* (chap. 9), is a tragic love story set among tribal peoples, in this case the Finno-Ugric Cheremys.[32] Exceptionally, the officer-narrator is male. Kizbek, the Tatar protagonist of "Nurmeka," is Durova's one strong female character (other than herself), but her obsession with reconquering Kazan from the Russians destroys her family.

It is clear that Durova, as she reports, really did read and absorb "all the horrors of Mrs. Radcliffe" (chap. 13), and the Gothic penchant for tales of mystery, concealment, and enigmatic identities furnished a pattern for much of her fiction. Durova's plots are more varied than Radcliffe's stories of menaced heroines, but, like the English author, Durova unmasks apparently supernatural events with rational explanations that turn out to be almost as improbable as the previous uncanny perception. A gypsy in "Nurmeka" twice repeats Durova's creed that "everything in the world happens very simply and naturally," but this is certainly not true of the world of her fiction. *Gudishki*, Durova's longest work (two hundred thousand words), was motivated by an incident from her early days in the cavalry: the discovery that there were twelve neighboring hamlets in Lithuania all named Gudishki (*Notes*, 1839, 50–69). Years later the wandering officer-narrator of the novel returns to the Gudishkis and hears from a local historian, a Jewish tavernkeeper, the rambling legend of the origin of the villages' common name in medieval times. (As with Durova's other complex narratives, the choice of a Jew as storyteller is purely formal. She makes no attempt to give him a distinctive diction.) *Gudishki* [Hooters], the Jew explains, was the nickname of the demonic stepchild of a noble family. The novel's main plot is about the tragedy arising from the boy's obsessive love for his stepmother. In *Buried Treasure* Durova pays tribute in the same extravagant fashion to the lore and mixed nationalities of her native Kama region. *Jarchuk, The Dog Who Saw Ghosts* is a confused and unlikely tale set in seventeenth-century Bohemia.

The themes of thwarted love, deception, strong goals passionately pursued, and, in "Nurmeka," a transvestite masquerade reflect Durova's own romantic life and nature. In fiction her voice was freed from the modesty and deprecating humor that constrained her as her own protagonist, and the grand sweep of her style kept the critics sympathetic or only gently critical as the tales grew longer and more confused and improbable. Many years later, when a guest asked Durova why she had given up writing, "the old woman replied, 'Because I couldn't write now the way I did before, and I don't want to appear in the world with just anything.'"[33] It is difficult indeed to imagine Durova constraining her pen to produce the "physiological sketches" of downtrodden urbanites that characterized the Russian natural school of the 1840s. Whatever the reason, after four years of intense literary activity in both Peterburg and Moscow, she returned to Elabuga for good.[34]

## RETIREMENT YEARS

In 1928 Jury Tynjanov published "Lieutenant Kizhe," a short story that seems as prescient of the atmosphere of Stalin's court in the twentieth century as it was a reconstruction of that of the mad Emperor Paul at the end of the eighteenth. Kizhe is a nonexistent lieutenant, created by scribal error in the daily duty roster submitted to Paul. Nobody dares to admit to the mistake for fear of incurring the emperor's capricious wrath.[35] Profiting by royal attention to his unusual name, the paper-work Kizhe rises meteorically to the rank of general. "Aleksandrov" had about him something of the same fabulous and inviolable air. It is striking that even those who knew or at least suspected that Aleksandrov was a woman—her own family, ladies of the regiment (chap. 5), Kutuzov (chap. 9), colleagues in the Lithuanian Uhlans (chap. 10), Adjutant General Zakrevsky in Peterburg (chap. 12), and General Gren of the Izhevsk Munitions Factory (chap. 13)—accepted her imperially sanctioned male persona as totally as Paul's cowed subordinates went along with the fiction that they were serving with an officer named Kizhe.

Over forty years later, Durova recalled the despair that overcame her in 1816 when, dressed for the first time in a civilian frock coat, she realized that her shield of invisibility was gone: "the first sentry I passed did not come to attention . . . as he was supposed to at the sight of an officer." No sentry would ever again salute her. God knows, she was not addicted to military formalities, but the cavalry had been her existence, and, as she said, "I could not bear this complete estrangement from the main element of my life.[36] The premonition Durova had as she watched the Big Dipper one night in Polish Galicia (chap. 5) came true:

> The years will pass, decades will pass, it will remain the same, but I. . . .
> My thoughts were carried forward sixty years into the future, and, in fright, I got up. My shako, my saber, my ardent steed! Eighty years old!

Her retirement lasted for fifty years; she was 83 when she died.

Durova portrayed herself as a martyr to filial duty, but her retirement was not entirely due to the wish to succor her father. Aleksandrov's career was not as meteoric as Kizhe's. It is apparent from the 1839 *Notes* that, vexed at being passed over for promotion, she first submitted her retirement early in 1815, only to withdraw it when Napoleon's last eruption onto the continent brought the promise of a new campaign. Waterloo ended her hopes of seeing further action, and the promotion of junior officers over her must have rankled.[37] Durova's disguise was dual: she was not only of the wrong sex to be a soldier, but fated, like Peter Pan, never to grow up. The occasional petulance and fierce need to defend her autonomy that she displays in the later pages of *The Cavalry Maiden* are most readily comprehensible as the frustrations of a woman over thirty who looked, and was frequently treated, like a mere boy. Whatever her motives for leaving the cavalry, it is hard to imagine that there could ever have been a comfortable niche for Durova-Aleksandrov in the Russian army of the Arakcheev epoch. Her account of a brief stint of duty in Peterburg in 1815 (chap. 12) shows how galling she found the new emphasis on rigid discipline and protocol.

In retirement Durova took solace at first in rambles and rides around the Sarapul region:

> . . . getting up at three o'clock in the morning, saddling my own horse, flying on it across mountains, valleys, and forests, or making my way on foot up dizzying heights, descending into ravines, bathing in rivers and streams, I had no time to turn my thoughts to the past—alas! to my woe, irrevocable.[38]

But provincial society had no more lasting appeal to her now than it had during her trips home on leave. Despite his pathetic appeals for her to come back and care for him, her father had married a peasant woman, and, soon after her own retirement, her brother Vasily also left the army and returned home.[39] Within a year Durova left for Peterburg, where she reportedly applied to rejoin the cavalry and was turned down. She spent a year or two there with her uncle Nikolaj Durov and her cousins the Butovskys, who lived in the bucolic suburb of Kolomna.[40] She traveled to the Ukraine to visit her maternal relatives before going back to Sarapul in 1822. After her father's death in 1826, her brother Vasily replaced him as the town's mayor. In 1830 or 1831 Durova moved with Vasily to a new civil post in Elabuga.[41] From there she launched her unlikely foray into the literary world in 1836, and she returned to Elabuga for good in 1840.

The few people who have left us descriptions of Durova as a guest in the two capitals during the late 1830s saw her as a kind of *monstre sacré*, a George Sand without any of the French author's glamor. She is described as a middle-aged, rather ugly woman with cropped hair who usually wore a frockcoat, sat with her legs crossed, smoked a pipe, chose to join the men for discussions of military matters, and escorted the ladies into dinner.[42] The disaffection was mutual: the "or . . ." of the title of her memoir *A Year of Life in Peterburg, or The Disadvantages of the Third Visit* refers to Durova's disillusioned discovery that if she made the mistake of accepting for a third time the hospitality of fashionable hosts who fawned over her as a novelty during the first visit and treated her politely during the second, she would find herself only a neglected figure in the corner. (I suspect that some of our current celebrities might find Durova's Law of Lionization still valid.)

In Elabuga Durova won a kinder reputation, despite her eccentric dress and manner and her demand to be addressed as "Aleksandr Andreevich." (There is a legend that she refused to respond to a letter from her son asking her blessing on his marriage because he called her "Mama"; a second request headed "Dear parent" [*roditel'*] fared better.) Durova shared her household with a pack of dogs rescued from the streets and spent a good portion of her days tending and walking them. She must have mellowed: the regimental museum of the Lithuanian Hussars preserved a few specimens of the handwork she had so loathed as a child. Early in the liberal 1860s when the "woman question" came to the fore and Russian women in substantial numbers began seeking broader opportunity, curious and admiring visitors came to visit Durova in Elabuga. Menshov described her as a lively, pleasant old woman still very much in touch with the world and contemporary affairs. This assessment is borne out by an (unpublished) article she wrote in 1858 on the need for women to participate in the impending reforms of the reign of Alexander II:

Durova in the 1830s. Engraving by A. Brjullov.

Durova in the 1860s. From a photograph belonging to N. I.
Ushakov. *Istoricheskii vestnik*, 1901, *9*.

In our times a women who is bored, who cannot find a way to occupy herself, and who languishes in inactivity, is more out of place than ever. Now more than ever Russian society needs active, hard-working women who sympathize judiciously with the great events taking place around them and are capable of adding their mite to the structure of social welfare and order which is being erected by common efforts. Now Russian society has need more than ever not of women-cosmopolites but of Russian women in all the fine sense of the word![43]

Durova was unfailingly sympathetic to fellow citizens in distress and generous to the point of improvidence. At her death in 1866, she left but a single ruble of the yearly pension of one thousand rubles she had drawn since 1824. The only woman to win the St. George Cross until the last year of World War I, Durova was buried with military honors.[44] In 1901 a new monument was erected over her grave in Elabuga, and since 1962 a marble bust stands in a nearby park.

## Durova's Posthumous Reputation

Durova's journals have not been equally honored. By 1887 *The Cavalry Maiden* was such a bibliographic rarity that V. P. Burnashev-"Bajdarov" could publish an unceremonious plagiarism and represent it as the result of conversations with Durova in 1830. Even with long passages taken directly from *The Cavalry Maiden*, Bajdarov imposed the masculine voice and preoccupations of the military memoir onto Durova's journal. He followed the outlines of *The Cavalry Maiden* closely, however, and his plagiarism served to stimulate new interest in her remarkable story. Valuable archival materials and a spate of articles about Durova began to appear. In 1890 the feminist critic, Ekaterina Nekrasova, published a short biography in a popular historical magazine; the article, although not completely accurate factually, does justice to Durova's free spirit. Colonel A. A. Saks of the Lithuanian Uhlans collected materials, documents, and souvenirs for the regimental museum and in 1912 published the short biography that is still the basic source of information about Durova's life.

Because she omitted the truth about her unhappy marriage, Durova was open to legitimate suspicion about the accuracy of other aspects of her tale. Some commentators found it more convincing to portray Durova as an adjunct to a male lover than as a person who served nearly ten years in the cavalry from a desire for freedom and a sense of vocation. In 1906 the *Russian Biographical Dictionary* could not decide between her own version of events and the variant requiring a lover, and in 1937 Veresaev repeated the Sarapul gossip about a Cossack captain in his brief

sketches of people whose lives touched Pushkin's. Her life adapted easily
to the demands of light romantic fiction as the story of a girl who runs
away in 1812 to fight Napoleon, finds love, and happily returns to the
domestic hearth at the end of hostilities. In 1908 Churilova-"Charskaja"
portrayed her most attractively as just such a heroine in A Daring Girl.
The novella set a generation of girls longing for adventure.

One striking characteristic of the bibliography of works about Durova
is the total absence of any interest in this uncomfortably loyal subject of
Alexander I during the first twenty-five years of Soviet power. Her story
surfaced only in World War II, as the propaganda machine began crank-
ing out patriotic exhortations. Durova became a model of female heroism. Borisova and Nikolskaja pulled out all the stops in their 1942 Kama
Foundling (a fond nickname supposedly given her by her Cossack comrades). Wyszemirski, the companion of her first days in the Polish Horse,
is transformed into a Cossack who sees through Aleksandrov's disguise
and falls in love with her; he becomes a Mason, lives a chaste life
mourning his thwarted love, and is killed at Borodino. Durova's life in
Turzysk is described through the eyes of her adoring orderly Zanudenko
(the "damned old mustaches" of chap. 10). The historical Aleksej Burtsov (d. 1813), whom Davydov addressed as "hussar of hussars" and "dare-
devil, rake, boon drinking pal" [era, zabijaka/ Sobutyl'nik dorogoj], is
inserted gratuitously into the tale.[45] He becomes Aleksandrov's protector
during the 1812 Russian retreat. The two of them are sent together to
join Davydov's partisans, and Aleksandrov is persuaded to disguise himself as a peasant girl to spy on the French (doublecross-dressing?). After
Moscow falls, Commander-in-chief Kutuzov not only appoints Durova his
orderly, but takes her to sleep in his room and nurses her through a
contusion-induced fever. (In view of Kutuzov's reputation as a woman-
izer, this is no happier an invention than pairing Aleksandrov with the
dissipated Burtsov.) It is a reflection of the tragedy of the Stalin epoch
and the haste to get Durova's example before the Soviet public that the
authors of Kama Foundling did not work closer to the known historical
record. But fiction has its privileges, and Durova herself might have
laughed at the extravagance of the fairytale.

Durova would certainly have disliked another fictional portrayal which
appeared that same year. Lipskerov and Kochetkov's four-act blank verse
play with occasional songs, Nadezhda Durova (Moscow-Leningrad, 1942),
stresses a historically distorted hostility toward the female sex. Like Kama
Foundling, it betrays the haste of its conception to fulfill the urgent needs
of propaganda. Durova travels by magic carpet. She leaves with the
Cossacks in late June 1812 after the news of Napoleon's invasion reaches
Sarapul; she is promoted to officer for heroism by early August, mainly
because Alcides is the fastest horse in either army; and she is called to

Moscow between the battles of Smolensk and Borodino for an interview
with a sinister Arakcheev and an indignant emperor who reproaches her
with violating the religiously ordained subordination of women. In *The
Cavalry Maiden* Durova described her fellow soldiers as titillated at the
possibility that one of their number is not what he seems, but in the play
she persuades Alexander I to let her remain with the armies only by
pointing out the demoralizing effect it would have on her colleagues to
learn that the most courageous officer in the regiment is a woman. Her
colonel is preparing to expel her anyway when Kutuzov intervenes.[46]

I imagine that Durova might also have been offended by Jakov
Rykachev's short biography (1942). He sketched her life accurately, but
with undue emphasis on the loneliness of her army days. He misuses her
frank passages on the fatigue and physical stress she underwent to make it
quite clear to Soviet women that a military career was not for them.
Victor Afanasev's introduction to the 1984 *Selected Works*, the most
positive Soviet assessment of Durova's life and works to date, also stresses
her isolation:

> . . . On bivouac, while her fellow officers carouse at the common table
> and carry on their masculine conversations (of course, in the boldest of
> terms), she with an alienated expression stands apart—away from people,
> the campfire, and the heat which she so desperately needs—closer to the
> nocturnal darkness; or she sits alone in her tent with a book.[47]

Durova's ambiguous situation certainly led to a degree of isolation. She
had no desire to share many of the officers' off-duty amusements and,
especially in early days, she was wary of revealing herself. But, as she
gained confidence in her new way of life, Durova approached something
like androgyny in her psychological accommodation to the role of young
soldier grafted onto a basic connection to her own sex. Far from accepting a guarded isolation, Durova describes herself as meeting and interact-
ing with both men and women as an integrated person who all too often
forgot to pay due caution to the problems her persona might pose for her
new friends. Female loneliness and isolation in Russian society and
within the family are a prominent theme of tales by nineteenth-century
Russian women writers. It is ludicrous that a text as full of the joy of life
as *The Cavalry Maiden* should be characterized among them.[48]

Durova would seem to be a natural precursor of the Communist
heroine who sacrifices her personal life to the greater good of country and
party in so many Soviet novels. However, judging by the timid, heavily
expurgated edition of *The Cavalry Maiden* (amounting to about half
Durova's text) that appeared four times in the USSR from 1960 to 1979,
it was not easy for the Soviets to come to terms with her addiction to a

wandering life and the preference she expresses for foreign lands; her independent, even insubordinate, spirit; her adoration of her personal liberator, Alexander I; her skeptical attitudes toward masculine prerogatives; and her defiance of the stereotype of oppressed womanhood.[49] It is pleasant to report that the complete 1836 text of *The Cavalry Maiden* was at last published in the USSR for the two hundredth anniversary of Durova's birth in 1983. In 1985 *Maiden* appeared in tandem with a selection of Denis Davydov's military reminiscences.

Translation may not always be treason, as the Italian saying would have it, but it does involve compromise at every turn, and I think translators are well-advised to explain their choices. The text of *The Cavalry Maiden* is Durova's 1836 edition. To reproduce her spirited prose I have tried to use vocabulary attested in English in the early nineteenth century, but the grammar and syntax follow modern norms that seem better representative of what her contemporaries perceived as a brisk, impulsive style. Durova blithely admitted to knowing nothing about punctuation. Like her earlier Russian editors, I have applied my own norms. I have cut out endless exclamation points and considerably reduced the number of spaced dots. The few parentheses in the text are Durova's; they seem to be later interpolations, second thoughts as it were, to the lost journal manuscripts. The 1985 Soviet edition retains Durova's run-on paragraphs, but I have broken them up and imposed arbitrary chapters. All headings are Durova's, whether they appear at the beginning or in the middle of one of my chapters.

Durova may have become accustomed to using masculine grammatical forms for herself in speech and letters, but in her autobiographical works and some of her fiction she retained a female voice. In the Russian text, where adjectives and past-tense verbs are gender-marked, the reader is reminded in virtually every sentence of the anomaly of a woman acting out the life of a male persona. (Durova's description of her meeting with Pushkin quoted above is a good example.) There is no way to reproduce the effect in English.

One review of *The Cavalry Maiden* (*Syn otechestva*, 1837) criticized it for "gallicisms," and there were a few I found troublesome. I substituted "parlor," "drawing-room," "anteroom" as appropriate for Durova's use of *zal* [salle] for any public room and "imbued with" or some such phrase for Durova's *dyshat'* [respirer] in a metaphoric sense. One that defeated me totally was *umen'e zhit'* which I left as *savoir-vivre*.

To give some idea of the diversity of peoples Durova deals with and her polyglot vocabulary, I have tried to transcribe the names of her fellow officers and local citizens according to their nationality and to leave foreign words and phrases in the original with footnotes where they seem helpful. I have followed modern usage in transcribing the Polish and Ukrainian phrases Durova reports hearing. The Polish names are in forms attested in Polish sources, even when they differ slightly from Durova's transliteration. The stress on the first syllable of the names Stánkovich and Dýmchevich is Durova's. Her pseudonym is left in transliterated Russian (*Aleksandrov*); the tsar's name is in the English form *Alexander*. The place names of villages and small towns that Durova describes as owned and inhabited by Poles are in the Polish forms given in Max Vasmer and Herbert Bräuer's *Russisches Geographisches Namenbuch* (10 vols., Wiesbaden, 1964–1981). "Little Russia" was the name for the Ukraine east of the Dnepr, which came under Russian rule after 1654. Durova uses the term for the nationality and language as well, whereas I translate them as "Ukrainian."

I have been eclectic in the translation of military terms, which in any case came into Russia from various sources as Peter the Great and his successors adopted West European models. I have retained the Russian *versta* since it is conveniently close to a kilometer; other measures have been translated into traditional English ones. All dates are in the Julian calendar which in nineteenth-century Russia lagged twelve days behind the Western (Gregorian) one. Where it seemed useful to refer to specific dates in European history in the footnotes, I have put both.

I use the Library of Congress transliteration system for Russian except that, in order to have a single letter for the English y in both Russian and Polish, I have substituted the international *jot* (*j*) for ligated *i*. In the text, but not in the footnotes, proper names have been simplified by eliminating hard and soft signs and using -y for the -ij of Russian proper names (Podjampolsky, for example, rather than the peculiar-looking but correct Pod"jampol'skij).

All footnotes are mine. I had fun tracking Durova through the swamps of Lithuania, into Galicia, on the difficult retreat to Moscow, across the Bohemian mountains, into Holstein, and down the dark streets of St. Petersburg. The need to keep annotation to a minimum clashed with my desire to share some of the more interesting or amusing secondary evidence I ran across as I checked the personalities, places, and facts mentioned in *The Cavalry Maiden*. I hope that I struck a reasonable balance and that the notes both reflect the joy of the research and help to place Durova in her times and her society.

## ACKNOWLEDGMENTS

The Russian and East European Center and the Research Library of the University of Illinois at Urbana-Champaign has furnished unstinting support for the research connected with my translation of *The Cavalry Maiden* (Summer Research Laboratory, 1983–1984) and my investigation of other Russian women writers (1978, 1980–1985). Jeanne Tatro of Millikan Library, California Institute of Technology, patiently tracked down volumes through Interlibrary Loan for me. Harold Zirin endows a permanent Zirin Fellowship in exchange for domestic, gardening, and editorial labors; he, Daniel, Dana, and Diane Zirin furnish moral support in their own inimitable ways. Barbara Heldt offered me collaboration and encouragement from start to finish. Helena Goscilo supported the project at the beginning and gave me generous help with Polish. Tom Beck initiated me into some of the *arcana* of Russian military historiography. Valentina Lindholm checked some difficult passages in Russian. Kenneth Craven helped me with the paper, "A Woman in the 'Man's World': The Journals of Nadezhda Durova," which I read at the conference on *Autobiography and Biography: Gender, Text, and Context,* sponsored by the Center for Research on Women, Stanford University, in April 1986. E. J. W. Barber acted as proofreader and cheered me on with her enthusiasm. Janet Rabinowitch is the editor who appreciated the importance of Durova's text and took a chance on it. William Mills Todd III read the manuscript; I am grateful for his generosity and useful suggestions.

I came late to the fellowship of women, and it is all the more precious to me. *The Cavalry Maiden* is Durova's to dedicate, but I must say that I thought a great deal about the gallant women in my own life as I worked on hers—and most particularly, about my loving and beloved mother, Mary Noble Fleming.

—MARY FLEMING ZIRIN

## NOTES

1. See the bibliography of works by and about Durova at the end of this book. Items listed there are referred to by author in the footnotes or, for Durova's works, by abbreviated title.

2. "Table-Talk (36): O Durove," dated Oct. 3, 1835, *Polnoe sobranie sochinenij* (Moscow-Leningrad, 1937–1959), vol. 12, 167–68. Pushkin reports that they discussed such desperate measures as robbery of a military payroll and direct appeals to the tsar, to Rothschild, and to the English public, which even then was known for its fascination with eccentrics.

3. *Zapiski* (Kazan', 1960), 144.

4. Pushkin's correspondence with Durova and her brother has been published in various editions of his works and recently in: *Perepiska A. S. Pushkina* (Moscow, 1982), vol. 2, 490–505. The excerpt from *The Cavalry Maiden* appeared in *Sovremennik [The Contemporary]* (1836), 2:53–132. What Pushkin chose, or the censor permitted him to publish, was the beginning of chap. 7 up

to Durova's billeting with the Uniate priest; chap. 8 minus the tale of the goose; chap. 9 omitting the passages about Moscow on fire, Durova's note to Stackelberg, and "The Tatar's Tale"; chap. 10 without the coachman's comment on French bodies, the French orphan's story, and "A Night in Bohemia"; and chap. 11 to the return to Russia, ending with the words: "Yes, at times like that one's *native land* does not count for much." Pushkin's text uses initials for many people who were identified by name in *Maiden* when it appeared in full later that year.

5. Letter, c. June 10, 1836.

6. "All That I Could Recollect" [Vse, chto ja mog pripomnit'], written in 1860 and first published from archival sources in *Nedelja*, 1962, No. 26, 7).

7. Durova's influence on the subsequent development of Russian autobiography has yet to be investigated. For a chronology of Russian autobiographical literature, see Toby W. Clyman, "Autobiography,"in *Handbook of Russian Literature* (New Haven: Yale University Press, 1985), 27–29. Natal'ja Dolgorukaja's record of her experiences in Siberian exile in the 1730s was published in a magazine for young people in 1810; see Charles E. Townsend's edition and translation, *The Memoirs of Princess Natal'ja Borisovna Dolgorukaja*, (Columbus, Ohio: Slavica, 1977). "Chistoserdechnoe priznanie" [A Heartfelt Confession], a short unfinished autobiography by the playwright Denis Fonvizin (1745–1792), appeared in 1830; it was the first work in Russian literature to give weight to childhood experience. Barbara Heldt's *Terrible Perfection: Women and Russian Literature* (Bloomington: Indiana University Press, 1987) includes a section on women's memoirs from the late eighteenth century to recent times with particular discussion of works by Catherine the Great's friend Ekaterina Dashkova, Durova, Nadezhda Sokhanskaja, Ljubov' Blok, Marina Tsvetaeva, and Evgenia Ginzburg.

8. For a recent review of the genre, see John L. H. Keep, "From the Pistol to the Pen: The Military Memoir as a Source on the Social History of Pre-Reform Russia," *Cahiers du Monde russe et sovietique*, XXI, 3–4 (July-December 1980): 295–320. Keep does not include Durova's journals in his survey. Military memoirs that appeared before 1835 (when Durova began revising her journals for publication) include: I. M. Murav'ev-Apostol, "Pis'ma iz Moskvy v Nizhnij Novgorod," *Syn otechestva* (1813–1814); F. N. Glinka, *Pis'ma russkogo ofitsera* (Moscow, 1815); V. I. Shtejngel', *Zapiski o pokhode 1812–1813 gg.* (Moscow, 1814–1815); D. V. Davydov, *Opyt teorii partisanskikh dejstvij* (Moscow, 1821); and V. S. Norov, *Zapiski o pokhode 1812 i 1813 godov ot Tarutinskogo srazhenija do Kul'mskogo boja* (1834).

9. Adam Mickiewicz, *Pan Tadeusz, or The Last Foray in Lithuania*, trans. Watson Kirkconnell (New York: Polish Institute of Arts and Sciences in America, 1981). These lines (90–93) from Mickiewicz's epilogue (used as a prologue in the Institute edition) are to be found only in Polish editions published between the two world wars.

10. *War and Peace*, book 2, part 2.

11. See William Edward Brown, *A History of Russian Literature of the Romantic Period*, 4 vols. (Ann Arbor: Ardis, 1986), 1: 276–84, for an outline of Davydov's life and works.

12. Reuel K. Wilson's *The Literary Travelogue: A Comparative Study with*

*Special Relevance to Russian Literature from Fonvizin to Pushkin* (The Hague: Martin Nijhoff, 1973), summarizes the genre's development abroad and in Russia. See also Brown, 2: 145–48, on the Russian travel sketch and Glinka's *Letters*.

13. Nikolaj Polevoj, *Syn otechestva,* 8 (1839): bib., 87–89.

14. Letter, August 5, 1835.

15. For a broader summary of the position of women in Russia than this simplistic outline of the tiny fraction (1 percent) of the population counted among the nobility [*dvorianstvo*], see Dorothy Atkinson, "Society and Sexes in the Russian Past," in *Women in Russia,* ed. Dorothy Atkinson, Alexander Dallin and Gail Warshofsky Lapidus (Stanford: Stanford University Press, 1977), 3–38; and Richard Stites, *The Women's Liberation Movement in Russia* (Princeton: Princeton University Press, 1978), Part One.

16. Marina Warner, *Joan of Arc: The Image of Female Heroism* (New York: Alfred A. Knopf, 1981), 10. See also Warner's chapter on the image and significance of the virgin warrior.

17. Prince Potemkin costumed a regiment of "Amazons" to greet Catherine the Great and the Austrian Emperor Joseph on their trip to the Crimea in the spring of 1787 (G. Esipov, "A Regiment of Amazons During the Reign of Catherine II," *Istoricheskij vestnik,* [1886] 1: 71–75; "Shidianskaia, Elena Ivanovna," *Russkij Biograficheskii slovar',* 23 [St. Petersburg, 1911]: 275). For the *byliny,* see V. Ja. Propp and B. N. Putilov, eds., *Byliny,* 2 vols. (Moscow, 1950), 1: 57–59.

18. The testimony from Joan of Arc's trial is the major exception. Mary Elizabeth Perry is currently working on the career of Catalina Erauso, a nun who ran away from her convent in Spain in the early seventeenth century to fight and serve as a teamster in the New World; it is not clear that any of three extant Erauso "autobiographies" is genuine, but her life and exploits are well attested through records of her testimony before civil and ecclesiastic authorities (Huntington Library Seminar in Women's Studies, February 7, 1987). For a survey of extant first-person tales by English and American women, see: Estelle Jellinek, "Disguise Autobiographies: Women Masquerading as Men," *Women's Studies Int. Forum,* Vol. 10 No. 1 (1987), 53–62. During the Napoleonic era Thérèse Figueur (nicknamed "Sans-Gêne") served and fought in the cavalry with little pretense of being a man; her oral memoirs were later published as *Un ancien du 15e dragons,* (Paris, 1936). The story of Maria Bochkareva, who fought for two years in World War I as a common soldier, is largely forgotten. After the March 1917 revolution, Bochkareva was commissioned and formed a troop of women called the *Death Battalion* who were determined to revive the flagging campaign against Germany. For Bochkareva's memoirs, see Maria Bochkareva, *Yashka: My Life as Peasant, Officer, and Exile,* as set down by Isaac Don Levine (New York, 1919); and for an eyewitness account, Bessie Beatty, *The Red Heart of Russia* (New York, 1918), 90–114. The heroism of Soviet women in all roles during World War II is well documented.

19. V. Belinskij, *Polnoe sobranie sochinenij,* (Moscow, 1953), 2: 236.

20. *Notes* (1839), 283.

21. "All That I Could Recollect."

22. Durova enlisted under the name of "Sokolov" rather than running the

risk of using her father's name. She refers twice to Arakcheev's nomination to the post of War Minister, whereas the second passage should refer to the nomination of Barclay de Tolly to succeed him in 1810. She mistimes her service as Konovnitsyn's orderly in August 1812. (These lapses are footnoted where they occur in the text.)

23. Letter dated November 21, 1861, to Vsevolod Mamyshev, who was collecting materials for a biographical dictionary of the military heroes who held the St. George Cross (Saks, 21).

24. *Voennaja entsiklopedija*, (St. Petersburg, 1912), vol. 9, 243.

25. Blinov, 416.

26. Chap. 6. Denis Davydov's letter passing on to Pushkin the gossip about this supposed affair is included in Appendix B.

27. Chap. 3 and Appendix A.

28. Durova was a pioneer in Russian fiction as well as in autobiography. In the late 1830s Elena Gan, Maria Zhukova, and Durova became the first Russian women writers to publish substantial bodies of prose. There is no evidence that they knew one another, but their works all share the traits of the late romantic school.

29. The Soviets reprinted "Pavil'on" for the first time in the 1984 edition of Durova's selected works—unfortunately, in the magazine version to which she objected.

30. *Notes*, 283–84.

31. The radical critic Maria Tsebrikova cited "Fate's Toy" as an early example of "realism in social relations" (*Nedelja*, 13–14 [1876]: 435).

32. In the Soviet Union the Cheremys are called Marijtsy.

33. Men'shov, 65.

34. Afanas'ev speculates that a volume of verse published by an otherwise unknown "Aleksandrov" (Moscow, 1859) might have been by Durova also (*Izbrannoe* [1984], 25).

35. The error is as if an American army clerk, interrupted at the end of the word "lieutenants" while writing "Lieutenants incl. Johnson, Fitzgerald. . . ." on returning to the page produced "Lieutenants Tsincl, Johnson, Fitzgerald. . . ." Never mind that the error is improbable in either Russian or English; the tale it introduces is wry and witty.

36. "All That I Could Recollect."

37. In any army scaling down after a war, promotions become few and far between. Durova's first platoon leader in the Polish Horse, Konstantin Boshnjak (chap. 1) did not do that much better. Like Aleksandrov, Boshnjak was the child of a retired cavalry officer and provincial civil servant. He was seven years younger than Durova (just the age she assumes in *The Cavalry Maiden*). Like Pushkin's fictional Grinev in *The Captain's Daughter*, Boshnjak was enrolled as a sergeant-major in the cavalry at the age of three. From 1800 he was a member of the elite Corps of Pages, and by 1807 he had already reached the rank of lieutenant. Despite these advantages, Boshnjak retired in May 1816, at the rank of captain. (O. P. [fon-]Frejman, *Pazhi za 183 goda (1711–1894): Biografii byvshikh pazhej c portretami*, part 1 [Friedrichshamn, 1894], 140.) Durova was promoted from cornet to lieutenant immediately after Borodino and retired at the next highest rank of staff (junior) captain.

38. "All That I Could Recollect."

39. Blinov, 416.

40. Kolomna is the setting of Pushkin's jocular verse tale of a widow who catches the outsized "female" cook hired by her daughter shaving in the kitchen ("Little House in Kolomna," 1830).

41. See Blinov for a full account of Vasily's eccentric and unsavory career, 417–19.

42. A. Ja. Panaeva, *Vospominanija* (Moscow, 1972), 62; T. P. Passek, *Iz dal'nikh let* (Moscow-Leningrad, 1931), 341–43; N. V. Sushkov, "Oboza k potomstvu," (unpublished memoir in the Lenin Library; quoted in Smirenskij [1960], xvi).

43. Smirenskij, xxiii.

44. For accounts of her last years and funeral see Kutshe, "Durov-Aleksandrov" and Lashmanov.

45. Davydov's two epistles, "K Burtsovu" (1804) are among his most famous glorifications of cavalry exploits on and off the battlefield. Durova never mentioned Burtsov.

46. A. K. Gladkov's 1941 *Davnym-Davno* [Long, Long Ago], a frothy verse play about a girl warrior of the Napoleonic epoch who faints at the sight of a mouse, served as the basis of the popular 1962 Soviet film *Gusarskaja ballada* [A Hussar Ballad]. Gladkov, however, has denied that he found Durova in any way inspirational (*Teatr: Vospominaniia i razmyshleniia* [Moscow, 1980], 329–30).

47. *Selected Works*, 11–12.

48. Among the scores of works with this theme are: Elena Gan's famous unfinished novel, *Naprasnyj dar* [A Vain Gift], published in 1843; Avdot'ja Panaeva's "Semejstvo Tal'nikovykh" [The Talnikov Family], 1848, and, sixty years later, her daughter E. Nagrodskaja's *Anja;* the novel *Bol'shaja medveditsa* [Ursa Major], 1865–1871, and many other tales, including "Bratets" [The Brother], 1858, reprinted in *Povesti i rasskazy* (Moscow, 1963), 33–91, and "Ridneva" (1875) by N. Khvoshchinskaja ("V. Krestovskij, psevd."); Ol'ga Shapir's *Bez ljubvi* [Without Love], 1886; and Maria Krestovskaja's "Imjaninnitsa" [Maria'a Name-Day], 1892. Other authors who treated the theme repeatedly include: Sof'ja Engel'gardt ("Ol'ga N."), Praskovja Lachinova ("P. Letnev"), Maria Markovich ("Marko Vovchok"), Nadezhda Merder ("N. Severin"), and Elena Apreleva-"Ardov."

49. These editions include: "My Childhood Years," the period from September 1806 to late December 1807 (cutting off before her interview with the tsar), and the months from September 1812 (after the fall of Moscow) to May 1813. The 1984 *Izbrannoe* adds some incidents from the Russian retreat in June-August 1812.

# THE
# CAVALRY
# MAIDEN

# "My Childhood Years"

My mother, born Aleksandrovicheva, was one of the prettiest girls in Little Russia. At the end of her fifteenth year, throngs of suitors came to seek her hand. My mother's heart preferred hussar Captain Durov to all the many others, but unfortunately this was not the choice of her father, a proud, arbitrary Ukrainian *pan*. [1] He told my mother to put out of her head the fantastic idea of marrying a *Muscovite*, and a soldier at that. My grandfather ruled his family with an iron hand: any order of his was to be blindly obeyed, and there was no possibility of either placating him or changing any of his announced intentions. The consequence of this unreasonable severity was that one stormy autumn night my mother, who slept in the same room as her elder sister, stealthily rose from her bed, picked up her cloak and hood and, in stocking feet, crept with bated breath past her sister's bed, quietly opened the door into the drawing-room, quietly closed it, dashed nimbly across the room and, opening the door into the garden, flew like an arrow down the long lane of chestnuts that led to a wicket-gate. My mother hastily unlocked this little door and threw herself into the captain's arms. He was waiting for her with a carriage hitched to four strong horses who, like the wind then raging, rushed them down the Kiev road.

They were married in the first village and drove directly to Kiev, where Durov's regiment was quartered. Although my mother's act was excusable in light of her youth, love, and the virtues of my father, who was a very handsome man of gentle disposition and captivating manners, it was so contrary to the patriarchal customs of the Ukrainian land that in his first outbreak of rage my grandfather pronounced a curse on his daughter.

For two years my mother never stopped writing to her father to beg his forgiveness, but to no avail: he would hear none of it, and his rage grew in proportion to their attempts to mollify it. My parents finally gave up all hope of appeasing a man who considered obstinacy a mark of character. They ceased writing letters to her implacable father and would have resigned themselves to their lot, but my mother's pregnancy revived her

My translation of Durova's memoir of childhood appeared in *The Female Autograph* (*New York Literary Forum 12–13*), 1984; paperback: University of Chicago, 1987. It has been revised somewhat for this edition.

1. Ivan Il'ich Aleksandrovich (died c. 1789) was a provincial civil servant who had an estate near Pirjatin in the Poltava region. Durova's mother, Nadezhda, was born about 1765 and died, according to her daughter's account, in 1807. The hussar was Andrej Vasil'evich Durov, born in Ufa province to the descendants of a Polish family (originally Turowski) who were resettled there from their native Smolensk-Polotsk region after Russia hegemony began in the 1650s (Judin, 413–14).

flagging courage. She began to hope that the birth of her child would restore her to paternal favor.

My mother passionately desired a son, and she spent her entire pregnancy indulging in the most seductive daydreams. "I will give birth to a son as handsome as a cupid," she would say. "I'll name him Modest. I will nurse him myself, bring him up, teach him, and my son, my darling Modest, will be the joy of my life. . . ." So my mother dreamed but, as her time drew near, the pangs preceding my birth came as a most disagreeable surprise to her. They had had no place in her dreams and produced on her a first unfavorable impression of me. It became necessary to send for an *accoucheur*, who insisted on letting blood. The idea was extremely frightening to my mother, but there was nothing she could do about it; she had to yield to necessity. Soon after the bloodletting I came into the world, the poor creature whose arrival destroyed my mother's dreams and dashed all her hopes.

"Give me my child!" said my mother, as soon as she had recovered somewhat from her pain and fear. The child was brought and placed on her lap. But alas! this was no son as handsome as a cupid. This was a daughter—and a *bogatyr* of a daughter at that![2] I was unusually large, had thick black hair, and was bawling loudly. Mother pushed me off her lap and turned to the wall.

In a few days Mama recovered and, yielding to the advice of her friends, ladies of the regiment, decided to nurse me herself. They told her that a mother who nurses her child at the breast finds that the act alone is enough to make her begin loving it. I was brought; my mother took me from the maid's arms, put me to her breast, and gave me to suck. But I evidently sensed the lack of maternal love in that nourishment and therefore refused her every effort to make me nurse. Mama decided to exercise patience to overcome my obstinacy and went on holding me at the breast, but, bored by my continued refusal, she stopped watching me and began talking to a lady who was visiting her. At this point, evidently guided by the fate that intended me for a soldier's uniform, I suddenly gripped my mother's breast and squeezed it as hard as I could with my gums. My mother gave a piercing shriek, jerked me from her breast, threw me into the arms of her maid, and fell face down in the pillows. "Take her away; get that worthless child out of my sight, and never show her again," said Mama, waving her hand and burying her head in a pillow.

I was four months old when the regiment in which my father was serving received orders to go to Kherson. Since this was a domestic march, Papa took his family with him. I was entrusted to the supervision

2. *Bogatyrs* were the warrior heroes of the Russian epic songs called *byliny*.

and care of my mother's chambermaid, a girl of her own age. During the day the maid sat with Mama in the carriage, holding me on her lap. She fed me cow's milk from a bottle and swaddled me so tightly that my face turned blue and my eyes were bloodshot. At our night's halts I rested, because I was handed over to a peasant woman brought in from the village who unswaddled me, put me to her breast, and slept with me all night. Thus after each day's march I had a new wetnurse.

Neither the changing wetnurses nor the agonizing swaddling impaired my health. I was very robust and vigorous, but incredibly vociferous as well. One day my mother was totally out of sorts; I had kept her awake all night. The march started at daybreak and Mama settled down to sleep in the carriage, but I began crying again and, despite all my nurses's attempts to comfort me, bawled louder by the hour. Vexed beyond measure, Mama flew into a rage and, snatching me from the arms of the maid, threw me out the window! The hussars cried out in horror, jumped off their horses, and picked me up covered with blood and showing no sign of life. They would have returned me to the carriage, but Papa galloped up to them, took me from their arms and, in floods of tears, placed me on his saddle. Trembling and weeping, as pale as a corpse, he rode on without saying a word or turning his head in the direction where my mother rode. To the astonishment of everyone, I came back to life and, against all expectations, was not permanently maimed. The shock of the fall just left me bleeding from the nose and mouth. Papa raised his eyes to heaven with a joyful feeling of gratitude, and, clutching me to his breast, he went over to the carriage and said to my mother, "Give thanks to God that you are not a murderess! Our daughter is alive, but I will never return her to your power; I'll care for her myself." And with this he rode off and carried me with him until that night's halt without a word or glance toward my mother.

From that memorable day of my life my father entrusted me to God's providence and the care of flank hussar Astakhov, who was always at Papa's side in quarters as well as on the march.[3] I was in my mother's room only at night; as soon as Papa got up and went out, I was taken away, too. My tutor Astakhov carried me around all day, taking me into the squadron stables and sitting me on the horses, giving me a pistol to play with, and brandishing his saber while I clapped my hands and laughed out loud at the sight of the scattering sparks and glittering steel. In the evening he took me to hear the musicians who played various pieces at dusk, and I listened until I fell asleep. Only slumbering could I be brought back inside. If I were not sleeping, I became numb with fear

---

3. Durova's biographer, Colonel Saks, says that the practice of using personal orderlies as nannies to officers' children was still common in the first decade of the twentieth century (5).

and clung howling to Astakhov's neck at the mere sight of my mother's room. From the time of my aerial journey out the carriage window, Mama no longer interfered in any way in my life. She had another daughter to console her, this one really as handsome as a cupid and, as the saying goes, the apple of her eye.

Soon after my birth my grandfather forgave my mother and did so in the most solemn way: he went to Kiev, asked the archbishop to absolve him of his impetuous oath never to pardon his daughter, and, once he had obtained pastoral absolution, finally wrote to my mother that he forgave her and blessed her marriage and the child born of it. He asked her to come and see him both to accept the paternal blessing in person and to receive her dowry. My mother had no way of taking advantage of this invitation until Papa was forced to retire. I was four and a half when my father realized that he would have to leave the army. There were two cradles in his quarters in addition to my cot; such a family made life on the march impossible. He went to Moscow to seek a position in the civil service, and my mother took me and the other two children to live with her father until her husband's return.[4]

Once she took me from Astakhov's arms, my mother never knew a single calm or cheerful moment. Each day my strange sallies and knightly spirit angered her. I had memorized all the words of command and was wild about horses, and when my mother tried to make me knit shoelaces, I wept and begged her to give me a pistol, as I said, *to click.* In short, I was making the best possible use of the upbringing Astakhov had given me. Every day my martial propensities grew stronger, and every day my mother liked me less. I never forgot anything that I had learned in the constant company of the hussars; I ran and galloped around the room in all directions, shouting at the top of my voice: "Squadron! To the right, face! From your places, charge—CHARGE!" My aunts laughed out loud and Mama, driven to desperation by it all, could not contain her vexation. She took me to her room, stood me in the corner, and drove me to bitter tears with abuse and threats.

My father obtained a post as mayor of a district capital and moved his entire family there.[5] My mother, who had come to dislike me whole-heartedly, seemed bent on doing everything she could to intensify and confirm my already invincible passion for freedom and the military life.

4. Children continued to be born to the Durovs regularly every two years or so until the turn of the century. Only four of them survived to adulthood: Nadezhda; Kleopatra, born in 1791; Vasilij, the first and only son, 1799; and Evgenija, 1801 (Blinov, 415).

5. The city where Durova grew up was Sarapul, on the Kama river in the western foothills of the Urals.

She never allowed me to enjoy the fresh air of the garden, or even leave her side for half an hour. I had to sit in her room all day and weave lace. She herself taught me to sew and knit, and when she saw that I had neither inclination nor skill for those pursuits and that everything ripped and broke in my hands, she lost her temper, flew into a rage, and whipped those hands painfully.

I turned ten. My mother was careless enough to tell my father in my presence that she no longer had the strength to cope with Astakhov's ward, the hussar upbringing was deep-rooted, the fire in my eyes frightened her, and she would rather see me dead than with such propensities. Papa replied that I was still a child, and she should pay no attention to me. As the years went on, I would take on other propensities, and all this would pass. "Don't take these childish ways so much to heart, my friend," said Papa. But fate decreed that my mother would not believe or follow her husband's good advice. She continued to keep me in seclusion, denying me every youthful joy. I submitted in silence, but oppression matured my mind. I resolved firmly to shake off my heavy yoke and began in an adult way to work out plans for doing so. I decided to take every means to learn to ride horseback and shoot firearms and then, in disguise, to leave my father's house. In order to begin realizing the radical change in my life that I contemplated, I never missed a chance to slip away from my mother's supervision. These chances came whenever visitors arrived to see Mama. They kept her occupied and I, beside myself with joy, ran out into the garden to my arsenal—that is, the dark corner behind the shrubbery where I stored my bow and arrows, a saber, and a broken gun. Busy with my weapons, I was oblivious to everything else on earth, and only the shrill cries of the maids searching for me brought me running in alarm to meet them. They led me to the room where punishment was always waiting.

Thus passed the two years until I turned twelve. Just then Papa bought himself a saddlehorse, an almost untameable Circassian stallion. My father, who was an excellent rider, broke this handsome beast himself and named him Alcides. Now all my plans, intentions, and desires were concentrated on this steed. I decided to do all I could to accustom him to me—and I succeeded. I gave him bread, sugar, and salt; I took oats from the coachman on the sly and spread them in his manger; I stroked and caressed him, speaking to him as if he could understand me, until at last I had the haughty steed following me as meekly as a lamb.

Almost every day I got up at dawn, stealthily left my room, and ran to the stable. Alcides greeted me with a whinny. I gave him bread and sugar and led him out into the yard. Then I brought him over to the porch and mounted his back from the steps. His quick starts, frisks, and snorts did not alarm me in the least; I held onto his mane and let him run with me

all around the yard. I had no fear that he would carry me outside the
gates, because they were still locked. On one occasion this pastime was
interrupted by the arrival of the groom who, with a shriek of fear and
astonishment, rushed to stop Alcides as he galloped past with me. But
the steed arched his head, reared, and broke into a run around the yard,
frisking and kicking. It was fortunate for me that Efim was so numb with
fear that he lost the use of his voice; otherwise his shout would have
alarmed the household and drawn me harsh punishment. I quieted
Alcides easily, caressing him with my voice and patting and stroking
him. He slowed to a walk and, when I embraced his neck and pressed my
face against it, he stopped at once because this was the way I always
dismounted or, more accurately, slid down off him. Now Efim approached
to take him, muttering through his teeth that he would tell my mother,
but I promised to give him all my pocket money if he would say nothing
and permit me to lead Alcides back to the stable. At this promise Efim's
face cleared; he smiled wryly, stroked his beard, and said, "Well, so be it,
if that rogue obeys you better than he does me!" Triumphantly I led
Alcides into the stable and, to Efim's astonishment, the savage steed
followed me meekly, arching his neck and bending his head to nibble
lightly at my hair or shoulder.

With each passing day I grew more bold and enterprising, afraid of
nothing on earth except my mother's wrath. It seemed quite odd to me
that other girls of my age were frightened of being left alone in the dark;
on the contrary, I was prepared in the dead of night to go into a
graveyard, a forest, a deserted house, a cave, or a dungeon. In short, there
was nowhere I would not have gone as boldly at night as in the daytime.
Although I, like other children, had been told tales of ghosts, corpses,
wood goblins, robbers, and water nymphs who tickled people to death,
and although I believed this nonsense with all my heart, none of it
frightened me. On the contrary, I thirsted for dangers and longed to be
surrounded by them. If I had had the least freedom, I would have gone
looking for them, but my mother's vigilant eye followed my every step and
impulse.

One day Mama and some ladies went for an outing into the dense pine
forest on the far side of the Kama. She took me with her, as she put it, to
keep me from breaking my neck alone at home. This was the very first
time in my life that I had been taken out into the open where I could see
dense forest and vast fields and the wide river! I could barely catch my
breath for joy, and we no sooner came into the forest than I, out of my
mind with rapture, immediately ran off and kept running until the voices
of the company were no longer audible. Then my joy was complete and
perfect: I ran, frisked, picked flowers, and climbed to the tips of tall trees
to see farther. I climbed slender birches and, holding tight to the crown,

leaped off; the sapling set me down lightly on the ground.[6] Two hours flew like two minutes! In the meantime they were searching for me and calling me in chorus. I heard them, but how could I part with such captivating freedom? At last, completely exhausted, I returned to the company. I had no trouble locating them, because the voices had never stopped calling me. I found my mother and the other ladies in a terrible state of anxiety. They cried out in joy when they caught sight of me, but Mama, who guessed from my contented face that I had not strayed, but gone off of my own volition, flew into a violent rage. She poked my back and called me a damned pest of a girl, sworn to anger her always and everywhere!

We returned home. Mama pulled me by the ear all the way from the parlor to her bedroom. She took me over to the lace pillow and ordered me to get to work without straightening up or looking around. "Just you wait, you wretch, I'll tie you on a rope and give you nothing but bread to eat!" With these words she went to tell Papa about what she called my monstrous act, and I was left to sort bobbins, set pins, and think about the glories of nature which I had just seen for the first time in all their majesty and beauty. From that day, although my mother's supervision and strictness became even more unremitting, they could no longer either frighten or restrain me.

From morning to night I sat over work which, I must confess, was the vilest imaginable because, unlike other girls, I could not, would not, and did not want to acquire the skill, but ripped, ruined, and tangled it until before me lay a canvas ball with a repulsive, snarled strip stretching across it—my bobbin-lace. I sat patiently over it all day, patiently because my plan was prepared and my intentions resolute. At nightfall, when the house quieted down, the doors were locked, and the light in Mama's room went out, I got up, dressed stealthily, sneaked out across the back porch, and ran straight to the stable. There I took Alcides, led him through the garden to the cattleyard, mounted him, and rode out down a narrow lane straight to the riverbank and Startsev mountain. Then I dismounted again and led Alcides uphill, holding him by the halter because I didn't know how to bridle him and had no way of getting him to climb the mountain of his own volition. I led him by the halter across the precipitous slope until I reached a level spot, where I looked for a stump

6.        . . . And climb black branches up a snow-white trunk
          *Toward* heaven, till the tree could bear no more,
          But dipped its top and set me down again.

                    —Robert Frost, "Birches"

or hillock from which to remount. Then I slapped Alcides' neck and clicked my tongue until the good steed broke into a gallop, a run, and even a breakneck dash.

At the first hint of dawn I returned home, put the horse in the stable, and went to sleep without undressing. This was what led at last to the discovery of my nocturnal excursions. The maid who took care of me kept finding me fully clothed in bed every morning and told my mother, who undertook to find out how and why this came about. She herself saw me going out at midnight fully clothed and, to her inexpressible horror, leading the wicked stallion out of the stable! She thought I must be sleepwalking and did not dare stop me or call out for fear of alarming me. She ordered the manservant and Efim to keep an eye on me, and she herself went to Papa's room, roused him, and told him what had happened. My father, astonished, got up hastily to go and see this singular occurrence for himself. But it all ended sooner than they expected: Alcides and I were led back in triumph, each to his proper place. The servant whom Mother had ordered to follow me saw me trying to mount the horse and, unlike Mama, decided that I was no sleepwalker. He came out of ambush and asked me, "And where are you going, miss?"

After this affair my mother wanted without fail to rid herself of my presence at any cost and decided to take me to my old grandmother Aleksandrovicheva in Little Russia. I had entered my fourteenth year by then. I was tall, slim, and shapely, but my martial spirit was sketched on my features and, although I had white skin, bright rosy cheeks, sparkling eyes, and black brows, every day my mirror and Mama told me that I was very ugly. My face was pitted from smallpox, my features irregular, and Mother's continual repression of my freedom, her strict and at times even cruel treatment of me, had marked my countenance with an expression of fear and sadness. Perhaps I would at last have forgotten all my hussar mannerisms and become an ordinary girl like the rest if my mother had not kept depicting woman's lot in such a dismal way. In my presence she would describe the fate of that sex in the most prejudicial terms: woman, in her opinion, must be born, live, and die in slavery; eternal bondage, painful dependence, and repression of every sort were her destiny from the cradle to the grave; she was full of weaknesses, devoid of accomplishments, and capable of nothing. In short, woman was the most unhappy, worthless, and contemptible creature on earth! This description made my head reel. I resolved, even at the cost of my life, to part company from the sex I thought to be under God's curse. Papa, too, often said, "If I had a son instead of Nadezhda, I shouldn't have to worry about my old age; he would be my staff in the evening of my days." I would be ready to weep at these words from the father I loved so extravagantly. These two contradictory emotions—love for my father and aversion to my own sex—troubled my young soul with equal force. With a resolve and constancy rare in one so young I set about working out a plan to escape the sphere prescribed by nature and custom to the female sex.

Such was my frame of mind and spirit at the beginning of my fourteenth year when my mother delivered me to my grandmother in Little Russia and left me there.[7] My grandfather was no longer alive. The family consisted of my eighty-year-old grandmother, an intelligent and pious woman who had once been a beauty and was known for her unusually gentle disposition; her son, my uncle, a man in his middle years, comely, kind, sensitive, and insufferably capricious, who was married to a young woman of rare beauty from the Lizogub family of Chernigov; and, finally, my aunt, a spinster about forty-five years old.[8] I liked my uncle's young and lovely wife best, but I never remained willingly in the company of my relations; they were so grand, so devout, such implacable foes of martial propensities in a girl that in their presence I was afraid even to think about my cherished intentions. Although my freedom was in no way restricted and I could roam wherever I wanted from morning to night without fear of rebuke, I think they would have condemned me to ecclesiastic penance if I had even dared to hint at riding horseback, so unreserved was my relations' horror at the mere idea of such illicit and unnatural, to their mind, pursuits for women, and particularly girls.

Under the clear sky of Little Russia my health became perceptibly better, although at the same time I burned in the sun and turned black and even uglier than before. Here nobody corseted me or wearied me with bobbin-lace. With my passionate love for nature and freedom, I spent all my days either running around the forested parcels of my uncle's estate or floating on the Udaj in a large boat of the type that Ukrainians call a *dub*. Had they known about this latter pastime, they might not have permitted it, but I was careful to undertake my navigation after dinner when my young aunt's sharp eyes were closed in sleep. My uncle busied himself with household matters or read the newspaper while my spinster aunt listened with great interest. There remained only my grandmother to catch a glimpse of me, but her eyesight was already weak, and I rowed about under her windows in complete security.

7. The direct distance between Pirjatin and Sarapul is over fifteen hundred kilometers as the crow flies. The journey would have taken well over a month at best.

8. Durova's maternal grandmother was Evfrosin'ja Grigor'evna Aleksandrovicheva, born Ogrenovicheva. The son who inherited the Pirjatin estate was Porfirij; his young wife was Marfa Jakovl'evna, born Lizogub; and his spinster sister was named Ul'jana.

Nadezhda Durova, age 14.

In the spring, another of my aunts, Znachko-Javorskaja, who lived near the city of Lubny, came to see us. She took a liking to me and won my grandmother's permission to take me to stay with her for the summer.[9]

Here both my occupations and my pleasures were completely different. My aunt was a strict woman who observed inflexible order and propriety in everything. She lived expansively; she was on good terms with the best society among the landowners of the district; she had a good cook and often gave balls. I found myself in a new sphere. I never heard the female sex abused or reproached and began making my peace with women's lot, especially as I saw the polite and obliging attentions of men. My aunt dressed me very well and tried to rid my face of sunburn. My military dreams slowly began fading bit by bit from my mind. The position of women no longer seemed so dreadful to me, and at last I grew to like my new way of life. Acquiring a friend completed the pacification of my turbulent designs. Another niece, Ostrogradskaja, who was a year younger than I, was also living with my aunt. We two were inseparable. We spent the morning in our aunt's room, reading, drawing, or playing; after dinner we were free to roam until teatime and went off at once to the *levada* (which is what they called the piece of land that usually adjoins the garden, separated from it only by a ditch). I leaped the ditch with the ease of a wild goat, my cousin followed my example, and we spent our afternoon excursion flying throughout the open space of all the neighboring *levadas*.

My aunt, like all Ukrainian women, was very devout and observed and followed strictly all the rites prescribed by religion. Every holy day she attended high mass, vespers, and matins, and my cousin and I had to do the same. At first I was very reluctant to get up before dawn to go to church, but in our neighborhood there lived a lady landowner named Kiriakova with her son, and they always came to church, too. While we waited for the service to begin, Kiriakova conversed with our aunt, and her son, a young man of twenty-five, would join us, or rather me, because he spoke only to me. He was very good looking, with beautiful black eyes, hair, and brows, and a youthful fresh complexion. I became quite fond of the divine service and always rose for matins even earlier than my aunt. At last my talks with young Kiriak attracted my aunt's attention. She began observing us and questioned my cousin, who at once told her

9. In addition to the senior Nadezhda Durova and the unmarried Ul'jana, three other Aleksandrovich sisters can be traced in the pages of Vadim Modzalevskij's *Malorossijskij rodoslovnik* [Ukrainian Genealogy], 4 vols. (Kiev, 1908–1914): Praskov'ja Znachko-Javorskaja, Anna Ostrogradskaja, and Evrosin'ja (or Fedosia) Butovskaja, whose son edited Durova's *The Cavalry Maiden* in 1836.

that Kiriak had taken my hand and asked me to give him my ring, saying that then he could consider himself sanctioned to speak to my aunt.

Having received this explanation from my cousin, my aunt sent for me: "What does our neighbor's son talk to you about when we are together?" I had no gift for dissembling and at once told her everything that had been said to me. My aunt shook her head; she was not at all pleased. "No," she said, "that's not the way to ask for a girl's hand. Why declare himself to you? He should have come straight to your relations."

After that I was sent back to Grandmother. I pined for young Kiriak long afterwards. That was my first attachment, and I think that if they had married me to him then, I would have relinquished my martial designs forever. But the fate that destined me for a battlefield career decreed otherwise. Old Kiriakova asked my aunt to inquire about my dowry and, when she found out that it consisted of a few yards of ribbon, linen, and muslin, forbade her son to think of me.

I had entered my fifteenth year when one day my uncle received a letter that plunged us all into sadness and perplexity. It was from Papa. He was writing to my mother, begging her to forgive him and come home, and swearing to give it all up. None of us could understand anything from this letter. Where was my mother? Why was the letter addressed to her in Little Russia? Had she parted from my father, and if so, why? My uncle and grandmother were lost in conjecture.

Two weeks or so after the letter came, I was out boating on the Udaj when suddenly I heard the shrill voice of Grandmother's chambermaid: "Pannochko, pannochko! idyt' do babusii!"[10] This summons to Grand-mother frightened me. I turned the boat around and mentally bade farewell to my obliging *dub*, supposing that now they would order it chained to the pilings and that my excursions on the river were finished forever. "How did Grandmother happen to see me?" I asked, pulling up to the shore.

"Grandmother didn't see you," replied Agafja, "but Stepan has come for you. Your mother sent him."

Mama! For me? How can that be? Oh, beautiful land, must I really leave you? . . . I hurried to the house. There I saw the old servant who had been with my father on all his campaigns. Gray-haired Stepan respectfully handed me a letter. My father wrote that he and my mother wished me to come home right away, that they were tired of living apart from me. I found this incomprehensible. I knew that my mother disliked me, and thus it was Papa who wanted me with him. But why on earth had my mother agreed? No matter what I thought and how much I deplored the necessity of leaving Little Russia, the constraints on my

10. "Missy, missy, you're to go to your grandmother!" (Ukrainian)

freedom that awaited me, and the disagreeable exchange of a fine climate for a cold and harsh one, I had no choice but to obey. For two days they cooked, baked, and roasted; they gave me a huge basket of delicacies and packed everything. On the third day my venerable grandmother hugged me to her breast and, kissing me, said: "Go, my child! The Lord's blessing on your journey, and his blessings on your journey through life as well!" She placed her hand on my head and quietly invoked God's protection on me. The prayer of this righteous woman was heard: throughout my turbulent martial life I have often had occasion to experience the clear intercession of the Almighty. . . .

There is nothing worth describing about my journey under the supervision of old Stepan with his twelve-year-old daughter Annushka as my companion. It began and ended the way all such voyages do: we traveled with our own horses slowly and for a long time and at last arrived. As I opened the door to the parlor of my father's house, I heard my little sister Kleopatra saying, "Mama, come here! A young lady has arrived." Against my expectations, Mother received me kindly. She was pleased to see that I had taken on the modest and steadfast appearance so becoming to a young lady. Although in a year and a half I had grown a good deal and was nearly a head taller than my mother, I no longer had the martial appearance that made me look like Achilles in woman's dress nor the hussar ways that drove her to despair.

After a few days at home I found out why they had been forced to send for me. My father, never indifferent to beauty, had betrayed my mother in her absence. He took a pretty little girl, the daughter of a townsman, as his mistress. For a long time after her return Mama knew nothing about it, but one of her woman friends decided to do her the favor of disclosing the ruinous secret and poisoned her life with the cruelest venom of all—jealousy! My unhappy mother listened numbly to the story her recklessly obliging friend had to tell, heard her out, went away without saying a word, and took to her bed. When Papa came home, she did her best to speak gently and calmly to him, but how could that be within her power? From her first words the agony in her heart overwhelmed her. Sobs cut through her voice. She beat her breast, wrung her hands, and cursed the day of her birth and the moment when she first knew love. She begged my father to kill her and thus spare her the unbearable torment of living with his disdain. Papa was horrified to see my mother in such a state. He tried to calm her and begged her not to believe absurd tales, but when he saw that she was too well informed about it all, he swore by God and his conscience to quit his illicit connection. Mama believed him, calmed down, and forgave him.

Papa kept his word for a time. He left his mistress and even arranged a marriage for her, but then he took her back again, and this time my mother, in despair, decided to part forever from her unfaithful husband; she set out for her mother's house in Little Russia, but stopped in Kazan. Unaware of this, Papa wrote to Little Russia to persuade her to forgive him and return home. Just then he himself got a letter from my mother. She wrote that she was not strong enough to remain away from him; she could not bear the thought of parting forever from a husband whom she still loved beyond measure even though he had wronged her so cruelly. She implored him to think twice and return to his obligations. Papa was moved; he repented and asked my mother to return. It was then that she sent for me, supposing that the presence of his beloved daughter would make him forget entirely the unworthy object of his attachment.

Unhappy woman! She was fated to be deceived in all her expectations and to drink the cup of grief to the dregs. Papa went from one attachment to the next and never came back to my mother. She languished, wasted away, fell ill, went to Perm to be treated by the famous Gral, and died at thirty-five, more a victim of misfortune than disease.[11] Alas! in vain I wash these lines with my tears. Woe to me, the first cause of all my mother's troubles! My birth, sex, traits, propensities—none of them were what my mother would have wished. My existence poisoned her life; constant vexation ruined her already naturally hot-tempered disposition and made her cruel. Even her exceptional beauty could not save her then. My father ceased loving her, and an untimely grave put an end to her love, hatred, suffering, and misfortunes.

My mother, who no longer took any pleasure in society, led a reclusive life. I took advantage of this circumstance to win permission from my father to ride horseback. Papa ordered a Cossack *chekmen* tailored for me and gave me his Alcides.[12] From that time on I was always my father's companion on his excursions outside the city. He took pleasure in teaching me to ride handsomely, keeping a firm seat in the saddle and managing the horse skillfully. I was a quick student. Papa admired my ease, skill, and fearlessness. He said that I was the living image of him as a youth and that, had I been born a boy, I would have been the staff of his old age and an honor to his name. This set my head awhirl, and this time for good! I was no child; I had turned sixteen. The seductive pleasures of society, life in Little Russia, and Kiriak's black eyes faded from my memory like a dream; brightly colored scenes of my childhood in camp among the hussars were sketched in my imagination instead. It all

11. Fedor Gral's life and benefactions are described in: Modest Kittari, "Vospominanija o doktore Grale," *Permskij sbornik* (Moscow, 1859), bk. 1, 42–49. Durova's mother was about forty-two when she died.

12. *Chekmen,* a long tunic with a fitted waist.

revived in my soul. I could not understand why I had not thought of my plan for nearly two years. My grief-stricken mother now described woman's lot in even more horrific colors. Martial ardor flared in my soul with incredible force; my mind swarmed with dreams, and I began searching actively for means to realize my previous intention: to become a warrior and a son to my father and to part company forever from the sex whose sad lot and eternal dependence had begun to terrify me.[13]

Before Mama went to Perm to seek treatment, a Cossack regiment arrived in our city to suppress the Tatars' incessant thievery and murder.[14] Papa often invited the colonel and his officers to dinner and went for rides with them outside the town, but I took the precaution never to take part in these excursions. I had to be sure that they never saw me in the *chekmen* and had no idea how I looked in men's clothing. I had a flash of inspiration when the Cossacks arrived in the city. Now I saw a sure way to carry out the plan I had undertaken so long ago. I saw the possibility of waiting for the Cossacks' departure and joining them for the journey to areas where regular army regiments were stationed.[15]

At last the decisive time came to act according to the plan as I had worked it out. The Cossacks received the order to move out, and they left on September 15, 1806. Their first full day's halt would be some fifty versts from the city. The seventeenth was my name-day, and the day on which, through fate, coincidence of circumstance, or invincible propensity, it was fixed for me to quit my father's house and take up an entirely new way of life.[16] On September 17, I awoke before dawn and sat by my window to await its appearance; it might well be the last I ever saw in my own land. What awaited me in the turbulent world? Would not my mother's curse and my father's grief pursue me? Would they survive? Could they await the realization of my colossal scheme? How horrible it would be if their death took from me the goal of my actions! These thoughts now clustered and now passed one after another through my head. My heart constricted and tears glistened on my lashes. Just then

13. During the seven years missing from this account of her years at home, Durova married Vasilij Chernov, a civil servant, on October 25, 1801. The birth of their son Ivan on January 7, 1803, was registered in Sarapul. After her husband was transferred to Irbit, Durova left him and returned to her father's house.

14. The Cossacks were people, mainly of Ukrainian and Russian stock, who had gradually been granted land on the frontiers and an autonomy unknown in Russia proper in exchange for service as auxiliary mounted police and cavalry.

15. By mid-1806 there was a strong probability that the Cossacks would be sent to Russia's western borders to reinforce the armies preparing to check the French in Prussia.

16. The routine on long marches was two or three days on the road, bivouacking at night, for each full day of rest in a populated settlement. Thus Durova's plan was to reach the site of the Cossacks' September 17th halt before they moved on early the following morning.

dawn broke. Its scarlet glow quickly flooded the sky, and its beautiful light, flowing into my room, lit up the objects there: my father's saber, hanging on the wall directly opposite the window, seemed to catch fire. My spirits revived. I took the saber off the wall, unsheathed it, and looked at it, deep in thought. This saber had been my toy when I was still in swaddling-clothes, the comfort and exercise of my adolescent years; why should it not now be my defense and glory in the military sphere? "I will wear you with honor," I said, kissed the blade, and returned it to its scabbard. The sun rose. That day Mama presented me with a gold chain, and Papa, three hundred rubles; even my little brother gave me his gold watch. As I accepted my parents' gifts, I thought sorrowfully that they had no idea that they were outfitting me for a distant and dangerous road.

I spent the day with my girl friends. At eleven o'clock in the evening I came to say good-night to Mama as I usually did before going to bed. Unable to suppress my emotions, I kissed her hands several times and clasped them to my heart, something I had never done before nor dared to do. Although Mama didn't love me, she was moved by these extraordinary effusions of childlike affection and obedience; kissing me on the head, she said, "Go with God!" These words held a great significance for me, who had never before heard a single affectionate word from my mother. I took them as a blessing, kissed her hand for the last time, and left.

My rooms were in the garden. I occupied the ground floor of our little garden house, and Papa lived upstairs. He was in the habit of coming to see me for half an hour every evening. He enjoyed hearing me tell him where I had gone and what I had been doing or reading. Now, as I waited for my father's customary visit, I laid my Cossack apparel on the bed behind the curtain, set an armchair by the stove, and stood beside it to wait for Papa to come to his rooms. Soon I heard the rustle of leaves under the footsteps of someone coming down the lane. My heart leaped! The door opened, and Papa came in. "Why are you so pale?" he asked, sitting down in the armchair. "Are you well?"

With an effort I suppressed the sigh that threatened to rend my breast. This was the last time that my father would come into my room with the assurance of finding his daughter there. Tomorrow he would pass it in grief, with a shudder. It would hold only a sepulchral void and silence!

Papa looked fixedly at me, "But what's wrong with you? You must be ill."

I said that I was only tired and chilled.

"Why don't you have them heat your room? It's getting damp and cold." After a short silence Papa asked, "Why don't you order Efim to run Alcides on a lunge? There's no getting near him. You yourself haven't ridden him for a long time, and you won't permit anyone else to do it.

He's so restive that he rears up even in his stall; you really must exercise him."

I said that I would order it done and fell silent again.

"You seem melancholy, my friend. Goodnight; go to bed," said Papa, getting up and kissing my forehead. He put one arm around me and pressed me to his breast. I kissed both his hands, trying to hold back the tears which were already flooding my eyes. The quivering of my body betrayed the emotions in my heart. Alas! Papa ascribed it to the cold. "You see, you're chilled through," he said. I kissed his hands once more. "My sweet daughter!" said Papa, patting my cheek. He went out. I knelt beside the armchair he had sat in and bowed to the ground before it, kissing and washing with my tears the spot where his foot had rested.

Half an hour later, when my sorrow had abated somewhat, I got up to take off my female clothing. I went over to the mirror, cut off my curls, and put them away in a drawer. I took off my black satin dressing-gown and began putting on my Cossack uniform. After I had tied the black silk sash around my waist and put on the high cap with a crimson crown, I spent a quarter of an hour studying my transformed appearance. My cropped hair gave me a completely different countenance. I was certain that nobody would ever suspect my sex.[17]

A loud rustle of leaves and the snort of a horse told me that Efim was leading Alcides into the rear yard. For the last time I stretched my arms to the image of the Mother of God which had received my prayers for so many years and went out. The door of my father's house finally closed behind me, and—who knows?—perhaps it might never be open to me again!

I ordered Efim to take Alcides by the direct road to Startsev mountain and wait for me at the edge of the forest. I ran hastily to the bank of the Kama and dropped my dressing-gown there, leaving it on the sand with all the trappings of female dress. I was not so barbarous as to intend for my father to think that I had drowned, and I was convinced he would not do so. I only wanted to make it possible for him to answer without confusion any embarrassing questions from our short-witted acquaintances. After leaving the clothing on the bank, I took a goat track which led directly uphill. The night was cold and clear, and the moon was shining at its fullest. I stopped for one last look at the beautiful and majestic view that opened out from the mountain: beyond the river, Perm and Orenburg provinces were visible to a boundless distance. Vast, dark forests and mirror lakes were displayed as if in a painting. The city at the foot of the precipitous mountain slumbered in the midnight hush. The

---

17. Durova's service record (Nov. 6, 1807) describes her as about 5′5″ tall and having a swarthy, pock-marked face, light brown hair, and hazel eyes (Saks, 18).

moon's rays played on and were reflected from the gilt domes of the cathedral and shone on the roof of the house where I grew up. . . . What were my father's thoughts now? Did his heart tell him that tomorrow his beloved daughter would no longer come to wish him good morning?

In the nocturnal silence Efim's shout and Alcides' powerful snort came distinctly to my hearing. I ran toward them, and I was just in time: Efim was shivering with cold and cursing Alcides, whom he could not manage, and me for my delay. I took my horse from his hands, mounted, gave him the fifty rubles I had promised him, and begged him not to say anything to Papa. Then I released Alcides' reins and disappeared in a flash from the dumbfounded Efim's view.

Alcides galloped at the same rapid pace for four versts but then, since I had to cover fifty versts that night to reach the hamlet where I knew the Cossack regiment had been assigned to halt, I reined in my steed's quick gallop and went at a walk. Soon I came into a dark pine forest some thirty versts across. Wishing to conserve Alcides' strength, I kept him walking and, surrounded by the deathly hush of the forest and the dark of the autumn night, I became absorbed in my own thoughts: And so I'm at liberty. Free! Independent! I have taken the freedom that is rightfully mine—the freedom that is a precious gift from heaven, the inalienable prerogative of every human being! I have found a way to take it and guard it from all future claims against it; from now to my grave, it will be my portion and my reward!

Storm clouds covered the sky. The forest became so dark that I could not see twenty feet ahead of me, and at last a cold north wind rose, forcing me to step up my pace. Alcides broke into a full trot, and at dawn I arrived in the hamlet where the Cossack regiment had spent their day of rest.

NOTES OF THE CAVALRY MAIDEN

# Chapter One

The colonel and his officers had long been awake and were all gathered in his quarters for breakfast when I came in. They were conversing noisily among themselves, but suddenly fell silent as they noticed me. The colonel approached me with a dumbfounded look, "Which troop are you in?"

I replied that I did not yet have the honor of being in any of them, but I had come to ask him for that favor. The colonel listened to me in astonishment, "I don't understand you. You are really not enrolled anywhere?"

"No, I'm not."

"Why not?"

"I haven't the right."

"What! What does that mean, a Cossack without the right to be enrolled in a Cossack regiment! What kind of nonsense is that?"

I said that I was not a Cossack.

"Well, who are you anyway?" asked the colonel, growing impatient. "Why are you in Cossack uniform, and what do you want?"

"I've already told you, Colonel, that I desire the honor of being enrolled in your regiment, although only until such time as we reach the regular army."

"But just the same I have to know who you are, young man, and, moreover, aren't you aware that nobody can serve with us except native Cossacks?"

"And I have no such intention; I am only asking you for permission to travel to the regular army in the rank and dress of a Cossack serving with you or your regiment. As to your question about who I am, I will say only what I can: I am a nobleman; I have left my father's house and am on my way to serve in the army without my parents' knowledge and volition. I cannot be happy in any calling except the military, and that is why I've decided in this instance to follow my own dictates. If you won't take me under your protection, I'll find some way to join the army on my own."

The captain watched me sympathetically as I spoke. "What shall I do?" he asked in a low voice, turning to a grizzled captain. "I haven't the heart to refuse him!"

19

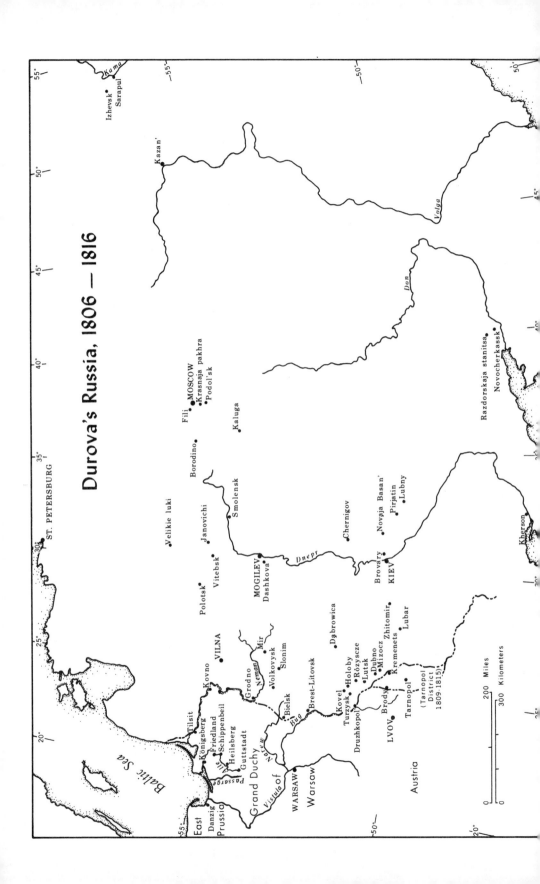

Durova's Russia, 1806 — 1816

ST. PETERSBURG

Izhevsk
Sarapul

Kazan'

MOSCOW
Fili
Krasnaja pakhra
Podol'sk

Kaluga

Borodino

Velikie luki

Janovichi

Smolensk

Chernigov

Novaja Basan'
Pirjatin
Lubny

Brovary
KIEV

Polotsk

Vitebsk

MOGILEV
Dashkova

Dnepr

Razdorskaja stanitsa
Novocherkassk

Kherson

VILNA

Kovno

Grodno
Neman
Mir
Volkovysk
Slonim

Bielsk
Brest-Litovsk
Bug

Dąbrowica

Kovel
Turzysk
Holoby
Różyszcze
Lutsk
Dubno
Mizocz
Kremenets

Zhitomir
Lubar

Druzhkopol
Turzysk

LVOV
Brody
Tarnopol

(Tarnopol
District
1809-1815)

Tilsit
Königsberg
Friedland
Schippenbeil
Heilsberg
Guttstadt

East
Danzig
Prussia

Grand Duchy
Passarge
Vistula

WARSAW
Warsaw

Austria

Baltic Sea

Kama

Volga

Don

200 Miles
300 Kilometers
0
0

"And why should you?" answered the captain indifferently. "Let him come with us."

"It might make trouble for us."

"How? On the contrary, his father and mother both will be grateful to you afterwards for giving him refuge. With his resolve and inexperience, he will come to grief if you send him away."

Throughout this brief exchange between the colonel and the captain, I stood leaning on my sword, firmly determined, if I were refused, to get on my mountain-bred steed and ride alone to my intended goal.

"Very well then, young man," said the colonel, turning to me, "come with us, but I warn you that we are now on our way to the Don, and there are no regular troops there. Shchegrov! Give him a horse from our stables."

A tall Cossack, the colonel's orderly, started to carry out the command, but I made haste to take advantage of a chance to play the part of a soldier under orders and said, "I have a horse, your honor. I'll ride him, if you will permit it."

The colonel burst out laughing. "So much the better, so much the better! Ride your own horse. What's your first name anyway, my gallant lad?"

I said that I was called Aleksandr.

"And your patronymic?"

"My father's name is Vasily."

"So, Aleksandr Vasilevich, on the march you will ride always with the first troop, and dine and be quartered with me. Go to the regiment now; we are about to move out. Duty officer, order the men to mount."

Beside myself with joy, I ran to my Alcides and flew like a bird into the saddle. The spirited horse seemed to comprehend my rapture; he went proudly, arching his neck and flicking his ears rapidly. The Cossack officers admired Alcides' beauty and praised me, too, saying that I sat my horse well and had a fine Circassian waist. I had already begun to blush and become confused by the curious stares fixed on me from all sides, but this state could not be allowed to last for long. I quickly recovered and answered their questions courteously and plausibly in a firm, calm voice, seemingly quite oblivious to the general curiosity and talk aroused by my apparition among the Army of the Don.

At last the Cossacks had their fill of discussing and looking over my steed and me and formed ranks. The colonel came out, mounted his Circassian steed, and commanded, "To the right by threes." The regiment moved out. The first section, composed for the purpose of men with good voices, struck up the Cossacks' favorite song, "The Soul Is a Good Steed." Its melancholy tune plunged me into revery: how long had it been since I was at home? In the garb of my sex, surrounded by girl friends, loved by my father, and respected by everyone as the daughter of the town mayor? Now I am a Cossack, in uniform, wearing a saber. The heavy lance tires my arm, which has not yet reached full strength. Instead of girl friends, I am surrounded by Cossacks whose dialect, jokes, rough voices, and loud laughter all trouble me. An emotion like a desire to cry constricted my breast. I bent to the arched neck of my steed, hugged it, and pressed my face to it. This horse was a gift from my father. It alone was left to remind me of the days I had spent in his house. At last my conflicting emotions subsided. I sat up straight again and turned my attention to the sad autumn landscape, swearing with all my heart never to permit memories to sap my spirit, but to go my freely chosen way with firmness and constancy.

The march lasted over a month. I was delighted with my new situation. I learned to saddle and unsaddle my horse and led him to water just like the others. On the march the Cossack officers often raced their horses and invited me to test the speed of my Alcides against them also, but I love him too much to agree to that. Besides, my good steed is no longer in the first bloom of youth; he is already nine years old, and, although I am convinced that there is no horse in the entire Cossack regiment who can equal Alcides in speed as well as beauty, I am not so inhumanly vain as to exhaust my comrade for the hollow satisfaction of prevailing over the scraggy chargers of the Don.[1]

At last the regiment reached the boundary of its lands and set up camp to await review, after which the men would be dismissed to their homes. The waiting and the review lasted three days. During that time I roamed the boundless Don steppe on foot with a gun or went riding. After the review, groups of Cossacks went their separate ways. It was a picturesque sight: a few hundred Cossacks, dispersing across the broad steppe, rode away from the site of the review in all directions. The scene reminded me of the scattered flight of ants when I chanced to fire a blank charge from a pistol into their hill.

Shchegrov called me to the colonel. "Well now, young man, our wanderings are at an end. And what about yours? What do you intend to do?"

"Go on to the army," I answered boldly.

"And of course you know where it is located? You know which road to take, and you have means for the journey?" asked the colonel with a wry smile.

His irony made me blush. "I will inquire about the place and the road, Colonel, and as to means, I have money and a horse."

"Your means are good only for the want of better. I pity you, Aleksandr Vasilevich! From your actions more than your words I've become con-

---

1. Durova has taken seven years off Alcides' age as well as her own.

vinced of your noble origins. I don't know the reasons which have compelled you to quit your father's house at such a young age but, if it is really a desire to serve in the army, then only your inexperience can conceal from you the endless difficulties you will have to overcome before you attain your goal. Think it over."

The colonel fell silent. I was silent also, and what could I say? Threatening me with difficulties! Advising me to think it over! Perhaps that might have been useful to hear at home, but since I have already gone two thousand versts, I can only continue and, whatever the difficulties, conquer them with a firm will. So I thought, but I kept my silence.

The colonel began again. "I see that you don't want to speak frankly with me. Perhaps you have your reasons, but I haven't the heart to let you go to certain destruction. Take my advice, remain here with me on the Don for now. The protection of a man of experience is indispensable to you. For the time being I offer you my home; live there until we set out on the next march. You won't be bored. I have a family, our climate, as you see, is very warm, there is no snow until December, and you can ride for pleasure as much as you like—my stable is at your service. Now we will go to my house, and I'll turn you over to my wife before I go on to join Platov in Cherkassk.[2] I'll be staying there until the next march, which won't be long in coming. Then you can travel with us as far as the regular army. Will you agree to follow my advice?"

I said that I accepted his proposal with sincere gratitude. It didn't take much wit to see how advantageous it would be for me to reach the regular army without attracting attention or arousing anyone's suspicion.

The colonel and I got into an open carriage and set out for Razdorskaja stanitsa, which was his home. His wife was greatly overjoyed by her husband's arrival. She was a middle-aged, comely, tall, plump woman with black eyes, brows, and hair, and the swarthy complexion common to the entire Cossack tribe. Her fresh lips smiled agreeably as she spoke. She took a great liking to me and was very kind to me, marveling that my parents let me, as she put it, "gad about the world" at such an extraordinarily young age. "You can't be more than fourteen, and here you are, alone in foreign parts. My son is eighteen, and I let him go to foreign lands only with his father, but alone! Oh, God! What might not happen to such a fledgling? Stay with us a while, you'll grow at least a little, you'll mature, and when our Cossacks are off on the march again, you'll go with them, and my husband will be like a father to you." As she talked, the colonel's good lady was setting the table with various treats—honey, grapes, cream, and sweet, newly pressed, wine. "Drink, young man," said my benevolent hostess. "What are you afraid of? Even we women drink it by the glassful, and our three-year-old children drink it like water."

2. Matvej Platov was *ataman* (commander) of the Don Cossacks from 1801 until his death in 1818.

I had never tasted wine before, and so I drank the nectar of the Don with great pleasure. My hostess kept her eyes fixed on me. "How little you resemble a Cossack! You're so pale, so slender, so shapely—like a young lady. That's what my women think; they've already told me you're a girl in disguise!" And with this, the colonel's wife burst out laughing artlessly, without in any way suspecting how well her women had guessed, and what a faint heart her words gave the young guest whom she was so cordially plying with treats.

From that day I took no pleasure in staying with the colonel's family, but roamed the fields and vineyards from morning to night. I would have liked to leave for Cherkassk, but I feared new questions. It was not hard to see how badly the Cossack uniform concealed my striking difference from the native Cossacks; they all shared a distinctive countenance, and therefore my appearance, manners, and even my way of expressing myself were the object of their curiosity and speculation. Moreover, as I found myself continually remarked, I often became confused, blushed, avoided conversation, and went off into the fields all day even in bad weather. [3]

The colonel had not been home for a long time; his duties kept him in Cherkassk. My monotonous and idle life was becoming unbearable. I decided to leave and search out the army, although my heart quivered at the idea that I could expect the same questions and the same curiosity everywhere. But at least, I thought, they would be somewhat incidental, unlike here, where I served as the continual object of remark and speculation.

I decided to leave the next day at dawn and went home before nightfall to inform my hostess of my departure and prepare my horse and gear. As I came into the yard, I noticed an unusual bustle and scurry among the colonel's servants; I noticed a great number of carriages and saddle horses. I entered the parlor, and the first person I met was the newly returned colonel. A crowd of officers surrounded him; none of them, however, was among those with whom I had come to the Don.

3. In the 1839 *Notes* (48–49), Durova recorded her impression of the Don Cossacks' way of life: "Of the pure patriarchal customs of the Army of the Don in its native land, I found the most noble to be that all their lieutenants, captains, and even colonels did not disdain to work in the fields! It was with great respect that I watched these valiant warriors, who had grown gray in martial exploits, whose bravery made their weapons dreaded, upheld the government which they served, and did honor to the land where they were born—it was with great respect, I say, that I watched them cultivating that land: they themselves mow the grass of their fields, they themselves rake it into stacks. How nobly they make use of the time when they are at rest from warriors' occupations! How can one not honor people whose entire life, from childhood to the grave, is dedicated to the good either of their country or their family? How can one not prefer them to those who pass the best years of their lives tormenting defenseless hares and giving their children's bread to packs of borzoj hounds?"

"Hello, Aleksandr Vasilevich," said the colonel in response to my bow. "Have you gotten bored here in our land? Gentlemen, permit me: this is a Russian nobleman; he will accompany us to our destination." The officers bowed slightly to me and went on talking about their march. "Well now, how have you passed your time, Aleksandr Vasilevich? Have you come to love our Don, and isn't there anything on the Don you've come to love as well?" The colonel accompanied this with a sly, ironic smile.

I blushed as I caught the sense of the last question, but I replied politely in the spirit of the joke that I had done my best to avoid becoming so attached to their beautiful land that I would pay for it with later regrets.

"You did very well," said the colonel, "because tomorrow at first light both we and you must bid farewell to our quiet Don! The Ataman regiment has been entrusted to me, and we have orders to march to Grodno province. There you will have a chance to join any regular regiment that suits you; there are lots of them there."[4]

At three in the morning I saddled Alcides and led him to the Cossack ranks. But since the colonel wasn't there yet, I tied up my horse and went into the parlor where the officers were all assembled. A great number of young Cossack women had come to see their husbands off. I witnessed a moving scene. Shchegrov, who was always at the colonel's side on the march, was with him on the Don also; his father, mother, wife, and three lovely grown daughters had come to see him off and once more bid him farewell. It was affecting to see the forty-year-old Cossack bowing to the ground to kiss the feet of his father and mother and receive their blessing, and afterwards himself blessing in exactly the same way the daughters who fell to his feet. This parting ritual was completely new to me and made a most mournful impression on my soul! "This," I thought, "is how children should part from their father and mother. But I—I ran away! Instead of a blessing, reproaches of aggrieved parents have pursued me, and perhaps. . . ." Horrible thought!

Absorbed in these sad reflections, I didn't hear them all go out, leaving the parlor empty. A rustling noise behind me caught my attention and wrenched me from my mournful reveries most disagreeably. One of the colonel's women was creeping up behind me, "And why are you still standing here alone, young lady? Your friends are mounted, and Alcides is running around the yard," she said with the look and ironic smile of a true satan. My heart shuddered and suffused with blood. I made haste to get away from this *Megaera!*

4. The officer who commanded the Ataman regiment during the 1807 Prussian campaign was Stepan Balabin, which fits with Durova's use below of the initial "B." for her benefactor's son (*Voennaja entsiklopedija*, vol. 3 [St. Petersburg, 1911], 228).

The Cossacks were already in formation. Nearby my Alcides was pawing the ground with impatience. As I rushed to catch him, I met the colonel's stern gaze: "In your situation you should aways be first; for you it's imperative, Aleksandr Vasilevich," he said, riding out before the ranks. At last the traditional "To the right by threes" set the regiment moving. Soon "The Heart Is a Good Steed" rang out again, and the scenes of our earlier life on the march were renewed, but I am no longer the same girl. Having aged a few months, I have grown bolder, and I am no longer thrown into confusion at every question. The officers of the Ataman regiment, better educated than the others, remarking in my deportment the courtesy that serves as a mark of good upbringing, treat me with respect and seek out my company.

In early spring we arrived in the little town of Druzhkopol on the banks of the Bug. The Brjansk Musketeers under Colonel Liders are quartered here also. The officers of the two regiments are often together. Their way of life seems deadly to me: they sit in a stuffy room from morning to night, smoking pipes, playing cards, and talking nonsense. The colonel asked me whether I wanted to enlist in the Brjansk regiment.

"God forbid, Colonel," I replied. "If there were only infantry on the terrestrial globe, I would never have come to join up; I don't want to serve on foot."

"Well, just as you please. You'll get your chance yet; you're still all too young."

I love to go out walking at night alone in the forest or the fields. Yesterday I strayed quite far from the town and was still on my way home well after midnight. Absorbed as usual in my thoughts, I was walking fast and paying no attention to my surroundings. Suddenly a groan, hollow and apparently coming from under the ground, broke into the nocturnal hush and my reveries. I stopped, looked around, and listened closely. Again I heard a groan and saw that I was ten paces away from a graveyard and that was where the groans were coming from. Not the least trace of fear perturbed my soul. I approached the graveyard, opened the enclosure, went in, and began walking around the graves, stooping and listening. The groans were resounding throughout the graveyard, and I went on from one grave to the next, until at last I ended up behind the church and heard to my surprise that the groans were being carried on the wind from the direction of a swamp half a verst away.

Since I had no idea what this could mean, I hurried to reach the colonel's quarters in time to catch Shchegrov awake and recount the incident to him. And, in fact, I found Shchegrov still vigilant and very angry. I was to some extent under his supervision, my prolonged absence at night had frightened him, and so my story was very badly received. He told me with vexation that it was foolish of me to drag about graveyards at night sniffing the graves like a jackal and that this strange taste would end up giving me the pleasure of contracting the swamp fever from which a great number of soldiers in the Brjansk regiment were dying; and he ended his sermon by remarking that if, instead of coming to them just out from under my mama's wing, I had taken the time to let the milk dry a bit on my lips, I would know that the groans I heard came from a bird living in the swamps called a bog-bull—that is, a bittern. The old Cossack's grumbling took away any wish on my part to ask why this bird does not cry, sing, or whistle, but groans. I went to bed without another word.

The colonel's son studied with the Jesuits in Lubar. He invited me to visit him there to feast my eyes on the extraordinary girth and enormous size of two of his teachers. We are quartered ten versts from Lubar, and so I rode my horse there. I stopped at the tavern where the colonel always stays. Entering the sort of spacious room one usually finds in every tavern, I saw a young Jewess chanting her prayers. She was standing before a mirror, quietly whining her psalms while simultaneously blacking her eyebrows and listening with an ironic smile to a young infantry officer who was saying something to her in a low voice. My entrance interrupted this scene. The Jewess turned toward me, quickly looked me over, and came up so close that her breath felt warm on my face. "What can I do for you?" she asked, almost whispering. I replied that I was asking her to care for the horse I was leaving at her tavern.

"Will you be spending the night here?" she asked, still in the same mysterious way.

"I'll spend the night at the Jesuit monastery, or maybe here—I don't know for certain."

At the mention of the Jesuit monastery, she turned away from me without a word, ordered a worker to take my horse, resumed her previous pose before the mirror, and started humming through her teeth again, bending toward the officer, who once more began talking to her. I left them and went to make sure that Alcides was well placed. Seeing all his needs satisfied, I went directly to the *klasztor* of the Jesuit fathers.

The monstrous obesity of young B.'s teachers, the reverend fathers Hieronim and Antonio, was in fact horrifying to me. The huge mass of their bodies exceeded all probability; they were almost totally unable to stand, but remained sitting and recited the entire church service seated in their cell. Their breathing was like a hollow roar. I sat down in a corner and stared fixedly at them in consternation and a kind of dread. The young Cossack pinched his nose and stopped his mouth in order to keep from laughing out loud at the odd sight of me together with his two monsters in cassocks.

At last the call to supper interrupted the reverend fathers' pious rumblings, the young scamp's grimaces, and my consternation. We took our places. The rascal B. whispered in my ear that hospitality obliged him to seat me between his teachers so I could have the full pleasure of their conversation. I tried as quickly as I could to sit down beside him, but I failed: a huge hand gripped mine, and a voice rang out in a low roar almost at the ceiling, "Wouldn't you like to take the seat between us? I beg you humbly, here, if you please!"

That supper was a genuine ordeal for me. Since I don't speak Polish, I didn't know how to answer my terrible neighbors to the right and left. Moreover, I had another fear, that of overeating on the delicious food of Poland. I was deathly hot, I blushed incessantly, and sweat stood out in drops on my forehead. In short, I was in torment and extremely comical. But at last the chairs scraped loudly, and the huge fathers got up. Their muttered prayers floated over my head like the distant rumble of thunder. After the completion of all possible formalities, I was overjoyed to find myself outside the monastery enclosure. My first impulse on going out the gates was to put distance at a near run between me and the walls of the hospitable retreat in which it was so melancholy to live and so difficult to breathe.

The Ataman regiment is on its way to Grodno. The Cossacks are sharpening their lances and sabers. There is no approaching Alcides; he snorts, frisks, and kicks. My good steed! What lot awaits us?[5]

We have arrived in Grodno. The regiment will be here for only two days, and then it will go abroad. The colonel sent for me: "Now you have a good chance to enlist in any of the cavalry squadrons forming here which suits you. But take my advice. Be frank with the commander of the regiment you decide to join. That alone isn't enough to get you accepted as a cadet, but at least you will win his favorable disposition and good opinion. And, meanwhile, make haste to write your parents to send you the necessary proofs of nobility without which you can either be rejected outright or, at the very least, remain for a long time in the ranks."[6]

I thanked him for the advice and for the protection which he had so long extended me and at last bade him farewell. The next day the Cossacks went abroad, and I remained behind in Grodno.

5. Napoleon defeated the Prussians at Jena in October 1806. The succeeding Russian movement into Poland was met by the French with the occupation of Warsaw in November. After a series of clashes culminating in the bloody and indecisive battle of Eylau in the winter of 1806–1807, the Russians and French withdrew to prepare for a decisive spring campaign in East Prussia.

6. A cadet—the Russians used the German word "Junker"—was a nobleman who enlisted as a common soldier.

*Grodno.* I am alone, totally alone! I'm staying in a roadside tavern. Alcides incessantly neighs and paws the ground; he too has been left alone. From my window I can see passing throngs of uhlans playing music and dancing. They are amicably inviting all the young men to join in their merriment. I am going to find out what is going on.

It is called the *verbunok!*[7] God help me, if there is no other way of joining a regular regiment except through the *verbunok!* That would be extremely disagreeable. While I was watching this dancing expedition, the swordbelt-wearing cadet who was in charge of it (or, as they call him, the *namiestnik* or deputy), approached me: "How do you like our life? It's gay, isn't it?"[8]

I replied that it was indeed and walked away from him. The next day I learned that this regiment was the Polish Horse, that it was recruiting to bring the regiment up to strength after heavy losses in battle, and that it was commanded by a captain.[9] Once I had gathered this information, I searched out the quarters of the deputy who spoke to me yesterday. He told me that, if I wanted to enlist and serve in their regiment, I could address my request to their Captain Kazimirski and that there was absolutely no need for me to dance with the throng of riffraff worming its way into the regiment. I was overjoyed by the possibility of joining the army without submitting to the odious ritual of dancing in the streets, and I told the deputy so. He could not help laughing: "But it's all done voluntarily, you see, and anyone who doesn't want to take part in our *bacchanalia* can easily avoid it. Would you like to come with me to see

7. The *verbunok* was a common recruiting ritual in Hungary and Poland. Denis Davydov speaks of printers dealing unceremoniously with his poetry "the way they used to recruit [*verbovali*] various tramps for hussar regiments: at noisy dinners and merry feasts, amidst uproarious revelry" ([Autobiography], *Voennye zapiski* [Moscow, 1940], 36).

8. The "swordbelt cadet" in Russian was *portupej-junker,* a term applied to a cadet who had been promoted to sergeant and was eligible for and awaiting an opening for commission; the Polish equivalent was *namiestnik.*

9. In the reign of Emperor Paul I (1796–1801) three regiments of Russian light cavalry, all lance-bearing and designated from 1806 as uhlans (lancers)—the Polish Horse (Konnopolskij), Lithuanian (Litovskij), and Tatar (Tatarskij) regiments—were formed in the lands Russia acquired by the three partitions of Poland between 1772 and 1795. Paul wanted "to furnish a suitable occupation for the large numbers of Polish nobility" (Faddej Bulgarin, *Vospominanija* [St. Petersburg, 1846], part 2, 157). Durova was to end up serving in two out of three of these regiments. The light cavalry consisted of hussars and uhlans. Their functions were similar to those of the Cossacks; on campaign they made up the advance- and rear-guards, carried out reconnaissance and picket duty, and in battle covered the flanks of the infantry; in peacetime they were frequently assigned to patrol the borders. Uhlans carried sabers and a brace of pistols; the first ranks bore lances, and the best marksmen in the rear ranks had carbines (A. A. Kozhevnikov, "Armija v 1805–1814 gg.," *Otechestvennaja vojna i russkoe obshchestvo,* vol. 3 [Moscow, 1912], 67). That a captain instead of the usual colonel was commanding the Polish Horse is an indication of the severity of the death toll in the winter campaign.

Kazimirski? He'll be very pleased to acquire such a recruit. And, besides, I'll cheer him up for the rest of the day when I tell him about your misgivings." So saying, the deputy burst out laughing wholeheartedly, and off we went.

From the deputy's room we had to cross the large public room that, as I said before, is to be found in every tavern. It was full of uhlans and prospective recruits, all of them dancing and singing. I clutched the deputy's arm and tried to get through the noisy crowd as quickly as I could, but just then one of the uhlans clamped his arm around my waist, flew with me into the circle, and with a stamp of his foot prepared to begin the mazurka in which a few couples were already capering and sliding helter-skelter. The deputy freed me from the arms of these en-chanted dancers, his laughter redoubled by this unexpected incident. At last we arrived at Kazimirski's quarters.

Cavalry Captain Kazimirski is about fifty years old, with a noble and at the same time martial appearance. All the features of his agreeable face are imbued with good nature and valor. As I came in, he evidently took me for a Cossack officer, bowed politely, and asked, "What can I do for you?"

I said that I wished to serve in the Polish Horse and, since I knew that he was in charge of bringing the regiment up to strength, I had come to ask him to let me enlist.

"You, enlist in the Polish Horse!" said the captain in astonishment. "You're a Cossack. You belong to the Army of the Don, and you should be serving there."

"My attire has deceived you. I am a Russian nobleman and, conse-quently, I can choose any form of service I wish."

"Can you prove it?"

"No. But if you are willing to trust my word alone that I really am a Russian nobleman, I will know how to value your indulgence, and at the end of the campaign I pledge to furnish the regiment with everything necessary to confirm the truth of my words."

"How do you come to be wearing a Cossack uniform?"

"My father did not want to enroll me in the army. I ran away in secret, joined company with a Cossack regiment, and came here with it."

"How old are you? What's your name?"

"I'm in my seventeenth year. My name is Durov."[10]

The captain turned to one of the officers of his regiment: "What do you think? Shall we take him?"

"It's up to you. But why shouldn't we? There's a war on, we need men, and he promises to be a gallant lad."

10. According to her service record, Durova enlisted under the name of Aleksandr Sokolov.

"But if he's a Cossack and trying to escape his own folk for some reason by enlisting in a regular regiment?"

"It's not possible, Captain! It's written on his face that he's not lying. At that age they haven't learned to dissemble. Besides, if you turn him down, he will just go on to someone who won't be so overly cautious and you'll lose a good recruit. . . ."

This entire exchange was in Polish. The captain turned to me. "I agree to accept your word, Durov! I hope that your conduct will justify my trust."

I would have liked to say that it would not be long before he saw for himself whether I was worthy of the honor of being accepted as one of the warriors with the enviable good fortune of serving Alexander, but I kept silent, fearing they would take this as an unseemly boast. I said only that I had a horse and would like to serve on him if I could.

"Impossible!" said the captain. "You will be given an army horse. However, you can keep him with you until you get a chance to sell him."

"Sell him! Alcides!" I cried involuntarily. "Oh, God preserve me from that misfortune! No sir, Captain, I have money. I'll feed my horse at my own expense, and I won't part from him for anything on earth."

Kazimirski was himself a cavalryman from the cradle; my attachment to the best of wartime comrades pleased him greatly. He said that my horse could have a place in his stable and feed as well, I could ride him when we went abroad, and he himself would undertake to secure permission for me to serve on him. After this he sent for one of the uhlans on duty with him and put me under his supervision, ordering him to teach me to ride in formation, wield a saber, shoot, master a lance, and to saddle, unsaddle, pack, and curry my horse. When I have learned something about all of that, he is to give me a uniform and put me on duty. The uhlan listened to the order and took me at once to the *muster-room*—which is what they call the cottage, sometimes merely a shed, where young soldiers are instructed in all that pertains to military service.

Every day I get up at dawn and head for the muster-room; from there we all go together to the stables. My uhlan mentor praises my quick comprehension and constant readiness to practice evolutions, if need be from morning to night. He says that I'll be a gallant lad. I must confess, however, that brandishing the heavy lance—especially the completely worthless maneuver of swinging it over my head—makes me deathly tired, and I have already hit myself on the head several times. I am also ill-at-ease with the saber; it always seems to me that I will cut myself. I would more readily suffer a wound, however, than display the slightest timidity.

I spend all morning in training and then go to dine with Kazimirski, who quizzes me with paternal indulgence, asking me whether I like my present pursuits and what I think of the military craft. I replied that I have loved the military craft from the day of my birth; that martial pursuits have been and will be my sole exercise; that I consider the warrior's calling the noblest of them all and the only one in which it is impossible to admit any vices whatsoever because fearlessness is the primary and indispensable quality of the warrior. Fearlessness is inseparable from greatness of soul, and the combination of these two great virtues leaves no room for vice and low passions.

"Do you really think, young man," asked the captain, "that it is impossible to have qualities meriting respect without being fearless? There are many people who are timid by nature and have outstanding qualities."

"I can well believe it, Captain. But I also think that a fearless man must surely be virtuous."

"Perhaps you're right," said the captain with a smile. "But," he added, patting me on the shoulder and twirling his mustaches, "let's wait for ten years or so, and also for your first battle: experience can be rather disillusioning."

After dinner Kazimirski lay down for a nap, and I went to the stable to give my horse his midday portion of oats. After this I was free to do whatever I wanted until six in the evening.

However exhausted I get from brandishing all morning that sister to the saber, the heavy lance, and from riding in formation and jumping obstacles, my fatigue passes after half an hour of rest, and from two to six I roam the fields, mountains, and forests on foot, fearlessly, tirelessly, and without a care. Freedom, a precious gift from heaven, has at last become my portion forever! I respire it, revel in it, feel it in my heart and soul. It penetrates and animates my existence. You, young women of my own age, only you can comprehend my rapture, only you can value my happiness! You, who must account for every step, who cannot go fifteen feet without supervision and protection, who from the cradle to the grave are eternally dependent and eternally guarded, God knows from whom and from what—I repeat, only you can comprehend the joyous sensations that fill my heart at the sight of vast forests, immense fields, mountains, valleys, and streams and at the thought that I can roam them all with no one to answer to and no fear of anyone's prohibition. I jump for joy as I realize that I will never again in my entire life hear the words: *You, girl, sit still! It's not proper for you to go wandering about alone.* Alas, how many fine clear days began and ended which I could watch only with tear-stained eyes through the window where my mother had ordered me to weave lace. This mournful recollection of the oppression in which my childhood years were passed puts a quick end to my cheerful capers. I remain downcast for an hour or so as I recall life at home, but fortunately I recollect it less and less each day, and just the mere thought that my liberty is as boundless as the horizon makes me giddy with joy.

The captain has ordered me and one of my comrades, Wyszemirski, assigned to the first platoon under the command of Lieutenant Boshnjakov. The platoon is quartered in a landowner's impoverished village surrounded by swamps.

What a famished land this Lithuania is! The inhabitants are so poor, pale, gaunt, and dispirited that it is impossible to look at them without pity. The clayey land, scattered with stones, rewards poorly their laborious efforts to fertilize and cultivate it. Their bread is as black as coal and mixed with something prickly as well (gravel). It is impossible to eat; at least I can't manage to finish a single slab of it.

We have been stationed here for over three weeks. They have given me a uniform, a saber, and a lance so heavy that it feels like a log; they have given me woolen epaulets, a plumed helmet, and a white crossbelt with a pouch full of cartridges. It is all very clean, very handsome, and very heavy. However, I hope to get used to it. But what I will never be able to get used to are the tyrannical army boots—they are like iron! Until now I wore soft and deftly sewn shoes, my foot was light and free, but now! Oh, my God! It is as if I were nailed to the ground by the weight of my boots and huge clanking spurs. I would gladly order the Jew shoemaker to make me a pair of boots, but I have so little money. What cannot be changed must be endured.

From the day I put on my government boots, I could no longer roam around the way I used to and, since I am perishing from hunger every day, I spend all my free time in the vegetable patch digging up leftover potatoes with a spade. By working diligently for four hours straight, I succeed in uncovering enough to fill my cap. Then I carry my booty in triumph to my hostess to cook. This grim woman always tears the cap full of potatoes from my hands with a grumble, spills them into a clay pot still grumbling, and, when they are done, puts them in a wooden bowl and shoves them along the table to me in such a way that a few of them always roll onto the floor. What a malicious woman! She has no obvious reason to begrudge me the potatoes; theirs are already harvested and hidden away somewhere. The fruit of my indefatigable labors is only those which were left very deep in the ground or somehow escaped the workers' attention.

Yesterday my hostess was pouring milk when I came in with my cap full of potatoes. She was startled and I, overjoyed, began begging her most earnestly to give me a little milk with my potatoes. It was terrible to see the spite and hatred that swept across her face. Cursing roundly, she poured the milk into a bowl, tore my cap from my hands, spilled all my potatoes onto the floor, and then, however, rushed at once to pick them up. This last action, the reason for which I could only conjecture, made me laugh.

Our platoon commander, Lieutenant Boshnjakov, has taken Wyszemirski and me into his quarters. Being well brought up, he treats us both as it becomes a gentleman to treat equals. We are living in the landowner's house. They have given us—our officer, that is—a large room separated by a hallway from the rooms of our host. Wyszemirski and I are the total masters of this chamber, because our lieutenant is almost always out and rarely sleeps at home. He spends all his time in a neighboring village at the house of an elderly landowner, a widow. She has a pretty daughter, and our lieutenant's valet tells us that he is mortally smitten with her. The wife of our landowner, a young lady of rare beauty, is very unhappy that her lodger does not stay in his own quarters. Every time she sees me or Wyszemirski she asks with a charming little burr, "What does your officer do at NN's? He is there from morning to night and night to morning!" From me she hears only one answer: "I don't know." But Wyszemirski finds it amusing to assure her that the lieutenant is afraid of losing his peace of heart and thus flees his dangerous quarters.

I have become accustomed to my fetters—that is, to my army boots—and now I run as lightly and tirelessly as before. But the heavy oak lance still nearly breaks my arm off in drill, especially when I have to swing it over my head. What a vexatious maneuver!

We are on our way abroad! Into battle! I am both happy and sad. If I am killed, what will become of my old father? He loved me.

In a few hours I shall leave Russia and be in a strange land! I am writing to my father where I am and what I have become. I write that I fall to his feet and embrace his knees, imploring him to forgive my flight, give me his blessing, and permit me to follow the path essential to my happiness. My tears fell on the paper as I wrote, and they will speak for me to my father's heart.

I had no sooner carried the letter to the post when the order was given to lead out the horses—we are moving out right away. I am being permitted to ride, serve, and go into battle on Alcides. We are on our way to Prussia, and, as far as I can tell, we are in no great hurry. Our marches are moderate, with halts as usual every third or fourth day.

On the third march Wyszemirski said that the next halt was not far from the hamlet of an uncle, with whom his sister lives and is being brought up. "I'm going to ask the captain for permission to ride over there for a day. Will you go with me, Durov?"

"If they let me, I'll be glad to go," I answered.

We went to see the captain. When he heard what we wanted, he sent us off at once, merely ordering Wyszemirski to take good care of his horse and emphasizing to us both that we had to be back in the squadron without fail on the second day. Off we went. The estate of landowner Kunat, Wyszemirski's uncle, was five miles from the village where our squadron would spend the day and, although we trotted all the way, we did not arrive until the dead of night.[11] The silence was broken only by a monotonous knocking sound from inside the high fence that enclosed the spacious yard of the manor; it was the watchman making his rounds and hitting something against a board. The gates were not locked, and we rode unhindered into a smooth, broad yard covered with green grass. But as soon as our horses' hoofbeats were heard in the still of the night, a pack of loudly barking watchdogs instantly surrounded us. I started to dismount anyway, but when I caught sight of a new arrival running up to us, a dog nearly on a level with my horse, I got back into the saddle and resolved not to get down even if we had to wait until dawn for someone to chase away the beasts attacking us. At last the watchman came into sight carrying his clapper. He recognized Wyszemirski at once and was delighted. At his first sign the dogs retreated to their kennels. Servants appeared, brought lights, took our horses and led them off to the stables, and invited us into the overseer's house, because the masters were asleep and the doors locked tight all around.

I don't know how the news of Wyszemirski's arrival penetrated the locked doors of the house, but his sister, who was sleeping near her aunt's bedroom, heard of it and came at once to see us. She was a very pretty child about thirteen years old. She curtseyed solemnly before her brother, saying "Jak sie masz?" and rushed in tears to hug him. I couldn't understand the contrast.[12] They served us supper and brought rugs, pillows, straw, and sheets to make up beds for us. *Panna* Wyszemirska rebelled against these arrangements. She said that the bedding was unnecessary, it would soon be daytime, and her brother would surely rather sit and talk to her than sleep. The overseer laughed and gave her the choice of going to her room and letting us go to sleep or staying and lying down between us to talk to her brother. The little girl said, "Wstydź się, pane ekonome!"[13] and went away, after kissing her brother and bowing to me.

The next day they called us to coffee with *pan* Kunat. The imposing-

11. The distance is in Polish miles, which equal about 4 1/2 English ones.

12. "How do you do?" (Polish) The formal manners of the Polish nobility within the family were frequently remarked on.

13. "For shame, honorable overseer!"

looking Polish gentleman was sitting with his wife and sons in an old-fashioned parlor lined with crimson damask. The chairs and sofas were upholstered in the same fabric and decorated with a fringe which had undoubtedly once been gold but was now all tarnished and blackened. The room had a gloomy air completely at odds with the kind and good-natured appearance of its owners. They embraced their nephew, bowed politely to me, and invited us to share their breakfast.

The entire family took the greatest liking to me. They asked me my age and where I came from and, when I told them that I lived not far from Siberia, Kunat's wife shrieked in surprise and looked at me with new curiosity, as if an inhabitant of Siberia were a supernatural being. Throughout Poland people have a strange concept of Siberia. Kunat looked up on the map the city where my father lives and assured me with a chuckle that I was mistaken in calling myself a Siberian; on the contrary, I was an Asian. I saw paper and pencil on the table and asked permission to sketch something. "Oh, gladly," answered my hosts. I had not practiced this agreeable art for a long time and was so glad to have the chance to draw a picture that I sat over my voluntary task for more than two hours. When I had finished sketching Andromeda on the cliff, I was showered with praise by Kunats young and old. I thanked them for their indulgence to my mediocre talent. I would have liked to present the picture to *panna* Wyszemirska, but the elder lady took it from my hands, saying, "If you have no use for it, give it to me. I will tell everybody that a Polish Horse soldier, a native of Siberia, drew it!"

Kunat heard her. "Excuse me, my dear, you're wrong. Durov is an Asian. Here, see for yourself," he said, dragging the huge map over to his wife's table.

The next day we said goodby to the Kunats. They rode with us for about ten versts in an open carriage. "Sketch a landscape of our village, Durov," said Kunat's wife. "It will remind you sometimes of people who have come to love you like a son." I said that I would never forget them even without that. At last we parted. The Kunats' carriage turned back, and we proceeded at a light gallop.

Wyszemirski was quiet and sullen. His saddlebags were filled with various provisions and loomed over the flanks of his horse in two large mounds. At last he began talking. "Let's go at a walk; Uncle's gifts have overloaded my horse's back. Why did I go to see them? Strangers are dearer to them than family! They were occupied only with you, and I might as well have not been there at all. What good are relations like that!"

Wyszemirski's pride was suffering cruelly from the clear predilection his family had shown me. I tried to placate him. "What do I care, Wyszemirski, whether your uncle and aunt were occupied with me, when your sister never once glanced at me and never said a word to me the entire time we were with them? Would you like to trade? You take your uncle and aunt's attention, and give me the caresses, tears, and kisses of your sister."

Wyszemirski sighed, smiled in a wry, melancholy way, and began telling me that his little sister complained of too strict custody and constraint. At once I remembered my life in my father's house, Mama's strictness, my cruel bondage, the endless hours bent over work; I remembered—and my face clouded with sorrow. I sighed in my turn, and the two of us traveled the rest of the way in silence.

Today our squadron rejoined the regiment. Tomorrow Captain Kazimirski must present us all for review by Major-General Kachowski, and tomorrow also we will all be assigned to other squadrons.

The review is over. Kazimirski had the courtesy not to put me in the ranks of the recruits, but presented me individually to Kachowski. He assigned me to the *leib*-squadron commanded by Captain Galéra.

At last my dreams have come true! I am a warrior! I am in the Polish Horse, I bear arms, and, moreover, fortune has placed me in one of the bravest regiments of our army!

# Chapter Two

*May 22, 1807. Guttstadt.* For the first time I have seen a battle and been in it. What a lot of absurd things they told me about the first battle, about the fear, timidity, and the last, desperate courage! What rubbish! Our regiment went on the attack several times, not all at once but taking turns by squadron. I was berated for joining the attack with each new squadron. However, this was honestly not from any excess of bravery, but simply from ignorance; I thought that was how it was done, and I was amazed when the sergeant-major of another squadron, alongside which I was racing like a whirlwind, shouted at me, "Get the hell out of here! What are you galloping here for?" I returned to my squadron, but, instead of taking my place in formation, I went on riding around nearby. The novelty of the scene absorbed all my attention: the menacing and majestic boom of cannon fire, the roar or kind of rumble of the flying balls, the mounted troops galloping by, the glittering bayonets of the infantry, the roll of drums, and the firm pace and calm look with which our infantry regiments advanced on the enemy—all this filled my soul with sensations that I have no words to express.

I came close to losing my priceless Alcides. While I was riding around, as I said before, near my squadron and looking over the curious scene of battle, I caught sight of several enemy dragoons surrounding a Russian officer and knocking him off his horse with a pistol shot. He fell, and they prepared to hack at him as he lay. Instantly I rushed toward them with my lance tilted. I can only suppose that this scatterbrained audacity frightened them, because in a flash they abandoned the officer and scattered. I galloped over to the wounded man and stopped above him; for a couple of minutes I watched him in silence. He lay with his eyes closed and gave no sign of life; he obviously thought that it was the enemy who stood over him. At last he risked a glance, and I at once asked him if he wanted to get on my horse.

"Oh, be so kind, my friend!" he said in a barely audible voice. At once I dismounted from my horse and with great effort managed to raise the wounded man, but here the aid I could render him came to an end: he fell chestdown across my arm and I, barely able to keep my feet, had no idea what to do and how to get him onto Alcides, whom I was also holding by the reins with my other hand. This situation would have ended very disadvantageously for us both—that is, for the officer and for me—except that fortunately a soldier from his regiment rode over to us and helped me to seat the wounded man on my horse. I told the soldier to

38

send the horse to Recruit Durov in the Polish Horse regiment, and the dragoon told me that the officer I had saved was Lieutenant Panin of the Finnish Dragoons and that they would return my horse immediately.

The officer was carried off to his regiment, and I set out for mine. I felt at a complete disadvantage, left on foot among charges, gunfire, and swordfights. Seeing everywhere men either flying by like lightning or quietly galloping in various directions with complete confidence in their good steeds, I exclaimed, "Alas, my Alcides! Where is he now?" I deeply repented having so rashly given up my horse—and even more when my captain, after first asking me with concern, "Did they kill your horse, Durov? Are you wounded?" shouted at me in vexation, "Get away from the front, you scamp!" when he heard how I happened to be wandering about on foot. Quickly, albeit sadly, I headed for the spot where I saw lances with the pennons of the Polish Horse. The men I passed said with compassion, "Oh, my God! Look, what a young boy has been wounded!" Nobody who saw an uhlan on foot in a uniform covered with blood could think anything else. As I mentioned, the wounded officer had lain chestdown across my arm, and I have to assume that his was a chest wound, because my sleeve was all bloody.

To my inexpressible joy, Alcides has been returned to me—not quite the way I hoped, but at least returned. I was walking pensively through the fields to my regiment, when suddenly I saw our Lieutenant Podwyszącki riding away from the enemy position on my horse. I was beside myself with joy and, without stopping to wonder how my horse had turned up under Podwyszącki, ran over to stroke and caress Alcides, who also expressed his joy by frisking and neighing loudly.

"Is this really your horse?" asked the astonished Podwyszącki.

I recounted my adventure to him. He too had no praise for my rashness. He said that he had bought my horse from Cossacks for two gold pieces. I begged him to return Alcides and take from me the money he had paid for him.

"Very well, but let me keep him today. My horse was killed, and I have nothing to ride in action!" And with this he spurred Alcides and galloped off on him. I was close to weeping as I saw my comrade-in-arms in strange hands, and I swore with all my heart never again to give up my horse as long as I live! At last this agonizing day came to an end. Podwyszącki returned Alcides to me, and our army is now pursuing the retreating enemy.

*May 24. On the banks of the Passarge.* What a strange affair! We made so little haste to pursue the enemy that he managed to cross this little river, on the banks of which we are now standing, and met us with gunfire. Perhaps I don't understand anything about it, but it seems to me we should have stayed on the enemy's heels and crushed him at the crossing.

*The same spot, on the banks of the Passarge.* We have been standing here doing nothing for two days now—and there is nothing to be done. In front of us jaegers are exchanging fire with enemy skirmishers across the river. Our regiment is stationed directly behind the jaegers but, since we have absolutely nothing to do, we have been ordered to dismount. I am perishing from hunger! I don't have even a single rusk. The Cossacks who captured my Alcides took from him the saddlebags with rusks, raincape, and valise. I got my horse back with only a saddle, and everything else was gone. I try sleeping to forget how hungry I am, but it doesn't help.

At last the uhlan who was assigned to supervise me and still holds a mentor's authority, noticed that my saddle was missing its bags and that my face was pale. He offered me three large moldy rusks. I took them eagerly and laid them in a hole filled with rainwater to moisten them a bit. Although I had not eaten for nearly two days, the rusks were so large, bitter, and green that I could eat only one of them.

We are still standing on the same spot. The skirmishers are exchanging fire, and so the uhlans are lying on the grass. From boredom I went for a walk around the hills where Cossack vedettes are posted. Coming down off a knoll, I saw a horrible scene: two jaegers, who had evidently wanted to take shelter from the gunfire or simply to drink their liquor at leisure, both lay dead. Death had found them in their refuge; they were both killed by a single cannonball which tore away the chest of the one sitting higher up, pierced the side of his comrade, who was sitting somewhat lower, ripped out his intestines, and lay there with him. Beside them also lay their canteen of vodka.

Shuddering, I left the dreadful sight of the two bodies. I returned to the regiment, lay down in the bushes, and went to sleep, only to be roused very quickly and disagreeably; a cannonball fell close to me, and a few more came flying after it. I jumped up and ran ten paces away from the spot, but I didn't have time to snatch up my cap and left it behind. It lay on the grass, and against the dark green its bright crimson color made it look like a huge flower. The sergeant-major ordered me to go pick it up and I went, albeit rather reluctantly, because balls were falling thick and fast into the shrubbery. The reason for this sudden rain of fire onto us was our pennons: we had driven our lances into the ground by our horses. The multicolored pennons playing in the wind and fluttering in the air attracted the attention of the enemy. Suspecting from them that we were in the woods, he directed his cannon fire there. Now we have been led farther off and ordered to lay the lances on the ground.

In the evening our regiment was ordered to mount. Until late at night we sat on our steeds and waited for orders to move out. We have become the rear-guard now and will cover the army's retreat. So our captain tells us. Since I was deathly tired from sitting on my horse so long, I asked Wyszemirski if he did not want to get down. He said that he would have dismounted long ago if he wasn't expecting the regiment to leave at any minute.

"We'll hear it and can be back on our horses in a flash," I said, "but now let's lead them across the ditch and lie down on the grass there."

Wyszemirski followed my advice. We led our horses across the ditch and lay down in the bushes. I wound the reins around my arm and instantly fell asleep. I heard my name repeated twice, I felt Alcides nudging me with his head, snorting, and pawing the ground, I felt the earth trembling under me, and then everything became quiet. My heart shrank. I understood the danger and made an effort to wake up, but I couldn't. Although Alcides, my priceless steed, was left alone, hearing his comrades in the distance and free because the reins had slackened and fallen off my arm, he did not leave me, but kept on incessantly pawing the ground and snorting, bending his muzzle to me. At last with difficulty I opened my eyes and got up. I saw that Wyszemirski was gone. I looked at the spot where the regiment had stood—it was gone, too! I was surrounded by a nocturnal darkness and quiet that under the circumstances was quite dreadful. The hollow reverberation of horses' hooves convinced me that the regiment was riding away at a trot. I made haste to mount Alcides, and justice demands that I admit that my foot was slow to find the stirrup. Seated, I loosed the reins, and my steed, my excellent, trusty steed, jumped the ditch and carried me right through the shrubbery at an easy, rapid run right to the regiment; in a quarter of an hour he caught up with it and took his place in the ranks. Wyszemirski said he thought it was the end of me. He said that he himself was very alarmed when he heard the regiment departing and, therefore, after calling me twice, he had left my fate in God's hands.

*May 29 and 30. Heilsberg.* The French fought furiously here. Oh, man is horrible in his frenzy! Then he combines all the qualities of the wild beast. No, this is not bravery! I don't know what to call this wild, bestial daring, but it is unworthy of being called fearlessness. Our regiment was able to play only a small active part in this battle: it was the artillery which pounded, and the victorious bayonets of our infantry which struck home. But we took some punishment anyway; we were covering the artillery, which is a most disadvantageous situation, because the insult is taken without response—that is, no matter what happens, you must stand your ground without moving.

Even now I do not see anything frightening in battle, but I see many men as white as sheets, I see them duck when a shell flies over as if they could evade it. Evidently in these men, fear has more force than reason. I have already seen a great many killed and severely wounded. It is pitiful to watch the latter moaning and crawling over the so-called field of honor. What can mitigate the horror of a position like that for a common soldier? A recruit? For an educated man it is a completely different matter: the lofty feeling of honor, heroism, devotion to the emperor, and sacred duty to his native land compel him to face death fearlessly, endure suffering courageously, and part with life calmly.

For the first time danger was so close to me that it could not have been closer. A grenade landed under the belly of my horse and at once exploded. Whistling fragments flew in all directions. Stunned and showered with dirt, I barely kept my seat on Alcides, who gave such a leap to the side that I thought he was possessed by the devil. Poor Wyszemirski, who screws up his eyes at every bullet, says that such a violent caper would have thrown him. But the most astonishing thing is that not a single fragment struck either me or Alcides! This is so extraordinary that my comrades cannot stop marveling at it. Oh, it is clear that my father's prayers and my old grandmother's blessing are preserving my life amid these terrible, bloody scenes.

It has been raining heavily ever since morning. I am shivering; nothing I have on is dry. Rain streams unimpeded onto my helmet, across my helmet onto my head, down my face, under my collar, over my entire body, and into my boots. It fills them and runs in several streams onto the ground. I am quivering like an aspen leaf in every limb. At last we have been ordered to pull back; another cavalry regiment is going to take our place. And it is long overdue! We have been standing here almost the entire day. We are soaked to the bones and stiff with cold, we no longer look at all human, and, moreover, we have lost many men.

When our regiment took up a position beyond the range of enemy bullets, I asked the captain for permission to make a quick trip into Heilsberg, which is a verst away from us. I needed to get Alcides shod— he has lost a shoe—and, besides, I wanted to buy something to eat. I was so hungry that I even looked with envy at a chunk of bread one of our officers was holding. The captain permitted me to go, merely ordering me to return as quickly as possible, since night was falling and the regiment might change position. Alcides and I, both of us shivering from cold and hunger, raced like a whirlwind to Heilsberg. I put my horse into the first wayside tavern I came across and, seeing blacksmiths there shoeing Cossack horses, asked them to shoe mine also. I went inside. In the parlor a large fire was burning in a kind of hearth or fireplace of unusual construction. I sat down at once in the large leather armchair standing beside it and barely had time to give the Jewess money to buy me some bread before falling instantly into a deep sleep. Fatigue, cold from my damp clothes, hunger, pain in all my limbs from long hours on horseback, and my tender age not yet conditioned to endure so many combined rigors—all this exhausted my strength and betrayed me defenselessly into the power of a sleep as untimely as it was dangerous. I was wakened by someone shaking my shoulder with great force. I opened my eyes and looked around dumbfounded. I couldn't understand where I was, what I was doing there, or even what I myself had become. Although my eyes were open, sleep was still stupefying my mental faculties. At last I came to my senses, alarmed beyond measure. It was already the dead of night, and everything around me was cloaked in darkness. There was barely enough fire left in the hearth to illuminate the room. By the light of the alternately flaring and dying flame, I saw that the creature shaking my shoulder was a soldier, a jaeger, who from my elegant epaulets took me for an officer and kept saying, "Wake up, wake up, your honor! The cannon fire's getting stronger. Balls are falling on the city!"

I dashed headlong to the spot where I had left my horse. I saw that he was still standing there and looked at his hoof—unshod! There was not a soul in the tavern. The Jew and Jewess had run away—there was no point even thinking of bread. I led Alcides outside and saw that it was not as late as I thought. The sun had just set, and it was a fine evening, the rain had stopped, and the sky was clear. I mounted my poor, hungry, unshod Alcides. As I approached the city gates, I was horrified by the numbers of wounded crowding around them. I was forced to a halt. There was no way I could penetrate that throng of men on foot and horseback, women and children. Disabled cannons and pontoons were being carried through also, and everything was so crowded and crushed in the gates that I was driven to complete despair. Time was flying, and I could not even begin to stir, surrounded as I was on all sides by a throng incessantly streaming toward me with no sign of letting up.

At last it became completely dark. The cannon fire died down, and everything around fell silent, except for the spot where I stood. There the groaning, whining, screeching, swearing, and shouting nearly drove me and my steed out of our wits. Had there been any space at all, he would have reared, but since there was not, he snorted and kicked at whomever he could. God, how was I going to break out of this? Where would I find the regiment now? The night was getting not just dark, but black. What was I going to do?

To my great good fortune, I caught sight of some Cossacks forcing a path in some unfathomable way through that compressed mass of people, horses, and artillery. I saw them dashing adroitly through the gates and in a flash joined them and dashed through also, but only by badly bruising my knee and almost breaking my shoulder. Escaping into the open, I stroked Alcides' arched neck: *I'm sorry for you, trusty comrade, but there's nothing to be done for it; on your way at a gallop!* A light touch of my foot, and the steed took off at a run. I put all my faith in Alcides' instinct. I had no way at all of ascertaining the correct route; the night was so dark that it was impossible to see objects twenty paces away. I loosed the reins. Alcides soon stopped galloping and went at a walk, continually snorting and flicking his ears. I guessed that he was seeing or smelling something dreadful, but since I could not, as the saying goes, see my nose before my face, I had no way of avoiding any misfortune that might lie before me. It was evident that the army had changed position and I was left alone to blunder through unfamiliar fields surrounded by darkness and the hush of death.

At last Alcides began to climb such an extraordinarily steep slope that I had to clutch his mane with all my might to keep from rolling off the saddle. The darkness had gotten so thick that I couldn't see anything before me. I had no idea where I was going and how this journey might end. While I went on thinking and changing my mind about what I should do, Alcides suddenly began heading downhill at the same horrible steep angle at which he had gone up. Now there was no more time for reflection. To save my neck, I leaped hastily off my horse and led him by hand, stooping close to the ground to see where to put my feet and taking all the precautions necessary during such a perilous descent.

When Alcides and I stood at last on a level spot, I saw a dreadful and at the same time lamentable sight: countless numbers of dead bodies covered the field. They were quite visible: they were either totally stripped or wore only their shirts and lay like white shadows on the black earth. At a distance a number of fires could be seen, and the highway was right beside me. Behind me was the redoubt which Alcides had clambered up and I had descended in such fear. Having found out at last where I was and taking it for granted that the fires I saw were those lit by our army, I remounted my horse and began heading down the road toward the fires directly ahead of me; but Alcides turned left and took off on his own at a gallop. The route he chose was horrifying to me: he was racing among the dead bodies, jumping over them, stepping on them, leaping aside, or stopping and bending his muzzle to sniff a corpse and snort over it. I could no longer bear it and turned him back to the road. My steed obeyed me with marked reluctance and went at a walk, continually trying, however, to head leftward.

After a few minutes I heard the hooves of many horses and men's voices and at last caught sight of a group of mounted men riding directly toward me; they were talking about something or other and kept repeating, "Your Excellency!" I was delighted, taking it for granted that *His Excellency* would know which were the fires of the Polish Horse or, if he didn't, would allow me to join his suite. When they came close to me, the man in front—I assume it was the general himself—asked me, "Who goes there?"

I answered, "A Polish Horse soldier!"

"And where are you going?"

"To the regiment!"

"But your regiment is standing over there," said the general, gesturing in the direction that my trusty Alcides had so insistently tried to take, "and you are heading toward the enemy."

The general and his suite galloped off to Heilsberg, and, after kissing my priceless Alcides' ears several times, I left him at liberty to choose the way. Finding himself free, the trusty steed reared to express his delight, neighed, and galloped directly toward the fires glimmering to the left side of the road. There were no dead bodies on my route, and, thanks to Alcides' speed, in a quarter of an hour I was at home—that is, in the regiment.

The Polish Horse soldiers were already mounted. Alcides took his place in the ranks with a sort of quiet, amicable neigh. He had no sooner settled down than the command rang out: "To the right by threes, march!" The regiment moved out. Wyszemirski and our other comrades in my unit were delighted at my return, but the sergeant-major felt obliged to scold me: "You do foolish things, Durov! You won't keep your head on your shoulders. At Guttstadt, in the heat of battle, you decided to give up your horse to some wounded man or other. Are you really too half-witted to realize that a cavalryman on foot in the midst of combat is a creature bound to perish? At the Passarge you dismounted and went to sleep in the bushes when the entire regiment was expecting orders at any minute to go and go at a trot. Whatever would have become of you if you didn't have a horse who, no offense meant, is a great deal smarter than you are? They let you go into Heilsberg for half an hour, and you settled down by the fireplace and went to sleep, at a time when even to think about sleeping was impossible—that is, impermissible. A soldier has to be more than human. In this calling there is no question of age: he has to carry out his duties the same way at seventeen and at thirty and at eighty. I advise you to die on your horse and in the ranks, or else I warn you that you will either be taken prisoner in disgrace or killed by marauders or, worst of all, considered a coward." The sergeant-major fell silent, but his last phrase stung me cruelly. Blood rushed to my face.

There are, however, limits to human endurance. . . . Despite our sergeant-major's philosophizing about a soldier's obligations, I was drop-

ping from lack of sleep and fatigue. My clothing was soaked. For two days
I had neither slept nor eaten, I had been constantly on the march, and,
even when we stopped, I was on horseback with only my uniform to wear,
exposed without protection to the cold wind and rain. I could feel my
strength slipping away by the hour. We were riding three abreast, but
whenever we happened upon a narrow bridge or some other obstacle that
we could not cross as a unit, we went two at a time or sometimes even
singly. At such times the fourth platoon was forced to stand motionless
for several minutes in one spot. I was in the fourth platoon, and at each
beneficent stop I would dismount in a flash, lie down on the ground, and
instantly fall asleep. The platoon began moving, my comrades shouted
and called me and, since a frequently interrupted sleep cannot be a deep
one, I awoke at once, got up, and scrambled back onto Alcides, dragging
my heavy oak lance behind me. These episodes were repeated at even the
briefest of halts. My sergeant was losing his patience, and my comrades
were angry with me. They all told me that they would abandon me on the
road if I dismounted even once more: "After all, you can see that we doze,
but at least we don't get off our horses and lie down on the ground. Do it
our way."

The sergeant-major grumbled in a low voice, "Why do these whelps
wriggle their way into the army? They should stay in the nest."

I spent the rest of the night on horseback, dozing, sleeping, bending to
Alcides' mane, and rousing in fright, feeling as if I were falling. I seemed
to be losing my mind. My eyes were open, but objects kept altering in a
dreamlike way. I took uhlans for forest, and forest for uhlans. My head
was burning, but the rest of me was shivering; I was very cold. Everything
I had on was wet to the skin. . . .

Dawn broke. We halted and were permitted to kindle a fire and cook
kasha. Oh, thank God, now I could lie down and sleep by the fire; I could
warm up and dry out.

"You can't do that," said the sergeant-major, as he saw me sitting down
by the fire and rolling grass into a clump to put under my head. "You
can't. The captain has ordered the horses fed on grass. Take the curb-bit
out of your horse's mouth and lead him to pasture."

I joined the others and walked Alcides around the fields. He grazed the
dewy grass while I stood sadly beside him.

"You're as pale as a corpse," said Wyszemirski, approaching me with
his horse. "What's wrong with you? Are you sick?"

"I'm not sick, just cruelly chilled. The rain has soaked clear through
me, my blood has turned to ice, and now I have to go walking around on
the damp grass!"

"It seems that the rain soaked us all equally; why are we dry then?"

"You're all wearing greatcoats."

"And where's yours then?"

"The Cossacks took it, along with my saddlebags and valise."

"What miracle brought that about?"

"Have you forgotten already that I put a wounded dragoon officer on my horse and let it be used to return him to his regiment?"

"Well, yes, I remember. What about it?"

"This is what: when I found my horse again, he was already in Podwyszącki's hands. He bought it from Cossacks with just the saddle, and everything else had disappeared!"

"That's bad, comrade. You're the youngest of us all. You won't last long during these cold nights without a greatcoat. Tell the sergeant-major; he'll give you a coat left from those killed. They're sending huge piles of them to the wagon-train."

We talked for a while longer. At last the sun rose quite high, the day warmed up, my uniform dried out, and my fatigue passed. I would have been very cheerful if I could have hoped for something to eat. But there was no use even thinking of it; I had no share in the kasha that was on the fire. And so I began diligently searching the grass for berries. As the captain rode past the uhlans walking around the fields with their horses, he noticed my pursuit.

"What are you looking for, Durov?" he asked, riding up to me.

I replied that I was looking for berries. The captain must have guessed the reason, because he turned to the platoon sergeant and said to him in a low voice, "See that Durov and Wyszemirski get enough to eat."

He rode away, and the old soldiers said to his back, "If we have enough to eat, they should, too. They always think more about these whelps than about seasoned old soldiers."

"What fools you are, seasoned old soldiers!" said the sergeant-major, approaching us. "Who should we worry about if not children? I think you can see for yourselves that both of these recruits are scarcely out of their childhood.

"Come with me, children," said the sergeant-major jovially, taking us both by the arms. "The captain ordered us to feed you." We were given soup, roast meat, and white bread.

Seeing the horses grazing quietly and the uhlans asleep in the meadow, I decided there was no need for me to be the only one standing vigil. It was afternoon already, and the heat had become unbearable. I climbed down to the banks of the little river which flowed by our camp and lay down in the tall grass to sleep. Alcides was roaming around not far from me. My sound sleep was broken by a shout of "Curb your horse! . . . Mount!" and the tramp of uhlans running to their horses and with their horses into the ranks. I jumped up precipitately. The sergeant-major was already on his steed and hurrying the uhlans into formation; I looked around for Alcides and, to my horror, saw him swimming across the river, heading directly for the far bank. Just then the sergeant-major galloped up to me, "Why are you standing there without your horse?"

There was no time to hesitate! I plunged after my Alcides, and we came out together on the opposite bank. In a minute I curbed him, mounted, and swam back; I was standing in place before the troops had finished forming ranks.

"Well, at least that was a plucky recovery," said the sergeant-major, looking pleased.

*Schippenbeil.* Great God, what horror! This little village was almost completely incinerated. How many people were burned alive here! Oh, the poor wretches!

*June 1807. Friedland.* Over half of our brave regiment fell in this fierce and unsuccessful battle. Several times we attacked, several times we repulsed the enemy, and in turn we ourselves were driven back more than once. We were showered with caseshot and smashed by cannonballs, and the shrill whine of the hellish bullets has completely deafened me. Oh, I cannot bear them! The ball is a different matter. It roars so majestically at least, and there are always brief intervals in between. After some hours of heated battle, the remnants of our regiment were ordered to pull back a little to rest. I took advantage of it to go watch the operations of our artillery, without stopping to think that I might get my head torn off for no good reason. Bullets were showering me and my horse, but what do bullets matter beside the savage, unceasing roar of the cannons?

An uhlan from our regiment, covered in blood, with a bandaged head and bloodied face, was riding aimlessly around the field in one direction or another. The poor fellow could not remember where he was going and was having trouble keeping his seat in the saddle. I rode up to him and asked him which squadron he was from. He muttered something and swayed so violently that I had to support him to keep him from falling. Seeing that he was out of his senses, I tied his horse's reins to Alcides' neck and, supporting the wounded man with one hand, rode with him to the river to refresh him with water. At the river he came to his wits somewhat, slipped off his horse, and fell at my feet from weakness. What could I do? I couldn't abandon him—he would perish! There was no way of getting him to a safe place, and what place here was safe anyway? There was gun and cannonfire all around us, balls were skipping in all directions, shells were bursting in air and on the ground; the cavalry like a stormy sea was rushing forward and falling back, and amid this terrible upheaval I could no longer see the pennons of our regiment anywhere. Meanwhile, there was no time to lose. I scooped up water in my helmet and poured it over the head and face of the wounded man. He opened his eyes. "For God's sake, don't abandon me here," he said, making an effort to rise. "I'll get on my horse somehow; walk me back behind the lines of our army. God will reward your human kindness." I helped him to mount his horse, got onto Alcides, picked up the reins of the wounded man's horse again, and we rode toward Friedland.

The city's inhabitants were fleeing, and regiments were retreating. Scoundrelly soldiers in large numbers, who had run away from the field of battle without being wounded, were spreading terror among the retreating crowds, shouting, "All is lost!" "We're beaten to the last man!" "The enemy is at our heels." "Flee! Save yourselves!" Although I did not completely trust these cowards, I couldn't keep from worrying as I saw entire platoons of dragoons riding at a trot through the city. I regretted wholeheartedly the curiosity that had lured me to watch the cannonfire and the evil destiny that had sent me the wounded man. To leave him to the whims of fate seemed to me base and inhuman in the extreme—I could not do it! The unfortunate uhlan, his face numb with fear, turned his alarmed gaze to me. I understood his apprehensions.

"Can you go a little faster?" I asked.

"No, I can't," answered the unfortunate man and sighed deeply.

We continued at a walk. Men were running and galloping past us, shouting to us, "Step it up! The enemy's not far off!" At last we came into a forest. I turned off the highway and rode through the thickets without letting go of the reins of the wounded uhlan's horse. The forest shade and coolness revived my comrade's strength somewhat, but, to his woe, he put that strength to the worst possible use. He decided to smoke his pipe, stopped, struck a light, and took a puff of his repulsive tobacco. A moment later his eyes rolled up, the pipe fell from his hands, and he fell lifelessly onto the neck of his horse. I stopped, dragged him to the ground, laid him flat and, since I had no way of bringing him to his senses, stood beside him with both horses, waiting for him to recover. In a quarter of an hour he opened his eyes, raised himself, and sat up, looking at me with a crazed air. I saw that he was out of his wits. His head was covered with saber cuts, and the tobacco smoke had acted on him like liquor. "Mount your horse," I said. "Otherwise we'll get there too late. Get up, I'll help you."

He didn't answer me, but he did try to stand up. I assisted him to his feet. Holding the horses' reins in one hand and using the other to help him up into the stirrup, I came close to falling, because, instead of clutching the mane, the half-crazed uhlan put all his weight on my shoulder.

We rode off again. The crowds were still fleeing with the same shout, "Save yourselves!" At last I saw some passing artillery pieces. I asked my protégé whether he wouldn't like to stay with them: it would be easier for him lying on a caisson than riding horseback. He was obviously delighted by my proposal, and I at once asked the sergeant of artillery if he would take the wounded uhlan and his horse under his care. He agreed willingly and ordered his men at once to take my comrade off his horse, spread a few saddle blankets on the caisson, and lay him on it.

I quivered with joy at finding myself free and would have gone immediately to look for the regiment, if I could have found out from anyone where it was. I rode alone until nightfall, asking those who passed me if they knew where the Polish Horse uhlan regiment was. Some said that it was up ahead; others, that one part of the army had gone off somewhere to the side and my regiment was in that detachment. I was in despair! Night had fallen, and I had to give Alcides a chance to rest. I caught sight of a group of Cossacks who had kindled a fire and were cooking their supper.

I dismounted and went over to them, "Hello, friends! Are you planning to spend the night here?"

"We are," they replied.

"And how about the horses? Do you put them out to grass?"

They looked at me in astonishment. "Where else then? Of course we do."

"And they don't stray too far from you?"

"What do you want to know that for?" asked one old Cossack, staring intently into my eyes.

"I would like to let my horse graze with yours, but I'm afraid he'll get too far away."

"Well, take care of him then: hobble him with a tether and wrap it around your arm. Then the horse can't wander off without waking you. We keep ours on a tether."

And with this, the old Cossack invited me to share their kasha with them. Afterwards they hobbled their horses, tying them on tethers and wrapping the ends around their arms, and went to sleep. I walked around after Alcides in perplexity: I too wanted to lie down, but how could I leave my horse free to roam all night? I had no tether. At last I got the idea of tying a handkerchief around Alcides' forefeet. It was a delicate batiste handkerchief from a dozen that my grandmother had given me back in Little Russia. Only one of the dozen was left intact, and it went everywhere with me. I was very fond of it and washed it myself every day wherever I had a chance—in a brook, a river, a lake, or a puddle. I used this handkerchief to bind Alcides' legs, allowed him to graze, and went to sleep not far from the Cossacks.

Dawn had already broken when I awoke. The Cossacks and their horses were gone, and Alcides as well. Mortally alarmed and saddened beyond expression, I got up from the grass on which I had slept so peacefully. The saddled horses of dragoons were roaming the fields all around me. With a heart full of bitter regret, I began searching among them at random for Alcides. I had been walking about in one direction or another for half an hour when I caught sight of a scrap of my handkerchief gleaming white at a distance. I ran over to it, and, to my indescribable joy, Alcides came running up to me, frisking; he neighed and rested his head on my shoulder. One end of the white handkerchief was still trailing from his right leg, but the rest was ripped to shreds and scattered about the field. His curb, snaffle, and reins had been taken. It was useless to ask the dragoons about them: who could make them tell me or, more to the point, give them back? It was a horrible situation! How could I appear in the regiment looking like that? This was an excellent opportunity to learn egotism: to make a firm resolution, always and in every case, to think more of myself than of others. Twice I had yielded to feelings of compassion, and both times I had been very badly rewarded. Moreover, the first time the captain had called me a scamp, and what would he think of me now? The battle was still in progress when I decided to go watch the cannons and suddenly disappeared. What a horrible thought! I was afraid to dwell on it. . . .

When the dragoons heard the reason for my distress, they gave me a long strap to use for reins and said that my regiment could not be very far ahead; it had spent the night where they did, and I could catch it still on the spot. As I tied the repulsive strap to the halter Alcides was still wearing, I felt extremely vexed with myself. *Oh, my fine steed,* I was thinking, *you're in the hands of such a capricious fool of a girl!* But neither repentance nor regret nor vexation saved me from woe!

I reached the regiment, and this time it was not the captain, but Kachowski, our general, who told me that my bravery was scatterbrained and my compassion witless; I rushed into the heat of battle when I was not supposed to, went on the attack with other squadrons, rescued anyone and everyone I came across in the midst of combat, and, giving up my horse to anyone who decided to ask for him, was left on foot among the fiercest clashes; he was out of patience with my pranks and was ordering me to go at once to the wagon-train. Me, in the wagons! Every last drop of blood drained from my face. In my worst nightmare I never imagined anything so horrible as this punishment.

Kazimirski, who loves me like a father, looked with pity at the change in my face. He said something under his breath to the commander, but the other answered, "No! No, we have to protect him." Then he turned to me, speaking now in a much kinder tone, "I am sending you to the wagon-train in order to preserve a brave officer for our native land in times to come. In a few years you'll be able to make better use of that daring which now threatens to cost you your life with no benefit to anyone."

Oh, how little those hollow words of consolation meant to me! They were mere words, and the truth of the matter was that I was going to the wagon-train. I went over to Alcides to get him ready for the shameful journey. Embracing my trusty comrade-in-arms, I wept from shame and sorrow. My hot tears fell on his black mane and skipped and rolled down the saddle-frame. Wyszemirski is also being sent to the wagons, and why should that be? He is always in the proper spot, and he cannot be reproached for either witless daring or misplaced compassion: he has all the common sense and equanimity of an adult.

Everything was ready, and our funereal procession began: wounded horses, wounded men, and we two, in the prime of life and completely healthy, moving slowly, step by step, to our final resting place, to the damned wagon-train. There is nothing in the world I desire so fiercely as that Kachowski shall see no action for the rest of the campaign!

*Tilsit.* Here we were reunited with our regiment. Everyone with strength enough to hold a weapon is in the ranks. They say that we are going to Russia from here. And so the campaign is at an end, and my hopes and dreams with it: instead of splendid feats I committed scatterbrained pranks. Will I someday have a chance to make up for them? Napoleon's restless spirit and the uneasy crown on his head assure me of the possibility. Once again he will force Russia to take up its formidable arms, but will it be soon? And what will I be until then? Can I really remain a common recruit? Will they promote me to officer without proofs of my nobility? And how can I get them? My uncle has our charter if he would send it. But, no, he will never do so. On the contrary. Oh, God, God, why was my life spared?

I was so absorbed in these lamentable reflections that I failed to notice the captain galloping up to the spot where I stood. "What's this, Durov?" he said, touching my shoulder lightly with his saber. "Is this any time to be hanging your head and looking pensive? Sit alert and look cheerful. The emperor is coming!"

And with this he galloped off. Words of command rang out, regiments dressed ranks, trumpets sounded, and we dipped our lances to our adored tsar as, accompanied by a large suite, he dashed up to us on a fine horse. Our emperor is a handsome man in the prime of life; meekness and charity are expressed in his large blue eyes, greatness of soul in his noble features, and an uncommon amiability on his rosy lips. Our young tsar's kindly face depicts a sort of maidenly bashfulness along with his benevolent expression. The emperor rode past our entire formation at a walk, looking at the soldiers compassionately and pensively. Oh, how his paternal heart must bleed at the memory of the last battle! Much of our army perished on the fields of Friedland![1]

1. In the summer of 1807 Napoleon and Alexander I met for the first time on a raft in the middle of the Neman to begin negotiations. The resulting peace of Tilsit defined the French and Russian spheres of influence in Europe and freed both powers to wage wars elsewhere (Napoleon in Spain; Alexander I in Finland and on Turkish territory).

# Chapter Three

## THE TROOPS' RETURN TO RUSSIA

When we got back to our native land, the army dispersed by corps, division, and even regiment to different areas. Our regiment, the Pskov Dragoons, and the Ordensk Cuirassiers are all in one camp. Our tents are as large as ballrooms; each of them houses a platoon. The captain sent for me and Wyszemirski. He told us that wartime, when we could all lie around together in the straw, was over: now we must observe meticulously all the formalities and obligations of service; we must come to attention for all officers, present arms to them—that is, draw our sabers—on sentry duty, and respond to roll call in a loud, gruff voice. I have been assigned on equal footing with the others to guard our hay at night, to clean with a spade the *placówka*—that is, the square where sentries assemble in front of the guardhouse—and stand watch at the church and the powder-magazine. Every morning and evening we lead our horses to water at the river, which is a verst away from us. Sometimes I have to lead two horses and ride a third. In this event I manage to reach the river without trouble, but from there to camp my three horses and I fly like a whirlwind, and in our flight I hear the curses of uhlans, dragoons, and cuirassiers scattering behind me. None of them can manage their horses after they have been seduced by the bad example of mine, who know that they will get their oats back at the picket line. They carry me impetuously, frisking, kicking, and trying to break loose as they run, and I expect to be ripped off Alcides' back at any minute. Each time my inability to restrain the playful horses earns me a reprimand from the sergeant-major and the duty officer.

At last we are in quarters. My life is spent in the routine occupations of the soldier. At dawn I go to see my horse and curry and feed him. Then, covering him with his blanket and leaving him under the protection of the duty-soldier, I go back to my quarters where, to my pleasure, I am quartered alone. My present hostess is a kind woman who gives me milk, meat, and good bread. The late autumn has made taking walks much less agreeable to me. How happy I would be to have books! The captain has many; I don't think he would find it odd if I were to ask him for permission to read them, but I'm afraid to risk it. I would be very ashamed if, against my expectations, he were to say that a soldier has other things than books to occupy him. I will wait. There'll be time for reading yet. Can I really remain a common soldier all my life? Wy-

szemirski has already been promoted to sergeant. True, he has a patroness, Countess Poniatowska. At the very start of the campaign she
herself took him to Bennigsen and made him promise to put her nursling
under his personal protection.[1] But I am all by myself in the wide world.
Why should anyone worry about me? I can only rely on time and on
myself. It would be odd, indeed, if my commanders could not distinguish
me from soldiers taken from the plow.

*Kresy:* this is what the Polish Horse soldiers call the duty of carrying
orders from headquarters to the squadrons. "To be on *kresy*" means to be
sent out with such orders. Today it was my turn. Gałczewski, my platoon
sergeant, announced it to me: "You're on *kresy*, Durov."

"Gladly!"

And in fact I am glad for any novelty. In camp it made me very happy
to be ordered to clean the *placówka.* I worked with a will, scraping grass
from the earth with a spade, sweeping it into a pile with a broom, and
doing it as if that were the only thing I had ever done all my life. My
former mentor was almost always present during these labors; he would
pat me on the shoulder and say, "Zmorduieszie, dziecko! Pracuj powoli."[2]

In the evening an order was brought from headquarters, and
Gałczewski told me to take it immediately to the captain, whose quarters
are five versts away from our hamlet.

"I'll walk," I told Gałczewski. "I'd be sorry to exhaust Alcides."

"Exhaust him! It's only five versts. All the same, if you're sorrier for
Alcides' legs than your own, go ahead and walk."

Off I went. The sun had already set, and the evening was fine. The
road ran through fields sown with rye and in other spots wound in and out
of shrubbery. Nature is captivating in Poland! At least I prefer it to our
northern climate. At home even in midsummer we can never forget the
winter cold: it is always so near at hand. Our winter is a real one, terrible
and all-killing. But here it is so short, so indulgent. The winter snow
leaves tips of grass exposed to our contented gaze, and the sight of this not
quite concealed greenery gives our hearts a consoling presentiment of the
earth's reappearance with the first spring wind: there's the grass, and
here's warmth and spring. . . .

As I walked along daydreaming, storm clouds covered the sky, and a
warm, fine drizzle began. I stepped up my pace and, since the village was

1. General Leontij Bennigsen, a native of Hannover long in Russian service, was the
commander-in-chief whose sluggish pursuit of the French in the Prussian campaign
puzzled Durova.

2. "You'll tire yourself out, my boy. Take it easy." (Polish)

in sight, succeeded in reaching it before the rain started in earnest. The captain read the order, asked me whether our quarters were all right, and then said, "Since it's night already, you can return to your platoon tomorrow, but for now go and spend the night in the stables."

This was the last thing I expected, and I felt ashamed for Galéra. Had he lost his wits? It's true that he could not in his wildest dreams guess who I am, but why send me to the stables anyway? A fine bedroom that is!

The rain had already ceased; there was only an occasional drizzle. I set out on the return journey. But in order to get home faster, I decided to go as the crow flies, heading in the direction where I knew our village to lie. This meant leaving the road and cutting across the grainfields, and I did so without a moment of hesitation. How could the direct route be longer than the usual road? Things went tolerably well as long as I kept to the outskirts of the ryefield; the night was so light that I could make out objects clearly. Although the rain-soaked rye twined around me, my clothing was not wet clear through. At last the path began cutting into the middle of the field, and I came into tall, dense rye up to my shoulders. Burning with impatience to reach a clear spot as soon as I could, I began walking fast, no longer worrying about the dense rye which was depositing all its raindrops on my uniform. But no matter how I hurried, I couldn't see any end to the boundless flat fields of grain which undulated like the sea. I was tired, water was flowing off me in streams, and my rapid pace made me unbearably hot. I slowed down, consoled only by the thought that the night had to end sometime and in daylight I would at last see where our village was. Mentally resigning myself to the melancholy prospect of blundering through wet fields among the tall rye all night, I walked on quietly and cheerlessly. And what could be diverting about walking along up to my ears in rye with nothing but heads of grain to look at?

After half an hour of my forbearing journey and just when I had lost all hope of seeing anything resembling a village or a fence, I suddenly found myself at the village gates. Oh, how delighted I was! In a flash I opened them and tore, almost flying, to my quarters. Everyone was already asleep, the fire was out, and I fumbled around in the dark for a long time locating my valise, taking out clean linen, undressing, and changing. Then I wrapped myself up in my greatcoat, lay down, and fell asleep instantly.

Alcides! Oh, mortal pain in my heart, when will you be stilled? . . . Alcides, my priceless Alcides! Once so strong, indomitable, unapproachable, allowing only my infant hand to govern you. You who carried me on your spine so obediently in my childhood years; who passed with me across the bloody fields of honor, glory, and death; who shared my rigors, dangers, hunger, cold, joy, and contentment! You, the only creature of the animal kingdom who loved me! You are no more. You exist no longer.

Four weeks have passed since this unhappy event. I haven't picked up my pen. Mortal anguish burdens my soul. I go everywhere with head lowered in dejection. I carry out the duties of my calling reluctantly and, no matter where I am or what I do, sorrow is always with me and tears continually well up in my eyes. On sentry duty blood rushes to my heart! When I am relieved, I no longer run to Alcides. Alas, I walk slowly to his grave. They distribute the evening ration of oats, I hear the cheerful neighing of our steeds, but the voice that made my soul rejoice is silent. . . . Oh, Alcides, Alcides, my joy is buried with you! . . . I don't know whether I have the strength to describe the tragic death of the unforgettable comrade of my youthful years and life under arms. The pen trembles in my hand and tears cloud my vision. However, I am going to write it. Someday Papa will read my notes and pity my Alcides.

The horses stood all together in one large squadron stable, and we took them to water as a squadron just as we had in camp. The bad weather, which did not allow us either to drill or ride them, caused our horses to become restive and impossible to manage on the way back from the waterhole. On the most ill-fated day of my life, to my eternal regret I decided to take Alcides by the reins. Before, I had always ridden him and led the other horses; now to my grief I did the opposite. As we were going to the river, Alcides frisked lightly without pulling at the rein; he kept rubbing his muzzle against my knee or nibbling playfully at my epaulets. But on the way back, when all the horses began frisking, rearing, snorting, and kicking, and some, breaking loose, started to play and squeal, my unfortunate Alcides was carried away by their example. He reared, leaped aside, tore the reins from my hands and, borne by his evil fate, took off like an arrow, jumping low wattle fences and hedges on the run. Oh, woe, woe to me, the ill-starred witness of my most horrible misfortune! I was watching Alcides' rapid gallop, I saw him jump . . . and a mortal cold swept over my body! Alcides jumped a fence which had sharpened stakes rising nearly three feet above it. My strong steed could jump that high, but, alas! he couldn't clear the stakes. The weight of his body dropped him directly onto the fence. One of the stakes plunged into his belly and broke off. With a cry of despair I set out at a gallop after my unfortunate friend. I found him in his stall; he was trembling all over, and sweat was streaming off him. The fatal fragment was still in his belly, a fourth of it visible from outside. Death was inevitable. I ran up to him, hugged his neck, and burst into tears. My good steed rested his head on my shoulder, sighed heavily and, at last, five minutes later fell and stretched out convulsively. . . . Alcides, Alcides! Why didn't I die there also? When the duty officer saw me embracing the lifeless body of my horse and covering it with kisses and tears, he said I was behaving like a foolish child and ordered it dragged into the fields. I ran to the captain, begging him to order Alcides' body left in peace and to give me permission to bury him myself.

"What! Your poor Alcides is dead?" asked the captain with concern as he saw my tear-stained eyes and pale face. "What a shame! You loved him so. Well, what's to be done? Don't cry. I'll tell them to give you any horse in the squadron. Go on now, bury your companion."

He sent his orderly with me, and the duty officer gave up trying to prevent me from carrying out the sad task of burying Alcides. My comrades, moved by the extremity of my grief, dug a deep hole, lowered Alcides into it, covered him with earth, cut turf with their sabers, and used it to edge the high mound under which the only creature who loved me rests in eternal sleep.

When their work was done, my comrades returned to the squadron, and I stayed behind and wept on Alcides' grave until late at night. The philanthropic captain gave orders that for two days I was to be allowed to mourn and relieved of all duties. I spent almost the entire time at my steed's grave. Despite cold wind and rain, I stayed there until midnight; when I got back to my quarters I didn't eat anything and went on weeping until dawn. On the third day my platoon leader sent for me and told me to pick a horse; the captain had ordered them to give me any one I chose.

"I'm grateful for the favor," I replied, "but all horses are alike to me now; I'll take whichever one it suits you to give me."

When I was going to tend Alcides, I did it eagerly, but now I find this occupation very disagreeable. With a deep sigh, I led my new horse into the stall where Alcides died and covered it with the blanket which had covered him only three days earlier. I no longer weep, but I roam the yellowed fields joylessly. I watch the cold rain splashing on my Alcides' grave and soaking into the turf on which he frisked so cheerfully.

Every morning my first steps are to Alcides' grave. I lie down on it and press my face to the cold earth, and my hot tears sink into it along with the raindrops. I return in thought to my childhood years, recalling the many joyful hours this fine steed's rare affection and obedience afforded me. I recall those magnificent summer nights when I led Alcides up Startsev mountain by a path climbed only by goats. It was no effort for me to follow the path; my little footsteps fitted as neatly on it as the goats' hooves, but my good steed risked slipping and smashing himself to bits. Nevertheless, he followed me obediently, albeit trembling with fear at finding himself at such a dreadful height and over a precipice! Alas, my Alcides, so many woes and dangers passed you by without doing you the least harm. It was my recklessness, my disastrous recklessness, that brought you at last to your grave. This thought torments, lacerates my soul. . . . Nothing cheers me now; the very shadow of a smile has vanished from my face. Whatever I do is done mechanically, from habit. I ride off to drill with a dead indifference, I come back in silence when it is over; I unsaddle my horse, return it to its place without even glancing at it, and go away without a word to anyone.

The commander-in-chief has sent a sergeant for me; I am wanted at headquarters. Whatever for? But I have been ordered to turn in my horse, saddle, lance, saber, and pistols to the squadron, so evidently I shall not be coming back here again. I shall go to bid farewell to Alcides.

I wept on his grave just as inconsolably as on the day of his death and, bidding him *farewell forever,* for the last time kissed the earth which covers him.

*Polotsk.* There is about to be some sort of major upheaval in my life. Kachowski asked me whether my parents agreed to my serving in the army or whether I enlisted against their will. I told him the truth at once: my father and mother would never have let me join the army; but, driven by an invincible propensity for arms, I ran away from home on the sly with a Cossack regiment. I may be only seventeen,[3] but I am experienced enough to realize at once that Kachowski knows more about me than he admits, because he listened to my answer without the slightest sign of surprise at my parents' odd way of thinking in refusing to let their son join the army, whereas the first choice of all the nobility for their children is a military career. He said only that I was to go to Vitebsk to see Bux-höwden with his adjutant, the honorable Neidhardt, who was also present.[4]

When Kachowski gave me my orders, Neidhardt at once exchanged bows with me and took me to his house. He left me in the drawing-room and joined his family in the inner rooms. A quarter of an hour later, one head and then another began peeping out at me through the half-open door. Neidhardt himself didn't come out; he dined, drank coffee, and stayed there for a long time, all of which I spent alone in the drawing-room. What odd people! Why didn't they invite me to dine with them?

Toward evening we left Polotsk. At post stations Neidhardt drank coffee and left me to stand by the carriage while the horses were changed.

Now I am in Vitebsk, staying in Neidhardt's quarters. He has become a

3. Twenty-four.
4. In late 1807 Friedrich Wilhelm Buxhöwden was the commander in charge of rebuilding the western army after the Prussian campaign. His adjutant, Aleksandr Neidhardt, was a general still on active duty when Durova published *The Cavalry Maiden* in 1836.

different man; he talks amicably with me and, like a courteous host, treats me to tea, coffee, and breakfast. In short, he behaves as he should have from the beginning. He says that he brought me to Vitebsk on orders from the commander-in-chief, and I am to report to him.

I am still staying with Neidhardt. We breakfast together in the morning; then he goes off to join the commander-in-chief and I stay in his quarters or go for a walk. But now it is deep autumn, and the mud is deep as well. Since I cannot find any place for a human to walk, I go to the tavern in which Neidhardt always dines. There I wait for him and we eat together. After dinner he leaves, and I stay on in the parlor of the mistress of the tavern. I always have a good time there; the tavernkeeper, a kindly, jovial woman, calls me *uhlan-panna*[5] and says that if I were to let myself be corseted, she would bet her entire tavern and its income against a *złoty* that there would not be a girl in all of Vitebsk with a waist as slender and pretty as mine. With these words she goes at once to fetch her corset. This makes her daughters laugh uproariously, because there is room in that corset for all of them and me together.

Five days have passed, and I am still staying in Vitebsk. At last this evening Neidhardt told me that tomorrow I am to see the commander-in-chief; he has been ordered to take me there at ten o'clock in the morning.

On the next day Neidhardt and I went to see Count Buxhöwden. Neidhardt led me into the count's study and left at once. The commander-in-chief greeted me with a kindly smile and began by asking me, "Why were you arrested? Where's your saber?"

I said that all my weapons were taken from me in the squadron.

"I will order them all returned to you. A soldier should never be sent anywhere without weapons."

After that he asked me how old I was and then went on to say: "I've heard a great deal about your valor, and I'm very pleased that all your commanders report only the best of you. . . ." He paused for a minute and then began again. "You are not to be alarmed by what I have to tell you. I must send you to the emperor; he wishes to see you. But I repeat, don't be alarmed. Our emperor is the embodiment of grace and magnanimity; you will learn that from experience."

It did alarm me, however. "The emperor will send me home, Your Excellency, and I will die of sorrow!" I said this with such deeply felt grief that the commander-in-chief was visibly moved.

"Have no fear of that. The emperor will refuse you nothing as a reward for your fearlessness and outstanding conduct. And since I was ordered to

5. Uhlan Miss. (Polish)

make inquiries about you, I will add my own report to the testimony of your regimental and squadron commanders, your platoon sergeant, and Captain Kazimirski. Believe me, they won't take away from you the uniform to which you have done such honor." With this, the general bowed politely to me as a sign to leave.[6]

Entering the anteroom, I found Neidhardt in conversation with Aide-de-camp Zass. They both came over to me, and Neidhardt said, "The commander-in-chief has ordered me to turn you over to M. Zass, His Imperial Majesty's aide-de-camp. You are to travel with him to Peterburg. And so, permit me to wish you a safe journey."

Zass took my arm. "Now you are to accompany me to my quarters. From there we'll send for your things from Neidhardt's, and very early tomorrow morning we are going back to Polotsk, because Buxhöwden has ordered your weapons returned to you without fail." The next day we left Vitebsk very early and soon arrived in Polotsk.

*Polotsk.* Zass went to see Kachowski and returned an hour later, saying that, to his surprise, Kachowski dined at noon and insisted that he stay, and so he had reluctantly eaten.

"Tomorrow we leave here very early, Durov. Getting up at dawn must be nothing new to you?" I said that I never got up at any time except dawn.

In the evening soldiers from my platoon came to see me and called for me to come out. I did so. What kind people! It was the platoon sergeant and my mentor, the man who had taught me everything that an uhlan needs to know on foot and horseback.

"Farewell, dear comrade," they said. "God grant you good fortune. We've heard that you're on your way to Peterburg; praise us there." "We praised you here when the general asked about you, particularly me," said my mentor, twirling his graying mustaches. "After all, it was me who Kazimirski ordered to be your nurse. The chief took me into his room and spent an hour asking me everything, down to the last detail, and I told him all about it, even how you cried and rolled on the ground when your Alcides died."

A deep sigh escaped me at this reminder. I bade farewell to my fellow soldiers, gave my instructor my year's pay, and went back inside in a most melancholy frame of mind.

At last we are on our way to Peterburg. Our open carriage barely moves; we drag along rather than ride. At each station as many as twelve horses are harnessed to it, and all together they are not worth two decent ones. They are more like calves than horses, and often, as they struggle

6. Buxhöwden's report to Alexander I is included in Appendix A.

hopelessly to pull the carriage out of the deep mud, they end up lying down in it themselves.

Something droll happens to us at almost every post-station. At one we were served bloody sugar with our tea.

"What's the meaning of this?" asked Zass, pushing away the sugar bowl.

The stationmaster was in the next room waiting to see the effect produced by the sugar. At Zass's question he put in an appearance and said on a note of triumph, "My daughter cut her hand chopping the sugar, and this is her blood!"

"Well, take away your blood, you numbskull, and order them to serve us clean sugar," said Zass, turning away in revulsion. I laughed wholeheartedly at this novel way of proving hospitable zeal.

At another station Zass started shouting at the stationmaster because he was drunk, said rude things to us, and refused to give us horses. The stationmaster's wife heard the loud voices and jumped out at Zass with fists flying and, capering with fury, cried piercingly, "What sort of lawless land is this? How dare they abuse the stationmaster!" The stunned Zass could find no way to free himself from this female satan until he thought of tweaking her nose. The remedy proved successful. The *megaera* ran off squealing, and the stationmaster went after her.

We waited half an hour for horses, but, when we saw that none were coming, we settled down to drink tea. Zass sent me as an envoy to the stationmistress to negotiate for cream. Our enemy was happy to make peace, and I returned with a cupful. An hour later horses were brought, and we parted very amicably from the stationmaster and his wife who, as she wished me in particular a safe journey, covered her nose with her apron.

## MY FIRST VISIT TO THE CAPITAL

*Peterburg.* So this is our bright, clean, magnificent capital, a memorial to the invincible courage, great spirit, and heroic resolution of the immortal PETER!

We arrived three days ago. I am staying with Zass, and every day I go to look at the monument to Peter the Great.[7] How worthy he is of the appellation! Peter would have been great no matter what station in life he was born to. His majestic appearance corresponds fully to the vast genius once governed by his great soul.

7. Etienne Falconet's famous equestrian statue, erected by Catherine the Great (1766); in Pushkin's narrative poem "The Bronze Horseman" it is a symbol of progress and imperial might.

My fate has been decided. I have been with the emperor! I saw him and spoke with him. My heart is filled with a happiness so ineffable that I have no words to describe my feelings. The greatness of my good fortune stuns and enraptures me! Oh, Emperor! From this hour my life belongs to you. . . .

When Prince V.[8] opened the door of the emperor's study for me and closed it after me, the emperor at once approached and took my hand. He led me over to his desk, rested one hand on it and, continuing to hold my hand in his other one, began questioning me in a low voice with such a gracious expression that all my timidity disappeared and hope once again revived in my soul. "I have heard," said the emperor, "that you are not a man. Is that true?"

I could not immediately pluck up the courage to say, "Yes, Your Majesty, it's true." I stood for a minute with downcast eyes and remained silent; my heart was throbbing fiercely, and my hand trembled in the tsar's. The emperor waited. At last, as I raised my eyes to him and uttered my reply, I saw that the emperor was blushing; instantly I began to blush, too. I lowered my eyes and did not raise them again until the moment when an involuntary impulse of sorrow threw me to the emperor's feet.

After he had questioned me in detail about all my reasons for joining the army, the emperor greatly praised my fearlessness. He said that this was a first example in Russia; all my commanders had only the highest praise for me and called my courage peerless; he was very pleased to verify it; and, therefore, he wished to reward me and return me with honor to my father's house, giving—

The emperor had no time to finish; at the phrase *return home* I cried out in horror and fell immediately to the emperor's feet. "Don't send me home, Your Majesty," I said in the voice of despair. "Don't send me back! I will die there. I will surely die! Don't make me regret that there was no bullet marked for me in this campaign. Don't take away my life, sire! I wanted to sacrifice it to you of my own free will. . . ." As I said this, I was hugging the emperor's knees and weeping.

The emperor was moved. He raised me to my feet and asked in an altered voice, "What is it you want then?"

"To be a warrior! To wear a uniform and bear arms! That is the only reward you can give me, sire! For me there is no other. I was born in an army camp. The sound of trumpets was my lullaby. From the day of my birth I have loved the military calling; by the age of ten I was devising ways to enlist; at sixteen I reached my goal—alone, without help from anyone! I held that glorious post through my courage alone, without patronage or subsidy from anyone. And now, Your Majesty, you want to

8. Saks (19) identifies "Prince V." as Court Minister Petr Volkonskij.

send me home! If I had foreseen such an end, nothing could have prevented me from seeking a glorious death in the ranks of your warriors." I said all this with my arms crossed as if before an ikon, looking at the emperor with tear-filled eyes.

The emperor listened to me, trying in vain to conceal how moved he was. After I finished speaking, he spent a minute or two in evident indecision; at last his face brightened. "If you presume," said the emperor, "that permission to wear a uniform and bear arms is your only possible reward, you shall have it!" At these words I began to quiver with joy. The emperor went on, "And you will call yourself by my name—Aleksandrov. I have no doubt that you will make yourself worthy of this honor by the distinction of your conduct and actions. Never forget for a moment that this name must always be above reproach, and I will never forgive you for even the shadow of a spot on it. . . . Now tell me, what regiment would you like to be enrolled in? I will promote you to officer's rank."

"In this matter permit me, Your Majesty, to surrender myself to your will," I said.

"The Mariupol Hussars is one of our most valiant regiments, and the officer corps comes from the best families," the emperor told me. "I will order you enrolled there. Tomorrow you will receive from Lieven as much as you need for the journey and for your uniform.[9] When everything is ready for your departure to the regiment, I will see you again."

With these words the emperor bowed to me. At once I went over to the door and, since I didn't know how to open it, took hold of the bronze knob and began twisting it this way and that. When the emperor saw that I would not be able to leave without his aid, he came over, opened the door for me, and watched me as far as the next door, which I managed by myself.

As I entered the anteroom, I found myself instantly surrounded by pages who vied in asking me questions: "What did the emperor say to you?" "Did he promote you to an officer?"

I didn't know how to answer them, but Zass came over to me along with another aide-de-camp, and the throng of imps retreated respectfully. The aide-de-camp who approached me along with Zass asked me, "Are you fifteen?"

I replied that I was already in my eighteenth year.

"They wrote us wonders about your fearlessness," he said with a polite nod.

Zass put an end to this conversation by taking my arm. "It's time we were going, Prince," he said to his colleague, and we left the palace.

9. Count Khristofor Lieven, Alexander I's counselor at Tilsit.

As we went down the stairs, he asked, "Durov, would you like to make the acquaintance of a relation of mine, the wife of General Zass?"[10]

I answered that I would be happy to.

"Well then, we'll go directly to her house for dinner, and afterwards all of us together will show you the Hermitage. You'll find much to interest you there."

Mme. Zass received me very courteously. After dinner we went to the Hermitage, where my attention was drawn foremost to the pictures; I dearly love painting. The general's wife said that it would take me at least a month merely to look at the pictures. "But just look here," she said, pointing out a bouquet made of rubies, diamonds, emeralds, and other precious stones. "Look, this is incomparably more interesting."

I don't agree with her. What are mere stones in comparison with a fine product of the brush which is imbued with life? I was very taken with four full-length depictions of two girls. In the first they were pictured in childhood and in the others, in youth, but in such a way that, when you looked at the grown girls, you immediately recognized the lovely children who had been so enchanting in their infant beauty. I looked at a depiction of Cleopatra. I sought in it the empress who chose death over humiliation and saw only a woman with a puffy, sallow face, in whose features there was no expression, not even one of pain. A leech was crawling up her bared arm, making its way toward her shoulder; this droll asp was unworthy to wound an empress. I would wager my head that no one in the world could recognize the Empress of Egypt in this depiction; I knew it was she only because Zass pointed her out and told me so. "That's the renowned Cleopatra!" Would he have had to tell me if the portrait were worthy of her?[11]

Today is Sunday. I dined with the general's wife. In the evening she, her young niece Jurkovskaja, Zass, and I went to the theater. It was evident that they were going only for my sake. No person of good taste goes to the theater on Sunday when they usually present a *rusalka* or some other such farce.[12] And, indeed, one of the parts of the rusalka was

10. Mme. Zass was most likely the wife of Aleksandr Zass's elder brother, the distinguished general Andrej Zass.

11. *The Death of Cleopatra* is by the seventeenth-century French painter Pierre Mignard. Of the paintings in the Hermitage in 1808, the ones most likely to be those of the two girls described by Durova are double portraits by Anthony Van Dyck: *Portrait of Philadelphia and Elizabeth Carey*, both girls under ten years of age, and *Portrait of Ladies of the English Queen's Court, Anne Kirke and Anne Dalkeith*. The family resemblance that Durova fancies she sees would be that common to Van Dyck's portraits. (*Gosudarstvennyj Ermitazh, Otdel Zapadnoevropejskogo iskusstva, Katalog zhivopisi*, t. II, [Leningrad-Moscow, 1958], 61.)

12. Although Durova speaks of it in generic terms, *Rusalka [The Water Nymph]* was a four-evening adaptation to Russian of the German operetta, *Das Donauweibchen*, which,

playing today. The artist who portrayed Lesta did her best to mutilate the role. She had absolutely no understanding of the character she was playing; in the *chiton* of the rusalka she grimaced, put on airs, spoke haughtily, smiled ironically, and kept looking at the *parterre* with no concern for her Vidostan. I never spent a duller evening in my life; the play and the actress bored me to tears. When I got back into the carriage, the general's wife asked me what I thought of the performance. I answered frankly that the play seemed to me a compound of absurdities and the leading actress completely out of character in the role. My candor was apparently not appreciated. They replied stiffly that Peterburg actresses are considered the very best.[13]

Today a new effort was made to astonish, engage, and entertain me. Once again it failed, and all this from the strange means taken. They decided to show me *Chinese shadows*, but since I am neither a child nor a peasant woman, I stopped watching the contraption after the first scene.[14] It must be assumed that the general's wife gives me no credit either for good upbringing or good taste. Be that as it may, her kind intentions merit my gratitude.

I have seen the emperor again! His first words as he greeted me were, "They tell me that you saved an officer! Did you really rescue him from the enemy? Tell me what happened."

I recounted the incident in detail and named the officer. The emperor said that his was a famous name and that my fearlessness on this one occasion did me more honor than everything else during the campaign, because it was based on the greatest of virtues—compassion! "Although your deed serves as its own reward," the emperor went on, "justice demands that you receive that which is owed you by statute as well: the

---

despite Durova's grumbles, was one of the most popular musical plays of the time. (*Istorija russkogo dramaticheskogo teatra*, vol. 2, 515–17).

13. The actress who usually played Lesta in 1807–1808 was Sofia Samojlova (*Letopis' russkogo teatra* Pimen Arapov, ed. [St. Petersburg, 1861], 172, 182). To be fair, her debut performance as Lesta (under her maiden name of Chernikova) was reported by one theater-goer as superior to that of her competitors in Berlin and Vienna (S. P. Zhikharev, *Zapiski: 1805–1807* [Moscow, 1891], 12.)

14. Shows featuring "Chinese shadows" were widespread throughout Europe in the late eighteenth century. They used the oriental technique of projecting "mobile paintings," cut out of cardboard or leather and illuminated from behind, onto a linen or oiled paper screen. The shows featured miscellaneous skits and such scenes as magicians working transformations, duck hunts, thunderstorms, battles, and the classic Chinese "broken bridge." See Charles Magnin, *Histoire des Marionnettes en Europe: depuis l'Antiquité jusqu'a nos Jours* (Paris, 1862), 182–86; and, for a description of a similar show in the Russian provinces in the middle of the nineteenth century, M. Semevskij, "Toropets," *Biblioteka dlja chtenija* (1863), 12:18–25.

Cross of St. George is awarded for saving the life of an officer!" With these words the emperor took a cross from his desk and with his own hands put it through the buttonhole of my uniform. I blushed bright red with joy and in my confusion seized both the emperor's hands to kiss them, but he would not permit it.

"I hope," said the emperor, "that this cross will remind you of me at crucial moments in your life." There is great significance behind these words. I swear that the adored Father of Russia will not be deceived in his expectations. This cross will be my guardian angel; I will cherish to the grave the memories connected with it, I will never forget the occasion on which I received it, and I will always—always!—see the *hand* which touches it now.[15]

I returned to Zass's apartment where I have been living ever since my arrival in Peterburg. I had not yet taken off my cartridge-pouch when I saw an old man entering after me and asking in a quavering voice, "May I see Recruit Durov of the Polish Horse regiment? I am his uncle." Hearing these words, I guessed that the man I saw before me was my father's younger brother, and my first thought was to flee.[16] Fortunately, I had no time to do anything so foolish. Zass responded to his question at once by pointing me out, and my uncle came over to me, embraced me, and said in a low voice, "Your mother is dead."

The words pierced me like a sharp dagger. I trembled and turned pale. I sensed that I was about to burst into floods of tears, and, unable to utter a single word, I took my uncle by the arm and led him out of Zass's apartment.

"Come home with me," said my uncle once we were out on the street. I got into his sleigh and rode all the way in silence, hiding my face and eyes in my greatcoat so that passersby would not see me crying.

At home my uncle told me that when my father received my letter from Grodno and learned from it that I had enlisted in the Polish Horse, he was alarmed by the singular step I had taken. Not knowing how to remedy it or what to do, he sent the letter to Mama. The consequences of this thoughtless act were disastrous. I had been so reckless as to write that it was my mother's excessive strictness which drove me out of my father's house and, in the event I was killed, I begged Papa to forgive me

15. Alexander I never could resist an impassioned appeal. For other young women who came under his patronage, see: Petr Bykov, "Russkie zhenshchiny-pisateli: A. I. Ishimova," *Drevnjaja i novaja Rossija* (1878), 8:316–23; Xavier de Maistre, "La Jeune Sibérienne," *Oeuvres* (Paris, 1825); and, for a summary of the two stories, Mary F. Zirin, "Alexandra Ishimova and *The Captain's Daughter*: A Conjecture," *Pacific Coast Philology*, vol. 15.2 (1980): 41–48.

16. According to Durova's later account ("All That I Could Recollect"), her uncle Nikolaj Durov was living in Peterburg to defend himself from charges of negligence which had cost him his post as a quarantine inspector in the Crimea.

the sorrow my death would inflict on him. Mama was confined to bed, dangerously ill and very weak. When this letter was brought to her, she took it and read it through; then, after a minute of silence, she said with a sigh, "She blames me," turned her face to the wall, and died.

I was sobbing like a five-year-old as I listened to this tale. How could I suppose that Papa would show her the letter? My uncle left me at liberty to abandon myself to my cruel grief and repentance and put off telling me the rest until the following day.

When my father got the letter back, he sent it to my uncle in Peterburg, asking him to find out whether I was still alive. My uncle showed the letter to some generals of his acquaintance and thus it reached the emperor who, they said, was moved to tears when he read it. He at once ordered inquiries made about me in the Polish Horse regiment and, if the reports proved favorable to me, my presentation to him in person. All my commanders showered praise on me beyond my merits and expectations. The result was the emperor's unprecedented grace: permission to dedicate my life to him in the ranks of his warriors.[17]

At last everything is ready for my departure. I have received a travel pass, regimental orders, and two thousand rubles for a hussar uniform and the purchase of a horse. My uncle is very angry because I won't say where I am going. I keep telling him that I am on my way home to Papa, but he does not believe me and says that sooner or later he will find out where I am.

17. Documents relating to the search for Durova are included in Appendix A.

# Chapter Four

*January 15.* From this, the happiest day of my life, I have begun a new existence. Brilliant, glorious prospects of a unique sort lie open before me, and, to crown my blessings, they are at the will and under the protection of the world's most powerful monarch!

Four days after my departure from Peterburg, I arrived in Vilna, where I planned on outfitting myself. A throng of Jews appeared with offers of every sort of service. In half an hour I had everything: quarters, servants, tailors; heaps of cloth, gold braid, fringe, morocco leather, tricorns, shakoes, plumes, tassels, spurs. In short, my room was turned into a shop full of wares, and all I had to do was choose. The Jews all talked at once, deafening me; I didn't know what to do until one quick Jew said to me stealthily, "The only way to get rid of them is by choosing a factor. Then he'll send this rabble packing and bring you a merchant from whom you can buy everything you need at a very reasonable price."

I asked him what a factor was.

"A factor," the Jew replied, "is the sort of servant who is quick, zealous, sharp-witted, tireless, and unbelievably cheap. Would having a servant like that suit you?"

I said it was exactly what I needed and begged him to choose one.

"Why choose?" said the Jew. "I myself will be your factor." He announced his title to the throng and at once began discharging his duties by sending away the other candidates for the post and making arrangements with merchants—also Hebrew, of course—to swindle me with the greatest possible lack of scruple. As all of us must, I paid the tribute these rogues exact from youth and inexperience. My uniform was well tailored; all my hussar attire shone with taste and resplendence. My cheap servant took from me only a ruble for his six days of service, but nevertheless I got to the regiment with only one ruble left out of the two thousand devoured by Vilna through the good offices of my zealous, cheap servant.

I have arrived in Kovel. My travel orders are good only this far, but the Mariupol regiment is not here; it is quartered in Lutsk and its environs. I don't know what to do. Lutsk is fifty versts from Kovel, and I have only one ruble. It is unlikely that anybody will take me to Lutsk for so little, and it is equally impossible for me to stay in Kovel without money waiting for a chance to leave.

I was pondering ways out of this disagreeable situation when I heard the crack of a whip. I glanced out the window and saw a lady in a *bryczka* heading for the tavern where I had stopped.[1] The Jewess ran to open the door. A well-dressed lady about thirty years old entered and at once turned her attention to me. She struck up a conversation, and when she found out that I was an officer from the regiment quartered in their neighborhood, would have liked to inquire about officers of her acquaintance. The Jewess, however, gave her no time for these questions; she began at once telling the lady that I was a new officer; I didn't know anyone in the regiment yet and had no way of getting to headquarters because my travel orders were good only to Kovel, and headquarters, as she well knew, was in Lutsk; and it would be kind of *panna* Nowicka to give the young hussar a ride in her *bryczka* as far as the village of Holoby, where he would be at home already because a Mariupol squadron was stationed there. All this she uttered in a single breath and so quickly that neither *panna* Nowicka nor I had a chance to think twice about the necessity of traveling together. This was pleasant for me: I saw in it a possibility to spare myself bother. But when it is proposed to an unmarried lady that she take a young hussar into her vehicle and ride thirty versts alone with him, she might well become embarrassed. To *panna* Nowicka's credit, however, it must be said that she at once offered me a seat in her *bryczka* without a trace of constraint and with a most amiable courtesy.

In two hours *panna* Nowicka finished her errands, which consisted in the purchase of sugar, tea, chocolate, and other such items, and we set off. The young woman was disposed to talk to me and made several attempts, but I answered only *yes* or *no* and that not always to the point, because I don't like the Polish language and have made no effort to learn it. My traveling companion's talkativeness put me in a dreadful plight. I sensed that my behavior was odd, but I knew of no way to remedy the woe and so remained silent. Poor Nowicka! Fate saw fit to send her the most graceless of all hussars as her comrade on the road. At last she too stopped talking, started yawning, rested her head on the pillow—and fell asleep. In this agreeable fashion we rode all the way to the town of Holoby, where Nowicka at once woke up and ordered the coachman to drive to Captain Ageev's quarters. The vehicle dashed off, bounding across the ruts, and stopped before a tiny whitewashed house. "Here are your captain's quarters," said Nowicka, bowing politely to me. I blushed for the foolish role I had played with this kind young woman. I would have liked to express my gratitude in Polish, but I was afraid of coming out with nonsense, and these misgivings made me blush even redder. At last I got out of the vehicle in silence and bowed to the *panna* just as

1. *Bryczka*, a light, open carriage. (Polish)

mutely, and her good steeds whisked my traveling companion up to the porch of the huge manor.

There was nobody in the captain's quarters except his orderly. Ageev was at headquarters. The old hussar served me tea and asked, "Your honor, will you sleep here or travel farther?" When I learned that it would be at least two days before the captain returned to the squadron, I decided to spend the night in his quarters. Questioning the orderly, I found out that Holoby belongs to the widow of *wojewoda* Wilga, Wilszina as the Poles call her, a very hospitable and charitable old lady of about eighty; that a number of young and pretty *szlachcianki* live with her, and she arranges marriages for them from her own purse; and that officers of the squadron frequently dine with her, but there never has been nor ever will be a ball at her house.[2]

"Why is that?" I asked the loquacious hussar.

"Because, your honor," he replied, "the lady's son, young *pan* Wilga, lost his wife, whom he loved passionately. Her death shattered his health and, to some extent, his reason, so that he shuns people in general, not even excepting his mother and his children."

Very early the next morning I saw by the porch a large wicker basket sitting on a sledge that was harnessed to two emaciated horses. The hussar came in, set my breakfast down on the table, and said, "The *kurmanka* is ready, your honor!"

To keep from revealing my ignorance, I did not ask what sort of beast the *kurmanka* was and why it was ready namely for me. After breakfast I said to the hussar, "Please see whether there'll be horses for me soon."

"They're ready now. There's the *kurmanka* standing in front of the porch," replied the hussar, pointing out the window.

At last the riddle was solved. This wicker basket is called a *kurmanka*—I think only when horses are harnessed to it, however; without them it becomes a big basket again. Be that as it may, I must go to headquarters in it. Oh, Fortune, be merciful to me! See that I don't encounter any of my future comrades in arms. I am joining the regiment in a most inglorious way.

I got into my straw-filled basket. The bridleless horses took off at a trot, and throughout the journey the coachman kept waving a long switch over them and shouting, "Wio, wio! Iss, iss!"[3] This is evidently the way they incite their horses to a run.

*Lutsk.* When I got to the city, I followed the custom of all travelers and newcomers and stopped at a tavern. I dressed as if for inspection and went

2. *Wojewoda*, a provincial administrator; *szlachcianka*, a Polish noblewoman.
3. "Wio, wio!" is "Hup, hup!" or "Off we go!" (Polish); "iss" is probably just a sibilant encouragement.

to report to the battalion commander, Major Dýmchevich. I handed him the packet Count Lieven had given me. When he was through reading it, Dýmchevich said to me, "Go to the regimental adjutant, and tell him that I ordered you placed in my squadron. Give him these papers." Then he asked me several questions about our Grand Duke Konstantin Pavlovich, but when he realized that I knew nothing at all about him, he repeated his order for me to see the adjutant and from there to set out at once for the squadron.

I had to spend my last ruble getting to Rożyscze, where Dýmchevich's squadron is quartered. The commander of the squadron, a junior captain, received me with all the pomposity of a superior officer which, however, was very unbecoming to him, in view of both his insignificant rank and his appearance: he is extremely short and snub-nosed, and his face has a common look about it. His first question was, "Do you have a saddle horse?"

I answered that I did not.

"You'll have to buy one," he said.

"I thought I had the right to take one from the regiment."

"So you do. But a hussar officer can't serve with only a regimental horse. You will need three horses: for yourself, for your orderly and pack, and a third in reserve."

I said that I had no orderly and no money to buy a horse.

"You can have an orderly tomorrow if you like, and nobody cares whether you have money or not, but you will need the horses without fail. Now be so good as to go to the hamlet of Berezolupy and take command of the fourth squadron until the return of its regular commander, who is away on leave. . . ."

Since I wasn't getting much pleasure from the company of this queer fellow, I went off at once to my village. There I was assigned to the quarters which Dokukin occupies in the house of the lady landowner of the village. *Pani starościna* received me with maternal kindness and asked me to dine each day with her because, as she said, "I see that you have no cook of your own." The *starościna* treats me just like her two grandsons, boys of twelve. They and I both get a cup of warm milk in the morning. We live almost in a single room; only a plank partition separates my bedstead from their beds. They say their prayers, study, shout, bang about, and quarrel just as if I were not there. Moreover, every morning these imps beg me to allow them to clean my boots, a favor which, on my part, I am only too happy to grant them.

A gentleman named Malchenko offered to sell me a horse for one hundred rubles in silver, which he will not expect me to pay until I receive money from home. I agreed. They brought the horse, who would have been tolerable if only he did not hold his ears so strangely. Malchenko praised him to the skies. I felt ashamed to tell him that his horse's ears hang down to the sides, and the bargain was struck. After that Malchenko asked me whether I knew how to drill with a carbine and, when I said I didn't, he told me, "You'll have to learn; it's indispensable. You have to know what you will be obliged to teach the soldiers. Order one of the veteran hussars to show you all the motions with the carbine. You can master it in two weeks; it's not at all difficult."

The *starościna* has an eighteen-year-old granddaughter, a pretty girl, but one with the most absurd propensity for falling in love with anyone and everyone—peasant, coachman, valet, cook, officer, general, priest, or monk! The current object of her affections is her brothers' teacher, a sallow, dry, repulsive pedant. In order to be with this Adonis, she spends all morning in our room.

Every morning old Grebennik, the flank hussar of my platoon, brings me a carbine, and I spend over an hour learning to order arms, slope arms, and present arms. The maneuver for ordering arms is very difficult for me. Much to my instructor's disgust, I perform it awkwardly and sluggishly. Every time he commands me to order arms, he adds, "Don't spare your foot, your honor. Toss it more boldly!"

I tried to obey him and not spare my foot, as he put it, but I bruised it so cruelly on the gunstock that it hurt for a month. At last I mastered carbine drill.

Emperor Alexander ordered me to write to him about everything I might need through Count Lieven. And so I wrote to the count, asking him for a grant of five hundred rubles. Two months later I received it, but not through Lieven. Count Arakcheev sent it and wrote me to address all my needs to him, because he had taken over Count Lieven's post with the emperor.[4] When the money came, I paid my debt to Malchenko, and now I do not know what to do with my lop-eared horse. Besides the damned ears he has other odd habits: he won't leave the other horses, rears, and always starts galloping from the hind foot.

The Mariupol regiment has been ordered to assemble near Lutsk, where our corps commander Dokhturov will inspect it. But first we must pass examination before our divisional commander, Count Suvorov.[5] So

4. Lieven became ambassador to Berlin. Count Aleksej Arakcheev was the first to hold the title of War Minister, a post he was named to on January 13, 1808, even before Durova left Peterburg. For the text of the letter Count Lieven wrote to Arakcheev explaining that dealing with Durova was a part of his new duties, see Appendix A.

5. Dmitrij Dokhturov was named to command the VI Corps in 1809. Count Arkadij

there we were, riding out onto the green plain in our white uniforms glittering with gold and with fluttering plumes in our shakoes. In this dress attire, white with gold, many of us resemble pretty girls more than courageous soldiers, especially those like me who are eighteen or younger.

It must be assumed that my lop-eared steed has always been back in the ranks, because the commanding role he had to play clearly terrified him. He kept trying to work his way, jibbing, back into the formation, and, when I goaded him with my sharp spurs to force him to move out front, he arched his head and reared. Judging from this start, I was expecting lethal tricks from him when the maneuvers began, and that's how it turned out. The count rode past our entire regiment at a walk, attentively inspecting the entire formation; then, moving a few paces out before the center of the regiment, he said loudly, "Honorable officers!" The entire brilliant assembly rushed as fast as the wind to their commander, but it took several stiff blows with the saber before my devil kicked his hind legs and took off at a melancholy gallop, waving his ears smoothly. Suvorov was gracious enough to wait until I joined my comrades before giving us his orders, which consisted of the exact maneuvers we would perform for Dokhturov and which would come when. "And now, gentlemen," added the count, "this will be merely a rehearsal. To your places, please." We all flew back to the regiment, and this time I went like a whirlwind. We stopped in front of the formation and dressed ranks. The command rang out, "By platoon, to the right, wheel! March!" The entire regiment made the motion smoothly and in good order, but my demon started jibbing, kicking, snorting, and arching his lop-eared head with all his might. Foreseeing no good end to such a beginning, I ordered the sergeant to take my place before our platoon and, giving my horse two or three *Fuchteln* with all my might, forced him to carry me posthaste down the Lutsk road.[6]

Watching this scene, Suvorov merely said with a wry smile, "The young officer doesn't care to drill with us."

The maneuvers before the chief of our corps ended without further woe for me; the battalion commander gave me his horse. After the inspection and drill all the officers went to dine with Suvorov. The count has such charming and obliging manners! The officers and men love him

---

Suvorov, born in 1784, was the only son of the fabled eighteenth-century Russian field-marshal, A. V. Suvorov. Young Suvorov drowned on April 13, 1811, while trying to force his carriage across a swollen ford on the Rymnik in Rumania—at the very spot where his father won a famous victory over the Turks in September 1789. See "Arkhiv M. I. Golenishcheva-Kutuzova-Smolenskogo," *Russkaja starina* (1872), 2:262.

6. *Fuchteln,* blows with the flat of a sword. (German)

like a father, a friend, one of their own comrades, because to their mind he combines all these qualities.

It will soon be three years since I left my father's house. We are on our way to camp for six weeks of maneuvers, but when we arrive back in our quarters, I will ask for leave.

Today, to my shame, I fell off my horse. I could have said: and to my misfortune, because I fell just as the entire regiment went on the attack. Podjampolsky had given me his horse, a young and frisky stallion. Our maneuvers were finishing well; all that remained was the attack by the regiment as a whole. At the command, "From your places, charge— charge!" my horse reared and bounded out ahead. His sudden motion tore the scabbard of my saber loose from its front strap, and it fell between his legs. The horse began to buck at a full run and on the third toss threw me over his head to the ground. I fell and instantly lost consciousness. In a flash the regiment came to a total halt. This posed no difficulty for such excellently trained men and horses: at the first com- manding shout, "Halt!" the regiment stopped as if planted on the spot. Officers lifted me up off the ground, unhooked my *dulam* or *dolman*,[7] undid my necktie, and shouted for the doctor to let blood quickly! But, to my great good fortune, I came to, and the fuss and any further undressing came to an end. I retied my necktie, hooked up my *dolman*, threw away the torn swordbelt, and remounted my horse. I took no further part in the drill, however, but merely rode after the regiment.

After the maneuvers Dýmchevich sent for me and, as I approached him, rode with me apart from the other officers. He began by saying, "You fell off your horse today? . . ." I tried to tell him that the horse threw me. He repeated in a stern voice, "You fell off your horse! A hussar can only fall with his horse, never off it. I don't want to hear any more about it. Tomorrow the regiment returns to quarters, and tomorrow you are to go to the reserve squadron to the riding master and learn to ride."

*The small town of Turzysk.* I am living with our regimental riding master, Lieutenant Wichmann, and every morning I spend an hour and a half and every evening an hour riding on the blanket with no saddle. I am having a good time here. Wichmann and I spend every afternoon at the house of Lieutenant-Colonel Pavlishchev, the commander of the reserve squadron. The Pavlishchev family is fond of me and treats me like one of their own. His eldest daughter is as pretty as a cherub, a genuine spring rose! Pure virtue shines in her eyes and suffuses the features of her innocent face. She is teaching me to play the guitar, which she plays

---

7. The fitted hussar jacket with standing collar and loop fastenings in gold braid.

extremely well, and tells me with childlike gaiety about the amusing things she has seen and heard.

In the Roman Catholic church here there is an icon of the *Najświętsza Panna*—that is, the Virgin Mary—with the babe at her feet, leaning on a globe. Legend has it that this picture was painted at the behest of a previous owner of Turzysk, Prince Ossoliński. The prince fell passionately in love with the daughter of a peasant. He divorced his wife, born Princess O., gave his mistress the education befitting a great lady, and married her. In the first year of their marriage they had a son; the happy prince, wishing to see the image of his dearly beloved wife and son everywhere, ordered an icon of the Mother of God painted with the features of his young princess. I spent a long time studying the image. The princess is charming, with a gentle and captivating countenance. Her son is the usual pretty child. Both of them died early and tragically. When the powerful and proud O. family saw that the birth of a son had firmly cemented Ossoliński's marriage to his peasant girl, they lost hope of seeing the first princess Ossolińska restored to her previous station and ordered the mother and son poisoned. The objects of Ossoliński's tender attachment suffered a cruel death before his eyes. Although he survived his loss, he grew to hate society, renounced it, and became a monk. The estate passed into the hands of the counts Moszyński; one of them, a very old man, owns it now. I also saw a portrait of Ossoliński's first wife, Princess O. What touching beauty! Sadness and revery are portrayed in her black eyes. She has delicate dark brows, rosy lips, and a pale, but comely face, all the features of which express an intelligence and gentleness that are quite enchanting. I am astonished at Ossoliński![8]

I am still taking riding lessons. To my vexation, Wichmann is an ardent hunter and, willy-nilly, I have to go out hunting with him. Beside all the discomforts and disagreeable aspects of this barbaric pastime, the pitiful squeal of a tormented hare is enough to depress me for the entire day. Sometimes I resolutely refuse to participate in these murders, but then Wichmann threatens that if I do not go hunting I will never learn to keep a firm seat in the saddle. Hunting, he says, is the only way to attain perfection in the equestrian art; and so once again I go out galloping at breakneck speed across various groves, islands, swamps, and tussocks, freezing from the fine sleet which turns my greatcoat and gloves to ice. At

8. *Polski Słownik Biograficzny* [Polish Biographical Dictionary], vol. 24 (Wroclaw, 1979), 412–15, lists a Józef Ossoliński (c. 1758–1834) who owned the town of Turzysk and had two wives, the first from a branch of the Ossoliński family and the second, a Cossack girl named Matriona Pęcherzowna by whom he had a son who died at six. There is no hint that the death of his second wife and son was unnatural, but the rumor must have been still afloat twenty years afterward. Durova used the tale as the basis for her story, "Count Mauritius"; see the section "Durova's Fiction" in the Introduction.

last we stop to rest in some ramshackle little hut or other and eat ham which has such a disgusting salty taste that one bite is enough to make me spit it out and eat my bread without it. These hunters are people under a spell of some sort. Everything seems different to them than to the rest of us: they find the hellish ham which I can't even put in my mouth, a delicacy; the harsh autumn, a propitious season; furious galloping and headlong somersaults with their horse, healthful exercise; and low swampy spots overgrown with stunted shrubbery, a beautiful landscape. At the end of the hunt, the hunters' discussion of it begins, opinions and anecdotes in jargon of which I can't understand a single word.

Amusing scenes take place in the society of the gentlemen hunters! Among the most desperate of them are Dýmchevich, Merlin, Soshalsky, and Wichmann. I think that even a dying man would burst out laughing if he could see Dýmchevich when he hears hounds barking as they find the trail; he is deeply moved, weeps, and, wiping away his tears, says, "Poor hounds!" Not long ago he went for an outing by carriage with Pavlishchev's eldest daughter. When he caught sight of a hare running across the fields, he was so carried away that he forgot the presence of the lady, the absence of the dogs, and the absolute impossibility of chasing the little beast from an open carriage and began shouting at the top of his voice, "Tally-ho! Tally-ho! . . . Halloo, halloo!!" His sudden transports frightened the young lady, the coachman, and even the horses.

A new commander-in-chief, Meller-Zakomelsky, has arrived in the regiment. He immediately demanded that I come to headquarters. I had to leave the fine company of the reserve squadron, to which I have become extremely attached. Meller sent for me to tell me that I have been granted leave for two months and to find out why I had not applied through the command but directly to the emperor.

I replied that, since I had permission to do so, I made use of it only in order to get leave as soon as possible. Meller ordered me to go to see Count Suvorov in Dubno. He said that there I would find Komburlej, the governor of Zhitomir, from whom I must get my travel orders.[9]

*Dubno.* The count is making preparations to give a splendid ball tomorrow. He told me that I would not receive my travel orders until after the celebration and that I must dance at his ball—he is imposing it on me as a duty. I heard him out and then went to see his adjutant, Count Kachowski. There I found many officers of my regiment drinking tea. Shortly afterward Suvorov came in, too, wearing his dressing gown and

9. Baron Egor Meller-Zakomel'skij was the son of one of Catherine the Great's generals. M. I. Komburlej governed Volhynia from 1806 until 1817; he had an estate in Zhitomir.

slippers. He lay down on Kachowski's bed and said that he was escaping from the unbearable bustle and dust raised by the sweeping, cleaning, and tidying of the entire house for tomorrow's festivities. Kachowski served him a glass of tea. Two hours later Suvorov went back to his own rooms, and an entire cartload of straw was brought into Kachowski's room, spread over the floor, and covered with rugs. Some morocco leather pillows were tossed on top of them, and this made up a spacious bed for his guests. I wished my fellow officers good night and went back to the tavern where I was stopping.

The innkeeper's daughter, *panna* Dobrowolska, unlocked for me the glass doors leading directly from the street into the parlor. "I've been waiting supper for you for a long time," she said. "There's nobody here today. Come into my room." We went into her chamber, where they served us hazel-grouse, apples, white bread, jam, and a half bottle of malaga, which we finished.

## THE BALL

The spacious halls of Suvorov's house were filled with a brilliant society. Countless lamps flooded all the rooms with bright light. Music thundered. Lovely Polish ladies, waltzing, hung amorously on the elbows of our adroit, slender hussars. Suvorov has been extremely spoiled by the Polish ladies. They forgive him altogether too much for his handsome looks; he says anything that comes into his head—and the things that sometimes come into his head are marvelous! He noticed that I was not dancing nor even going anywhere near the ladies, and asked me the reason for this odd behavior. Stánkovich, my squadron commander who is, as the saying goes, a dashing hussar, hastened to answer for me: "He's afraid of women, Your Excellency. He is shy of them, doesn't like them, and knows nothing of any relations with them."

"Really!" said Suvorov. "Oh, that's inexcusable. Come along, young man, you'll have to make a start." And with this he took my arm and led me over to the young and lovely Princess Lubomirska. He introduced me to the lady by saying, "A la vue de ses fraiches couleurs vous pouvez bien deviner qu'il n'a pas encore perdu sa virginité."[10]

After this recommendation, unique of its kind, the count released my arm, the princess, with a barely perceptible wry smile, rapped him lightly on the cuff with her fan, and I returned to my comrades. Half an hour later I left the ball altogether. It was now past midnight, and I am used to

10. "From his rosy complexion, you can see at a glance that he hasn't yet lost his virginity." (French)

going to sleep early. Moreover, I am not fond of gatherings where there are many women. Stánkovich was not in error when he said that I fear them; I really do. A woman has only to look fixedly at me to start me blushing in confusion. I feel as if she sees right through me and guesses my secret from my appearance alone. In mortal dread I make haste to hide from her eyes.

# Chapter Five

## HOME LEAVE

Three and a half years have passed since my father last saw me. I have changed a great deal: I am taller and I've filled out, my face has changed from pale and oval to swarthy and round, and my hair, which used to be light brown, has darkened. I think that Papa won't recognize me right away. I traveled alone by hired carriage, with nothing but my saber to keep me company.

Stationmasters, taking me for a green youth, often made difficulties for me on the road. They would wait six hours before giving me horses so that I would order something—dinner, tea, or coffee; then the horses would appear. When they presented the bill, it was accompanied by words like: "With your travel allowance, here is what you still owe. . . ." This was usually quite a considerable sum, but I paid it without a word. Sometimes they refused me horses altogether in order to force me to hire private ones at double my allowance. Oh, this journey has inspired me with both dread and loathing of post-stations!

I arrived home at exactly the same time of night I quit the paternal shelter—one o'clock in the morning. The gates were locked. I took my saber and valise from the sleigh and dismissed my coachman for the return trip. Left alone in front of the locked gates of the house where my oppressed, joyless childhood was spent, I experienced none of the emotions that are so often written about. On the contrary, it was with a feeling of sadness that I walked along the palisade to the spot where I knew there were four loose stakes; through this aperture as a child I had often gone out at night to run around the square in front of the church. Now I used it to enter! How could I have ever imagined when I used to crawl through this hole in my white coarse linen frock, looking around timidly and listening closely, shivering from fear and the cold night, that someday I would come back in through this same aperture, also at night, as a *hussar?*

All the windows of the house were locked. I went up to those of the children's room and tried to take hold of the shutters to open them, but they were fastened somehow from the inside, and I didn't want to knock because I might frighten my little brother and sister. I went over to the building where Mama's women-servants live. Our two dogs, Mars and Mustapha, heard me crossing the yard and rushed me with loud barks which turned at once to joyful yelps. The dear, faithful beasts began twining themselves around my legs, jumping up on my chest, and racing

79

impetuously in rapture around the yard and back to me again. After I had petted and caressed them, I climbed the stairs and began going from door to door, knocking lightly at each. For a quarter of an hour I had no luck. The dogs both followed me, and both scratched at each door I knocked on. At last I heard the door into the hall open, and soon afterward a woman's voice asked, "Who's there?"

I recognized at once that the person questioning me was Mama's maid Natalja. "It's me. Open up, Natalja."

"Oh, my God, the young mistress!" shrieked Natalja joyfully, rushing to open the door. It took her a minute or so of clanking away at bolts and locks before the door opened and I came in, holding my saber under my arm, accompanied by Mars and Mustapha. Natalja stepped back dumbfounded. "Oh, God save us! Is it really you?" She stood motionless before the door and wouldn't let me enter.

"So let me in, Natalja. What's the matter with you? Don't you recognize me?"

"Oh, ma'am, miss, how could I recognize you? If it weren't for the voice I'd never in my life recognize you." Natalja opened the inner door, helped me off with my greatcoat, and again gasped in surprise as she caught sight of the gold braid on my uniform. "What rich clothes you're wearing, miss! Are you a general, perhaps?"

For another quarter of an hour Natalja kept spewing nonsense and reaching out to touch my gold braid and the fur collar of my *mentik,* until at last I reminded her that I needed a bed made.[1]

"Right away, right away, ma'am. . . ." Then she added, talking to herself, "Maybe you shouldn't call her 'miss' anymore. Well, it'll take a while to get used to. . . ." She started out and then came back, "Would you like me to make tea? It'll be ready in two minutes."

"Please, dear Natalja."

"Oh, ma'am, miss! You're just as nice as ever." Natalja began talking again. "I'll make tea this very minute. But what do they call you now, miss? I can hear that you don't talk the way you used to."[2]

"Call me just what everyone else does."

"But what are the others going to call you, ma'am—sir! Excuse me. . . ."

"That's enough, Natalja. Go bring the tea." The chatterbox went and then came back to take away Mars and Mustapha. Both of them were lying at my feet, and they growled at Natalja when she called them.

"Chase them out, miss, they should be outside."

---

1. The *mentik* was the short hussar cape worn on the left shoulder as padding in combat.

2. Natalja is confused by hearing Durova's use of masculine grammatical forms for herself.

"Later, later, Natalja. Do me a favor, go get the tea. I'm deathly cold."

Natalja went running off, and I was left to reflect that scenes like this would be repeated not only with all our own household, but with my father's circle of acquaintances as well. Imagining it all, I almost regretted having come. A quarter of an hour later Natalja appeared with the tea and some pillows.

"What time does Papa get up?" I asked her.

"The same as always, miss, at nine o'clock." After this reply she began grumbling to herself again, "I'll never get used to it. . . . What are you to do?"

I gave Mars and Mustapha each a hard biscuit and ordered them out; they obeyed me instantly.

At seven o'clock the next morning I put on my white *dolman*. Our regiment changed uniforms a long time ago, with dark blue prescribed instead of white, but Stánkovich's squadron, I don't know why, must wear white for another year yet.[3] To avoid motley ranks, he asked us to keep wearing white uniforms also. I agreed more willingly than anyone, because I love the combination of white and gold. When I was dressed, Natalja looked at me with fresh surprise: "You've changed a lot, miss. Your papa won't recognize you."

I went to see my sisters. They were already up and waiting for me. Papa joined us that very minute. I embraced his knees and kissed his hands; it was beyond my power to utter a single word. My father wept, hugged me to his breast, and said, smiling through his tears, that no feature of my face looked the way it had before, that I resembled a Kalmyk woman. At last my little brother came in, wearing the uniform of the Mining Institute. He had spent a long time conferring with Nanny about the proper way to greet me: should he just bow or kiss my hand? When Nanny told him he should do whatever he wished, he came running at once and threw himself into my arms. I kissed him and said to Papa that it would be a pity to leave such a fine boy in the Department of Mines; in three years Papa should allow me to take him with me into the hussar regiment.

"No, no, God forbid!" said Papa. "You can be whatever you want since you've already chosen your path, but the consolation of my old age, my Vasinka, will stay with me."

I said no more, wholeheartedly regretting that I had been so thoughtless as to grieve my father with a proposal that was both mis-

3. The change in the uniform of the Mariupol' Hussars was made late in 1809. Previously the regiment wore the navy-blue *mentik* over a white dolman; now both were prescribed as navy-blue (V. V. Zvegintsov, *Russkaja armija*, part 4: 1801–1825 [Paris, 1973], 358–59).

placed and premature. Meanwhile, my brother clung to me and whispered in my ear, "I'll go with you."

Although I love my father with all my heart, the idle life, lack of society, cold weather, and constant questions of our provincials depressed me so that I was almost glad to see the dawn of the day on which I was to start back to the regiment. The return journey was considerably more difficult than the earlier one, but not where horses were concerned. Nobody played niggardly tricks on me this time, because I said to any stationmaster who started telling me that he had no horses, "I will note in your book how many hours I spend here, and you'll answer for it if I am late getting back." And so they gave me horses very promptly everywhere; but the winter road had begun to break up, my hired vehicle was beyond comparison more heavily loaded than it had been before, and it was a dreadful bother to haul all that by myself. I didn't take a manservant; and, of course, there was no way I could have.

Returning to my comrades and the pursuits I love makes me feel like the luckiest creature on earth. My days pass merrily and serenely. I always get up at dawn and at once go out walking in the fields. I return after the horses have been tended to—that is, about eight o'clock in the morning. At my quarters my horse is already saddled and waiting. I mount him and ride out into the fields again, where I drill my platoon for an hour and a half. Afterwards I go off to headquarters or the squadron commander's and stay there until evening.

I presented my worthless horse to Wichmann in return for the riding lessons. He ordered him harnessed to a *drozhky,* and to our surprise he has become a fine steed. Thus shafts were the sphere for which nature intended him. I think it is the same way with human beings; they do well only once they have found their proper place.

I also gave Wichmann a hunting horn made from a beautifully carved elephant tusk. Papa had given me this rare object for Count Suvorov, but for some reason I felt ashamed to present it to the count, and so I gave it to Wichmann. I was instantly punished for disregarding Papa's wishes: Wichmann took this rare object as coldly and negligently as if it were a cowhorn of tobacco.

Our battalion has gone with Meller-Zakomelsky to Galicia.[4]

4. In 1807, by the terms of the treaty of Tilsit, the Duchy of Warsaw was constituted under French protection from the areas seized by the Prussians in the late eighteenth-century. The Russians picked up the Tarnopol district of Polish Galicia in 1809 when the French forestalled an Austrian attempt to mount a pan-Germanic campaign against Napoleon; the other Polish lands that Austria had held since the third partition were added to the duchy. The Mariupol' Hussars were sent to guard the new border and prevent defections of Polish soldiers from the Russian army.

Stánkovich's squadron and all its officers are remaining here under the designation of reserves and, together with the supply troops, will be under Pavlishchev's command. Since I am one of the officers of Stánkovich's squadron, I am staying here also, although I am very eager to go abroad and see action again; but Stánkovich says, "Don't volunteer to go where they don't send you; where they send you, don't refuse! This is the guiding rule for men of proven valor." His advice and the excellent company of the officers who are staying here with me helped me to watch with less regret the departure of our brave hussars abroad. Fate has arranged for the most amiable lady of the regiment to remain here also. I avoid women in general, but not the wives and daughters of my fellow officers. I like them very much; they are the finest beings in the world— always kind, always obliging, lively, bold, cheerful; they like to go horseback riding or for walks, to laugh, and to dance! They have no whims or caprices. Oh, the women of the regiment have nothing in common with women from other walks of life, with whom I would not willingly spend a quarter of an hour. It is true that my regimental ladies never miss a chance to make me blush by calling me *hussar miss* as a joke. Since I am always with them, I am used to the appellation, and sometimes I make so bold as to ask them, "What do you find girlish about me?"

"Your slender waist," they answer. "Your little feet and rosy cheeks that any of us would be eager to have. That's why we call you *hussar miss*, and, by your leave, we can't help but be a little suspicious that we are correct in giving you the name."

Since I hear jokes like this almost every day, I am so accustomed to them that they hardly ever embarrass me anymore.

We are stationed on the Galician frontier in the little town of *Kołodno*. This is a land border, and our duty is to patrol and supervise the reliability of the Cossack cordon. Kołodno belongs to Szwejkowski, whose wife is a beauty brought up in Paris. A long chestnut lane, as dark as night, leads from the porch of the manor to a little whitewashed house planted all around with lindens. The overseer lives in this house with his kind wife and two merry, playful, sweet daughters, and we pass all our days there. I notice that my comrades spend more time there than with the proud and beautiful Szwejkowska.

Officer Wątrobka told us that on one of his horseback excursions across the border he met and got to know Baron Czechowicz. He said that the baroness has a beauty more ravishing than any he could ever imagine, but, fortunately for all her husband's friends, her limited intelligence and lack of modesty serve as a strong antidote to the destructive force of her contagion, and, despite all the fascination of her indescribable beauty, nobody falls in love with her, because her words and actions destroy in a minute the impression produced by her celestial appearance.

The damned *ruchawka* has settled in near our borders. *Ruchawka* is what the Polish call their militia—more accurately, a crowd of riffraff. Furthermore, this entire ragged, barefoot, famished pack has decided to spread the fame of its exploits, prosperity, and freedom! To the shame of the men of our gallant Mariupols, some of them were seduced by this pack of lies and ran away to join the abominable *ruchawka*.

Stánkovich was outraged by this unprecedented act by hussars and sent Wątrobka and me with an entire platoon to locate our fugitives if we could, seize them by force, and bring them back to the squadron. Wąatrobka undertook this mission in a way that made our departure for the foray seem more like a raid against an enemy than a simple search. We crossed the border, stopped half a verst from the little town of * * *, and dismounted. I don't know what we were waiting for. Wątrobka is senior, he was in command and gave the orders, and I honestly don't understand why I was there also. Stánkovich does everything with a sort of excessive pomp.

We stood around in silence. I lay down on the grass and looked at the glittering constellation of Ursa Major. It reminded me of the merry times of nocturnal excursions during my childhood years. How often had I given my Alcides his head without bothering about where he went and, resting both arms on his withers, tilted my head and looked at those seven beautiful stars for a quarter of an hour at a time. Wholeheartedly engrossed in my memories, I became by turns the twelve-year-old child on Alcides' spine and the Polish Horse soldier; now I was amidst dense Siberian forests, now on the battlefields of Heilsberg, now at your grave, oh, my unforgettable steed! How many days, events, changes there have been since then! But now once again I see my favorite constellation. It is always the same, always as brilliant, the same seven stars in the same place. In short, it is always the same, but I. . . . The years will pass, decades will pass, it will remain the same, but I. . . . My thoughts were carried forward sixty years into the future, and, frightened, I got up. My shako, my saber, my ardent steed! Eighty years old. . . . Argentius, let's go, for God's sake, let's ride! What are we standing here for? . . . I mounted my horse and began putting him through close turns at a gallop. My disagreeable thoughts circled with me.

"Why are you trying to exhaust your horse?" asked Wątrobka.

"Why are we standing here wasting time?"

"Wasting time! I'll know when we should ride into town. . . . Well, the time has come. Mount! To the right by threes, march!"

Dreams vanished, and I was back in the material world. We mounted and set out for the town; we rode into it furtively, noiselessly and, taking

all due precautions, spread out in formation opposite the walls of a
*klasztor* of some sort. Wątrobka sent the sergeant and four hussars inside
to search for our fugitives. Our envoys returned emptyhanded, of course,
because the monastery was locked tight.

At dawn Wątrobka and I left our men and rode over to see the town
commandant, Colonel N., who is also the commander of the *ruchawka*.
Wątrobka had met the colonel before, but I was seeing him for the first
time. He received us in confusion and haste, asked us to be seated,
apologized for not being dressed, and went at once into the next room,
saying he would return in a minute. This reception seemed suspicious to
Wątrobka, and he said to me that we should leave at once. And so,
without waiting for our host, we left the room, rejoined our men, and
rode off. I found Wątrobka's action odd and asked him the reason for it.
He said that he had remarked that the commander's intentions were
hostile.

"But what could he do to us? After all, we have an entire platoon of
hussars."

"A fine thing that is! An entire platoon! And why are we here? We
couldn't justify ourselves by telling him that we've come looking for
runaway hussars and that if we find them we want to take them back by
armed force. That was arranged in secret, as an internal measure by our
squadron commander, excusable in cases like this. After all, there's
nothing agreeable about reporting that such a number of hussars have
been escaping across the border."

Our lack of success did not stop Stánkovich. He sent me to Tarnopol
to Prince Vadbolsky with a letter and a commission to bring back the
fugitive hussars if they were turned over to me. I had to go through the
little town where we made our nocturnal search. At the frontier post they
asked me whether I had a pass from their colonel.

"No."

"We can't let you through; get a pass."

I sent a hussar to the colonel to ask for a pass. The colonel ordered him
to ask me to come for it in person. I went.

"You should know your duty better, sir," said the Pole with a frown.
"You should report to the commander yourself, and not send a soldier. . . ." As he said this, he was hurriedly signing a pass. "You arrived
with armed men, searched the monastery, came to see me, and, when I
left the room for a minute to order coffee, you rode away as if you were
escaping from a den of thieves. Odd behavior for a Russian officer!"

And I had to listen to all that! For a minute or two I thought of
proposing to exchange shots with him, but apprehension that Stánkovich
would be held responsible restrained me. I postponed the challenge until
my return from Tarnopol, when we could meet at the border. In the

meantime I told him that he was at liberty to say whatever he liked, because I was alone there, surrounded by Poles and outside the borders of my state. As I talked, he handed me the pass with a polite nod and, extending his hand, said he hoped for my friendship, but I pushed away his hand with mine, replying that after all I had heard from him I had no wish to be his friend. He bowed and saw me to the door, and we parted.

I went farther. Stánkovich had ordered me to ride on to Brody if I did not find our runaway hussars in Tarnopol.

The Lithuanian Uhlans are stationed in Tarnopol. The commander, Prince Vadbolsky, sent one of his officers with me to Brody. Arriving in the town, we went at once to the Polish colonel's quarters and there found a numerous company and thundering music. The colonel received us very courteously and asked us to stay for dinner and join in their diversions. My comrade, Strakhov, agreed, and I was only too happy to listen to fine music and the merry conversation of the witty young Poles. We told the colonel why we had come, however, and asked him to order the fugitives turned over to us.

"Most readily," replied our courteous host. He immediately sent a *pan podchorąży*5 to bring our hussars and invited us to listen to his music and have a goblet of champagne while we were waiting. Half an hour later the *pan podchorąży* returned and, putting his hand to his fur shako, began telling his colonel deferentially that the hussars he had sent him for were not in the guardhouse.

"Where are they then?" asked the colonel.

"They've run away," replied the *podchorąży*, still in the same deferential tone.

The colonel turned to me and said, "I greatly regret that I cannot offer you my services in this matter; your hussars have escaped from custody!"

I would have liked to say that that did no great honor to their guard, but I didn't; and what good would it have done? There was no doubt that they had the hussars and that the colonel had no intention of giving them up.

The Polish officers could not stop admiring the excellent tailoring of my uniform; they said that their tailors weren't capable of giving a uniform such a fine cut. At dinner I sat beside an ancient mustached horseman who had served in the army since the days of the National Cavalry. After he had drunk a few goblets of champagne, he began pestering me by asking why I had taken down the French eagle in Lemberg and hung up the Austrian one instead.

I had no idea what he was talking about. Seeing that I was at a loss, Strakhov told the hot-tempered Nationalist that I had not been in Lvov when the incident took place.

5. Cadet. (Polish)

"How could he have not been there?" exclaimed the old uhlan. "I remember that uniform well!" and he went on reproaching me, saying, "Was that a nice thing to do?"

The colonel asked him to stop it, but he asked in the commanding tone that even drunken uhlans obey. The captain fell silent. Then Strakhov explained to me in a low voice that when our regiment was with Meller-Zakomelsky in Lemberg (or Lvov), it took down the French eagle from some place or other and replaced it with the Austrian crest; the Nationalist captain had witnessed this incident and, seeing me in the same uniform, took me, as he put it, for "one of those unruly cut-throats." After dinner I said goodbye to the Polish colonel and, leaving our runaway hussars to him as booty, returned to Kołodno.

Wątrobka invited me to visit the Baroness Czechowicz. "You have to get an idea of her beauty for yourself; my description is inadequate!" We rode over, but to my great good fortune we did not find her at home; we were received by the baron alone. In the garden I saw various amusement devices; Wątrobka said they were all designed to break the skull of anyone who used them. "The baroness," he added, "uses every means she can to get at the heads of her visitors, either through her beauty or her toys." We started back without waiting for our hostess's arrival. Wątrobka confessed to me that he had a motive for wanting me to meet the baroness: "The encounter between her brazen effrontery and your extraordinary bashfulness promised me a host of amusing scenes."

I was very unhappy with this devilish plan and told him that he was a bad comrade and from now on I would beware of him.

"As you wish," he replied. "But you are intolerable and comical in your virginal modesty. Do you know what I have to say to you? If I had a wife as modest and diffident as you, I would kiss her feet; but if I had a son with the same qualities, I would thrash him soundly. Now judge for yourself, shouldn't we take every means possible to break you of your comical diffidence? It doesn't become a hussar and is of no earthly use to him."

Stánkovich gives us some far from pleasant surprises. Just when we are as far as heaven is from earth from thoughts of agitation of any kind, he orders the alert sounded, and in a flash all is turmoil: hussars dash headlong, lead out their horses on the run, saddle them helter-skelter, mount, and race off impetuously, setting straight on the gallop whatever they couldn't finish standing still. Those who arrive within two minutes are rewarded by the captain, and those who come last also get a reward, but one of a completely different sort. One of those alarms cost me dearly. My knee was sore in the exact spot that presses against the saddle. I couldn't ride my horse, and the sound of the damned alert came as a shock to me. But there was nothing to be done: I sent my platoon rushing off and got on my horse, taking care to avoid putting pressure on my sore knee. But then, of course, I had to go at a run; my horse threw up his head and flew. For a while I managed to keep the necessary position in the saddle but, to my woe, there was a pit on my route, my horse jumped into it with all his force, and all was lost. My knee flowed blood, and I quivered from a pain which I cannot find the words to express. Suffice it to say that involuntary tears spurted from my eyes.

A few days later Stánkovich invited me to go with him to Kremenets to see Pavlishchev. I always enjoy my trips to the town. Its beautiful, romantic location at the foot of a mountainous cliff, over which the tumbled stone walls of Queen Bona's castle loom picturesquely, affords me an enchanting and varied excursion. I imagine that Kremenets got its name from the siliceous mountains that surround it.

I always pass time pleasantly at Pavlishchev's house with his daughter and cadet Drevich, an extremely well-bred young man. This unfortunate cadet has had a very strange fate. Despite his brilliant talents, noble actions, rather handsome looks, and distinguished lineage, nobody likes him, and he has spent nine years waiting for commission. The year before I met him, there was a horrible incident in which he played the leading role and that deprived him at once of rank, freedom, and tranquillity of conscience, as well as any wish to live: he inadvertently stabbed a hussar. He was tried for the death, confined for a year to the guardhouse, and then demoted to soldier with no hope of promotion. I learned of his misfortune by chance. Meller-Zakomelsky had not yet left with the battalion for Galicia, and the regiment was still stationed in Kremenets. It was a part of my obligations as duty officer to find out and report about the men under arrest. Entering the little closet where poor Drevich was confined, I asked him whether there was anything he needed: my present post made it possible for me to offer him some slight relief from his harsh situation.

"Oh, if you do not disdain the appeal of a murderer," he said mournfully, "I would ask you to permit me to breathe the air of those mountains where I used to pass so many happy hours."

I said that I couldn't do it on my own, but I would ask Gorich, and I thought that through him I would be able to get the commander-in-chief's permission for the outing. Gorich listened very courteously to my request and went in at once to see Meller. A minute later he returned and told me: "The general leaves you at liberty to do as you see fit in consideration of easing the prisoner's lot, but he asks you to observe due procedures."

I went to get Drevich and was witness to his joyful and at the same time grief-filled sensations at the sight of the beauties of nature. Two hussars with drawn sabers started after us, but I told them that I would guard him myself and that they should follow us at a distance. Several times Drevich came close to fainting, so greatly had the sedentary life sapped his strength.

Both of our squadrons have been ordered to march. Drevich has been placed under Colonel Pavlishchev's supervision. This worthy officer had no need of education in order to treat the prisoner in the most noble and tactful fashion; he simply followed the dictates of lofty virtue. "You are assigned," he told Drevich, "to my squadron under my surveillance until your affair is decided, but I cannot bear, I haven't the heart, to see you a prisoner in the guardhouse. Instead, I offer you my home, my table, and the custody of a friend. If you should decide to run away from me, I will, of course, take your place—that is, I shall be the soldier!"

There is no pen, there are no words, the human tongue is too impoverished, to express what Drevich felt; I will not attempt to describe it. But the result was that Drevich lived in his benefactor's house, loved him like a father, and was coming to terms with his lot when the verdict came: Drevich was to remain a soldier with no hope of promotion. Pavlishchev was obliged to use him in that rank on duty, and evidently his prolonged misfortunes, pangs of conscience over the murder—although unintentional it was still murder—and, as I had the opportunity to surmise, hopeless love for Pavlishchev's daughter made the unfortunate Drevich's life hateful to him. About two weeks after he was sentenced, he shot himself. He was found in the garden on a raincape with his head blown to bits. A carbine lay beside him.

We have arrived in Chernigov province and settled down in quarters in a sprawling hamlet called Novaja Basan. The landowner who lives here is Cheadaev, an old, reclusive, boring man, who has a sister just like him. We never go to his house.

There is a wedding in our neighborhood. Landowner M. is marrying his daughter to Captain I. of the Aleksandrijsk Hussars. We are all invited, and tomorrow we will go.

M. set aside one room for all the men: military and civilian, young and old, married and bachelor—they were all lodged there. As a hussar, of course, I was included in this company. One of the guests was a commission-agent, Plokhuta, a jovial, witty fellow seven feet tall who was a great storyteller. Among the host of curious incidents he related, I had the pleasure of hearing my own history: "Imagine, gentlemen," said Plokhuta to us all. "Imagine my surprise when, after dining in Vitebsk in a tavern together with a young uhlan, I heard that this uhlan was an amazon who had been in all the battles of the Prussian campaign and was now on her

way to Peterburg with an aide-de-camp whom our tsar had sent especially
to fetch her. Before then I hadn't paid any attention to the uhlan lad, but
after this news I couldn't stop looking at the heroine."

"What did she look like?" the young men shouted from all sides.

"Very swarthy," replied Plokhuta, "but she had a fresh color and a
meek gaze. To anyone who had not been forewarned, though, there was
nothing noticeable about her to betray her sex; she just looked like an
extremely young boy."

I was blushing hotly as I listened to this story, but, since the room was
already dark, I was prankish enough to ask Plokhuta whether he would
recognize the amazon if he were to see her now.

"Oh, without fail," replied the commission-agent. "I remember her
face as clearly as if I were gazing at her now, and no matter where I met
her, I would recognize her immediately."

"You obviously have a very good memory," I said, wrapping myself up
in my greatcoat. Plokhuta went on to recount something else, but I
stopped listening and at once fell asleep.

The next day we all went back to our Basan. Young Miss A. told me
the story of a comical mistake which could, however, have grave consequences. Two days after we returned from the wedding feast, I went to
see the lieutenant-colonel. Finding him occupied with business, I went
on into Miss A.'s room and found her deep in pensive thought. To my
question as to why she was so gloomy and if the reason wasn't that all the
dancing had tired her out, she replied with a sigh, "No, the dancing
wasn't tiring, but an incident during the dances is weighing on my mind.
I made a conquest, inadvertently, unintentionally, not only without
desiring it, but without even suspecting that such a disaster could happen
to me!"

I laughed at her sorrow and asked her how this extraordinary misfortune had come about. Who was this outcast of God, the conquest of
whom was causing her such bitter sorrow?

"It's all right for you to joke," said A., "I'm ready to weep. Just listen to
my story. You know what good friends I am with Katinka Aleksandrovicheva. Whenever our turn comes to clasp hands during the
dances, we always press each other's hand. I was absent-minded and
didn't notice that I was to give my hand to Ch., that young officer from
the Aleksandrijsk Hussars. When I felt someone take my hand, I at once
pressed it, assuming that the other hand was Katinka's, but when there
was no response I looked around and, to my inexpressible confusion, saw
Ch. holding my hand and looking at me with an expression of dumbfounded joy! I blushed and tried to avoid meeting his eyes. Yesterday Ch.
went to Stánkovich's wife with a proposal of marriage for me, wishing, as
he says, to be sure of my feelings before asking my parents for my hand.

But I haven't the slightest fondness for him, and I'm not at all ready to marry so soon. It will be to my woe if he ascribes my refusal to diffidence and comes to propose openly. Papa will give me to him. Ch. is rich!"

"Yes, you really made yourself trouble with that untimely press of the hand. I can't help marveling at the nobility of Ch.'s sentiments, however. One press of a young lady's hand led him to propose marriage, when another, a rake, could have pressed your hand thirty times and given you no peace afterward without ever bothering to propose a binding union. . . ."

The entrance of Miss A.'s father with Stánkovich and his wife interrupted our conversation. Miss A.'s apprehensions were well-founded. Ch. had made his proposal to her father, who eagerly accepted and, taking his daughter's consent for granted, was coming to tell her of it. There was much astonishment, tears, abuse, and bother before A. was finally spared this unwelcome match.

While I was out for an evening stroll near the mill, I saw our hussars setting up a straw dummy on the far side of the ditch. To my question as to why, they replied that tomorrow there will be a mounted drill with pistol shooting.

At six in the morning we were already in the field. Stánkovich commanded the squadron; Pavlishchev was inspector for the review. The first platoon went into action under the command of T., who was to be the first to jump the ditch, fire a pistol at the straw dummy, and at once slash it with his saber. His men would follow him and do the same. T. at once demurred, refusing to jump the ditch; to our general laughter he presented as the reason for his refusal that he would fall off his horse.

"How dare you say that!" shouted the inspector. "You are a cavalryman, a hussar! Aren't you ashamed to tell your superior to his face that you're afraid of falling off your horse? Break your neck, sir, but jump! Do what you have to do in mounted service, or don't serve!"

T. heard him out, but he still didn't dare to attempt the feat and remained only a spectator to his hussars, who performed outstandingly. Next came P., who galloped up smoothly, jumped the ditch phlegmatically, fired at the dummy indifferently, brushed its head with his saber, and stood quietly aside without worrying whether his platoon performed their evolutions well or badly.

My turn came next. At this time I did not have my own horse, and I was mounted on one of the warhorses, a fiery steed who was handsome but extremely easily startled. He dashed like a whirlwind up to the ditch and carried me across it like a bird, but the pistol shot made him leap to one side. For a quarter of an hour he knocked about here and there, rearing and carrying me rapidly away from the dummy which I had to slash. I lost patience completely and, hoping to end the fuss as quickly as

I could, struck my capricious steed with what I took to be the flat of the saber. The horse hurled himself at full speed at the dummy and even knocked it over. I didn't stop to worry about the reason for this quick obedience, but turned the horse around, jumped back across the ditch, and began to watch my hussars performing the same evolution. At last it was finished. The fourth platoon came onto the scene under the command of Wątrobka, who is an outstanding marksman and rider. It was my turn to become a mere spectator, and I rode over to join Stánkovich and Pavlishchev in watching the gallant antics of the last platoon.

"Why is there blood on your horse's leg, Aleksandrov?" asked Stánkovich.

I looked around. Blood was streaming across the hoof of my horse's hind leg and staining the green turf. Astonished, I began looking uneasily for the source of it and, to my deep regret, saw a broad wound on his croup which I had evidently inflicted with my careless blow of the saber. To Stánkovich's repeated question, "What's that from?" I had to tell him. Stánkovich's face distorted with vexation: "Leave the formation, sir! Go to your quarters! You have nothing to ride in the drill and no reason to be here. You'll wound all my horses for me!"

Stunned by this volley of reproach, I rode back to my quarters. I was not so much vexed at the captain's rebuke as saddened by my cruel behavior to the poor horse. When I got there, I ordered the wound washed with liquor and bandaged while I watched.

After the drill was over, everybody, T. included, went to Pavlishchev's quarters. When Pavlishchev asked where I was, the coward made haste to tell him, "Aleksandrov's busy washing his horse's wound with hot tears."

"How's that? What horse?"

"The one he was riding; he slashed its croup because it wouldn't charge the dummy."

"That couldn't happen to you, Grigory Ivanovich! The dummy would charge you before you went after it."

Displeased, the mocking fellow fell silent.

# Chapter Six

## Detached Duty—1810

*Kiev.* Stánkovich received orders to send an officer, a sergeant, and a private to serve as orderlies to the commander-in-chief of the reserve army, General Miloradovich.[1] My squadron commander got the fantastic notion of sending the youngest men to be orderlies, and under this disposition the choice fell on me, as Stánkovich says, the most youthful of all officers. It is a good thing I am no longer so young as I look—I have reached my twenty-first year—or else I don't know what Stánkovich could expect to gain by sending three striplings, alone and at their own disposal, to such a prominent post. Cadet Gravier is sixteen, the hussar eighteen, and from appearance no one would give me even sixteen. What outstanding orderlies!

At dawn my detachment and I set out for Kiev, where our corps headquarters is located. To escape the unbearable heat and spare our horses, I traveled at night from Brovari to Kiev. The dense pine forest was crisscrossed by a countless number of roads grooved deep in the sand. Since I didn't know that they all come out at the same spot, the banks of the Dnepr and Krasny traktir, I thought we had lost our way. As we went at random, following any road we happened on and surrounded by impenetrable thickets, I caught sight of something darting off the road into the forest. I spurred my horse and galloped over to the spot where something was hiding behind the trees. To my hail, "Who's there?" a peasant woman came out, gasping from terror. But when she saw three calm and amicable looking young hussars, she calmed down too and said, by now chuckling, "What a predicament that was! I was frightened of you, and you of me." Gravier found it very comical that the Ukrainian woman thought three armed hussars could be frightened of her.

"Can you tell us, my dear, where we're going? We want to get to Kiev."

"Well, so that's where you're going," replied the woman in her Ukrainian dialect.

"How can we guess where to turn? There are so many roads here!"

"No matter," said the peasant woman. "They all come out at the same spot, Krasnyj traktir, not far from the ferry."

We thanked her, rode off at a trot, and soon caught sight of the Dnepr gleaming in the moonlight. While the boatmen were waking up and

---

1. Count Mikhail Miloradovich was governor-general of Kiev from 1810 to 1812 as well as head of the reserve army.

preparing the ferry, the moon began to lose its luster, a sign of approaching daybreak. We got onto the ferry, and, by the time we got across, it was broad daylight. I rode directly to the house of our general, Ermolov. My cadet and hussar settled down to bivouac in his yard, and I went into the anteroom and lay down on the sofa without undressing. I got up half an hour before they roused Ermolov, put my uniform in order, and waited for him to wake up so that I could go in to see him immediately.

The general received me very kindly and courteously. Ermolov's manner is bewitchingly simple and at the same time obliging. I have remarked a trait in him that makes me think that he is unusually intelligent: he never assumes that any of the officers around him are ill-bred, ignorant, or lacking in *savoir vivre*. He speaks to each of them as an equal, without attempting to simplify his speech in order to be understood. He does not suffer from the ridiculous prejudice that the expressions and turns of speech of the patrician are incomprehensible to people of the middle class. This lofty trait of intelligence and kindness disposed me to see everything about our general in the most favorable light. Ermolov's features and countenance reflect a great and indomitable soul.[2]

K., Miloradovich's adjutant, sent for me. When I came in, I realized at once that he was expecting someone else. This rude, uneducated officer asked, without even offering me a chair, "Why didn't your squadron commander send the officer I designated for orderly?"

"Probably," I replied, "because your designation was incompatible with his internal dispositions for the squadron. We have a rotation of detached duty which no outsider need trouble about." I saw that my reply angered K. He is extraordinarily proud, like petty people in general. Notwithstanding my apparent youth, I had the pleasure of making K. my enemy.

On certain days I fly around from morning to night on my steed, Diamond, either alongside Miloradovich's carriage or with commissions from him to various officials in Kiev. In the latter case, he sends me only when the person for whom he has a message is a newly arrived general or one passing through; but when Miloradovich himself goes out in his carriage or on horseback, it is always my hussars and I who accompany him—and no other orderly ever rides after him. From this I conclude that

2. In 1810 General Aleksej Ermolov commanded the reserve troops who, like the Mariupol' Hussars, were assigned to guard the southern frontier with the Duchy of Poland (Galicia and Volhynia). The Russian *Military Encyclopedia* describes him as: "Ambitious and independent, . . . proud with superiors and amiable with equals and inferiors" (*Voennaja entsiklopedia*, vol. 10 [1912], 346). During his years as military commander in the Caucasus and diplomatic representative to Persia from 1816 to 1827, Ermolov confirmed the reputation for decision and ruthlessness he had won on the western borders.

he is fond of flash and opulence. It flatters his self-esteem to have a hussar glittering with gold braid posed beside his carriage window, ready at his beck and call to fly like an arrow wherever he orders.

K. took it into his head to inspect to see whether the orderlies—not only the soldiers, but also the officers—are properly dressed. What a scatterbrained notion! How can an infantry officer know the fine points of the accessories of the hussar uniform—and better than the hussars themselves at that? I ignored his order as one which could not apply to me; I didn't go to be inspected by him, nor did I send my hussars. K. was weak enough to complain to Ermolov who, as adjutant general, is our direct superior. Ermolov asked me why I had not reported to K.

"Because, Your Excellency," I replied, "K. doesn't understand anything about our uniform, and it would be odd indeed if a hussar officer needed an infantry man to instruct him on how to wear his uniform."

Ermolov did not insist further; he merely said, "K. got his orders from Miloradovich. Settle it somehow."

"Believe me, General, K. is lying. Miloradovich has wit enough not to send a hussar to a musketeer for inspection."

The affair ended with no further trouble. K. abandoned his pretensions.

Today they laid the foundation-stone for a veterans' home. When the ceremonies were over, we all dined in tents. The weather was unbearably hot. Before attending the foundation-laying Miloradovich, accompanied by his entire suite, made the rounds of the fortifications, some twenty versts in all. His little arab galloped quite calmly, without in the least fatiguing his rider, but I can't say the same for my Diamond, who had trouble matching his running pace to the light and smooth gallop of the steppe-bred horse. Irritated at not being given liberty to run as he liked, Diamond continually jumped, reared, made rushes, and tried to tear the reins from my hands. He exhausted me so completely that by the time we got to the tents my blood was seething in such a hot torrent through my body that I thought it would explode.

After the dedication we at once sat down to eat. I put a piece of ice in my wine glass. Golitsyn, who was standing beside me at the time, was horrified. "What are you doing?" he said. "You can catch your death of cold." While he was saying this, I swallowed my icy wine in a single gulp. "Aren't such rapid changes from hot to cold harmful to you?"

I replied that I was used to it. And, in fact, my health is unexampled. I am, so to speak, in the bloom of health, and I am not at all pleased with my scarlet cheeks. I once asked Lubarski, our regimental doctor, whether he knew of a remedy for excessive high color.

"I do indeed," he replied. "Drink more wine and spend your nights gambling and philandering. Two months of this laudable way of life, and your complexion will take on a most interesting pallor."

I am enjoying myself in Kiev. I have many agreeable acquaintances here, among whom I count the household of Masse, the local commandant. His nephew, Shlein, an officer in the cuirassiers, is a great chum of mine. Despite his sixty years, Masse is still a dashing fellow and gallops on horseback as briskly as the best of our hussars.

Yesterday there was a concert to benefit the needy. Miloradovich gave two tickets apiece to all his orderlies including me. The performers were all ladies; the leader of this musical society was Princess Kh., a young and beautiful married woman, whom Miloradovich courts tirelessly. I have had more than one opportunity to remark that luck in love makes our general very obliging in manner. When I meet him in the garden, I can always guess how the princess has been treating him: if he is in her good graces, he strikes up a conversation with us and makes jokes; if not, he walks past us gloomily, answers our salute coldly, and is not vexed when we come to attention, whereas in a cheerful frame of mind he cannot bear it.

Miloradovich gave a ball on the name-day of the widowed empress, a glittering, magnificent ball! The drawing-rooms teemed with guests; the large old-fashioned garden was beautifully illuminated, but strolling in it was not to be thought of. Miloradovich had decided to entertain his Apsheronsk regiment there, and this led to a droll incident later on. During the evening the countless glowing lamps, thundering music, and throngs of lovely ladies attracted the curiosity of our valiant colleagues in the garden. They came as close as they could to the glass doors of the drawing-room, which were open and guarded by two sentries. Masse saw that the throng of soldiers was getting denser by the hour and shoving at the doors, so that the sentries were barely able to keep them from bursting into the room. Since I was on duty that day, he called me over, "Aleksandrov, tell the sentries to shut the doors."
I started to carry out his order, but Miloradovich, who had heard what Masse said to me, stopped me and asked, "Where are you going?"
I replied that I was going to tell the sentries—
"I know," interrupted Miloradovich impatiently. "There's no need to shut the doors. Let them come in. The cadets can dance. Stay where you are." As he said this, he straightened his necktie once or twice, which was a sure sign of vexation, and went to tell the sentries not to hinder any soldier who decided to enter the room.
The result of this disposition was that in less than five minutes the drawing-room was teeming with soldiers who swarmed like bees through

the garden door and mingled in a flash with the guests. Masse shrugged his shoulders, Ermolov smiled sardonically, and the ladies retreated in consternation as they saw these hefty, coarse creatures at their side. The other orderlies and I laughed wholeheartedly at this odd spectacle. The ladies all gathered in one room; the men waited, smiling, to see how the scene would end. Miloradovich, who had not really expected such a noisy and numerous visitation from his fellow soldiers, said that he advised them to return to the garden where they could amuse themselves more freely, adding, "Fresh air is the native element of the Russian warrior!"

From this maxim the Russian warriors understood only that they were to return to the garden and quickly did so. Now Miloradovich himself commanded the door shut. Order was restored, music struck up, lovely ladies scattered throughout the drawing-room, and once again their sparkling gazes fell on hussars, uhlans, cuirassiers, dragoons—in short, on everything in mustaches and spurs. An officer of the Tatar Uhlans, Baron N., a young man both exceptionally handsome and exceptionally tall, was the apparent monarch of this entire huge, glittering assembly. The ladies and girls beamed the radiance of their eyes at him. It would be impossible to calculate all the rivalries, vexations, and transports of jealousy that he produced that evening. Miloradovich did not escape a fit of the latter. When the princess danced a quadrille with him, she continually kept turning her head to the next foursome where the baron was dancing.

Half an hour before supper the dances ended and everything quieted down. Some of the young men, and among them commission-agent P., a mischievous, garrulous rake, went with us—that is, with the orderlies—into the chamber adjoining the drawing-room. There P. began telling us about all the beautiful women he had chanced to see in Little Russia. "In Pirjatin," said P., "I saw a girl, a rare beauty named Aleksandrovicheva, and what do you think? She had such a barbaric name that I can't pronounce it or hear it without vexation: "Domnika Porfirevna!" Have you ever heard the like?

I started at the name: Domnika Aleksandrovicheva is my cousin, and I had reason to fear that a straight line would lead from her to me. My apprehensions were instantly justified; P. went on, "Besides her beauty and her comical name, Domnika is further remarkable as a close relation of that amazon there was so much talk of three years ago and who vanished God knows where afterward." Everyone began discussing and explaining that occurrence. I was silent, and, while I was deciding whether or not to join in the conversation, Davydov, one of our fraternity of orderlies who was sitting beside me, suddenly slapped me on the knee and exclaimed, "What are your amazons to us? We have our own little girl, don't we? He's slim as a reed, blushes at every word. . . ."

"Why are we hiding in here, gentlemen?" said Shlein, getting up and

taking me and dragoon Shtejn by the arm. "Let's rejoin the general!"
Everyone got up and trooped back into the hall after us.

How badly commanders calculate when, wishing to be rid of a badly
behaved officer, they send him off on detached duty. In the regiment he
and all his imperfections are hidden, and whatever mischief he gets up to
remains, so to speak, in the family. But once he is sent out on display to
the world, he plays solo and so abominably that all those who wear the
same uniform are ashamed to listen to him. An incident at yesterday's
ball gave me the pretext for this reflection. An uhlan orderly, T. A., saw
the possibility of drinking as much punch as he deemed fit and got so
drunk that his normally slitted little Kalmyk eyes were almost totally
shut. In this state of complete inebriation, he walked about among the
ladies, inviting each of them to dance, although the music had long since
ceased and preparations for supper were underway. The ladies smiled
wryly and kept retreating from this queer fellow's advances. He went on
roaming about the company until at last he stumbled onto old Masse and
stepped on his foot. The commandant's blood boiled at such effrontery.
He stopped A. with his hand and said to him, "Apparently, dear sir, you
can't see anything any more?"
"And what is there to see?" retorted T. A., trying to force open his
closing eyes.
"The people whose feet you're stepping on."
"Whose?" asked the drunken uhlan.
"Mine, mine, the commandant's; you stepped on my foot," said Masse,
losing patience.
"We're all commandants here," muttered A. and, with a wave of his
hand, set off around the hall again, swaying from side to side. The next
day he was sent back to the regiment.

Today there were maneuvers, a mock battle. Ermolov, who was commanding the troops designated to retreat, asked Miloradovich to give him
two of his orderlies. Miloradovich gave him the dragoon and the uhlan
and kept the hussar and the cuirassier for himself. Amid this vanity of
vanities, the charges, gunfire, and attacks, one unfortunate rider, sitting
his horse with his legs sticking out by half a yard, galloped past me,
caught on my spur, and tore it off. I soon learned the disadvantage of
having only one spur. I was the one whom Miloradovich sent everywhere, and throughout the maneuvers I flew around in my gold uniform
with my *mentik* on my shoulders, flashing like a glittering meteor amid
men shooting, marching, shouting "Hurrah!" and advancing with fixed
bayonets.
At last my horse was gasping for breath. Just then Miloradovich was
standing beside a deep ditch and looking over the position. Across the

ravine where our commander stood, there were jaeger skirmishers who, to their woe, were standing up when, according to the disposition, they should have been lying down. Miloradovich lost his temper, began jerking at his necktie, glanced at me, and said curtly, pointing toward the ravine, "Ride over to those skirmishers and tell their slow-witted officer to order them to lie down!" I touched my remaining spur to the horse, but when he saw that his path led into the deep ditch, he balked.

"What's the matter? Don't you want to obey me?" shouted Miloradovich. A blow with spur and saber forced my steed to hurl himself headlong into the ravine, and I, like Curtius, flew with my horse into the abyss.

After the maneuvers were over, when my poor Diamond was brought into the stables, he lay down as soon as they took off his saddle. The next day he was so changed that I did not recognize him.

The two months of my duty in the post of orderly to the commander-in-chief are over. Tomorrow I return to the squadron.

My service in the squadron began very unhappily. At dawn the duty sergeant galloped over to my quarters with the news that Cornet Poradowski had shot himself. In an instant I dressed, mounted my horse bareback, and dashed at a full run to Poradowski's quarters. Stánkovich was already there. The unhappy Poradowski was lying facedown in the middle of the room. His blood had collected in a large puddle by the door, his skull was shattered into several pieces which lay on the floor and benches, the carbine with which he shot himself lay beside the body, and two bullets had lodged in the ceiling. Stánkovich looked through all the dead man's letters and various notes, but he found nothing from which he could deduce a reason for the suicide. He ordered Poradowski's face and the fragments of his head wrapped in a kerchief and his body carried out to the crossroads, where they dug him a grave. The road runs beside it, and that evening, walking down it, I shuddered involuntarily as I came abreast of Poradowski's green mound: yesterday he and I walked along this road together. But today. . . .

We have been ordered to move out. What an inconstant life! We never get a chance to settle anywhere. We were just getting well acquainted with the neighboring landowners, and here we go again, rushing off afar. Our new quarters will be near Rovno, on Korwicki's estate, the town of Mizocz (on the Volyn).

Our squadron passed through Kiev. Ermolov rode with us as far as the city gates. He talked with me very kindly and asked me whether I missed anything in Kiev. When I said that I didn't, he praised me, saying, "Always conduct yourself that way, young man; I will respect you."

*Mizocz.* There are two remarkable objects here, a large riding-hall and a beautiful garden; otherwise it is all just like any other spot in Poland—nothing but tumbledown shacks covered with straw. We never use the riding-hall; we drill our good steeds in the open fields, but the garden! That's quite another matter. I always spend the time after dinner there. It has such a vast number of flowers, and such beautiful ones, that the sight of them makes me jump for joy. Nothing in the world could keep me from picking one of the roses, which grow taller than any I have ever seen. They are small trees, ten feet or more in height, strewn with the most charming roses, and the only way I can reach them is by severing the flower with the tip of my saber. One day a gardener arrived just in time to catch me at this exploit. Embarrassed, I showed him the severed rose and asked if I might sometimes pick a flower from the rose trees.

"Since you've already done so, you may," replied the gardener, chuckling. "Just don't damage the tree itself."

Yesterday Stánkovich got the idea of holding drill at midday. The dust and heat were unbearable. All the maneuvers took place at the full gallop to which Stánkovich, a dashing hussar, became accustomed when Wittgenstein was still chief of the Mariupol regiment. Yesterday this method nearly cut short the life of a poor Jew, the most cowardly creature on the face of the earth. Our final maneuver is the attack. At the command, "From your places, charge—charge!" we dashed off like madmen. Stánkovich chose to carry the attack to Mizocz, near which is a broad road with dust on it a foot deep. As we galloped onto this road, dust enveloped the squadron in a cloud so dense that not only could I not see where I was going, I couldn't even see the horse under me. Just then the commander's "Halt! Form ranks!" rang out suddenly, accompanied by a desperate wail right beside my stirrup. Alarmed, I brought my horse to a stop, and at the same time the dust cleared enough to allow me to see a Jew who had fallen by my horse's hooves and was shouting at the top of his voice, "Ratujcie!"[3] His pale face, horror-stricken eyes, disheveled sidelocks, and widely gaping mouth made him look like a monster. My horse snorted and reared, and the Jew crawled on all fours away from the halted formation; then he got up and, bent nearly double, ran off into the town. Later I found out that he had fallen from fright, but escaped unhurt because, as chance would have it, the galloping squadron chose that moment to halt. After the exercises I told my comrades about the incident.

"Well then," asked Wątrobka, "when you saw the Jew by your horse's hooves, all unstrung, with his yawning muzzle and goggling eyes, didn't the passage from *Phedre* come to your mind?

---

3. "Save me!" (Polish)

De rage et de douleur le monstre bondissant
Vient aux pieds des chevaux tomber en mugissant,
Se roule, et leur présente une gueule enflammée
Qui les couvre de feu, de sang, et de fumée[4].

*Dąbrowica*[5] We have parted company with the Aleksandrijsk regiment and arrived at quarters in the small town of Dąbrowica. It is the property of Count Plater, who lives three versts away.[6] I have made some agreeable new friends—and in a rather odd way. Dýmchevich, our battalion commander, occupies the main floor of a large stone house; we had no idea who was living on the floor above. One day I was the officer in charge of the guard, and as part of my duties I went to report to Dýmchevich. Climbing the porch steps, I heard the sounds of a pianoforte. The novelty of it and the excellence of the playing made me forget Dýmchevich, the report, and all the guards on earth. I went in the direction from which the bewitching harmonies were drifting: I climbed the stairs, walked down a corridor, and came to doors through which I could distinctly hear the music. I opened them and, to my surprise, found myself in a kitchen, where there was not, nor could there be, a piano. I stopped dumbfounded and continued listening: the music was coming from the next room. Driven by hussar enterprise, I went farther, firmly resolved to find out who was casting that beautiful spell on my hearing. I walked over to the other door and opened it, and an instant exclamation of "Oh, my God!" interrupted the music.

The lady who cried out was an elderly woman. She looked at me with a disturbed, inquiring appearance, but the young woman who had been playing the piano recovered at once from her initial confusion when I told her, as best I could in Polish, that her excellent playing had led me like one enchanted through the entire place against my volition and all propriety; and if my arrival through the kitchen seemed odd to her, I begged her to remember that I had no power to choose my way.

She answered in pure Polish dialect that the chance which afforded her my visit was a most agreeable one. They invited me to take a seat, and I asked her to go on playing. She did so at once. When she was finished,

4. Leaping with rage and pain the monster now
   Falls bellowing at the startled horses' feet,
   Rolls on his back, thrusts forth his flaming jaw,
   Engulfing them in fire and blood and smoke.

—Act V, Scene 4. Jean Racine, *Complete Plays*, tr., foreword and notes by Samuel Solomon (NY: Random House, 1967) vol. 2: 298–99.
   5. Dubrovitsa on modern maps.
   6. For the Plater family, see *Polski Słownik Biograficzny*, vol. 26 (Wroclaw, 1981), 641–47.

she began speaking to her mother in Russian. I was surprised at her correct speech and told her so. "I'm Russian," she replied.

"Oh, my God! Then why was I twisting my tongue every which way to speak to you in Polish?"

"I don't know," chuckled the young Vyrodova, this being my new acquaintance's surname.

This adventure had most agreeable consequences: the mother and daughter became so fond of me and so valued my company that they didn't want to spend a single day without me, and, if I didn't come on a certain day, they reproached me and resolutely opposed my failing to visit them for even twenty-four hours. I myself most willingly consented, because nowhere have I ever met with such intelligence, agreeable manners, affection, friendship, outstanding education, and brilliant talents, as those of the young Vyrodova.

The kindly old woman, Vyrodova's mother, loves me like a son, calls me Sashinka, and kisses me on the cheek.[7] I told Wątrobka, who is sharing my quarters, about these new friends. Although he is ill just now and unable to put on his uniform and, therefore, can't pay her a visit, his desire to see this Dąbrowica phenomenon was so great that he resolved to carry out some prank or other which would give him a means of entering their house. He thought of something, thought better of it, and at last got the idea of my sending him with books for Vyrodova: he would put on a soldier's tunic for the mission and, thus shielded by this aegis from the ladies' attention, would have full freedom to examine my *conquest*, as he calls her. I gave him the books, nearly laughing myself sick as I saw him transformed into a sick, thin, pale soldier with lackluster eyes and a crooked neck. Off he went, and I was left to await the outcome.

Wątrobka returned a quarter of an hour later and said that his campaign was a complete failure. The parlor maid took the book from him and, when he tried to look through a door that had opened a crack at the noise created by his arrival, the maid decided he was drunk, resisted, and pushed him out the door. I told him that Vyrodova's self-esteem will be flattered when she learns the reason for his transformation into a drunken soldier.

Countess Plater often comes to visit my friend, the young widow. This seventy-year-old lady is a great hunter, taking to the fields after hares, wolves, and wild boar, and also a crack shot with firearms. She frequently rides through Dąbrowica, and always past our guardhouse, on a white horse not much younger than its rider. Her groom follows her with a switch. When the countess deems fit to step up the pace, she has only to say the word, "Gallop!" At this command the groom touches his switch

7. Sashinka is a diminutive of Sasha, the most common nickname for Aleksandr.

to the horse, and it breaks into a smooth, easy gallop. We have all had both opportunity and time to remark that the white horse gallops only when there is a group of hussar officers assembled either in front of the guardhouse or on the porch of the commander's quarters. I do not understand why the countess is so unhappy with us; she calls us *capuchins!* Why? Can it possibly be because we so rarely visit her house? That is more her fault than ours. Who ever heard of a ball that ends at eight o'clock? That is the count's statutory suppertime, and often the toll of the fateful eight hours that silences the thundering music sounds just as unexpectedly and unwelcomely as the death knell, especially to some of our young hussars.

I don't know what to do! Money vanishes like smoke, and I can't understand where it goes. I don't play cards or drink liquor, I never buy anything; but no sooner do I turn my paper currency into silver than these *złoty, groszy,* and *dwudziestówki* drive me mad and scatter like ashes. I am ashamed to ask His Majesty for more money, and so soon at that, but there is no help for it. My father will not give me any, and I myself would not for the world begin troubling my kind parent. Oh, he is so poor, and already elderly! Shall I ever see the happy day when I will be in a position to aid him? Will God bless me with that joy? Will I ever be able to repay him for caring for me in childhood? Oh, height of bliss for dutiful children, shall I ever attain you?

His Majesty has granted me one thousand rubles. I received them from Arakcheev, who writes me that he has taken Count Lieven's place with His Majesty and, among other business, has been charged with making all my requests and wishes known to the emperor. He ended his letter with the assurance of his willingness to do everything he could for me.[8]

Today I'm on duty with the horse herd and will be at this post all week. A straw shelter has been erected for me in the middle of the meadow set aside to pasture our horses. The first day I covered nearly all the surrounding fields on foot, admiring our four-legged friends as they played and ran about.

Yesterday for the first time in my life I became frightened, and now I have some idea what fear is. Our herd is pastured seven versts from the squadron quarters, a distance I have often walked without the slightest fatigue. Yesterday I rode as usual to Stánkovich's quarters to report on the welfare of our steeds and stayed there for dinner. I turned my horse over to the hussar who had come with me and ordered him to return to the

---

8. It was Barclay de Tolly who replaced Arakcheev as War Minister on January 1, 1810.

herd, since I was planning to walk back. After dinner, when I wanted to leave, Stánkovich, who did not know that I had sent away my horse, began urging me to stay for tea. I agreed, considering that the evening would not be so hot. After tea Stánkovich said, "Where are you rushing to, Aleksandrov? Have supper with us. The moon is shining now, and it's a fine night; you'll ride back after supper."

The words *a fine night* convinced me to stay for supper. I began happily anticipating my nocturnal voyage through silent fields by the captivating light of a full moon. After supper I bade farewell at last to Stánkovich and, strapping on my sharp sword, set out. But I decided to avoid going the long way around from Stánkovich's quarters by cutting directly through vegetable plots and fields to the road that led from the hamlet to the spot where the herd was roaming. I would have gained greatly if this plan had succeeded, but I made a mistake in my reckoning. By the deceptive moonlight it all seemed flat and smooth, but, when I had to cross those areas, I thought that the ditches, pits, and plowed fields would never end. At first I jumped the ditches and gullies with ease and ran nimbly through the plowed fields, but when I saw a second field succeeding the first, then a third, then another field, and yet another, with no end in sight, my high spirits flagged and I began walking more slowly. At last the ditches and vegetable plots ended, but the fields still stretched like a black rug over the vast distance I had to cross whether I wanted to or not. With belated repentance I recalled the folk saying, "Only crows fly straight."

At last I came out onto the road. The moon was already near the zenith, and its light poured silver onto the boundless expanse of the fields. All around a deep silence reigned. As I came out onto the smooth and flat road where I no longer felt under my feet the tussocks which I stumbled over or the loose dirt which bound me, I started off at a quick, light pace. But suddenly horror and consternation brought me to a standstill. I stopped. A howl with nothing human about it rang out over the expanse of the fields and went on, uninterrupted, with such horrible wails, screeches, rumbles, and a kind of moaning that my heart and mind were seized with fear. I would have turned around and run, but the shame of an act so extraordinary for me, and the even greater shame of making it known to my comrades, made me see reason and keep going. I drew my saber and walked on toward the frantic howls, which went on bellowing, wailing, and roaring with the same force. I was straining my eyes in the effort to see what sort of creature had appeared in the fields, but I couldn't make anything out, and I needed all the force of reason and faith to resist taking this howling noise for the howl of an evil spirit. I covered another half verst before catching sight at last of something black approaching me, yelling frantically. I went faster. In less than a hundred paces I saw that it was a huge peasant. Reassured that this was no beast, no monster, no evil spirit, but merely a man, I sheathed my saber and, when I got closer to the peasant, asked him why he was yelling so.

He could not answer me. He was a mute from our hamlet who lived on alms. By means of various signs, he succeeded in making me understand that he was coming from a nearby village and, fearing wolves, was trying to imitate dogs barking in order to chase them off. As he explained all this, he used body motions so terrible that they alone would frighten anyone: he popped his eyes, gnashed his teeth, and snarled in a savage voice. I made a sign for him to go his way, and off he went with the same absurd wailing which had been so dreadful to me, but now became desirable and necessary. I was facing an actual danger, not supernatural or romantic, but of the simplest, crudest, and most horrible kind—the danger of being devoured by wolves. In Little Russia and here, these beasts prowl in great packs at night through the fields and around the villages. Now I walked rapidly, keeping an anxious eye on every object, and my anxiety increased proportionally as the mute peasant's beneficent wails died away in the distance. My heart was throbbing in anticipation of a danger against which neither strength nor courage nor skill with weapons would be of any use to me. What could I do against eight, ten, or even more, fierce and ravening beasts? These dispiriting reflections were most agreeably interrupted; my ears caught distinctly the hails of the sentries on guard with the herd, and even the songs they were humming in low voices.

When I got to my hut, instead of ordering a fire lit, I lay down on my straw bed without undressing. Since I expected dawn to break soon and didn't want to go to sleep, I began considering, examining, analyzing, and reviewing all the aspects of my adventures that night. It had to be admitted that I was frightened when I heard the yells of the deaf peasant. My fear vanished when I saw that it was a man yelling, only to be replaced by dread of encountering wolves. Why is it that in battle, within sight of thousands of horrible deaths nearby, there was no trace of fear in my soul? What does it mean? Are not pain, torment, death just the same whether they come from a bullet or enemy saber or from the teeth and claws of a ferocious beast? I cannot rationally fathom the real reason either for my fear or my fearlessness. Can it really be because death on the battlefield is linked with glory, and death in the field among wolves only with pain?

## A JOURNEY TO PETERBURG

The regiment is on its way to Slonim, and I have been granted twenty-eight days to go to Peterburg.[9] Barclay de Tolly has replaced Arakcheev;

9. In the chapter "Love" of her 1839 *Notes*, Durova explained that her trip to Peterburg

if only he will be as obliging to me as Arakcheev was! It is not likely. They say that he is a very stern man. It would be odd, however, if they have found someone even sterner than the count. But Arakcheev had two priceless qualities: a sincere allegiance to His Majesty and blind obedience to his will.

Once again I have seen our beautiful capital, the enchanting abode of our adored tsar, our dearly beloved, our gentle and merciful father. No, the human tongue is too poor to express so many virtues compounded! Every day I hear people speaking of our Alexander with so much love; I see heartfelt tears in the eyes of those who recount some deed of his, and all of his deeds are filled with grace and have the people's happiness for their goal. I must make an effort to stop writing about him. I would never finish if I were to heed the heartfelt feelings for him with which all the inhabitants of vast Peterburg are imbued.

Barclay de Tolly ordered me to report to him, and, when I entered his study, he handed me five hundred rubles with a very courteous air, saying that His Majesty the Emperor believes this sum to be sufficient to outfit me. What could I do? I took the money, bowed, and went to order the uniform and the other things. It would be a miracle to get a hussar uniform made for that amount, but since the age of miracles has passed, I decided to transfer into the uhlans.[10] I wrote expressing this wish and the reason for it to the War Minister and asked him, as was permitted me, to make my request known to His Majesty and, moreover, to grant me a sum of money for transfer to a new regiment and the complete uhlan uniform. After I had written this note and sent it to the War Minister, I made haste to leave Peterburg, assuming that the minister's first heated impulse would be to berate me and report nothing to His Majesty; but if I were gone, there would be nobody to berate, and in time he would realize that the money they had given me was too little for service in the hussars, which comes dear. What business is it of his, anyway? It is at His Majesty's pleasure.

I returned to Slonim, but I didn't find my regiment there; it has not yet arrived. Jews clustered around me offering their services but, when they found out that my gold was sufficent only for a uniform, they went away,

---

in the winter of 1810–1811 was to ask for transfer to another regiment, because she had found no other way to escape the infatuation that Olga Pavlishcheva, her colonel's eldest daughter (chap. 4 above), had conceived for the merry, enigmatic young Aleksandrov. The "Miss A.," whose anecdote about being courted at a ball is a transparent attempt to arouse Aleksandrov's jealousy, is also Olga (chap. 5); "Love" contains a more highly embroidered version of the same incident. In 1828 Olga's younger brother Nikolaj married Alexander Pushkin's sister. For their son Lev Pavlishchev's notes on his father's family, see: "Iz semejnoj khroniki," *Istoricheskij vestnik* (1888), 2:283–84.

10. Durova had originally hoped to transfer to another hussar regiment.

and I am alone, with no servant, living in the house of an old, retired sergeant of the guards who from morning to night tells me stories of his youth and service during Catherine's reign.

At last the regiment caught up with me. The squadrons have dispersed to quarters that are almost all in charming and romantic spots. Poland is nice in so many ways: it has cheerful and hospitable men, lovely and affectionate women, a propitious climate, picturesque places, and an obedient and helpful folk!

All our regiment is now together. The first battalion, which was stationed in Odessa, has come to Slonim also.

## Transfer to a New Regiment

*April 1, 1811.* I am on my way back to Dąbrowica. I am now an uhlan in the Lithuanian regiment. I have been transferred.

I parted with sorrow from my worthy comrades. I regretfully stripped off my splendid uniform and sadly put on a blue *kolet* with crimson facings. "What a shame, Aleksandrov," the elder Pjatnitsky said to me. "What a shame you've made such a disadvantageous transformation. The hussar uniform was made for you; I admired you in it. But that jacket! Why on earth did you decide to change?"

Colonel Klebek sent for me. "What does this mean, Aleksandrov?" he asked. "Why have you gone begging your way into another regiment? I'm very unhappy about it."

I didn't know what to answer. I was ashamed to say that the hussar uniform was too expensive for me because I didn't know how to manage my money. I bade a sad farewell to my valiant colleagues, the gold uniform, and the black steed; I got into a hired cart and headed at full gallop down the road to Pinsk. My orderly, Zanudenko, has been assigned to me in the uhlans, and he is sitting on the box, twisting his gray mustaches and sighing. Poor fellow! He has grown old in the hussars.

So here I am in Dąbrowica. While its chief, Tutolmin, is absent, the Lithuanian regiment is under the command of the Prince Vadbolsky whom I knew in Tarnopol. I don't think it will take me long to reconcile myself to the loss of the hussar uniform. The sight of uhlans, lances, helmets, and pennons rouses in my soul memories of service in the Polish Horse, action in battle, my unforgettable Alcides—all the events and dangers! It has all revived and is painted in vivid pictures in my imagination. Nothing can ever expunge from my memory that first year after I entered upon my military career, that year of happiness, complete freedom, and total independence, which were all the more precious to me because I found a way to attain them by myself, with no outside intercession. Four years have passed since those days. I am now twenty-one years old.[11] Ch. says that I have matured; when he saw me in Tarnopol, he took me for a child of about thirteen. It's not surprising. I have a very youthful appearance, and there is something childlike in my face. Everyone tells me so; even *panna* Nowicka, before my diverting company put her to sleep, exclaimed twice, "Mój Boze, tak młode dziecko i juz idzie do wojska!"[12]

I have been assigned to the squadron of Captain Podjampolsky, who was my colleague in the Mariupol regiment. It has pleased my good genius to see to it that here also my squadron comrades are educated men; Schwartz, Czerniawski, and the two Tornesi brothers are officers outstanding in the regiment for intelligence, deportment, and good breeding. Podjampolsky has yet to give me a platoon. I am staying with him, every day the platoon commanders come to see us, and we pass our time most cheerfully.

The chief of our regiment has returned. I am often at his house. He likes to live well and is very practiced at it. He often gives balls for the ladies from the neighboring estates. Countess Plater does not call the uhlans *capuchins,* and the count does not order the table set for supper at eight o'clock. On the contrary, we dance at their house until four in the morning, and the old countess takes a most lively and active part in our amusements.

The young widow Vyrodova has married Szaboniewicz, an adjutant in our regiment. She told me that after my departure for Peterburg Wątrobka made her acquaintance, was captivated by her, and succeeded in pleasing her, too. They spent every day inseparably: together they read, sketched, sang, played, and brewed coffee and drank it—in short, their life was paradise and their love genuine, with mutual respect and astonishment at each other's perfections —

I couldn't go on listening. "How did it come about then, permit me to ask, that after all that you are Szaboniewicz's wife?"

"Here's how it happened," she replied. "Your regiment was ordered to Slonim. Wątrobka parted from me with genuine grief and swore to be faithful, but with no mention of his hand. From Slonim he wrote to me very tenderly, but again without mentioning our eternal union. From this I concluded that his attachment was just one more like dozens he has had before. He likes testing the heart he has won, and, while he swears that our love is mutual, his is cooling. Since I had no desire to suffer that fate, I ceased answering his letters and forced myself to stop thinking of him.

11. Twenty-eight.
12. "Good heavens, such a young child, and he's already joining the army!" (Polish)

Love rewarded me for this insult to my affections: Szaboniewicz, a young and handsome uhlan, fell in love with me with all the force of his ardent soul and proved the truth of the words that he could not live without me; he offered me his hand, heart, and everything he has now and in the future. I married him, and now I am the happiest of women and thank God every day that he did not give me Wątrobka for a husband. It is a hellish life, my dear Aleksandrov, with a man who is always testing, who trusts nothing, and who, through a surfeit of experience, fears everything. My precious Juzio is not that sort; he trusts me absolutely, and I love him more each passing day." The beautiful *erotiada* ended her story by sitting down at the piano and asking me lightly, "And what pieces, Aleksandrov, would you like me to play for you?"

I named them, handed her the sheet music, and sat down beside her instrument to listen and dream.

Tutolmin is a handsome man. Although he is already forty-four years old, he looks at most twenty-eight. Not a single one of the eligible girls and young ladies from the neighboring estates is indifferent to him, they all have designs on him, while he! . . . I have never seen anyone look more coldly and carelessly on every sign of sympathy, attention, and concealed love. I ascribe it to his much too high opinion of himself. Oh, a heart filled with pride has no room for love!

Yesterday Schwartz and I went out for a ride. After wandering a long time aimlessly among sandy knolls and shrubbery, we strayed at last from both our wits and our way—that is, we lost the road and any idea of how to find it again. We circled for over an hour around the spot where we thought the road should be until we spied a nearby village. Schwartz, who had already begun to lose his patience and get angry, galloped off toward it, and I followed him. We came to the vegetable plots; in one of them a woman was spreading flax. Schwartz rode up to the plot and shouted, "Listen, aunty, what's the name of this village?"

"Shcho pan kazhe?[13] asked the peasant woman with a low bow.

"What's this village's name? Damn your bowing and scraping!" cried Schwartz with flashing eyes. The woman took fright and started telling us, drawling and stammering over every word, that the village had more than one name, that when it was built it was given a tricky sort of name, she could not remember what, but now—

"The devil with you, your village, and those who built it," said Schwartz, spurring his horse.

We dashed off. Schwartz was railing and cursing, and I was finding it hard to keep from laughing. After we had galloped in one direction for

13. What does the gentleman order? (Ukrainian)

half a verst, we saw another woman. She too was spreading flax, in a glade surrounded by shrubbery with a little-used road running through it.

"Let me question this woman," I said to Schwartz. "You only frighten them with your shouting."

"Go ahead and question her. You'll see what nonsense she comes out with."

I rode up to the woman. "Listen, my dear, where does this road lead?"

"I don't know."

"Can we get to Kornilovka by it?"

"No, you can't!"

"Well, can we get to the devil by it?" asked the impatient Schwartz, with malicious irony and in a voice that alarmed even me.

"You can, you can," said the intimidated peasant, bowing low to us both.

"Don't listen to him, my dear. Just tell us, don't you know how we can get to Kornilovka? Can we cut across the fields? It seems it can't be far away."

"And where did you come from?" asked the woman, glancing timidly at Schwartz. I told her. "Oh, then you've lost your way. You'll have to turn around and come back here again!" At this reply, as the saying goes, I died laughing.

"Your questioning went so well," said Schwartz, "Don't you want to follow her advice?" We rode off and, after blundering around for another couple of hours, we finally found our bewitched Kornilovka and rode into it. [14]

At last Tutolmin's steel heart has softened! The hour of his subjugation has struck. Countess Manuzzi, a beauty twenty-eight years old, has come to visit her father, Count Plater, and the fire of her black eyes has ignited our entire Lithuanian regiment! They have all become quite extraordinarily lively. They dance, improvise, twirl their mustaches, spray themselves with perfume, wash in milk, jingle their spurs, and cinch their waists à la circassienne! The countess is truly captivating in a white satin dressing-gown, her hair covered by a silk lace veil which falls halfway over her lovely, languid eyes. She sits in a large armchair and looks with sweet negligence and indifference at our uhlan Adonises, who walk around or stand striking splendid poses before her. She has just arrived and is tired. She bends her head enchantingly to her mother's shoulder and says in a low voice, "Ah, maman, comme je suis fatiguée." But the fire in her eyes and her contented smile say otherwise. The uhlans trust them more than her words and are in no hurry to leave. At last the drowsiness of the

14. In later years Grigorij Schwartz was known to boast that Durova ran away and enlisted in the cavalry out of love for him. See Denis Davydov's letter to Pushkin on the subject, Appendix B.

eighty-year-old count convinces the fascinated cavalry officers that perhaps the countess is in fact tired.[15]

The handsome Tutolmin and the beautiful Manuzzi are inseparable. A ball at Tutolmin's house is followed by a ball at Plater's. We dance day and night. After our drill, which takes place every day now with music and a full review, and always before the eyes of our inspector general Countess Manuzzi, we all go to the colonel's house. There we lunch, dance, and at last separate to our quarters to prepare for the ball that evening. The only heads that have not been turned by our new Armida are those of us who are old, who have not seen her, whose hearts are already taken, and, of course, mine. Everyone else is sighing.

It has all subsided. No music thunders. Manuzzi is weeping. Not a single soul from our regiment is at their house. Manuzzi weeps, and weeps bitterly, all alone in her bedroom. . . . And yesterday we were all leaping about joyfully in a sort of jumbled dance. Yesterday, when we parted, we agreed to meet earlier, dance longer, and once again inflict the old countess on our Gruzintsev for the entire evening. But that's how transient our earthly blessings are. *Move out in twenty four-hours!* Magic words! From them Manuzzi's tears are flowing. From them young soldiers are bustling about merrily. From them everyone who yesterday sang and danced today is gloomily reckoning up accounts and paying off sundry debts. Rejkhmar says he is stunned by the order. Although Solntsev, Czerniawski, Lizogub, the Nazimovs, and the Tornesis were all Tutolmin's trusty rivals in the realm of dalliance, they are not in the least despondent and by now have flown back to their squadrons. Tornesi and I rode to Strelsk.

"So you've finally come to your senses, have you?" Podjampolsky asked us. "I thought you'd be whirling around until you dropped!"

We said that the sound of the last cotillion was still ringing in our ears.

"Well, that's all very well, but now we're beginning a cotillion whose figures will apparently be rather difficult. Farewell, gentlemen! We have our hands full now."

We went back to our platoons.[16]

15. The *Polish Biographical Dictionary* characterizes Countess Konstancja Plater's marriage to Stanisław Manuzzi (1773–1823), a Polish magnate with extensive property in the Braslaw region of Belorussia, as follows: "His wife was very gregarious and high-spirited; this was very wearing to Manuzzi, who over the years became crotchety and took to drink" (*Polski Słownik Biograficzny*, vol. 19 [Wrocław, 1974], 506).

16. By January 1812 Napoleon's tolerance of another great power on the continent had so eroded that France began mobilizing forces to invade Russia. In April Alexander I, eager to see action as a military commander, came to Vilna to the headquarters of the Russian First Army under Barclay de Tolly. The border with Poland across which Napoleon might attack was five hundred kilometers long. The Lithuanian Uhlans were on their way to join the advance-guard of the Second Army which, commanded by the fiery, self-willed Petr Bagration, was assigned to cover the southern segment of the front.

# Chapter Seven

## THE WAR OF 1812

*March 11.* Today we bade our last farewell to the hospitable Plater house, our merry abode in Dąbrowica, and to all that loved and captivated us. We are on our way to Bielsk; we will sharpen our lances and sabers and go on from there.

The veteran uhlans say that whenever Russian troops move out, every sort of foul weather goes with them. This time we have to believe them: from the day we left, snow, cold, blustery storms, rain, and a penetrating wind have accompanied us. The skin on my face hurts so much I can't bear to touch it. I took the elder Tornesi's advice to wash it every night with whey. This remedy has lessened the pain somewhat, but I have turned black, so black that I can't think of anything blacker than I am.

Podjampolsky is occupied with accounts at headquarters. As the officer next in seniority, I have been left in command of the squadron. I am, however, caliph for an hour; in two days my reign will be over.

*Kastjuknovka.* Our squadron has been assigned to a day's halt in this hamlet. A blackened, sooty, smoke-saturated peasant shack with a tattered straw roof and an earthen floor, from outside resembling a squashed turtle, serves as quarters for four of us—Czerniawski, the two Tornesis, and me. The front corner of this hovel is our domain. Our orderlies have settled down by the threshold and the stove and are industriously occupied cleaning bits, curbs, and stirrups, oiling straps, and carrying out other such cavalry tasks. Could we really be expected to spend all day in that kennel and that company? We decided to ride over and visit the hamlet's owner, Sokolowski, for the day.

He received us very cordially, and we passed a merry, agreeable day with him. I was delighted to learn that he is the Sokolowski about whom Kotzebue wrote in his *A Memorable Year of My Life*. Kotzebue, apparently in error, calls him Sokolow. Sokolowski told us all about his own life in Siberia, how he desponded and hoped, went hunting, and waited with patience and philosophy for a change for the better. I asked whether Kotzebue's life in Siberia was the way he described it and whether he was sad.

"He led a merry life," replied Sokolowski with a chuckle. "He played cards every day and always won and, to all appearances, never seemed to worry much about what would happen to him next."[1]

The hamlet of * * *. We have stopped here, I don't know for how long. I have been assigned to quarters in the home of a Uniate priest. His young wife takes very tender pains to provide me with the best of everything she has in the house. Every morning she herself brings me coffee, cream, and sugar wafers, while for her husband she simply prepares a glass of warm beer and cheese. Her dinners are always delicious and refined, and, only in order to avoid angering her husband totally, she fixes one kind of dish to his taste which, it must be admitted, is rather coarse.

Yesterday our pastor was very angry about something. All through dinner he wore a frown and, with an agreeable sardonic smile, kept pushing away the dishes his wife set before him. Luckily his anger never reached the point of exploding into speech. Neither of us spoke to him, and we even tried to avoid meeting his eyes. His wife is expert at that maneuver.

My hostess tries my patience! She never lets a day pass without telling me, "You must surely be Polish!"

"What makes you think so?" I ask and get some extravagant nonsense in reply: "You speak so pleasantly; your manners are so noble!" She is out of her mind.

"Is it really your opinion that pleasant conversation and noble manners are the exclusive property of Poles? Permit me to ask, how have all the other nations so sinned against you that you deny them these advantages?"

Instead of replying, she laughs, changes the subject with jokes, and once again begins finding various Polish valors in me.

Trying all possible arguments to escape the honor of being a Pole, I told my hostess among other things that, if she notices something not

1. The German playwright August von Kotzebue had served in the Russian civil service from 1783 to 1795 in Reval, Estonia. In *Das merkwürdigste Jahr meines Lebens* (Berlin, 1801), he described his abrupt arrest as he crossed the Russian border on a return journey to Peterburg in 1800. By orders of the capricious and paranoid Emperor Paul, Kotzebue was sent across the continent to exile in the remote Siberian town of Kurgan. In the book he speaks at some length of his closest companion there, a Polish noble, also in exile, whom he does indeed call "Sokolow." After only three weeks in Kurgan, Kotzebue was just as abruptly summoned to Peterburg, where he received an apology of sorts from the emperor and an appointment as director of the German theater. Durova probably read the French edition of Kotzebue's indignant memoir, *Une année memorable de la vie* . . . (Paris, 1801); there is no evidence that she knew German in 1812.

completely Russian about me, it might be because there are particles of Ukrainian and Swedish blood in me; my grandmothers on the maternal and paternal sides were Ukrainian and Swedish respectively. My hostess began extolling the Swedes, praising to the skies their courage and firm and upright character. My host was becoming visibly impatient. To my woe, just then his favorite dish was served, buckwheat kasha with melted lard on top and fried bits of the same lard scattered over it. I don't know how or why, but in Poland these are called *swedes*. My host seized the dish, set it down before him, and in a frenzy began hitting those innocent bits with his spoon, saying over and over again, "I don't like swedes! I don't like swedes!" Sprays of lard flew onto my uniform and epaulets. I got up from the table hastily, wiping my face with a handkerchief.

"Oh, my God!" cried my hostess, trying to tear the spoon out of his hand, "he's gone mad, completely mad!"

A few days after this scene my hostess brought me morning coffee as usual. This time she didn't wait for me to take the cup from her hand, but put everything on the little table in front of me and, without saying a word, sat down pensively by the window.

"Why so melancholy, my pretty hostess?" I asked.

"Nic, panie poruczniku!"[2] After a minute of silence, she began speaking, "Will you remember me?"

"I will, I swear on my honor that I will!"

"Then give me a token of that promise."

"Certainly; what would you like?"

"This ring!" She took my hand and gently pressed my little finger, on which I wore a gold ring. This took me by surprise. In silence and confusion, I looked at the priest's young wife, whose black eyes were fixed on me. I didn't know what to do. The ring was a gift from the young Pavlishcheva, and I had sworn to her that I would never part with it. Meanwhile, my hostess was waiting for my answer and, of course, becoming flustered despite herself when she saw that I was not going to take it off instantly and hand it to her. . . .

"What's the meaning of this, my dear? Here you are, sitting with the lieutenant, and you've forgotten that I haven't yet had breakfast." It was my enraged host speaking. As he opened the door to my room, he saw his wife holding my hand and stopped on the threshold.

His wife rushed over to him, "Oh, my life, my soul, forgive me, please! I'll get it ready right away." And with this she tore past him like lightning, leaving him posed like a statue in the doorway directly opposite me. I was relieved by this fortunate turn in an affair which at first

2. It's nothing, Lieutenant. (Polish)

threatened to deprive me of the ring that was a precious token of friendship. I asked my landlord to come in.

"I have joyful news for you, Lieutenant," said my host, as he entered.

"What kind of news, Reverend Father?"

"Tomorrow you're off on the march."

"Tomorrow! But how do you know that?"

"I just came from your captain. I was going to ask him to quarter you elsewhere. I hope that doesn't offend you. I am not so rich that I can offer my table and all the amenities due an officer for more than two or three days, and you've been staying with me for about two weeks now. I told your captain all that, but he said he had just that minute received the order to move out, and that tomorrow at eight o'clock in the morning your squadron will leave here."

"I congratulate you, my amiable host! Of course, this news gives you more joy than it does me. The weather is not too favorable for a march right now: rain and snow and cold and dust all together! I thought we would be waiting here for spring to settle in for good."

"What can you do? When you're ordered, you have to go." With this, my host bowed to me with his sardonic smile and went to drink his warm beer.

And so we're to march! Well, and it's all for the best. If we must go, let's be off. In quarters like these, we just go uselessly soft. We become accustomed to delicacies, affection, gratification. White satin hands lightly pat our cheeks and tenderly tweak our ears. They give us sweets and jam, they make up a soft bed for us, and how easy, how agreeable it is to get into the habit of it all! Then suddenly we have to march, suddenly we must pass from comfort to rigors and change seats from a velvet sofa to a tempestuous steed, and so on: contrast in everything. . . . Before I had finished reflecting on all this, the captain sent for me.

"Well, brother," he said as soon as I opened the door to his room. "Bid farewell to your priest's wife and her black eyes. Tomorrow we march!"

"Thank God, Captain."

"Thank God? That's novel! Weren't you the *piękne dziecko* and the *czerwone jabłko?*[3] Ungrateful fellow! . . ."

The captain's joke reminded me that I was, in fact, an ungrateful woman. I could not repay my hostess's love either with love or the gold ring, but all the same I had to give her something as a keepsake, and, of course, it couldn't be money! I went back to my quarters. My hostess was sadly laying the table. My host stood by the window, playing a doleful tune on his violin and watching his wife sardonically.

There was still an hour before dinnertime. I went to my room to see if I

3. Pretty child; scarlet apple. (Polish)

could find something to give my hostess. I burrowed into my things and found two dozen Sarepta kerchiefs glistening iridescently. I bought them in Sarepta and sent them to Papa; but when I came to see him, he gave them back to me, and they were lying among my things unused. I took them out and spread them on the table. I went on inspecting my belongings and found in one corner of my valise a silhouette which had been taken while I was still in the hussars and wearing their uniform. I laid it beside the kerchiefs and went back to tossing about all the things in the valise. I finally tired of seeking without finding, and, to get it over with once and for all, I grasped the valise by the bottom, upended it, shook the contents out onto the floor, and sat down there myself. Just as I triumphantly snatched up a rhinestone belt buckle with one hand and a scarf my sister had given me with the other, my hostess entered.

"Dinner's ready. What are you doing there?"

"You wanted a keepsake of some sort. Make me happy by choosing whatever you like," I said, showing her the kerchiefs, the silhouette, the buckle, and the scarf.

"I chose the ring."

"That I can't give away; it was a gift from a friend."

"A sacred thing, a gift from a friend! Cherish it." She went over to the table, picked up the silhouette and, without even glancing at the other things, went to the door, saying that her husband was waiting dinner for me. Touched by her choice of gift, I ran after her, put my arm around her, and earnestly begged her at least to take the rhinestone belt buckle. "After all, you do like me, my dear little hostess! Don't you want to take something you can wear close to your heart?"

Without replying or even looking at me, she pressed my hand to her breast, gently took the buckle from it, and went downstairs without a word.

A minute later I followed her. My host was already seated at the table, and his wife was showing him the buckle. "What do I know about such things anyway?" he said, pushing away her hand and the buckle. He saw me and got up, asking me to take my seat. "And so, my dear, today we should treat the lieutenant to our best. After all, he's parting from us, and most likely forever. What are we having today?"

"You'll see." After this short reply, spoken as if in vexation, she took her place.

"My wife is angry with you," my host began by saying. "You are paying her too much for these two weeks during which we have had the pleasure of offering you a few trifling amenities."

"I haven't paid at all, it seems to me. A glittering trinket can't be considered payment; it is simply for. . . ." I almost said *remembrance*, but my hostess glanced at me, and I stopped short, as could be remarked, most inaptly.

My host finished the sentence, "A keepsake, isn't that so? But we would remember you even without it."

All afternoon and into the evening, my host was in a good mood. He joked, laughed, played his violin, kissed his wife's hands, and asked her to sing, "Vous me quittez . . ." while he accompanied her. He asked me to add my persuasions to his. "As yet you have no idea how beautifully my wife sings!" At last his wife's patience snapped; she glanced reproachfully at her husband with tear-filled eyes and left the room. This unsettled my host. In confusion and haste, he hung his violin on the wall and followed his wife.

I went to see the captain and stayed there until midnight with the intention of avoiding, if possible, seeing either of my hosts again that evening. But in this reckoning I was deceived. They were both waiting up to have supper with me, and apparently on the best of terms. When I saw my hostess nestling amorously on her husband's bosom, I began to think that my suspicions were unfounded, and, overjoyed by this discovery, I struck up a merry, amicable, and trusting conversation with her. But disillusion was soon to come. Her husband turned to the door to order something from their man, and during that time my hostess quickly pulled my silhouette out of her shawl, showed it to me, kissed it, and hid it again. All this took her only two seconds, and, when her husband turned back to us, she again clung close to his shoulder.

I got up at dawn and stopped in for a minute to see my host and his wife and wish them all future happiness, before setting off for the captain's to await the hour fixed for the march. That tease Tornesi rode beside me all the way, singing, "Nie kochajsie we mnie, bo to nadaremnie. . . ."[4]

We are moving at a leisurely pace, in short stages, and now once again we have been ordered to halt *until further orders,* and, as luck would have it, in the most disadvantageous quarters. This village is poor, vile, and ravaged, it must be assumed, by the owner's exorbitant demands. All four of us are quartered in one large cottage. Czerniawski and the elder Tornesi have settled on benches by the windows, and the younger Tornesi and I are on plank beds by the stove. Directly opposite us on the stove, close to the ceiling, sits an old woman who must be about ninety. I don't know why, but she continually takes hold of her nose with two fingers, saying in a most refined voice as she does so, "Hm!" and then applying the two fingers to the wall. In the first days Tornesi and I guffawed like madmen at this practice by our *sibyl,* but now we have gotten used to it and, despite her penetrating *hm's,* we sometimes forget that there is a creature drawing breath up over our heads.

4. "Don't fall in love with me; it's futile. . . ." (Polish)

Spring this year is a melancholy one, damp, cold, windy, and muddy. I have always considered making the rounds of our platoon stables a pleasant outing, but now I prepare for it reluctantly. I get dressed lazily and linger, looking out the window twenty times to see whether the weather might be clearing. But since there is nothing to be done except go, off I go, sticking to plank walks, clutching fences, jumping rivulets, picking my way across on rocks, and falling several times anyway into mud up to my calf. When I return from my muddy journey, I find my comrades already assembled: Czerniawski reads Racine; Cesar smokes his pipe and always puts a bit of aloe on top of the tobacco, telling us that is what the Turks do; Ivan Tornesi sometimes performs a ballet, *Ariadne on the Island of Naxos,* and always plays the role of Ariadne himself. This would make even a dying man laugh, and I instantly forget my difficult voyage through the muddy streets.

Podjampolsky has gone to headquarters for three days or so to draw up accounts of some sort. My comrades have been sent to procure oats and hay for our horses, and I am left as commander of the squadron and sovereign over the entire village by right of force. I have made so little effort to learn anything about the village except our stables that I was not even sure whether there was a post-station in it. This morning I had the chance to find out. Finished with all my official occupations and having nothing to do and nothing to read, I picked up one of Voltaire's tales to reread for the hundredth time. I began leafing through the book halfheartedly and in boredom and was about to lie down on my campaign couch, a bench with a rug on it, when the door suddenly opened and a young infantry officer entered. "I would like to know, please, who is in command of this squadron."

"I am."

"Be so good as to order them to give me horses. I am hurrying to my regiment; here are my travel orders. The Jew who keeps the station won't give me any horses; he says they are all out, but he is lying. I saw a great number of them being led to water."

"You shall have your horses right away. Please take a seat. Send for the man on duty!"

The duty-soldier came.

"Go immediately to the post-station and order any horses you find there harnessed to this officer's carriage, even if the Jew tells you, as they usually do, that he only has horses for couriers."

The soldier left and came back two minutes later with the Jew station-master. The Judas swore to us that he was not giving horses because he had only enough left for couriers.

"We'll see whether you give horses or not!" I turned to the duty-soldier. "I ordered you to see that horses were harnessed without fail. Why did you bring the Jew here?" The second I finished the question, the soldier and the Jew both vanished as if a whirlwind had swept them out the door, and ten minutes later the officer's carriage rolled up to the porch of my quarters.

The officer stood up. "Didn't you used to serve in the hussars?"

"I did."

"And surely in the Mariupols? And surely you're Aleksandrov?"

"Yes, but how do you know?"

"We knew each other in Kiev. We served together as orderlies to Miloradovich. You really don't remember me?"

"No."

"I'm Gorlenko."

"Oh, my God! Now at last I recognize your face. I'm glad to see you. Stay and visit a bit longer; tell me about our other comrades—where are Shlein, Shtejn, Kosov?"

"God knows. I've never met them from that day to this, any more than I have you. We'll all see each other somewhere. Now the time has come for a rampaging life—that is, incessant tramps, rides, campaigns, marches, now here, now there—our paths are bound to cross. I wasn't as friendly with them as I was with you. Do you remember how we always sat at the end of the table to get as far as possible from the general so we could help ourselves to candy? Your pouch was always crammed with a full day's supply for both of us."

"No, now you're joking. I don't remember cramming dessert in my pouch."

"But that's how I remember it. Good-by, Aleksandrov! Let's hope we'll still be the same when next we meet." He got into his vehicle and dashed off down the bumpy road in a cloud of splattering mud.

I went back inside my smoky hovel, very content with forcing the damned Jew to give us horses; I had not forgotten the quibbles and delays I experienced at post-stations when I was traveling on leave. As soon as Gorlenko told me they were refusing him horses on the pretext that they were all out, I remembered all the tricks of stationmasters and was overjoyed with the chance to take revenge on at least one of the class.

## A Foraging Expedition

My comrades have come back, Czerniawski with nothing, and Cesar with a trifling acquisition; Ivan brought back somewhat more. In two days it will be my turn.

At last I, too, was sent out after forage. Like the others, I was given a detachment and orders under the signature and seal of the regimental commander to make the rounds of the neighboring estates, demand oats and hay from the landowners, and take it all, giving them in exchange vouchers which they could send with their village elders to the squadron to obtain receipts. They could then go with these to headquarters again, where they would be given other receipts, and with these receipts the landowning gentlemen could present themselves at last to the commissariat and receive their payment in cash.

At dawn I left our muddy village and my smoky quarters with its hundred-year-old female inhabitant and three gallant lads, my comrades, that is, and set out on my journey, followed by twelve uhlans. My first sphere of action was the estate of *podkomorzy* L.,[5] thirty versts from our quarters. My commission seemed to me rather ticklish, and therefore I was very embarrassed to catch sight of *pan* L.'s house only ten paces away. How could I begin? What could I say? Perhaps this was a venerable person, elderly, the father of a family. He would receive me cordially, taking me for a guest—and then I would demand oats for almost nothing. I know, of course, that the Poles are reluctant to give up their provisions against our receipts and use any means they can to escape them. This is quite natural. However sure they may be of getting payment for the receipts, it is always more cheering and certain to receive cash instantly than to carry receipts hither and yon. But as I thus reasoned and reflected, blushing from the drama to come, I arrived anyway, rode into the yard, and went inside. My forebodings had not deceived me. . . .

I was met by a man about sixty years old. His face was sad, his gaze troubled. It was clear, however, that we, his uninvited guests, were not to blame: my uhlans were still out of sight, and I alone, looking as I do like a seventeen-year-old youth, could not alarm him. Therefore, the grief depicted on his good-natured face was some domestic one. Poles are always very courteous. He invited me to be seated before asking me to what he owed the honor of seeing me in his home. At last the beginning was made; the question I found so horrible had flown from my host's lips. I replied, blushing as red as a person can, that I had a commission from the regiment to locate whatever forage we could obtain and to buy—of course not for cash but against a receipt—

"I cannot be of service to you," said the landowner indifferently. "A week ago everything I have burned—oats, hay, wheat, rye—and I have just sent to the neighboring landowners to buy all that for myself, if they will sell. The fact that you gentlemen of the cavalry are quartered here is very profitable for those of us who have something to sell you, but it does the greatest injury to those like me who seek to buy."

During this conversation coffee was served. L. went on, "Your commission is a most awkward one. Forgive my candor, but no landowner will sell you the produce of his soil against a receipt. I myself would not do so, even if we had no other way of disposing of it. Judge for yourself, why

5. Chamberlain. (Polish)

should they give it up to you now when they have a chance to sell for cash?"

I stood up irresolutely, not knowing what to do: leave without another word, or show him my orders?

L. got up also. "Must you go so soon? I very much regret that I cannot fulfill your needs; it would be agreeable to have the pleasure of your company longer, if I were not griefstricken: yesterday I buried my son. . . ." He could not continue; his eyes blurred with tears and he sat down, no longer in a state to keep to his feet. I left hastily, mounted my horse, and rode off at a gallop with my uhlans.

Toward evening I arrived at the estate of *staróscina* T., and this time I entered the house somewhat more boldly. To my woe, here again I had old age to deal with. I was received by a lady of about eighty. When she heard what I needed, she sent for her overseer and invited me to amuse myself until he came. So saying, she opened the door to the next room, which was a spacious drawing-room where every sort of diversion had been assembled: shuttlecock, billiards, hoops, cards, cut-out pictures, harps, guitars. There I found a company of young people all busy playing the various games.

"These are my grandchildren," said my hostess, leading me into their circle. They immediately invited me to take part in their games. I at once agreed and threw myself wholeheartedly into the pleasure of playing each in turn. Catching and returning the shuttlecock, I could at the same time listen as one of the girls played enchantingly on the harp and another sang delightfully. How I wished that the overseer would take as long as possible to arrive! Within sound of the harp and the lovely voice, how could I think without shuddering of the order which lay like a sleeping viper on my bosom beneath my uniform? I had merely to pull it out, and they would all take alarm. But now, how merry these young people were! How fond they became of me. How amiably they pressed my hands, hugged me, and kissed me. The girls themselves picked partners for the dances and romped and ran about. Now we were nothing but a throng of fully grown children, and yet in an hour or two suddenly all would change; I would become a desperate uhlan with the power and possibility of seizing forage from them. . . . And my captivating hosts. . . . What would happen to their joyful countenances, their lively and merry chatter? Oh, why had all the oats not burned and one of the grandsons or granddaughters died here as well? Then it would be easier for me to go away with nothing, but as it was. . . . Here I was, already fifty versts from the squadron, and I had not yet done anything, and probably would not, because any landowner with the least drop of sense would not give me anything against a mere voucher. And here I was under orders to demand it and, in case I was refused, to take what we needed anyway, giving the landowners a voucher for it and sending it off to the squadron with their horses. . . . How could I think of it without despairing? At the least, for the first time ever I damned my rank of uhlan. Amid the dances, laughter, and romping, I winced whenever the door opened into our drawing-room.

Fortunately, the overseer did not arrive until suppertime, and to my great good fortune my hostess said that she could give me about ten quarters of oats and four loads of hay, if her people were paid for transporting it, and her elder and my sergeant took my voucher to the squadron along with the carts. I agreed with great joy and gratitude to all her dispositions and kissed her hand; I would have kissed it even if Polish custom and my attire had not so obliged me, because her indulgence had lifted a most horrible weight from my heart and spared me the need to stir the viper. Now I could carry it farther.

I dispatched the carts with the forage and returned to the merry company. They were waiting supper for me, and all the bother of the dispatch had delayed it by an hour. When we sat down at the table, my hostess placed me beside her. She began by saying, "You take your duties too seriously, young man. Is it really necessary to watch and wait until the carts are loaded and leave the village? That's going too far. From your appearance and youth I didn't expect to find you such a good soldier." The foolish old woman didn't realize that it was for her benefit that I had kept close watch over my uhlans; there were lots of places where they might have found something better than oats. Why will people always insist on judging by appearances? They urged me to stay the night, but I was already disillusioned and took no further pleasure in their company.

I left the *starościna's* house and decided to ride all night in order to visit another village at dawn, that of retired cavalry Captain M. of the Polish Army. The Jews had told me that he had a very large store of oats and hay and was prepared to sell. I hoped that fate would be merciful to me, that the viper would not wake.

When I got to the old Nationalist's house at ten in the morning, he received me with all the cordiality of the cavalryman. "Be seated, be seated, my dear uhlan, what can I offer you? You surely don't drink liquor yet, do you? Hey, Marusia!" Marusia, a tall, dried-up, gray-haired woman with a gloomy countenance responded to this hail. "Order coffee served to us, my dear."

It flattered my self-esteem greatly that Marusia (although she must have been close to fifty) looked at me kindly and with a wry smile, whereas her glance at the old soldier expressed both vexation and scorn. She replied that coffee would be ready right away, went out, and returned with it a quarter of an hour later. She told her master that the overseer was asking for him and took her place beside me to pour the coffee. This lack of ceremony did not surprise me; housekeepers for elderly bachelors have all the privileges of ladies of the manor, and in Poland they are almost all from the nobility—that is, they are *szlachcianki*.[6]

At last my host returned. When he learned the reason for my visit, he shook his head and shrugged his shoulders, "Well, if I don't give you my oats against your voucher, what then?"

"Then I won't have them," I replied.

"You are more reasonable than I expected, and that does you great honor. Why don't your superiors send you out with cash instead of the right to give vouchers?"

"I don't know. I think that it has to do with internal dispositions in the regiment. But vouchers are just the same as cash, after all. The only difference is in the time; you receive it somewhat later because you have to take them to headquarters."

The Nationalist burst out laughing. "Ah, how young you are yet, *kochany kolego!*[7] However, let's go. I assume that you have no time to lose. Let's go. I will order them to give you twenty quarters of oats. More than that I cannot and will not spare you from the amount I have set aside for sale only for cash. . . ."

I was so delighted with the twenty quarters, which was more than I had anticipated and would permit me to return to the squadron, freed at last from the loathsome *baranta*[8] that I seized the old Nationalist by the arm and ran off with the speed of a doe, dragging him with me.

"Slower, slower, young man! I can well believe that you find it agreeable to receive so much oats with so little bother, but my days of running are long since over. Besides, I was wounded in both legs, so let's go at a walk."

I regretted my untimely rapture and walked in silence beside my benevolent host. We passed through a beautiful garden and came out by his barns and granaries, where my sergeant and the overseer were standing. At last everything was prepared. I sent all my uhlans back with the plunder, keeping only one with me, since I was planning to spend that day with the amiable Nationalist and return on the next to the squadron. It gave me great pleasure to pull the orders out of my uniform, tear them into tiny pieces, and throw them into the lake. How happy I was! All my high spirits returned, and the retired captain took such pleasure in my company that he begged me most persuasively to stay with him for a day

6. "A Polish *panna* in the house is a creature known only to Poland. The *panna* is usually from the poor nobility and occupies the post of lady-in-waiting, companion, even servant (only from love for her masters); she sits down to meals with the landowner's family and usually serves as the butt of his jokes at the female sex in general. Their fidelity and complaisance are astonishing! Genuine *panny* are a vanishing species" (Faddej Bulgarin, *Vospominanija*, part 1 [St. Petersburg, 1846], 314, footnote).

7. Dear comrade. (Polish)

8. A word of Turkic origin for a marauding revenge raid.

or two longer: "Your blooming youth, liveliness, and high spirits recall to me and revive in my soul the happy days of my own boyhood. At your age I was just like you. Stay on, young man," he said, embracing me. "Make a gift of these two days to an old man who has come to love you like a son."

I stayed. To reward me for this concession, my host invited three or four families from neighboring estates to visit him. I had a very merry time at the gallant Nationalist's house; we danced, played every game imaginable, and ran through the rooms no better than five-year-olds, and even Marusia's frowns could not quiet the noise, talk, laughter, and dances; moreover, our host surpassed our expectations by keeping a huge table set with sweets, jams, and delicacies of every sort. Poor Marusia! She could not pass the table without making a convulsive grimace.

When the two days were over, I bade farewell to my kind host and returned to the squadron. Thus I came to the end of my disagreeable mission, and God grant that I never see the commencement of another like it! Returning home, I told the captain only that I had not resorted to forcible measures. Now Cesar and I are left alone in our quarters; Czerniawski and the elder Tornesi have gone off on another foray.

Today my comrades returned, and today also we are off on the march. How long can this continue? I have trouble understanding why we go by such fitful stages.

# Chapter Eight

We covered about a hundred versts and stopped again. They say that Napoleon has crossed our frontiers with an enormous army.[1] For some reason I have become more indifferent now. There are no more of those extravagant dreams, those flashes and transports. I think that this time I will not go on the attack with each squadron. I have undoubtedly become more sensible; experience has taken its customary toll even from my fiery imagination—that is, given it a conventional turn.

We are stationed in a poor little village on the banks of the Narew. Every night our horses are saddled; we are dressed and armed. At midnight half the squadron mounts and rides out of the hamlet to maintain the pickets and make the rounds on patrol. The others remain in readiness on horseback. It is a way of life very much like that described by Zhukovsky's dead man:

> My abode beside the Narva
> Is a cottage cramped and spare:
> As the moon o'er the valley courses
> And the stroke of midnight swells,
> Then we saddle up our horses
> And forsake our gloomy cells.[2]

That is exactly the way it is with us, the Lithuanian Uhlans: each midnight we saddle up and ride out, and the cottage I occupy is cramped, small, and right beside the Narew. Oh, how this situation has revived all my sensations! My heart teems with emotions, and my head with ideas, plans, dreams, conjectures; my imagination paints pictures for me glittering with all the rays and colors that exist in the kingdom of nature and of possibilities. What a life! What a full, joyous, active life! How can it be

1. Napoleon crossed the Neman on June 12/24 at Kovno and massed his armies for an attack centered on Vilna. The Russian First Army escaped, but the French forces succeeded in driving a wedge between it and the Second Army. For well over a month the Russians retreated, maneuvering to unite their two armies while Napoleon's forces tried to prevent that union. When the French attacked, by Durova's account the Lithuanian Uhlans were on alert on the Narew river west of the Second Army's position near Volkovysk. During the retreat into Russia, Durova's regiment served in the rear-guard as part of the Fourth Cavalry Corps under Major-General Karl Sievers, along with the Akhtyrsk Hussars (Denis Davydov's regiment), the Kharkov, Chernigov, Kiev, and Novorossijsk Dragoons, and a battery of horse artillery.

2. "Ljudmila" (1808) was the first of the Russian poet Vasilij Zhukovskij's three ballads based on Gottfried Bürger's "Lenore."

compared to that which I led in Dąbrowica? Every day and every hour now I live and feel alive. Oh, this way of life is a thousand thousand times superior! Balls, dances, flirtation, music. . . . Oh, God, what trivial and boring pastimes!

I honestly never thought to find a use for the two winecups of liquor that are distributed every day to us as well as the soldiers. But obviously nothing should be disdained. Yesterday, passing through a hamlet, our squadron had to cross a narrow dike. The leading detachment met some kind of obstruction and brought the squadron to a halt; others, still coming on, jostled us from the rear, and our horses, jostling and bracing themselves to keep from falling into the wide trenches bordering the dike, went wild and started kicking and rearing. In this chaos I was pressed into the middle of my platoon and so squeezed that, although I could see that the horse standing in front of me had every intention of striking me with its well-shod hoof, I was powerless to do anything but anticipate and suffer the blow with courage. The sharp pain made me gasp from the depths of my soul! The worthless horse had both the will and the opportunity to smash my leg to bits, because I was caught as if in a vice. Fortunately, as it prepared to repeat the blow, the squadron began to move and order was restored.

When we made camp, I examined my leg. I was horrified: it was bruised, bloody, and swollen, and it ached unbearably from the sole to the knee. For the first time in my life I would have been glad to get into a carriage; riding was torment, but I had no choice except to bear it. We have had no vehicles at all for a long time. Now the liquor has proved useful. Every day I wash my sore leg with it and every day, to my alarm, I see it turning a darker purple, although the pain is diminishing. The foot of the injured leg has become as black as coal. I am afraid to look at it, and I can't understand why the foot has turned black when the blow was midway between it and the knee. Kornilovich, our regimental doctor, says that my leg will have to be amputated. What rubbish!

What can it all mean? We are retreating, and in great haste, without once seeing action.

Today we marched through a trackless forest, and I thought we were rushing to intercept the enemy directly, but nothing came of it. We arrived on the run only to draw up in formation in high hemp fields. It was hardly worth the rush! Ahead of us there is fighting, however.

It's too bad that we have been left without a real commander. Tutolmin, the chief of our regiment, reported sick back in Bielsk and left us to the whims of fate. We are now under the command of Stackelberg, a lieutenant-colonel from the Novorossijsk Dragoons. Krejts, the commander of that regiment, heads our brigade.

We are still standing in the hemp. The weather is unbearably hot. Captain Podjampolsky asked me if I would like to bathe, and, when I replied that I would like it very much, he ordered me to take command of fourteen uhlans he was sending to fetch water from a nearby river, which is also not far from the fighting. "It will give you a chance to bathe," said the captain. "Be careful, though. The enemy is nearby."

"Why aren't we fighting them then?" I asked, dismounting from my horse for the walk to the river.

"As if we can all fight! Just wait, you'll get your share yet. Be off now, make it quick! Yes, and please, Aleksandrov, watch out that your falcons don't fly away."

I ordered the sergeant to lead the way, took up the rear, and in that order conducted my men to the river. Leaving the uhlans to fill their pots with water, wash, drink, and refresh themselves as best they could, I walked half a verst upstream from them, quickly undressed, and plunged with indescribable pleasure into the fresh, cold current. I could not revel in this bliss for long, of course. In ten minutes I got out of the water and dressed even more rapidly than I had undressed, because now shots could be heard quite close to us. I led my refreshed and heartened men to bring the salubrious liquid to their comrades.

Our entire squadron has been assigned to picket duty. It was my turn to lead out, post, and make the rounds of the vedettes. I was given a half-squadron for the task, while Podjampolsky settled down in the village with the other half. After the captain had instructed me on what to do in various circumstances, what precautions to take, and what to observe as I posted the sentries, I set out with my half-squadron uphill to the monastery where I was to station the first vedette. I occupied the designated points with half my men, keeping the others in readiness to relieve them at the end of their duty.

It was already midnight when I came back to relieve my sentries. As we approached a hamlet situated not far from the hilltop on which the monastery stood, I ordered the uhlans to ride on the grass, pressing their sabers to the saddle with their knees and staying far enough apart to keep their stirrups from clashing. At the hamlet I halted my men and rode on alone to make sure the enemy was not in hiding there. A dead silence reigned everywhere, all the houses had been abandoned by their inhabitants, everything was quiet and empty, and only the black depths of the peasants' open sheds and stables gaped dreadfully at me. Zelant, who has a bad habit of neighing when he is separated from other horses, now seemed to be holding his breath; he trod so lightly on the hard road that even I could not hear his hoofbeats. Once I had assured myself that there was nobody in the hamlet, I returned to my uhlans and led them through it to the foot of the hill. I left my men there and, taking two uhlans and a sergeant with me, rode uphill to the walls of the monastery to relieve the main vedette.

"We keep hearing something in the fields, your honor," said the uhlans, "and things keep looming up here and there, maybe men on horseback, but we can't make it out properly; it's most likely the French."

I said that the sentries were to fire on anyone who failed to give the password when challenged and, taking the newly-relieved uhlans with me, started back to the men I had left below. As I rode through the woods surrounding the monastery, I was astonished to see, walking toward me, one of the men who was supposed to be waiting for me at the foot of the hill.

"What's the meaning of this?" I asked. "What are you doing here, and without your horse?"

He answered that he had been knocked off his horse.

"What! Standing still?"

"No. The French attacked us. The sergeant you left in charge of us ran away first. There was nothing we could do, and we scattered in all directions. I was about to gallop off to let you know when my horse reared, threw me, and bolted."

"And where are the French?"

"I don't know."

"A fine thing that is!" I had no right to censure the soldier when the sergeant had run away, but I was extremely distressed and disturbed by the circumstance. As we came out of the woods, I caught sight of a group of mounted men who were milling about indecisively, now riding, now stopping, now reining in their horses and bending close to one another. I stopped to take a closer look, but when I heard them speaking Russian, I at once rode over to them and asked them who they were.

"Cossacks," one of them replied. "It's a good thing you stopped, or else we were going to strike you."

"And why strike someone without hailing him or asking the password, without finding out for sure whether it's the enemy or our men? And what do you mean by 'It's a good thing you stopped' anyway?"

"You should know, it was you running away from us just now. . . ."

This explained the entire affair. Some Cossacks, prowling about every-where as usual, had also visited the deserted village to see if anyone was there. From it they headed for the monastery and, when they saw a mounted detachment at the foot of the hill, took it for the enemy. While they were deliberating among themselves whether or not to go whooping after it,[3] my valiant men, taking them for the enemy also, decided that no good could come of waiting and, following the example of their scoundrel of a sergeant, galloped off headlong in all directions. This scattered flight and the speed of their horses saved them from pursuit by the Cossacks, who climbed the hill, looked around the monastery, and, not finding anything or anyone, came back down. When they saw me and my three uhlans, they took us for what they thought were the same Frenchmen who had fled at the mere sight of them, and, if I had not approached and begun questioning them, they would have struck at us with their lances.

"We were all set to give you a warm welcome!" said one dashing Cossack about fifty years old.

"You and who else!" I answered, vexed. "Our lances are harder than yours. You wouldn't have found a spot to flee to." And, without listening to any more of their talk, I went my way. I was distressed and disheartened beyond words. What can I expect in the future? How can I hope to win glory in battle with fellow warriors like these? At the slightest sign of danger they will run away, betray me, put me to shame. Why did I ever leave my valiant hussars? They are Serbs, Hungarians! They are imbued with courage, and glory is inseparable from them!

There is no hope for me in the future, but what else awaited me now? The cowards had doubtless already alerted our reserves. Podjampolsky might well have sent this hellish dispatch to headquarters: "A picket under the command of Lieutenant Aleksandrov was routed by the enemy who, by this action, broke through the forward line of vedettes!" And now the tranquillity and security of the army are disrupted, and all because Lieutenant Aleksandrov is either a coward or a blockhead, who let himself be routed without defending himself, alerting the reserves, or firing a single shot. Otherwise the enemy could not have broken so easily through the forward line of vedettes! And I was told that *even the shadow of a spot on the name of Aleksandrov would never be forgiven me!*.

Thoughts and emotions as black as night weighed on my mind and heart. I rode on at a walk in the company of the three uhlans left to me. Suddenly the forceful hoofbeats of a galloping half-squadron struck my ears. I glanced ahead and saw Cesar Tornesi racing like a whirlwind and, flying behind him, the half-squadron. As he caught sight of me, he cried out dumbfounded and brought his horse to a halt, "It's you, Aleksandrov! For God's sake, tell me what happened!"

"What could happen, brother? What happened, of course, is what is bound to happen with our cowards. They were frightened by Cossacks and ran like hares without even raising a weapon."

3. The Cossacks attacked with a blood-curdling cry.

"Podjampolsky is in despair. The sergeant said you had been taken prisoner, and the entire picket butchered."

"What a way to put it! Butchered! The rascals weren't sound asleep to be butchered; they could only be hacked down. What's that about Podjampolsky?"

"I tell you, he's in despair. 'How could he forget my words? I explained everything so clearly and in such detail to him!' said our valiant commander in grief and vexation. . . . But here he comes now. We were on our way to rescue you from the enemy even at the cost of the entire squadron. . . ."

I rode to meet Podjampolsky. "Don't blame me, Captain. I would rather be routed and taken prisoner than see myself covered with unwarranted shame." (It was the very first time that I had been given a mission and assigned a post entailing danger and demanding courage and vigilance, and this was how outstandingly I had carried it out.) I related the entire incident to the captain in detail. We returned to our village, leaving the poor sentries at their posts without relief until dawn. There was no longer time to change them.

However distressed and chagrinned Podjampolsky, the finest of officers, valiant and experienced, may have been when he received the absurd report from the sergeant who had fled the picket, he did not want to pass the news further without taking every means possible to rectify the unfortunate affair. He decided it would be better to perish with the entire squadron, battling to the last drop of blood, than to make such a shameful instance public. Thanks to this heroic resolve, my name was saved from defamation, but what had happened stamped such a deep distrust in my soul that I began to fear any detached duty or mission that was to be carried out together with my men. I will never, never be able to trust them again! What Ermolov said is true: *a cowardly soldier does not deserve to live.* The conclusion seemed harsh to me at the time, but now I see that it is a truth arrived at by the great mind of an extraordinary man. A lazy farmer, a spendthrift merchant, a freethinking priest—all have vices out of keeping with their calling and benefit, but their example does not attract others, and they harm only themselves: poverty and contempt remain their lot. But a cowardly soldier! I have no words to depict the magnitude of the evil one worthless, timid scoundrel can do to an entire army! And in this case think of the grief that might have been drawn onto my head, and all because a coward was frightened by his shadow, ran away, lured others after him, and very nearly became the reason for a lying dispatch and a false alert throughout the army. No, a timid soldier does not deserve to live. Ermolov is right!

These reflections occupied me until dawn. We relieved our sentries. The cowards were painfully punished, and the sergeant even more so.

After these exactions a new idea gives me no peace; it frightens and shames me, and I cannot get it out of my head. I blush as I pen these lines: isn't it all my fault? Don't I alone deserve the censure and punishment? I am an officer, and the detachment was entrusted to me; why did I leave them alone with a sergeant who had never yet been in battle?

We are moving by quick marches into the heart of Russia, with an enemy at our heels who believes in all simplicity that we are running to escape him! Fortune blinds. I often think of Starn's prayer before the altar of Odin, when he asks the god to cloud Fingal's mind with the credulity *that presages a great fall!*[4] Despite Napoleon's countless admirers, I make so bold as to think that, for one considered such a great genius, he is much too confident both of his luck and his capabilities, too credulous, rash, and uninformed. Blind luck, coincidence of circumstance, an oppressed nobility, and a deluded people all helped him to take the throne, but he will have difficulty in holding and occupying it worthily. The artillery lieutenant, whose unprecedented luck has cost him both wits and common sense, will soon be remarked through the emperor's robes. On the basis of only geographical information and the dispatches of spies, how could he resolve to come and conquer a vast, rich nation, one famed for the magnanimous spirit and selflessness of its nobility, the unshakable bulwark of the Russian throne, and for its well-ordered host of troops, whose strict discipline and courage, physical strength and sturdy constitution allow them to withstand all hardships; a nation that includes as many peoples as it does climates and, above and beyond all this, is buttressed by its faith and toleration? To see that glorious army retreating without giving battle, retreating so rapidly that it is hard to keep pace with it, and to believe that it is retreating for fear of encountering the enemy? To believe in the timidity of the Russian army within the borders of its native land? To believe and pursue it, trying to overtake it? What horrible blindness! It can lead only to a horrible end.

The French are making every effort to overtake us and fight, and we are making efforts just as great to get away without fighting. I find these tactics very reassuring. It is amusing to see the speed with which we are carrying our credulous enemy deep into our forests. I don't always find it so droll, however. When I imagine the dreadful end of our retreat, involuntarily I sigh and become pensive. The French are a foe worthy of us, noble and courageous, but evil fate in the guise of Napoleon is leading them into Russia. Here they will lay down their heads, and their bones will be scattered and their bodies rot.

4. Durova is citing Vladislav Ozerov's 1805 tragedy, *Fingal,* which used an incident described in James Macpherson's *Ossian* cycle.

I have not closed my eyes for two days, and I have hardly gotten down off my horse. Stackelberg sent me to occupy our campsites. He gave me four uhlans from each squadron, and the quartermasters of the Novoros-sijsk Dragoons and the Akhtyrsk Hussars are also riding with me. When I have occupied the campsite, I ride back to meet the regiment and see them settled into it. Then I await orders and, once I get them, set out again immediately. Our marches are quite long. Almost every time I leave at night and arrive at the next camp about noon. While sites are being assigned to the entire rear-guard, I wait my turn to receive our regiment's. Then I have to set off at once to meet the regiment and see each squadron to its proper place, and again, after waiting for the commotion to end and for new orders, I go my way.

Three days passed in that way. We were occupying a camp near the little town of Kadnevo. My strength was completely exhausted. Return-ing from the camp to town, I sent an uhlan to watch the road and let me know when the regiment appeared. I myself went to headquarters, intending to get something to eat and, if I got the chance, to sleep afterwards. While I was waiting for dinner, I lay down on our host's bed, and that is the last thing I remember. . . . I woke late at night, as-tonished that I had been allowed to sleep so long. There was no fire and nobody in the room. I got up hastily, opened the door into the hallway, and called my sergeant. He appeared. "Has the regiment really not come yet?" I asked.

He replied that it hadn't; only the Kiev Dragoons had arrived.

"Why didn't you wake me?"

"We couldn't, your honor. You were sleeping like the dead. We called you quietly at first, and then we shook you by the arms and shoulders, we sat you up and brought a candle right up to your eyes. At last we splashed cold water in your face, but it was no use: you didn't even stir. The mistress was here while all this was going on, and she began crying when she saw that we had no luck in waking you and were laying you back down on the bed: 'Poor child! He's dead to the world. Why do you take such young boys into the army?' She bent over you and listened to be sure you were breathing. I stayed with you and ordered an uhlan to go farther down the road to meet the regiment, but he soon returned with the information that our regiment has changed route and that only the Kiev Dragoons commanded by Emanuel have come here."

I went at once to the camp. They were not yet asleep, and there I found both my comrades, the dragoon and hussar quartermasters. The former asked Emanuel to take him under his command for the time being, but the hussar and I, informing ourselves as to the road our regiments had taken, set out to find them and very soon did so.

Sometimes there are minor clashes between our rear- and the enemy's advance-guard only so that we do not keep retreating without any action at all.[5]

Why on earth do we keep on running like this? . . . I don't know what to do. I am mortally afraid of falling ill. It will be ascribed afterwards not to the extremity of these rigors, but to the frailty of my sex! We are on the move day and night. Our only rest comes when they halt the regiment and permit us to dismount for half an hour. The uhlans at once lie down at their horses' feet, but I rest my elbows on the saddle and lay my head on my arms. I am afraid to close my eyes lest an involuntary sleep overwhelm me. Not only do we not sleep, we don't even eat. We are rushing somewhere. Oh, our poor regiment!

In order to fight off the sleep threatening to possess me, I try dismounting and walking, but my strength is so spent that I hasten to get back on my horse, and I have difficulty even lifting myself onto the saddle. Thirst parches my interior. There is no water anywhere except in the gutters beside the road. I dismounted again and with great clumsiness dipped some repulsive water, warm and green, from the very bottom of the gutter. I collected it in a bottle, got back on my horse with this treasure, and carried it for another five versts, holding the bottle before me on the saddle without resolution enough either to drink the muck or throw it away. But needs drive: I finally drank the hellish liquid.

If I had millions, I would trade them all for permission to sleep. I am completely exhausted. All my senses crave repose. . . . I got the idea of looking at myself in the shiny blade of my saber: my face is as white as a sheet, and my eyes have lost their luster. There is not such a marked change in the others, and that is undoubtedly because they know how to sleep on horseback while I can't.

That night Podjampolsky scolded Cesar and me because the men of our platoons were dozing, swaying in the saddle, and letting their helmets drop off their heads. The day after this reprimand, we saw Podjampolsky himself riding with closed eyes, quite sound asleep on his high-stepping steed. Gratified by this spectacle, we rode beside him to see how it would end. But Cesar was determined to pay him back for the reprimand: he spurred his horse and galloped past Podjampolsky, whose horse took off at

5. Durova's service record shows her as seeing combat on June 27 at Mir and July 2 at Dashkovka. The battle at Mir is usually described as pitting the rear-guard under the Cossack general Platov against the Polish cavalry of Jerome's French advance-guard, but Durova's regiment clashed with their fellow Poles there also.

a full run. We had the pleasure of seeing the alarm and haste with which Podjampolsky hurried to gather up the reins which had fallen from his hands.

An inexplicable spirit of discord has come over Cesar and me. We always start by riding out ahead of the squadron, talking very amicably at first; then we begin quarreling and, after exchanging polite, caustic remarks, separate to opposite sides of the road. During one of these sallies we rode off to the ditches at the side of the road, dismounted, and lay down. Fortunately we had not yet fallen asleep when the squadron caught up. Podjampolsky, who had assumed us to be with our platoons, was surprised and angry when he saw us settled tranquilly beside the ditches near the road. "Aren't you ashamed, gentlemen," he said. "Instead of looking after your soldiers to keep them from sleeping, falling, dropping their helmets, and ruining their horses, you rode off ahead and went to sleep on the road!"

Provoked by the same spirit of discord that set us against one another, we told him that less than two days ago he himself had felt and demonstrated that our present rigors are beyond human strength. Podjampolsky made no rejoinder, but simply ordered us to be without fail in our places and with our men. "We are obliged to set an example for them," he added kindly. "It will be easier for them to bear any rigor which they see their officers bearing on an equal footing. A soldier will never dare to grumble at any hardship that his officer shares with him." I felt the justice of Podjampolsky's words and resolved firmly always to be guided by them.

At last we have been granted a respite. With inexpressible pleasure I spread my greatcoat on some hay, lay down, and fell asleep instantly. I think I must have slept for ten hours, because it was already after sundown when I crawled out of my shelter—crawled literally, because the aperture serving as a door was just over a foot high. A lively and handsome scene met my eyes: throngs of uhlan, hussar, and cuirassier officers were walking around the camp. Soldiers were cooking kasha and cleaning their equipment. Orderlies and adjutants galloped to and fro. Our regiment's excellent music thundered, delighting the countless numbers of officers from every regiment who came to listen to it. When Stackelberg, a knowledgeable music-lover, became our commander, he undertook to improve our regimental band and brought it to such a high degree of perfection that it has no equal now in either the First or Second Western Armies.

Our regiment was settled near a chain of rather high hills. At nightfall countless bivouac fires were lit and noises resounded, soldiers talking and the hoofbeats and neighing of horses. I studied this noisy, animated spectacle for half an hour and then, I don't know why, I crossed over to the other side of the hills; as I descended into the valley, I no longer heard the slightest noise—it was as if the soldiers, the war, the army had never even existed! I climbed the hill again, watched the scene of ebullient activity and continual tumult and motion for a while, and then plunged once more into the peace and quiet of the valley. This rapid transition from great uproar to total silence made an impression on my soul, which I can't, however, either comprehend or describe.

Near Smolensk the emperor's manifesto was announced to us; it said that *the emperor will no longer restrain your valor and frees you to take revenge on the enemy for the tedium of the involuntary retreat which until now has been essential.* Our soldiers jumped for joy, and everyone's eyes glowed with courage and satisfaction. "At last!" said the officers. "Now it will be our turn to pursue them."[6]

*Smolensk.*[7] Again I hear the menacing, majestic rumble of cannons! Again I see the flash of bayonets! Memories of the first year of my martial life revive. . . . No, a coward has no soul. Otherwise, how could he see and hear all this and not blaze with courage? For two hours we waited for orders by the wall of the Smolensk fortress; at last we were commanded to march on the enemy. As the inhabitants of the city watched us go by in disciplined ranks, with heroic bearing and confidence in our own strength, they saw us off with joyful exhortations; a few, especially the old men, continually repeated, "God help you! God help you!" in an uncommonly solemn tone which made me shudder and deeply moved me. . . .

Our regiment is placed on both sides of the road. Podjampolsky's squadron is on the left, and farther to the left are bricksheds. The spot assigned to us is so awkward for cavalry maneuvers that we will not be able to withstand the enemy's first onslaught. The entire field is so pitted, strewn with scraggly bushes, and cut by ruts that in any rapid movement the squadron would have to jump either a ditch or a bush or a pit at every step. Since this was where they dug clay for the bricks, there are countless pits and, moreover, all of them are full of rainwater.

6. Alexander I issued a proclamation with this approximate wording from the fortress at Drissa on June 27 (the anniversary of Peter the Great's victory over the Swedes at Poltava in 1709). Alexander left the armies and returned to St. Petersburg in the second week of July. If Durova has placed the passage correctly, the proclamation was not read to the rear-guard until after the Second Army's union with the First near Smolensk in late July.

7. Napoleon concentrated his troops for a crossing of the Dnepr behind the Russian lines near Smolensk on August 1–2. The French attack on the city on August 4 found less then twenty thousand Russian soldiers commanded by Lieutenant-General Nikolaj Raevskij to defend Smolensk's medieval fortifications; they held off the French until the main armies could arrive.

We were ordered to delay the enemy. And so, in order to engage them, Podjampolsky put the squadron into battle formation and ordered the flankers to ride out. "Who among you, gentlemen, would like to take command of them?" the captain asked us.

The elder Tornesi volunteered immediately. He and twenty of our best riders went to meet the enemy. An hour later all of them returned except Tornesi, who had been cut down by the French. They said that in a heated outburst he rode straight into a crowd of them. No matter how they shouted at him, "Rendez vous! Rendez vous!" he paid no heed, but slashed at them right and left, until at last, enraged, they rushed him and finished him off in a flash.

When Podjampolsky asked the flankers how they could have allowed their officer to be cut down, they justified themselves by saying that Tornesi galloped into the throng of enemy soldiers and, refusing their demands to surrender, slashed and swore at them mercilessly, and they all suddenly rushed him. A number of sabers flashed over the unhappy Tornesi, and he fell to his horse's feet lifeless and disfigured.

We were all very attentively watching the battle already in progress to the right of the road, in which some of our squadrons were fighting outstandingly. We would have paid dearly for our idle neglect of other directions if our priest Wartminski, the most fearless man in the regiment, had not ridden over to us and pointed to our left with his riding-crop (his only weapon, which he used on horses and the enemy alike). We glanced where he was pointing and saw the enemy cavalry galloping up on our flank. Instantly Podjampolsky ordered, "Second half-squadron, left wheel!" and, once it was facing the enemy, ordered me to take command and immediately attack the onrushing horsemen. It was a thrilling moment for me! I no longer remembered the shameful flight of my uhlans from the picket; I saw only the possibility of winning glory. . . . But suddenly my order, "From your places, charge, charge!" merged with the thunderous voice of our commander resounding behind the lines, "Back! Back!" My half-squadron turned around instantly and galloped at breakneck speed down the highway, leaving me behind. The squadron was galloping in disarray in a dense throng across bushes, hummocks, and ruts. Zelant, my fiery, headstrong steed, tried to break loose under me, but I didn't dare give him his way. When overexcited, he has the bad habit of flinging up his head, and the choice before me was a very hard one: giving Zelant his way and at once falling with him into a pit or flying headfirst through a bush; or checking him and being overtaken by the enemy who flew at our heels. I chose the latter as less dangerous. I have long been familiar with the mediocrity of the French cavalry; I could be certain that there was not one horse in the entire detachment pursuing us who could match Zelant's speed; and so, checking my steed, I rode at a full gallop after the running squadron. But when I heard hoofbeats close behind me, I was carried away by involuntary curiosity and could not resist glancing back. My curiosity was well rewarded: I saw three or four enemy dragoons galloping after me two or three feet from my horse's hindquarters, brandishing their broadswords to strike at my back. At this sight, although I did not step up my running pace, I brought the flat of my saber down on Zelant's back, I don't know why. Dodging hummocks and pits, he carried me away from the enemy throng like a tempestuous whirlwind.

When we reached a smooth spot, we repaid the enemy for our chaotic flight: the squadron, obeying the voice of their officers, took only a minute to form ranks and rush like a menacing storm cloud to meet the enemy. The earth groaned under the hooves of our ardent steeds, the wind whistled in the pennons on our lances, and it seemed as if death with all its horrors was racing ahead of our brave uhlans' formation. The enemy could not withstand the sight and, trying to get away, was caught, beaten, scattered, and driven off with a much greater loss than we had sustained when we were forced to retreat so impetuously across the hummocks and ruts.

Now our squadron has been placed to the right of the road, and jaegers are occupying the hummocky field. "It should have been done long ago," says Podjampolsky, twisting his mustaches in vexation. We are here to guard the fortress, and so we stand without fighting, but in readiness— that is, on our horses with lances tilted. In front of us skirmishers from the Butyrsk regiment are exchanging fire with the enemy. A valiant, first-rate regiment! Immediately after it went into action, the enemy's bullets began falling short of us.

We will be on the same spot until tomorrow. The Butyrsk regiment was relieved by another, and now the bullets not only do not fall short, they are wounding us. Podjampolsky finds this very disagreeable. At last, tired of seeing one after another of us carried behind the lines, he sent me into Smolensk to Stackelberg to tell him about our critical position and ask him what he ordered done. I did as I was commanded; I told Stackelberg that many men were being wounded and asked him for orders.

"To stand," replied Stackelberg. "To stand without stirring even a pace from the spot. It's odd that Podjampolsky should send someone to ask."

I took great satisfaction in carrying this fine answer back to my captain. "Well?" shouted Podjampolsky to me from a distance, "what are the orders?"

"To stand, Captain."

"Well, stand it is," he said quietly and turned back to the front with the dauntless air that is so typical of him. He would have tried to encourage the soldiers somewhat, but he saw to his satisfaction that they had no need of it: the faces and eyes of our brave uhlans were cheerful. Their recent victory has given their features an animated heroism. Their entire appearance says: *Woe to the enemy!*

Toward evening the second half-squadron dismounted and, since that freed me to leave my place, I went over to the captain to ask him about everything which had puzzled me that day. Podjampolsky was standing by a tree, resting his head on his arm and watching the crossfire without a trace of concern. It was evident that his thoughts were elsewhere.

"Tell me, Captain, why did you send me to Stackelberg instead of the sergeant? You were trying to protect me from the bullets, weren't you?"

"It's true," replied Podjampolsky pensively. "You are still so young, you look so innocent, and amid these terrible scenes you're so cheerful and carefree! I saw you galloping after the rest of the squadron during our chaotic flight from the bricksheds, and it seemed to me that I saw a lamb pursued by a pack of wolves. Blood rushes to my heart at the very thought of seeing you killed. I don't know why, Aleksandrov, but it seems to me that if you were killed it would be a lawless act of murder. God spare me from witnessing it! Oh, bullets do not pick and choose. They are as likely to pierce the heart of a boy in the bloom of youth as the breast of an old warrior!"

I was surprised by my captain's melancholy mood and his extraordinary concern for me, which I had not remarked before. But then I remembered that he has a brother he loves dearly who remained in the Mariupol's, alone and at the mercy of fate and his own wits, and I found it quite natural that my look of immature youth and the dangers of the war reminded him of his brother, still a child himself, and the situations he might face in the heat of this war.

Night fell. The second half-squadron got back onto their horses, and the first dismounted. The gunfire ceased. I asked the captain for permission not to remount; he agreed, and we went on talking. "Explain to me, Captain, why so many of our officers are being wounded. There is such a dense mass of soldiers that it would be easier to kill more of them. Are they really aiming on purpose at the officers?"

"Of course," answered Podjampolsky. "That is the most effective way of disrupting and weakening enemy forces."

"Why is that?"

"Why? Because one brave, competent officer can do the enemy more harm with his knowledge, sagacity, and skill in using both the advantages of the landscape and the mistakes of the opposing side—particularly when he is an officer endowed with the lofty sense of honor which makes him face death dauntlessly and act coolly no matter how great the danger—such an officer, I repeat, can do more harm to the enemy than a thousand soldiers with nobody to command them. . . ."

We went on talking in the same vein for two hours or so. I listened attentively to the opinions and observations of Podjampolsky, who is the best officer in our regiment, brave, experienced, and as strict with himself as with others. The second half-squadron's turn to dismount put an end to our conversation. The captain got back on his horse and told me that I could sleep for half an hour now if I wished. I did not force him to repeat the offer twice, but at once took advantage of his permission. I bundled myself up in a soldier's raincape and lay down under a tree, resting my head on its roots.

At dawn, through a light sleep, I felt something smack against my helmet. Wide awake, I uncovered my head and saw Lieutenant-Colonel Lopatin and Podjampolsky standing near me. They were discussing something, looking and occasionally pointing toward the enemy skirmishers. I was ashamed that they had caught me asleep and hastened to get up. Just then a spent bullet struck my helmet. This explained the earlier noises. I gathered up the bullets lying beside me and carried them over to show the captain. "Well, what of it?" he said, laughing. "Do you really find it such a wonder?"

"Yes indeed! After all, they didn't get this far by rolling, they flew, so why didn't they wound me?"

"They didn't have the force. That's enough now, get back on your horse. We're being relieved immediately."

A squadron of dragoons arrived to take our place, and we went into the fortress and settled down to rest under the walls.

Smolensk has been surrendered to the enemy! During the night our rearguard climbed the heights across the river. Raevsky looked with regret at the blazing city. Someone in the crowd of officers surrounding him blurted out, "What a beautiful picture!"

"Especially for Engelhardt," interjected one of the general's adjutants. "He has two houses on fire there."[8]

We are still retreating! Why on earth did they announce to us that the emperor would no longer restrain our courage? It seems as if our valor has not been put to much of a test. As I see it, we are retreating into the heart of Russia. It will go badly for us if the enemy stops in Smolensk! Only Napoleon's boundless presumption ensures us of the opportunity to lure him farther. It is all beyond my comprehension, however. Was it really impossible to meet and rout the enemy at our nation's borders? Why these dangerous tactics? Why lead the enemy so far into the middle

8. After two days of indecisive fighting, on the night of August 5–6 the Russians began moving out of a Smolensk reduced to fire and ruins by the French artillery. On October 15 the Smolensk landowner Pavel Engelhardt was shot by the French as a Russian spy.

of our land? Perhaps there is some excellent goal behind it, but the troops may lose heart before we attain it or figure it out. Already one hears from all sides conclusions and conjectures, each sadder and more absurd than the last.

My turn came to serve as orderly to Konovnitsyn.[9] The general likes to come as close to the enemy as possible and seems to regard any and all dangers as trifling. At least he is as calm in the midst of battle as in his own room. A skirmish started. The general rode up to the forward line, but since his suite immediately attracted the enemy's attention and bullets, he ordered us to disperse. I don't know why, but we were slow to obey him, and in the interval his horse was wounded under him. The enemy concentrated their fire on our group, and this forced Konovnitsyn to retreat a little from the line of flankers. When we all turned to follow him, I didn't notice that my vexatious Zelant, who has a long stride, was moving out ahead of the general's horse. Seeing this, Konovnitsyn asked me very sternly, "Where are you going, sir? Don't you know that you should ride behind and not ahead of me?" In shame and vexation I checked my horse. The general undoubtedly thought that it was fear that made me go faster.

Konovnitsyn needed to send someone to the left flank to find out from General Sievers if, in case of retreat, the roads were safe and convenient for his withdrawal, if he had enough men, and if he would need reinforcements. I was the one who reported to receive his orders. "Oh, no," said Konovnitsyn, taking one look at me, "you're too young. You can't be trusted with this; send someone older."

I blushed. "Won't Your Excellency be so good as to try me? Perhaps I might be in condition to understand and carry out your orders."

"Ah . . . very well! Excuse me," said Konovnitsyn hurriedly and in a courteous tone. He gave me his orders, adding that I should go as quickly as possible. I was no sooner out of sight when, uneasy with the idea of trusting me, he sent a second orderly in my tracks with the same instructions. This was clearly an act of God's intercession, because the enemy immediately occupied the areas I passed through on my way to see Sievers. On the way back I met the second orderly and found out from him that there were enemy skirmishers along my previous route.

I returned to Konovnitsyn and recounted to him in great detail the

9. Durova could have served as Konovnitsyn's orderly only after he was assigned to replace Platov as commander of the rearguard. He took up the post on August 19, a day or two after Kutuzov's arrival at the front (below). Petr Konovnitsyn had a long and distinguished career as "one of the outstanding combat generals of Alexander's epoch. He liked the soldiers, knew how to talk to them, and took very good care of them; the soldiers in return were extremely attached to him and performed miracles of bravery under his command" (*Voennaja entsiklopedia*, vol. 13 [1913], 120).

position of Siever's detachment, routes, crossings, supplies—in short, everything I had been ordered to find out. After hearing my report, Konovnitsyn praised me highly, asked my forgiveness for his doubts about entrusting the mission to me because of my youth and, evidently trying to make up for it, sent only me everywhere the rest of the day, saying with each mission, "You're more reliable than the others." After I had spent the day rushing through the fields from one regiment to the next, I was worn out, tired, perishing from hunger, and no longer at all pleased with my new fame as a reliable orderly. Poor Zelant resembled a *borzoj*.

The sun had already set by the time we made camp. I had no sooner dismounted than I had to get back on my horse again. Podjampolsky said that it was my turn to fetch hay for the entire regiment. "Here are ten men from my squadron; the others will be along right away. Good luck to you!" He added in a low voice, "And can't you get us something to eat? A goose or a chicken? There's been nothing but bread for days now. I'm sick to death of it!"

Fifty uhlans reported to my command, and I set out with them down the first road we crossed, looking for haymaking, since at this season the harvest is already underway. The night was very warm, but also very dark; there was no moon. We had gone about six versts from camp when we saw a village about half a verst away. It took us only three minutes to reach it, because we were so delighted by our quick find that we headed for it at a trot. A broad meadow adjoined the village; we could see a little river, and beyond it a few scraggy clumps of trees. I ordered the uhlans to take their horses to the meadow and remained alone in the abandoned village. Tying up my horse, I went to take a closer look at the deserted dwellings. There was something dreadful about seeing all the doors left open. Gloom, silence, and desolation reigned everywhere. Nothing was closed; stables, sheds, granaries, storerooms, and houses were all agape. Cattle and sheep, however, were walking, lying, and standing around in the yard, and geese were sitting in flocks. Poor geese! The sight of them reminded me of Podjampolsky's appeal, reminded me that one of them surely must die. Oh, how ashamed I am to write this! How ashamed to confess such inhumanity! With my noble saber I cut off the head of an innocent bird!! It was the first blood I had ever shed in my life. And, although it was the blood of a bird, please believe me, you who will someday read my *Notes*, that the memory of it weighs heavily on my conscience.

An hour later my uhlans returned, leading horses piled high with hay. "Haven't you made those loads too heavy?" I asked when I saw the huge sheaves hanging on their horses' flanks.

"No, your honor, hay is light, you know."

I believed them. I didn't suspect at all that a weight unknown to me was concealed there, that the hay had been bound up into those awesome mounds for a purpose. I remounted, ordered them to bring the dead goose, and rode ahead of my detachment who walked and led their horses by the reins. We had already gone more than halfway and were about two versts from camp when an uhlan suddenly galloped up. "Hurry, your honor, the regiment's leaving soon!"

I ordered my men to go as fast as they could. They broke into a run and, naturally, the horses began to trot. I was astonished to see sheep falling off horses here and there in my detachment. Before I had the chance to ask them why they had collected so many, another uhlan galloped up with orders from the regiment to abandon the hay and hurry back. I ordered the men to leave everything on the spot—hay, sheep, and my goose—and to mount and return to the regiment at a trot. We caught up with it already on the march.

"What does this mean, Captain? Why is the regiment moving on so soon?"

"That's an odd question, what does it mean! We're ordered, and we go. We're not on an outing; this is war!"

I said no more. The captain was out of sorts, undoubtedly from hunger. I was hungry, too, and besides, I got no sleep at all that night.

We have a new commander-in-chief: *Kutuzov!* I heard the news while I was standing in a circle of orderlies, adjutants, and many other officers crowded around the campfire. The hussar general Dorokhov stroked his gray mustaches and said, "Let's hope to God that Mikhajlo 'Larionovich gets here as soon as possible and stops us. We keep on running as if we were rolling downhill."

Kutuzov has arrived! Soldiers, officers, generals—all are ecstatic. Misgivings have given way to calm and confidence. Our entire camp is ebullient and imbued with courage.[10]

A cold, piercing wind has turned my body to ice. My greatcoat not only has no batting; it has nothing, no lining at all. My *kolet* is lined with taffeta, and that is my only protection against a wind as cold as winter.

*Borodino.* In the evening our entire army settled down in bivouac near the village of Borodino. Kutuzov intends to give the battle that everyone

---

10. Mikhail Kutuzov was named commander-in-chief replacing Barclay de Tolly on August 8; he left Peterburg on August 11 and reached the front a week later. The armies heard the news only a day or two before his arrival. Durova's service as Konovnitsyn's orderly, which she placed earlier, took place during the succeeding march to Borodino.

has so long wished and waited for. Our regiment as usual occupies the front line. [11]

Tonight, no matter how I curled up in a ball and muffled myself in my greatcoat, I could neither warm up nor fall asleep. Our shelter was set up *à jour*, and the wind whistled through it like a broken window. My comrades, who have warm greatcoats, are sleeping peacefully. I would have been glad to lie near a fire, but none has been lit.

*August 24.* The wind has never let up. The signal cannon began to rumble menacingly at dawn. Its roar carried, rolling and echoing, throughout the entire vast space occupied by our army. Overjoyed to see daylight, I at once left my restless lodging. Before the boom of the cannon had completely died away, everyone was on his feet. In a quarter of an hour everything was in motion, preparing for the battle. The French are coming toward us in dense columns. The whole field has turned black, covered with their countless multitudes. [12]

*The 26th.* [13] A hellish day! I have gone almost deaf from the savage, unceasing roar of both artilleries. Nobody paid any attention to the bullets which were whistling, whining, hissing, and showering down on us like hail. Even those wounded by them did not hear them; we had other worries!

To my great displeasure our squadron went on the attack repeatedly. I have no gloves, and my hands are so numb from the cold wind that I can barely flex my fingers. When we are standing still, I return my saber to its scabbard and bury my hands in the sleeves of my greatcoat, but when they order us to attack, I have to take out the saber and hold it barehanded in the wind and cold. I have always been very sensitive to cold and bodily pain in general. Now, bearing the brutal north wind to

---

11. The Russian armies reached the vicinity of Borodino on August 22. After a thirteen-hour battle the preceding day at Kolotsk Monastery, the Russian rear-guard took up a position southwest of Borodino near the village of Shevardino.

12. On August 24 the French attacked the exposed Russian rear-guard on the army's left flank at Shevardino; after a day of fierce fighting, the Russian troops retreated to join the main line of troops stretching south from Borodino.

13. Well over two hundred thousand troops took the field at Borodino on August 26; over a third of them were either killed or wounded that day. The Fourth Cavalry Corps, including Durova's regiment, was stationed between Raevsky's redoubt (a heavily fortified artillery position known in French sources as "la grande Redoute") and three minor fortifications (*flèches*) just south of it. The left flank of the Russian army was vulnerable, and the corps spent the day rushing to the defense of the redoubt and the *flèches* as they repeatedly changed hands. In *War and Peace* Pierre Bezukhov finds Raevsky's redoubt overrun with French and barely escapes with his life.

which I am exposed without protection day and night, I can feel that my courage has diminished since the start of the campaign. There is no timidity in my soul, my face has never changed color, I am calm, but I would be overjoyed to see an end to the fighting.

Oh, if only I could get warm and sense again that I have arms and legs! Now I cannot feel them.

My wish has been granted. How is not important; at least it has been granted. I am not in battle, I have warmed up, I can feel my arms and legs, and my left leg in particular gives me very tangible proof that I still have it: it is swollen, blackened, and aches unbearably. I received a contusion from a cannonball. The sergeant-major caught me before I could fall off my horse, supported me, and led me away from the lines. Despite the many battles I have been in, I had no concept at all of a contusion. I thought that receiving one did not count as being wounded, and, therefore, when I saw no blood on my knee, I returned to my post. Podjampolsky glanced around, saw me standing ahead of our line, and asked in astonishment, "Why did you come back?"

"I'm not wounded," I replied.

The captain, assuming I had been hit by a spent bullet, was reassured, and we continued to hold our position under fire until nightfall. Then the enemy began lighting us with incendiary balls which skipped picturesquely past our lines. At last even this sport ended, and everything quieted down. Our regiment moved back a little and dismounted, but Podjampolsky's squadron remained on horseback. I no longer had the strength to bear the torment I was suffering from my aching leg, the cold that turned my blood to ice, and a cruel ache in all my limbs (I think, because I had not been off my horse even for a minute all day). I told Podjampolsky that I could no longer keep to the saddle and that, if he would permit it, I would go to the wagon-train, where staff-doctor Kornilovich could see what was wrong with my leg. The captain agreed. At last the time has come when I went willingly to the wagons I had previously so scorned. I went without being seriously wounded! What can valor do against the cold?

Leaving the squadron I set out in the company of an uhlan down the road to the wagon-train, barely suppressing groans of pain. I was unable to go any farther than Borodino, however, and stopped in that hamlet, which was packed from one end to the other with wounded. After searching in vain for a cottage which would take me in and meeting refusals everywhere, I decided to enter and take a place without asking consent. I opened the door of a large peasant cottage, as dark as the grave, and was greeted by twenty voices shouting painfully at me from the gloomy depths, "Who's there?" "What for?" "Shut the door!" "What do you want?" "Who's that who came in?"

I replied that I was an uhlan officer, wounded, and had not been able to find quarters, and I asked them to let me spend the night there.

"Impossible!" "Impossible!" cried out several voices at once. "There's a wounded colonel here, and we're cramped as it is. . . ."

"Well then, the wounded colonel should know from his own experience how hard it is to look for quarters in that condition and, no matter how cramped you are, you should offer to let me stay with you and not drive me out."

To this sermon someone replied curtly, "Well, stay if you like. There's nowhere for you to lie down."

"That's my concern," I said, and, overjoyed to find myself in warmth at last, I crawled onto the stove and lay down on the edge of it, not only wearing all my weapons, but without even removing my helmet. My limbs began to thaw and the pain to subside, but my contused leg was as stiff as a board. I couldn't move it even slightly without pain. Worn out from cold, hunger, fatigue, and pain, I fell into a profound sleep in a minute.

At dawn I must have tried to turn over. Since I was sleeping on the very edge of the stove, the motion caused my saber to hang off it and start clanking. Everybody woke up and they all began shouting, "Who's there?" "Who goes there?" Their voices testified to a sharp fright. One of them cut short the alert by reminding his comrades about me, expressing himself in a most obliging way: "That's the uhlan fussing about, the one the devil brought us last night."

After that they all went back to sleep, but I could not: my leg was terribly painful, and a high fever had succeeded yesterday's chill. I got up and, seeing through a crack in the shutters that dawn was breaking, opened the door and went out, quitting the hospitable shelter where I had spent the night. My uhlan stood on the threshold with both our horses. The excruciating pain I felt when I had to put the weight of my left foot into the stirrup pressed involuntary tears from my eyes. Before we had gone half a verst, I was ready to dismount, lie down in the fields, and abandon myself to the will of fate. My leg was swollen and causing me unbearable pain. Fortunately, my uhlan caught sight of a cart in the distance which had only an empty barrel lying on it in which liquor had been carried to the army. He galloped off immediately and brought the cart over to me. They threw away the empty barrel, and I took its place, lying on the straw where it had lain. The uhlan led Zelant by the reins, and this was the way I came to the wagons, where I found my good friend, the regimental paymaster Burogo. Now I am sitting in his warm hut, wearing his sheepskin coat, and holding a glass of hot tea in my hands. My leg is bound with bandages soaked in alcohol. I hope this will help somewhat for lack of any better remedy. Kornilovich is not here; he is with the regiment.

I have completely recovered. Good soup, tea, and warmth have returned the strength and flexibility to my limbs. It is all as forgotten as a
dream, although my leg still hurts. But why think about that? Besides, it
really does seem to me that my contusion is the lightest possible.

After spending two days in Burogo's hut, I hurried back to the regiment. I was given a small detachment, twenty-four uhlans in all, to take
with me to bring the squadron up to strength.[14]

14. Once Kutuzov assessed the heavy toll of the day's combat at Borodino, he decided
not to renew the battle, and the Russians again took up the retreat toward Moscow.

# Chapter Nine

We are retreating toward Moscow and are now only ten versts away. I asked Stackelberg for permission to make a quick trip into the city to order a warm jacket tailored, and, when he said I could, I turned my horse over to an uhlan and set out with a pair of half-dead nags I hired in the village. I was hoping to stay in the Kremlin with my father's faithful friend and comrade-in-arms, Mitrofanov, but I found out that he had gone away. While I was inquiring after him, I made visits to a number of the inhabitants of the vast building where he had his apartment. One of these forays took place on the rooms of a merchant's young wife. She began talking as soon as she saw me opening her door, "Come in, come in, officer, kind sir! I beg you humbly, be so good, be seated. You're limping; it's from a wound, of course, isn't it? Would you like some tea? Katenka, tea, and be quick about it."

Saying all this, she seated me on the sofa and Katenka, a sweet child of fourteen, a blooming beauty of the merchant type, was already standing before me with a cup of tea.

"So, sir, is our arch enemy far off? They say he's coming to Moscow."

I replied that he would not be permitted to enter Moscow.

"Oh, God grant! What should we ever do then? They say he is forcing everyone to take his faith."

How could I answer such questions? The little one piped up also in her thin voice, "We hear that he brands all the prisoners over the heart." She pointed to her own heart as she said this.

"That could well be," I replied. "I've heard something of the sort, too."

They would have gone on plying me with questions, but I stood up and told them that I had to hurry back to my post.

"The Lord be with you then, sir," said both sisters, accompanying me through the corridors to the staircase.

My jacket was finished. I put it on and would have liked to leave the city immediately, but that was not so easy to do. The enemy was not far off, many coachmen had left Moscow, and those who remained asked fifty rubles to take me to headquarters; since I did not have even one ruble, let alone fifty, I set out on foot. After walking about three versts on paving, I was compelled to lie down on the ground just outside the city gates. My leg had begun to ache and swell again, and I could no longer put any weight on it. Fortunately, a supply-wagon loaded with saddles, sweatcloths, canteens, knapsacks, and other such petty military supplies came by. There was an officer with it, and I asked him to give me a ride on the wagon. At first he refused, saying that he couldn't abandon any of the supplies and there was no room for me. But I persuaded him to make a place for me by submitting to him that not only an officer, but even a common soldier, is dearer to the emperor than twenty such wagons.

At headquarters I climbed down, thanked the officer, and went limping off in search of Schwartz in order to beg a horse from him; mine had remained with the regiment. I found Schwartz in Count Siever's quarters. We had not seen each other since the action at Borodino; he was surprised to see me and asked why I was not with the regiment. I told him about the contusion and the pain, and Moscow and my jacket, and ended by adding that I would like to get back to the regiment as soon as I could and needed a horse in order to do so. Schwartz gave me a hideous Cossack horse with a thin, elongated neck. It was wearing a vile saddle with an enormous bolster. On this steed, which even in its best years had had neither fire nor speed, I returned to the regiment. I was burning with impatience to mount my brisk, proud Zelant and was greatly vexed to learn that he had been sent with the reserve horses to a village five versts farther off.

We passed through Moscow and stopped two or three versts beyond it. The main army went farther.

Soon afterward our ancient capital burst into flames at many spots. The French are totally improvident. Why did they set fire to our beautiful city and the magnificent quarters they had leased at such great cost? What strange people! . . . All of us watched with regret as the fire intensified and covered almost half the sky with a bright glow. The surrender of Moscow has left us in a bewildered state; the soldiers seem frightened by it. Sometimes the words escape them, "It would have been better to perish to a man than give up Moscow!" Of course, they say this in low voices to one another, and in such cases an officer has no obligation to hear it.[1]

There is a small village situated on our left flank with not a single person left in it. I asked the captain how long we would be standing here.

"Who can tell?" he replied. "We are not allowed to light fires, so evidently we have to be prepared to go at a moment's notice. But why do you want to know?"

"Just so I could go take a quick nap in the nearest house. My leg is very painful."

1. The Russian armies passed through the city on the night of September 1–2; the fire, set at the instigation of Moscow governor Fedor Rostopchin, broke out at about eight o'clock on the evening of the second.

"Go on then. Let the sergeant stand outside the cottage with your horse. When the regiment leaves the spot, he will rouse you."

I promptly ran to the homestead, entered the cottage and, seeing that the floors and benches were broken, found no better place than the stove. I climbed up on it and lay down on the edge. The stove was warm; it had evidently been recently heated. The closed shutters made the cottage rather dark. Warmth and darkness, two blessed comforts! I fell asleep at once.

I think I must have slept no more than half an hour, because I woke quickly to repeated exhortations, "Your honor, your honor! The regiment has left. The enemy's in the village!"

Fully awake, I hastened to get up, and, as I began putting weight on my left hand, I felt something soft under it. I turned to look, and, since it was dark, I bent very close to the object I had rested my hand on. It was a dead man, evidently a militia recruit. I don't know whether I would have lain down on the stove if I had seen this neighbor first, but now it didn't even occur to me to be frightened. What odd encounters there are in life, and particularly in the present war![2] I left the silent inhabitant of the hut to his eternal rest and went out into the street. The French were already in the village and firing at any and all of our men. I rushed to mount my horse and caught up with the regiment at a trot.

Stackelberg sent me for hay for the regimental horses and, willy-nilly, I had to ride the horse which was stubborn, lazy, and ugly as a donkey. I sent my troops on ahead and rode after them, pondering my disagreeable situation. With this steed, shame and woe awaited me at the first action: it could neither run toward the enemy nor carry me away from him. . . .

"That's where our reserve horses are," said one of the uhlans to a comrade, pointing toward a nearby hamlet. It was a verst distant from the road down which I was leading my detachment. The idea that I could get my horse back flashed into my mind, calming and dispelling all my gloomy thoughts. I charged the sergeant to lead the detachment at a walk to the forest nearby, and I myself did not so much gallop as jolt my way as fast as I could to the village where I hoped to find our reserve horses.

Fate had no mercy on me. I didn't find my horse there. These were not our regiment's reserves; the uhlan horses were still farther away, three versts from this hamlet. Suffering from a vexation that can only be imagined, I went on riding the unhappy, hungry donkey who would not

2. In the 1839 *Notes* (201), Durova remarked on the habituation to death that takes place during an extended campaign: "In our present life there is nothing so ordinary and nothing that attracts less attention than death. This is its dominion, and it is exactly here that nobody thinks about it or fears it; everyone finds it beneath notice. 'And where's such-and-such?' 'Killed.' 'Well, then send me so-and-so.' 'He's been killed, too.' 'Well, you fool, don't just keep parroting *killed, killed.* Send for a sergeant who's still alive.' "

go except at a walk, and a very lazy walk at that. It was the most tormenting state I had ever experienced. If I were given my choice between taking part in two more battles of Borodino or having to ride that horse for two days, I would choose the former immediately without a second's hesitation.

I located and took my Zelant, but it cost me dearly. Determined to escape from my disagreeable situation no matter what, with spurs and saber I forced my poor horse to carry me at a trot to the second hamlet and there, to my delight, the first object that met my eyes was Zelant. I changed mounts and flew like an arrow to the forest where I had sent my detachment. I hoped to locate it by its tracks, but I was bewildered by the great number of roads leading right, left, and crosswise, and all covered with countless traces of hooves. I took a guess, rode three versts down a road which appeared to me to be wider than the rest, and came to a manor of handsome architecture. The flower bed before the porch giving onto the garden had been completely trampled by horses. Rich silks and laces trailed along the lanes; traces of pillage were visible everywhere. Finding nobody at all there and having no idea how to locate my troops, I decided to return to the regiment.

When he saw me alone, Stackelberg asked, "So where are your men?"

I told him frankly that, wishing to fetch my horse from the nearby hamlet, I ordered the detachment to go at a walk to the forest and wait for me there, but when I got back I couldn't find them at the designated spot and now I didn't know where they were.

"How dare you do such a thing?" shouted Stackelberg. "How dare you leave your troops? You shouldn't have left them alone for even a second. Now they're lost: that forest has been occupied by the enemy. Go, sir! Find me those men, or I will report you to the commander-in-chief and you'll be shot!"

Stunned by this fusillade, I went back to the damned forest, but the enemy skirmishers were already in it.

"Where are you going, Aleksandrov?" asked an officer of the *leib*-squadron, who was standing in the forward line of our skirmishers.

I replied that Stackelberg had chased me out to look for my foragers.

"And have you really lost them?"

I told my story.

"That's all trifling, brother. Your foragers surely must have gone the long way around in safety, and by now they should be in the hamlet occupied by our rear-guard's reserve horses. Go there."

I followed his advice and, in fact, found my men with their loads of hay in the village. To my question, "Why didn't you wait for me?" they said they heard galloping and gunfire in the forest and thought it was the enemy. Having no wish to be taken captive, they rode farther, eight versts or so. There they found hay, loaded it on their horses, and came to wait for me. I took them to the regiment, presented them to Stackelberg, and then rode directly to the commander-in-chief.

I felt deeply insulted by Stackelberg's threat to have me shot, and I no longer wanted to remain under his command. Without dismounting, I wrote a note in pencil to Podjampolsky: "Inform Colonel Stackelberg that, since I am not eager to be shot, I'm going to see the commander-in-chief, with whom I will try to remain in the post of orderly."[3]

When I got to headquarters, I saw written in chalk on a set of gates the words: *To the commander-in-chief.* I dismounted and went into the hall, where I met some sort of adjutant.

"Is the commander-in-chief here?" I asked.

"Yes," he replied in a polite and cordial tone. But the adjutant's appearance and voice changed instantly when I said that I was looking for Kutuzov's quarters. "I don't know; this isn't it. Ask over there," he said curtly, without looking at me, and at once walked away.[4]

I went farther and again saw on some gates: *To the commander-in-chief.* This time I had found the place I wanted: in the anteroom were several adjutants. I went up to the one whose face seemed to me kinder than the others. It was Dzichkanets.

"Announce me to the commander-in-chief; I need to speak to him."

"About what? You can declare it through me."

"No, I can't. I must speak to him myself, and without witnesses. Don't refuse me this indulgence," I added, bowing courteously to Dzichkanets.

He went at once into Kutuzov's room. A minute later he opened the door, said to me, "If you please," and with this returned to the anteroom. I entered and, not only with due respect but with a feeling of reverence, bowed to the gray-haired hero, the venerable, great old military leader.

"What can I do for you, my friend?" asked Kutuzov, looking fixedly at me.

3. The military historian D. P. Buturlin, who served with the Fourth Cavalry Corps during the French retreat from Moscow, wrote an unflattering sketch of the commander of the Lithuanian Uhlans: "Colonel Stackelberg is a very stiff, taciturn, dull German, and stronger in body than in intelligence, besides. Military regulations guide him in all his actions and impulses, and he is brave only because regulations prescribe that all soldiers be brave" (*Russkaja starina* [1894], 11:197).

4. Durova's cool reception reflects the armies' confused command structure. "After the terrible losses at Borodino and during the rear-guard battles on the way to Moscow, the Russian army melted away to such a degree that its division into two armies became completely superfluous, especially since both armies were already seeing joint action. The existence of two separate army headquarters in addition to that of the commander-in-chief only hampered, delayed, and confused direction" (S. P. Mel'gunov, "Vozhdy armii," *Otechestvennaja vojna i russkoe obshchestvo*, vol. 4 [Moscow, 1912], 103). On September 7, when the various headquarters were located in Podol'sk, Kutuzov named Konovnitsyn as his adjutant-general in charge of restoring order to the chain of command.

"I would like the good fortune to be your orderly for the rest of the campaign, and I have come to ask you to grant me that favor."

"What's the reason for this extraordinary request and, even more so, for the way you propose it?"

I told him what had forced me to take this resolution and, carried away by recollection of the undeserved insult, spoke with emotion, fervor, and in bold terms; among other things, I said that I had been born and raised in an army camp and had loved military service from the day of my birth, that I had consecrated my life to it forever, that I was ready to shed my last drop of blood defending the welfare of the emperor, whom I revered as I did God, and that, with this way of thinking and the reputation of a brave officer, I did not deserve to be threatened with death. . . . I stopped, overcome with emotion as well as a degree of confusion: I had remarked the slight, ironic smile that appeared on the commander-in-chief's face at the words *brave officer,* and it made me blush. I guessed his thoughts and, in order to justify myself, decided to tell him *everything.*

"In the Prussian campaign, Your Excellency, all my commanders praised my daring so much and so unanimously—even Buxhöwden himself called it *peerless*—that, after all that, I consider I have a right to call myself brave without fear of being taken for a braggart."

"In the Prussian campaign! Can you really have been in the army then? How old are you? I assumed you to be no more than sixteen."

I said that I was in my twenty-third year and that in the Prussian campaign I served in the Polish Horse.[5]

"What's your name?" asked the commander-in-chief hastily.

"Aleksandrov."

Kutuzov stood up and embraced me, saying, "How glad I am at last to have the pleasure of meeting you in person. I have heard about you for a long time. Stay here with me, if you like. It will give me great pleasure to offer you a respite from the onerous rigors of the war. As for the threat to shoot you," added Kutuzov with a wry smile, "you shouldn't take it so much to heart. Those were hollow words, spoken in vexation. Go now to Adjutant-General Konovnitsyn, and tell him you're to be a permanent orderly on my staff."

I started out, but he called me back. "You're limping. Why is that?"

I said that in the battle of Borodino I received a contusion from a cannonball.

"A contusion from a cannonball! And you're not under medical care? Tell the doctor to examine your leg immediately."

I replied that the contusion was very slight and my leg hardly hurt me at all. I was lying when I said it: my leg was very painful and bruised all over.

5. Durova turned twenty-nine that month.

Now we are living in Krasnaja pakhra, at Saltykov's house.[6] We have been given a sort of plank hut, in which all of us (that is, the orderlies) huddle together and shiver from cold. Here I found Shlein, who was with me as orderly to Miloradovich in Kiev.

I am wasted by fever and quivering like an aspen leaf! . . . I am sent out to various places twenty times a day. To my woe, Konovnitsyn remembered that when I was his orderly I turned out to be the best of the lot. "Oh, hello, old friend," he said when he saw me on the porch of the house occupied by the commander-in-chief. And from that day I had no peace. Whenever someone had to be sent off in a hurry, Konovnitsyn shouted, "The uhlan orderly to me!" And the poor uhlan orderly dashed like a pale vampire from one regiment to the next, and sometimes from one wing of the army to the other.

At last Kutuzov sent for me.

"Well now," he said, taking my hand as I entered. "Is it more peaceful here with me than in the regiment? Have you rested up? How is your leg?"

I was forced to tell him the truth: my leg hurt unbearably, I ran a fever from it every day, and I managed to stay on my horse only mechanically, by habit, but I was weaker than a five-year-old child.

"Go home," said the commander-in-chief, looking at me with paternal compassion. "You really have lost weight, and you're terribly pale. Go home, rest, recover, and then come back."

At this proposal my heart constricted. "How can I go home now when not a single man is leaving the army?" I said sadly.

"What's to be done? You're ill. Will it be any better for you to be left behind in hospital somewhere? Go! We've stopped here without action for now, and perhaps we'll be here for a long time. In that case you'll succeed in finding us still in the same place."

I saw the necessity of following Kutuzov's advice. I could not bear up under the rigors of wartime life for even another week. "Will you permit me, Your Excellency, to bring my brother back with me? He is fourteen already. Let him begin his military career under your command."

"Very well, bring him," said Kutuzov. "I will take him onto my staff and be like a father to him."

Two days after this conversation Kutuzov sent for me again. "Here are your travel orders and money for horses," he said, handing me the one and the other. "Go with God! If you should have need of anything, write directly to me; I'll do all that is in my power. Goodbye, my friend." The great general embraced me with paternal tenderness.

6. Kutuzov's headquarters was in Krasnaja pakhra from September 8 to September 16.

Fever and the cart jolt me unmercilessly. I have a courier's orders, and for this reason all the coachmen gallop headlong, paying no heed to my orders to go slow. They are so frightened by my crimson stripes and lapels that, although they hear me telling them as I get into the carriage, "Go at a trot," they do not trust their ears. Urging their dashing steeds to a breakaway pace from the start, they stop them only at the porch of the next station. There is no ill without some good, however: I am no longer chilled; the agonizing jolting gives me an incessant fever.

In Kaluga a man, evidently an official of some sort, came to the post-station, waited until everybody else had left the room, approached me as quietly as a cat, and asked even more quietly, "Won't you permit me to know the content of your dispatches?"

"My dispatches! It would be a funny thing if couriers were told what is written in the papers they travel with! I don't know the content of my dispatches."

"Sometimes it is known to the honorable couriers. I'm discreet; nobody will find out anything from me," my tempter went on whispering, with a cordial mien.

"Nor from me. I am as discreet as you are," I said, standing up in order to get away from him.

"In a word, my dear fellow! Moscow—"

I didn't hear the rest; I got into my vehicle and drove off. Scenes like that one were repeated in many places and with many people. Evidently interrogating couriers was for them no novelty.

*Kazan.* I stopped for dinner at the Noblemen's Assembly. The horses were ready and waiting and my dinner nearly finished when a clerkish creature with a light step, squinting eyes, and a sly countenance entered the room. "Where do you deign to go?"

"To S . . ."[7]

"You are coming directly from the army."

"Yes, I am."

"Where is it located?"

"I don't know."

"How can that be?"

"Perhaps it has moved to some other spot."

"And where did you leave it?"

"In the field between Smolensk and Moscow."

"They say that Moscow has been taken, is that true?"

"Of course not!"

"How can that be? You don't want to tell me. Everybody says that it has been taken, and that must be right."

---

7. Sarapul.

"And if it's right, what more do you want?"

"Then perhaps you agree that the rumor is correct?"

"Not at all! Farewell, I have no time for talking or listening to nonsense about Moscow." I started to leave.

"Wouldn't you like to come see the governor? He has invited you to his house," said this sly character in a completely different tone.

"You should have told me that from the beginning instead of amusing yourself questioning me. But now I don't believe you and, besides, a courier is under no obligation to make visits to anyone."

The official rushed out precipitately, only to reappear two minutes later: "His Excellency most earnestly requests you to call on him. He has sent his carriage for you."

I went at once to see the governor. The honorable Mansurov began by expressing his gratitude for my prudence with regard to indiscreet questions.[8] "I was very pleased," he said, "to hear from my clerk how cautiously you answered him. I am greatly obliged to you for it. A scoundrel who broke away from the army tried to make trouble for me here; he spread so much nonsense and so alarmed the minds of our inhabitants that I was forced to put him under guard. Now I ask you to be frank with me: has Moscow been taken?"

I hesitated to answer. It would be ridiculous to deceive the governor, but there was another official standing there, and I did not want to respond to this vital question in his presence. The governor guessed my thoughts. "This is a close friend, my second self. I beg you not to conceal the truth from me. The emperor himself favors me with his confidence. Moreover, I need to know Moscow's lot in order to take rational measures for the city; unruly Tatars are gathering in crowds and waiting for a chance to take to violence. I have to forestall it. And so, has Moscow really been taken?"

"I can assure Your Excellency that it was not taken, but voluntarily surrendered, and this is our enemy's last triumph in the Russian land: his destruction is now inevitable!"

"On what do you base your conjectures?" asked the governor. His face expressed regret and alarm at the words of Moscow's surrender.

"These are not conjectures, Your Excellency, but complete conviction: the warrant of our enemies' destruction is the composure and cheerful look of all our generals, including the commander-in-chief himself. It would be unnatural of them to retain that composure of spirit after admitting the enemy into the heart of Russia and surrendering our ancient capital to him were they not assured of his quick and inevitable destruction. Take this into consideration, Your Excellency, and you will have to agree with me."

8. Boris Mansurov was governor of Kazan' from 1804 to 1814.

The governor talked with me a long time, questioning me about the operations and the present situation of the army. At last he bade me farewell and said many flattering things to me, ending up by telling me that Russia would not have had to resort to the extreme measure of surrendering Moscow if all the officers in the army were like me. Such praise from a man like Mansurov would turn the head of anyone—and me most of all, who can expect a host of rumors, conclusions, speculations, and slander whenever my sex is revealed. Oh, how indispensable the testimony of men like Mansurov, Ermolov, and Konovnitsyn will be to me then! . . .

## THE TATAR'S TALE

Vast, dense, impenetrable primeval forests begin beyond Kazan. In winter the highway that runs through them is as narrow as any country lane. The latter roads have the added advantage over the former of being sometimes shorter and always cheaper. This last circumstance was not unimportant to me, and from the second station I turned off the highway onto a small road which took me deeper into the thickets of the pine forest every hour. Night fell. Nothing stirred in the primeval forest, and the only sounds were my coachman's exhortations and the doleful songs of an old Tatar who had ridden with me from Kazan. He had asked me for permission to ride on the box of my carriage and, in return, served me on the road.

"Gajda, gajda, Khamitulla!" he sang in the drawling and melancholy melody of his people; it was the refrain of some never-ending song.

Weary of listening to the same thing for an entire hour, I asked him, "What is this Khamitulla, Jakub, that you keep dinning into my ears?"

Jakub turned around crossly on the box. "What is Khamitulla? Khamitulla was the handsomest man of all our folk!"

"Of your family, Jakub, or the entire Tatar tribe?"

Jakub didn't answer. I thought that he was angry again as usual, but the gray-haired Tatar looked somberly into the depths of the forest and sighed. I left him to what were evidently thoughts of Khamitulla and covered my head with my greatcoat, intending to go to sleep.

Suddenly Jakub swung around to face me: "Barin!9 We are now riding through the very forest where Khamitulla so long hid and wandered, where the mere mention of his name and his supposed robberies inspired horror in travelers, where they searched for him, pursued him, and at last captured him. Poor Khamitulla! I couldn't believe my eyes when I saw him in chains, a kind and upright person, a model son, brother, friend!

9. Master! (Russian)

In chains for a crime, for robbery! What would you think, *barin*, what was his crime, what sort of robberies? Would you like to know?"

"Yes indeed, Jakub. Tell me."

"I like to speak of him. I marvel at him and mourn his grievous fate with all the heartache of a father. . . . Yes, I loved Khamitulla like a son.

"He was seventeen when I paid the *kalym*[10] for my second wife and went to live with my father-in-law in the village of * * * to help him in his labors. The house of Khamitulla's father was next to ours. At that time I was forty-two years old; I had no children of my own, and I became wholeheartedly attached to the gallant youth, who loved me like a father, too. He was not only the handsomest of our young men, but the finest marksman and boldest rider as well. Sometimes after he had tamed a bad-tempered, unbroken horse, he would bring it to me and say, 'Look, Jakub, these are the only sort I like to ride. What good are the meek ones? Oh, if only there were no meek horses in the world!'

"I laughed. 'Why on earth, Khamitulla, do you want all of us to break our necks riding frenzied horses? It's fine for you—you're young, strong, a famous rider, but I and your old father, what would we do?'

" 'True! I never thought of that. . . .' And, at a run, the scamp led his beloved horse off to graze.

"But there came a time when neither a good steed nor a taut bow could divert Khamitulla any longer. His fiery steeds flew over hill and dale with sweeping manes, but Khamitulla never thought to saddle any of them. He took pleasure in staying home and passing now and then by the window of Zugra, the daughter of one of the richest Tatars in the village. Zugra was a tall, swarthy, stately Tatar girl, with black eyes and brows, of course, although charms of that sort are no rarity among Tatar girls: almost all of them have black eyes. But the blackness of Zugra's eyes and brows was somehow a captivating black! Something in them made Khamitulla's heart ache cruelly."

"But, Jakub, how did your Khamitulla manage to see his beloved? After all, your Tatar girls are hidden from men."

"But not from those whom they seek to please; then they are very skillful in letting themselves be seen. It was enough that Khamitulla could tell the charming blackness of his Zugra's eyes and brows from twenty other pairs of eyes and brows which were just as black. 'Her eyes blaze, and her brows are lustrous! I swear it to you, Jakub, I swear on the Koran,' the young lover would repeat before me.

" 'Are you in your right mind, Khamitulla? Have you really no comrades of your own age, that you come to talk such nonsense to me, and even swear to it on the Koran?'

10. Bride-price. (Tatar)

" 'Comrades! Tell my comrades about Zugra? Oh, they know about her only too well, and I am surely not about to pour oil on the flames.'

" 'Well, what do you want then? Have you asked your father to pay the *kalym* for her?'

" 'Yes, I have.'

" 'And what did he say?'

" 'It is not money, but a fortune! Zugra's father wants a *kalym* that no one in the village can pay, least of all I.'

" 'In that case there's nothing to be done, Khamitulla. Be sensible, try to forget her, master yourself. Do something useful—trading, for instance. Go to Kazan.'

" 'I have to go anyway,' said my young friend dejectedly, 'and I will go. My father is sending me to sell *khalaty*;[11] I will be there until spring.'

" 'And how soon do you leave?'

" 'In a week.'

"I was delighted to hear it. I assumed that in Kazan, a beautiful and populous city, amid worries, diversions, and a variety of objects of interest, the young Tatar would have no time to fret about his passion. Little did I know Khamitulla!

"He went; he wrote often to his father, accounted in detail for his sales, sent him the money he had earned, made no attempt to hasten his return, and never once mentioned Zugra. I was delighted, thinking that absence had worked its effect, that the lad had quieted down, but little did I know Khamitulla!

"In the meantime, while he was trading, pining, despairing, hoping, and awaiting the first flowers of spring in order to return to the paternal roof, Aburashid, Zugra's father, was receiving proposals of *kalym* for her from far and wide. The old Tatar's greed grew in measure with their increase in value. At last a rich merchant came from a far-away town and offered a price that Aburashid could no longer resist: Zugra was pledged and given in marriage. On the evening of the day when Zugra shed bitter tears on a magnificent collar on her breast, the gift of her young husband—on that very evening Khamitulla arrived.

"No one saw on the face of the young Tatar any sign of the sorrow, let alone the frenzy or despair that could have been expected judging by his first impulse when he heard about Zugra's wedding. I chanced to be the first to meet him as he rode into the village and, supposing it would be easier for him to hear the fatal news from me, I told it to him with all the affection and consolation of a father. At the first words Khamitulla turned as pale as a sheet and began trembling in all his limbs. Convulsively he snatched up an axe which was lying in his cart, but he recovered instantly and, to my inexpressible astonishment, listened quite

11. Robes. (Turkic)

coldly to the entire history of the matchmaking, the tears, the resistance, and, at last, the wedding of his poor Zugra. I was delighted by this indifference and blessed the fickleness of the human heart. But, oh, *barin,* little did I know Khamitulla!

"That night Zugra disappeared from her husband's bed and Khamitulla from his father's plank bench. Neither of them was anywhere to be found. Zugra's husband nearly went out of his mind; he rode into the city and presented a complaint. A court came; searches and sweeps began. At last it was discovered that Khamitulla was living with his Zugra in a primeval wilderness forty versts across—the forest we are passing through right now. Well, how could it be possible to find him here, much less capture him? I was wholeheartedly delighted at this circumstance; it eased my fears for Khamitulla at present. But what would happen later? Where could he take refuge in winter? What would he eat, what would he wear? How could he live in the forest in that season which in our land is so terrible? . . .

"Meanwhile, Zugra's father and husband rode out in the forest every day, accompanied by an escort of all their relations. The district police were also searching for Khamitulla who, as rumor had it, was here and there taking bread, and sometimes even money, from passersby without, however, ever doing anyone the slightest injury. Almost all the summer passed in these searches and rumors. Autumn came. Common talk had already proclaimed Khamitulla an outlaw, although he never raised a hand to anyone, and, if he did take something from them, it was always such a small amount that it could serve only to buy bread. But the district police now brought volunteers into the search and began hunting for the outlaw Khamitulla with all the zeal of active officials.

"One rainy night, when the moon had already set and it was so dark that nothing could be seen at two paces, I sat up later than usual. For some reason I was melancholy. Thoughts, most mournful thoughts, drifted through my mind one after the other—they were all of Khamitulla. The resolution of my beloved boy's sad tale was fast approaching; winter would reveal all and end all. Horrible! At last I went to bed. I could no longer keep my eyes open, and I think that I must have gone to sleep, but a light tap at the window and the whisper of a familiar voice roused me swiftly from my bed in horror and involuntary joy. 'Khamitulla,' I cried out in tears and could say no more; the words died away. I could only press my poor friend's trembling hand. I could not ask him into my cottage, I could not offer him shelter, warmth, food. It was enough to break my heart! 'Khamitulla, run for it! The village is full of volunteers. The commissioner himself is searching for you. Run quickly!'

"'Come out to me, Jakub,' said Khamitulla in a voice that I could barely hear. 'Come out to me, come with me outside the village, into the forest. I have much to tell you.'

"I went out, and we walked arm and arm out of the village into the fields. A verst from us the dark forest loomed; we took cover in it. I wanted to stop there. 'No, my father, let's go farther. I have need of you. You will render me a service, perhaps a final one. . . .'

"I had no strength to speak and walked on in silence, following where Khamitulla led me. A torrential rain lashed my face and head mercilessly—in my haste I had rushed out without a cap. We walked for over half an hour at the quickest possible pace.

"'Here,' said Khamitulla, suddenly stopping and halting me. 'Here, Jakub, is my poor Zugra! . . .' He rushed over to a kind of hillock that looked like a haycock or a heap of straw. I went after him and saw him bringing a woman out from under a pile of pine branches; it was Zugra! With moans that rent my heart, Khamitulla pressed her to his heart, 'Zugra! My Zugra! My only earthly blessing! We must part. . . .' He fell in despair to the grass and embraced the knees of the weeping Zugra. She sat down beside him, pulled his head to her breast, embraced him, pressed her lips to the exhausted youth's pale face, and kissed him passionately, shedding the bitterest of tears. . . . I was sobbing violently. Oh, *barin!* What emotions sometimes lie concealed beneath our rough exterior and in the depths of the wild, impenetrable forests of our cold land!

"When the first gusts of the cruelest of all the pains of love—the pains of parting—had spent themselves somewhat, Zugra began to speak, 'Let us submit to our fate for a time, my sweet friend. Let us part until you find a place where we can once again be together. I will go to my father, but not to my husband, not for anything! He is no husband to me! They did not ask my consent. Let my father return the *kalym*. I am yours, yours forever. I have had no other husband.'

"'Oh, Zugra, Zugra, we are parting forever!' said the young Tatar dejectedly; then, becoming gradually more and more frenzied at the thought of eternal separation, he began to beat his breast savagely, crying in a despairing voice, 'Zugra! I will never see you again. Kill me, Jakub! Kill me! What is life to me without Zugra?'

"Meanwhile dawn was beginning to break. I tried to bring Khamitulla to his senses and, pointing out to him the light in the east, said that if he did not want to be seized by the volunteers he should decide on something immediately. 'I still don't know why you brought me here to the forest. You spoke of some service or other; what can I do for you? In me you have the heart and hand of a father; make use of them, demand of me anything that can ease the cruelty of your lot. . . .'

"Khamitulla stood up, embraced Zugra once more, and long held her in his arms, pressing her convulsively to his breast. . . . At last he turned her over to me and, turning so pale that not even a dead man could be paler, said in a fading voice, 'Take her, Jakub! Hide her at first from the wrath of her father and husband and the jeers of malicious people. Take my Zugra . . . Zugra, Zugra! . . . Jakub, why don't you want to kill me?'

"Fearing a new outburst of despair, I seized the young Tatar girl by the arm and ran with her as fast as my strength allowed to the outskirts of the village. Her tears were choking her.

"When I got home, I turned Zugra over to my wife and went to the council hut to learn what measures were underway for the capture of Khamitulla. They told me that all the paths into the forest were posted with guards, the lieutenant-colonel himself had taken charge, and the late season furthered all their maneuvers, because the falling leaves bared the forest and permitted them to see deep into the thickets. The unfortunate Khamitulla was sure to be captured! Returning home, I found Zugra asleep. The poor thing was thin and pale. She quivered incessantly and, through her sobs, pronounced indistinctly, 'Khamitulla! Oh, Khamitulla!'

"It would take a long time, *barin*, to tell you all that I learned from Zugra about their life in the forest, their inexpressible happiness, and, at last, the mortal anguish and forebodings of woe that constricted their breasts at the sight of the falling leaves. The forest grew barer with each passing day, becoming for them not a refuge, but a transparent dungeon. It was then that Khamitulla decided to entrust Zugra to me and flee somewhere farther off until a more propitious time. But in this he could not succeed: the district police, commanded by the chief himself (an army lieutenant-colonel), undertook such active measures that, after a few days of continual pursuit and sweeps, my poor friend, my stalwart, brave Khamitulla, despite heroic resistance, was seized, fettered, carried off to the city, and put in prison. They tried him, and . . . but no! I can't go on talking about it. The memory has once again aggravated the ancient wound in my heart. He was innocent of human blood, but they treated him like a killer. The main crime charged against him was that in a skirmish with the volunteers he wounded the police chief and left him sprawled dead to the world on the road. That was the only blood which Khamitulla shed in the course of all his disastrous wanderings in the forest. . . ."

The Tatar hid his face in his hands and sighed deeply or, more accurately, moaned, bending his head almost to his knees. . . . I allowed some time for this outburst of grief to settle before asking him, "What became of Zugra?"

"Her father took Zugra back. She threatened to kill herself if she were returned to her husband. Her beauty, unhappy love, silent grief, and inconsolable tears made her an object of the keenest sympathy to all, but she was dead to everything except her memories of Khamitulla. She wept for him day and night, sitting behind her curtain, and it was she who composed the song that you heard from me. In it she portrays the happy time of their love in the primeval wilderness, dread of approaching separation, fright at the resounding voices of the volunteers searching the forest for traces of her dear one . . . and, at last, the final parting! All our village sings this song."

"And what does the chorus mean, 'Gajda, gajda, Khamitulla'?"

" 'Gajda' means 'hurry' or 'go' or 'let's go' depending on how the word is used." Jakub fell silent.

Wilderness, primeval wilderness, in your impenetrable depths, the lair of ferocious beasts, burned a love that words cannot express! Khamitulla is long gone, but his name still resounds in the places where he was so happy, where he loved and was loved peerlessly. How often has the echo of the forest repeated his name, pronounced now in the whisper of love, now in the stern voice of a tracker, now, at last, in the doleful song of a Tatar girl, poor bereaved Zugra?

I am home at last! My father greeted me in tears. I told him I had come home to warm up. Papa cried and laughed as he examined my greatcoat, which has lost all its color and is riddled with bulletholes, scorched, and in spots burned through. I gave it to Natalja, who says she will make a dressing-gown out of it.

I told my father how kindly disposed the commander-in-chief is toward me and convinced him to let me take my brother back with me. He agreed to what is for him a cruel separation, but only under the condition that we wait until spring; I did my best to persuade Papa that this was impossible for me, but he refused to listen. "You can go," he said, "as soon as you're well again, but I will not send Vasily off in the winter at such a tender age and in such troubled times! No, no, go alone if you want. He'll have time yet; he's not even fourteen."

What can I do? It will take time for Papa to get used to the idea of parting with his dearly beloved son. I cannot wait that long, and so I wrote to Kutuzov that: "as eagerly as I desire to be back under his glorious banners, I cannot hope for the happiness of standing under them beside my brother, because my elderly father does not want to send an immature boy off to the bloody field of battle in this harsh season and urges me, if possible, to wait for warm weather," and now I don't know what I should do.

I received an answer from Kutuzov. He writes that I have every right to carry out my father's will; that, since I was sent home by the head of the army, I am not obliged to account to anyone except him for the length of my absence; that he permits me to wait at home until spring; and that I will lose nothing in the men's opinion by doing so, because I shared the dangers and rigors with my comrades to the end, and the commander-in-chief can testify personally to my fearlessness.

This letter was in the handwriting of Kutuzov's son-in-law, Khitrovo. Papa knew his hand well, because Khitrovo had lived for a time in V***, and my father had occasion to correspond with him. I showed the letter to Papa, and my elderly father was so touched by the renowned military leader's grace and consideration to me that he could not help weeping. I would have liked to preserve the letter as a souvenir of the kindly disposition toward me of the greatest of Russian heroes, but Papa took the piece of paper for himself and made me blush twenty times a day by showing it to everybody and letting them all read it. I was forced to carry it off on the sly and burn it. My father was outraged when he found out what I had done and reproved me sternly, reproaching me with unforgiveable indifference to the flattering attentions of the first man in the state. I listened to Papa's rebuke in polite silence, but at least I had the pleasure of putting a stop to the endless readings of Kutuzov's letter.

There are five captured French officers living here, three of them very well-educated men. Their confidence in Napoleon's common sense does honor to their own. They point to Smolensk on the map and tell me, "Monsieur Alekzandr, Fransh here." I don't have the heart to disabuse them of their happy delusion; why should I be the one to tell them that the reckless French are in a trap?

At last, after any number of postponements, Papa has decided to let my brother go, and it is high time! The snow has already completely melted, and I am burning with impatience to return to martial action. Once I was free to make preparations for my departure, I set about them so energetically that in two days everything was ready. Father gave us a light open carriage for two, as well as a manservant, to Kazan, but from there we will go on alone. My father was very reluctant to let my brother go without a servant, but I suggested to him that the consequences might be very disagreeable, since there is nothing to keep a valet from telling all he knows. And so it was decided that we will travel alone.

# Chapter Ten

## 1813

On Monday, May 1, at dawn we left our father's house. My conscience reproaches me for not yielding to Papa's request that we not depart on that day. He is superstitious and considers Monday unlucky, but I should have honored him, particularly in this instance. A father was sending away a beloved son and parting with him as if with life itself. Oh, I was wrong, quite wrong! My heart never ceases reproaching me. I imagine that Papa will grieve and brood much more now than if we had followed his will and left a day later. Humans are incorrigible. How many times before have I repented behaving stubbornly just because I considered it my right to do so? We are never so unjust as when we consider ourselves justified. And how could, how dared I, oppose my will to my father's—I, who consider that a father should be revered by his children like a deity? What demon clouded my mind?

Three stations before Kazan our carriage was smashed to pieces. We were thrown off a slope into a broad ditch and the carriage broke apart, but fortunately neither of us was injured. Now we are riding in a cart. How strange my fate is! How many years have I been traveling around in exactly the type of vehicle I despise?

*Moscow.* Mitrofanov had grievous news for us: Kutuzov is dead![1] This leaves me in a most difficult position: my brother is enrolled in the Department of Mines and still registered there, and I carried him off without getting a written release from his superiors. How will I ever get him into the army now? If Kutuzov were alive, this rash act would not have mattered, but now I am going to have endless troubles. Mitrofanov advises me to send Vasily home, but, at the first mention of it, my brother said resolutely that nothing on earth could force him to return home and that he would not serve anywhere except in the military.

*The Smolensk road.* As we rode through the forests, for a long time I couldn't understand why the wind sometimes wafted a bad smell from the thickets. At last I asked our driver about it and received an answer that

1. Kutuzov, already in failing health, fell ill and died in April 1813 on campaign in Silesia.

could not be more horrible, spoken with the total indifference of the Russian peasant: "There's a Frenchman rotting somewhere."

In Smolensk we walked along the demolished fortress walls. I recognized the spot near the bricksheds where we were so awkwardly situated and retreated in such disarray. I pointed it out to my brother and said, "Right here, Vasily, my life was in danger."

The flight of the French has left horrible traces: their bodies are rotting in the depths of the forests and contaminating the air. Poor wretches! No one's presumption and conceit have ever been punished as harshly as theirs. Horrors are recounted about their lamentable withdrawal.

When we returned to the post-station, the stationmaster was not at home; his wife asked us to come into the parlor and fill out the travel orders ourselves. "The horses will be here right away," she said, sitting down to her work and giving a tender kiss to the sweet-faced little girl who stood beside her.

"Is this your daughter?" I asked.

"No. She's French, an orphan. . . ."

While our horses were being harnessed, our hostess told us the touching story of this pretty child. The French came to Russia certain of victory and permanent residence, and, in this certainty, many of them brought along their families. During their disastrous withdrawal or, more accurately, flight, these families tried to hide in the forests, both from the killing frost and the Cossacks. One such family settled in the forest on the outskirts of Smolensk. They made a shelter for themselves, lit a fire, and were busy cooking a meager sort of meal, when suddenly the Cossack whoop resounded through the forest. Poor wretches! To them might well be applied the verse: *Jusqu'au fond de nos coeurs notre sang s'est glacé.* [2]

They scattered at hazard in all directions, intent only on reaching the densest part of the forest. Their eldest daughter, a girl of eight (the one who now stood before us, leaning against the knee of her benefactress and weeping at her own tale), ran into an impenetrable thicket and, wearing only a thin white frock, went on crawling through the deep snow until nightfall. The poor child, numb with cold, at last crawled out onto the highway at sunset; she had no strength left to walk and was creeping along on her hands and knees. Just then a Cossack officer rode by. He might not have seen her, but the little girl had the presence of mind to

2. Another quote from Racine's *Phedre* (Act V, Scene 4): "To the depths of our hearts our blood froze." (My translation.)

gather her last strength and cry out to him, "Mon ami! Par bonté, prenez moi sur votre cheval!"[3]

The astonished Cossack halted his horse and, looking closely at the object stirring on the road, was moved to tears when he saw that it was a child, almost half-naked because her clothing was in tatters. Her hands and legs were numb with cold. She fell at last and lay motionless. The officer took her in his arms, mounted his horse with her, and rode into Smolensk. As he passed the post-station, he saw the stationmaster's wife standing at the gates.

"Do me a favor, take this little girl under your care."

The stationmistress replied that she had nowhere to put her; she had many children of her own.

"Well, then, I'll smash her head against the corner right here before your eyes to spare her further suffering!"

Thunderstruck by this threat and already imagining that she saw it actually carried out, the stationmistress hastily snatched the unconscious little girl from the officer's arms and carried her inside. The officer galloped off.

For over two months the child lay near death. The poor thing was badly frostbitten. Skin peeled in shreds from her arms and legs and her hair fell out, but at last, after a high fever, she came back to life. Now this little girl lives with the stationmistress as a beloved daughter. She has learned to speak Polish and, thanks to her very young age, does not regret the lost advantages to which she is entitled by the nobility of her origins: she is from the leading family of Lyons. Many distinguished ladies to whom the stationmistress told the story just as she did to us have offered the touching orphan a home, but she always embraces the stationmistress and replies, "Mama brought me back to life; I will never leave her." As she ended her tale with these words, the stationmistress began to cry and hugged her sobbing child to her breast. This scene moved us to the depths of our souls.

They took my courier's travel orders from me and gave me others only as far as Slonim where all the officers who for some reason or other were left behind by their regiments are staying under the command of Kologrivov.[4] This is the lot that awaits me also. On the road we joined forces with Nikiforov, a hussar officer, who is very courteous and oblig-

---

3. "My friend! Be so good, take me on your horse!" (French)

4. General Andrej Kologrivov was appointed commander of the cavalry reserves in late 1812 and charged with replenishing the supply of both men and horses. The success of his mission was described by the future playwright A. S. Griboedov in his article, "The Cavalry Reserves" (*Vestnik Evropy* [Messenger of Europe] [1814], 15: 228–38).

ing, but rather odd. My scamp of a brother takes pleasure in angering him at every station.

*Slonim.* Here I am back in Slonim, but how altered it all is! I can't even locate my former quarters with the old guardsman. Kologrivov received me with a most stern and commanding air, "Why did you stay home for so long?" he asked.

I replied that it was due to illness.

"Do you have a certificate from a doctor?"

"No, I don't."

"Why not?"

"I saw no need to get one."

This odd reply angered Kologrivov greatly. "You, sir, are a scamp—"

I left before he had a chance to finish this obliging word. And so: what am I to do now? I have an under-age brother on my hands, whom I can't enroll in the regiment because he is still registered in the Department of Mines. What on earth am I to do with him? So I thought, hiding my face in my hands and resting my elbows on the Jews' large table. A gentle tap on the shoulder forced me to glance around at God's world.

"Why so pensive, Aleksandrov? Here are your orders from Kologrivov. You must report to Captain Bibikov in Lapshin and receive from him horses which you will pasture in the green meadows, on the silken sward!"

I wasn't in a joking mood. What am I to do with my brother? Where can I leave him? To take him with me into the regiment, to introduce such an immature youth to the broad picture of uhlan life, God forbid! But what on earth am I to do? Oh, why didn't I leave him at home? I was too clever by half when I broke my father's heart by parting him from his dearly loved son, and it has brought me nothing but bother and vexation. . . . My appearance was so altered by sorrow and disquiet that Nikiforov, our comrade on the road, was moved by it. "Leave your brother with me, Aleksandrov. I will be to him all that you could, and he will see the same friendship and the same care from me that he would from you yourself." The noble Nikiforov's proposition lifted the weight from my heart. I thanked him with all my heart and turned my brother over to him, asking the latter to lose no time in writing to Father to ask for his discharge from the Department of Mines. I gave him all our money, bade him farewell, and rode off to Lapshin.

Captain Bibikov, Ruzi, Burogo, and I have been charged with fattening up the exhausted, wounded, and emaciated horses of all the uhlan regiments. To my part fell one hundred and fifty horses and forty uhlans to look after them. The hamlet in which I am quartered is fifteen versts from Lapshin and surrounded by forests and lakes. I spend days at a time riding or wandering on foot in the dark forests and bathing in lakes as clean and clear as crystal.

I occupy a spacious shed. This is my parlor. Its floors are strewn with sand, and the walls are decorated with garlands, bouquets, and wreaths of flowers. In the center of it all stands a luxuriant couch—luxuriant in the full sense of the word: four short stumps support three wide boards, on which have been spread some three quarters of fine, sweet-smelling hay, almost all from the blossoms alone. It is covered with a kind of velvet rug in vivid, glowing colors, and a large, black morocco-leather pillow with crimson embroidery completes the splendor of my bed, which also serves as my sofa and armchair. On it I sleep, lie, sit, read, write, dream, dine, sup, and fall asleep.

It is now July. I am never bored for even a single moment of the long summer day. I get up with the dawn at three o'clock—that is, I wake up—and right away the uhlan brings me coffee, which I drink from a glass, along with black bread and cream. After this breakfast I go to inspect my flock in their places in the stables. In my presence they are led to the waterhole. From their cheerful and brisk capers I see that my uhlans are following their superior's example: they are not stealing and selling the oats, but giving them all to these fine and obedient beasts. I see their bodies, previously distorted by emaciation, taking on their old beauty and filling out; their coats are becoming smooth and glossy; their eyes glow, and their ears, which were all too ready to droop, now begin to flick rapidly and point forward. After I have stroked and caressed the handsomest of them, I order the one which frisks most cheerfully saddled for me and go for an outing wherever I am lured by curiosity or a captivating view.

At twelve o'clock I return to my woven brushwood parlor. There a bowl of very tasty Ukrainian cabbage-soup or *borshch* and a small piece of black bread are ready for me. After I have eaten this dinner, which always leaves me a little hungry, I go out again wandering on foot either through the fields or along the river. I return home for a couple of hours to write a few lines, lie down for a while, dream, build castles in the air and tear them down again, and take a quick look through my *Notes* without correcting anything in them—and why bother to correct them, what for? It is my family who will read them, and one's kin are easily pleased. Late in the afternoon I go for another walk. I bathe and at last return to be present during the evening watering.

After all this, my day concludes with a scene that is repeated every evening without fail: it is the time for field-work now, and so at nightfall all the young wives and girls return from the fields, drawling a song (the most repulsive singing I have ever heard!). They head back to the village in a dense throng. On the outskirts my uhlans are waiting for them, also standing in a throng. The two groups meet and mingle, the singing dies away. Talk, loud laughter, squeals, and oaths (the last always from the men) are heard, and with this hubbub they all run into the village and at last separate to their homes. I, too, go to lie down on my luxuriant, sweet-smelling couch and fall asleep instantly. But tomorrow it will be the same routine and the same scenes. . . .

Tranquillity, joy, cheerful dreams, good health, and high color are all inseparable from me in this present way of life, and I have never yet felt bored for even a minute. Nature, by implanting in my soul a love of freedom and her beauties, has given me an inexhaustible source of joys. As soon as I open my eyes in the morning a feeling of pleasure and happiness rouses throughout my entire being. I can't even imagine anything sad; in my imagination everything sparkles and glows with a bright radiance. Oh, Your Majesty! Our adored father! There is never a day on which I do not mentally embrace your knees. To you I owe a happiness that has no equal on earth, the happiness of being completely free: to your indulgence, your angelic kindness, but most of all your intelligence and the great spirit powerful enough to perceive a potential for deeds of high valor in the weaker sex. Your pure soul did not presume anything unworthy in me or fear that I would abuse the rank you granted me. Truly, His Majesty fathomed my soul. My thoughts are completely innocent. Nothing occupies them except the beauties of nature and the duties of my post. From time to time I am carried away by dreams of returning home, high rank, magnificent rewards, and the heavenly bliss of easing my father's old age by giving him prosperity and abundance in everything! This is the only time that I weep. . . . My father! My indulgent, magnanimous father! May God the All-Merciful grant me the ineffable joy of being the comfort and staff of your old age. . . .

I have remarked that there is in the air some obscure, vague rumor of my presence in the army. Everybody talks about it, but nobody knows anything; everybody considers it possible, but nobody believes it. More than once I have been told my own story with all possible distortions: one man described me as a beauty, another as an eyesore, a third as an old woman, a fourth gave me giant size and ferocious looks, and so on. . . . Judging from those descriptions I could rest assured that nobody's suspicions would ever rest on me, if it were not for one circumstance that threatens at last to draw my comrades' attention: I should be wearing mustaches, but I haven't any, and, of course, I never will. The Nazimovs, Solntsev, and Lizogub often laugh at me already, saying, "So, brother, when are we to expect your mustaches? You're not by chance a Laplander, are you?" They are only joking, of course. They suppose me to be at most eighteen years old. But there are times when the conspicuous

courtesy of their behavior toward me and the decorum of their words
serve notice that, although they are not quite convinced that I shall
never have mustaches, they at least strongly suspect the possibility. My
fellow officers, however, are very amicably disposed toward me and think
quite well of me. There is no way I can lose their good opinion: they have
been the witnesses and comrades of my life under arms.

I have been ordered to turn over all my horses and men to the senior
sergeant of my detachment and set out for the squadron of our regiment
commanded by Staff Captain Rszęsnicki. There are two of them. The
elder is an eccentric fellow, a real *Schleicher*[5]: he knows all, has seen all,
been everywhere, and does everything, but he dislikes his duties and pays
them little heed; his element is headquarters. But his brother is a fearless,
experienced, upright officer, who is devoted wholeheartedly to the din of
camp and a sharp saber and a good steed. I am delighted to be in his
squadron; I can't bear worthless squadron commanders: to be with them
in wartime is woe, and in peace, both laughter and grief.

When I got to Rszęsnicki's squadron, I found it mounted and ready to
march. This came as a complete surprise to me, and I found the rapid
transition from total tranquillity to great activity and commotion very
disconcerting.
"Hello, my dear Aleksandrov," said Rszęsnicki, "I have been expecting
you for a long time. Do you have a horse?"
"Neither horse nor saddle, Captain. What shall I do?"
"You will have to remain here for a day and find a saddle to buy. Take a
horse from the reserves. But do try to catch up with the squadron at the
next halt."
After this he and the squadron left, and I went to see our Lieutenant
Strakhov. There I found many officers from our regiment, and one of
them sold me a rubbishy French saddle-frame for one hundred and fifty
rubles. I could see that this price was scandalous, but what was I to do?
He could have asked five hundred rubles for his saddle, and I would still
have had to pay it.
The next day I rose with the dawn and at once set out on the tracks of
my squadron. At about five o'clock in the afternoon I got to the hamlet
where it was supposed to halt for the day. The first object that met my
eyes was the sergeant-major, wearing nothing but a shirt and roped to the
porch. At first I did not notice it and tried to hand him my horse. Then
at last I saw that he had been tied there and tied up my horse, too.
"How do you come to be tied there?" I asked the poor prisoner.
"You can see for yourself, by the arms," he replied rudely.

---

5. *Schleicher*, an intriguer. (German)

In Brest-Litovsk we had to undergo inspection before crossing the border. Two straight hours of heavy rain drenched us from head to foot. At last, soaked to the bones, we crossed the Russian frontier. The sun came out of the clouds and began to shine brightly. Its rays and the warm summer wind soon dried our uniforms.

Our detachment is made up of squadrons from various uhlan regiments; our commander is Colonel Stepanov. Some squadrons of mounted jaegers have joined us also. They are commanded by Seidler, who is a colonel, too, and apparently senior to ours.

*Prussia.* We are on our way to the fortress of Modlin, and we will be under the command of Kleinmichel.[6]

Yesterday it rained all day and a cold wind was blowing. We had to cross a river, and, although it was not a wide one, the ferry could take no more than ten horses, and our crossing promised to be quite prolonged. The faces of all our uhlans became so blue and black from cold that they no longer looked human. The cold wind accompanied by incessant fine drizzle was worse than winter frost. I decided to go warm up in the little house on the hillside above the river. I scrambled up the steep slippery path and entered the parlor where a fire burning in the fireplace was spreading a salutary warmth, only to be greeted by a stern, "Why did you come here?" The question came from Colonel Stepanov, who had settled down to wait for his detachment to finish crossing.

I replied that, since the Lithuanian squadron had not yet begun to cross and its turn was still some time away, I had come to warm up a little.

"You should be in your place," said the colonel drily. "Go back immediately!"

I went, in my thoughts cursing wholeheartedly the colonel who had driven me from the warm, dry parlor into the cold, the damp, and the dark night. As I approached the bank, I saw that my squadron was making ready for the crossing. I was duty officer and supposed to be present constantly both while the squadron crossed and on the march. I boarded as many men and horses as the ferry could hold and went off to the little cabin on deck where a peat fire was burning in a small castiron stove and a German woman was making coffee for all who wanted it. Her soft bed stood right beside the stove. I knew that our squadron's crossing would take an hour and a half, and therefore I ordered the duty sergeant, whom I knew to be a reliable man, to look after it and inform me when it was over.

---

6. A six-week summer truce in the campaign to drive Napoleon out of Prussia ended on August 3/15. Andrej Kleinmichel commanded the Russian reserve battalions who besieged the strategic French-built fortress at Modlin (on the confluence of the Vistula and the Narew just north of Warsaw) while the war swept west past it into Prussia.

After making these judicious arrangements, I sat down on the German woman's bed and ordered coffee from her. Drinking two cups of it took off the chill. The cabin was not merely warm but even too hot; I was not at all eager to go out on deck, however, where it was still rainy and windy. While I waited to be told that the entire squadron had crossed, I sank into the soft, deep pillows, and I don't remember or know how I fell so soundly asleep. When I woke, there was not a noise to be heard from wind or rain or people. Everything was quiet, the ferry was not stirring, and there was nobody in the cabin. Astonished by this, I quickly got up and opened the door. I saw that the ferry was standing at the riverbank, the vicinity was empty, there was nobody in sight anywhere, and day was breaking. "What does this mean?" I thought. "Can they really have forgotten about me?"

I went up the hill and saw an uhlan holding my horse. "And where's the squadron?"

"It left long ago."

"Why didn't they rouse me?"

"I don't know."

"Who led the squadron?"

"The colonel himself. . . ."

I mounted my horse. "Which squadron crossed last?"

"The Orenburg Uhlans."

"A long time ago?"

"Over two hours."

"Why didn't you tell me when our squadron left?"

"Nobody knew where you were."

"And the duty sergeant?"

"He just told me to hold your horse and wait here on the bank."

"Are our quarters far off?"

"About fifteen versts."

I set off at a light trot, very unhappy with myself, my uhlan, the duty sergeant, the wind, the rain, and the colonel who had driven me out so ruthlessly. The morning became fine, the wind and rain ceased, the sun came out, and at last I caught sight of our regiment in its quarters near a dense forest. I rode up to my comrades and found them tranquil and satisfied (well fed, that is). They had had a good breakfast and were getting ready to march. And so all I could do, hungry and without a chance to dismount, was to join the squadron and go on to our next quarters.

*Modlin.* We got to Modlin on August 10th. Tomorrow our squadron will be on picket duty. Rszęsnicki stationed us all at posts spread out over two versts. I am in the center, in charge of the entire picket. Ilinsky and Ruzi, on the flanks, must notify me every morning of everything that happens at their posts, and I send a report directly to the captain. Now I am living in a small cave or dugout. By night half my men stand in readiness by their saddled horses, and the other half rest.

Yesterday Rszęsnicki sent me a bottle of excellent cream as a reward for a minor clash with the enemy and four prisoners.

Modlin evidently has a large supply of balls and powder. Our men have only to appear in the fields for cannons to open fire on them; sometimes they do these honors for one man. This strikes me as extremely comical: how can they possibly hope to hit one man with a cannonball?

We have left Modlin and are on our way to join our own regiments. Ours is stationed near Hamburg.[7]

*Bohemia. October.* The view of the Bohemian mountains is extremely picturesque! I always ride up onto the highest of them and watch our squadrons stretching along the narrow road in a motley, sinuous strip.

The weather has turned cold and raw again. We are surrounded by dense fog, and our journey across the spine of the Bohemian mountains is taking place in this impenetrable cloud. How many beautiful views are concealed by this undulating gray shroud? A severe toothache completes my misery.

## A Night in Bohemia

"Your honor, you're duty officer for the squadron tomorrow."
"Do we march early?"
The sergeant-major who was announcing my duty to me replied that the orders were to be at the assembly point at four in the morning.
"Very well. You may go."
I am dead tired today. As soon as we got to quarters, I turned Hurricane over to Kindzersky and, setting out along the first path that met my eyes, followed wherever it led. I spent all day climbing mountains, descending into valleys, and running from one beautiful spot to the next. I wanted to be everywhere I saw a fine landscape, and there were a host of them. My excursion ended only after sunset, and, even in my rush to return to the squadron, I couldn't resist stopping for another quarter of an hour to feast my eyes on the evening fog as it began filling the narrow mountain ravines like whitish smoke. At last I got home—that is, to the

7. Durova's service record lists her as taking part in the blockade of Modlin from August 10 to October 20, 1813.

squadron (forgive me, dear Papa, I keep forgetting that you do not like it when I use the word *home* to speak of the squadron)—and the first thing that met me was the duty roster. I called my orderly. "Zanuda, wake me at dawn tomorrow."

"Don't be *perturbed,* your honor; the general-march will rouse you."

"Oh, yes, I forgot. Well, there's no need then."

Can there be anything more vexing than the *general-march* at dawn? Before it was even completely light out, the trumpeters were in formation under my windows, playing the piece which has the magic power not only to drive out sleep but to get even the laziest of our armed estate up and dressed instantly. Although I am considered one of our most energetic officers, I never longed so badly as I did now to stay in bed for another half hour. But here came Ruzi, throwing the door wide open and flying into my room in full uniform. "What! You're still lying around? What about your duty? Get up, get up! What a queer fellow you are! Didn't you hear the general-march?"

"How could I help but hear it, with ten trumpets playing right in my ear?"

"Ten trumpets yet, what splendor! There are only two trumpeters riding around the village. But anyway, get up. You know the captain has no time for jokes."

"So that's what you've dreamed up to frighten me."

"Get up. I'm off to lead out the squadron."

Ruzi left, and I got dressed in five minutes. For some reason I thought that full uniform meant wearing my plume, and I ordered Zanuda to give it to me. But when he brought it, I could not make out what on earth damned old mustaches was carrying: it was a sort of long, yellowish-brown paintbrush. "What's that, Zanuda?"

"Your honor's plume."

"My plume! Where have you been keeping it?"

"In the valise."

"And undoubtedly without a case?"

"Without a case."

"Give it here, you worthless fellow!" In vexation I tore the plume from the hands of the confounded Zanuda, inserted it into my helmet, and went to join my comrades. Zanuda grumbled after me: "Handsome is as handsome does. Who does he expect to impress with his plume?"

The officers burst out laughing in chorus as they glimpsed my frowning brow and the plume, which looked like nothing on earth. "Oh, how sweet you are today, Aleksandrov!" "How becoming that plume is! Today you and it are made for each other." "And why such adornment, if you'll permit us to ask?"

"I'm duty officer."

"What of it?"

"I'm supposed to be in full uniform."

"Including a plume?"

"Yes."

"How comical you are. . . ." "That will do, brother, throw that rubbishy thing away before it breaks your neck in today's wind." I paid no heed.

We set out. On the march Ruzi turned the duty over to me, and, since he is in the fourth platoon, we rode together behind the squadron. "Aleksandrov, do you know where we'll be spending the night?"

"Yes. On Baron N.'s estate."

"Oh, yes. But you really haven't the least idea of the pleasures in store for us."

"What are they then?"

"We are quartered in the castle itself. The baron is rich as Croesus and hospitable. Today's march is a short one, we'll get there long before evening, and the baron surely has daughters and a fortepiano. Oh, I foresee something delightful!"

"You're crazy, Ruzi. Who assured you that the baron will be disposed to entertain us?"

"The Germans say that he's a very nice man and likes to lead a merry life."

"Well, and the daughters? What if they don't exist?"

"There'll be daughters. . . ."

The wind was getting stronger by the hour. "Let's cross to the other side, Ruzi. It seems that you told the truth when you said the plume would break my neck. This vexatious wind is ripping it from side to side." We crossed the road.

All Ruzi's hopes were fated to be dashed that day. The clear sky turned overcast, at first with light cover and then with stormclouds, and at last it became totally cloaked in a black, impenetrable shroud. A noisy, wind-driven rain streamed down on us and drenched the defenseless uhlans unmercifully. Before we could get our capes on, everything we wore was soaked. Our escorts led us God knows where, and the short march dragged on so long that we arrived at our quarters in the dead of night.

Soaked, shivering, spattered with red clay, we halted at last before Baron N.'s opulent castle. Oh, how joyfully I sprang off my horse; I couldn't believe that I was back on solid ground! All day on horseback! All day in the rain! My limbs were completely numb. One doesn't soon forget a march like that one.

"Why have you dismounted, Aleksandrov?" asked the captain. "Have you forgotten that you're duty officer? Remount and show the men to their quarters."

"I can do it just as well on foot, Captain," I replied and, taking Hurricane by the reins, started off in front of the squadron.

The captain had a twinge of conscience. "Come back, Aleksandrov. The sergeant will see the men to their billets. . . ."

We mounted a clean, well-lit staircase that was as smooth as glass; we entered magnificent, sumptuously furnished rooms and settled down to rest in armchairs and sofas. Everything we chanced to touch suffered an ill fate: walking, standing, or sitting, we left traces everywhere of the red clay that had spattered us from head to foot—or, more accurately, from foot to head.

Our affable host invited us to take our seats at the table. The captain and my comrades sat down immediately. They began talking noisily and clashing their goblets, glasses, plates, spurs, and sabers. Supposing themselves secure from the rain and wind for the rest of the night, they gave themselves up lightheartedly to the pleasures of a sumptuous table and cheerful conversation.

I took advantage of their zealous efforts at supper to go into the bedroom or, rather, into the room set aside for us. The door leading from it into the dining room was open, and some beds stood in a row along the walls. The baron was to be pitied for making our beds with such fine linens. The only mercy I could do the baronial opulence was to remove my clay-plastered boots; still wearing everything else, I lay down on one feather quilt and covered myself with another. How nice it all was, clean, white, soft, delicate, resplendent! It was all satin, batiste, lace—and there in the middle of it lay a damp uhlan spattered with red clay! I found my situation so amusing that I laughed myself to sleep.

I was awakened by a loud, heated dispute between our captain and Major Nichvalodov of the Orenburg Uhlans. "Your clerks wrote it down wrong," said the captain.

"Excuse me," said Nichvalodov courteously, "but yours read it wrong."

They argued, shouted, and at last decided to read the disposition again, and it turned out that Nichvalodov was correct: we were in the wrong quarters! What horrible news! In a flash I sprang out of my warm refuge. The captain was already looking around for me. "Where is the duty officer? Aleksandrov! Go and order the men to play the alert—and as loud as they can!" When he saw that I was not budging from the spot, he asked in surprise, "Why are you just sitting there?"

Nichvalodov replied for me that I was in my stocking feet.

"What a fine orderly! Well, sir, go in your stockings if you must!"

Fortunately the orderly came in with my boots. I quickly put them on and went off at a run to avoid hearing the captain's derisive exclamations, "What a fine duty officer! Why didn't you take off all your clothes?"

The wind was howling and gusty, it was pouring rain, and the night could not have been darker. Our trumpeters were standing in the courtyard. "Go around the village and play the alert as loud as you can," I told them. They rode off. We had no other means of assembling our men from their billets in the village, which stretched for some three versts along the mountain ravines.

In an hour and a half the squadron was assembled. We mounted our horses; escorts with torches took places before, behind, and at both sides of the squadron; and we set out, shivering and cursing the march, the storm, the captain, and the distance to our quarters: we had two more miles to go.

After we had gone half a verst, the captain suddenly halted the squadron. The brain of our indefatigable superior had suddenly been struck by the preposterous notion of leaving me behind alone to wait for men who, as he supposed, had not heard the alarm or could not reach the assembly point in time. "Assemble them all, Aleksandrov, and bring them after us to quarters!"

A fine disposition this was, but there was nothing to be done—I couldn't argue. I stayed, the squadron went on, and, when the noise of the horses' hooves sloshing through the mud died out altogether, the wild howl of the wind took possession of the surroundings. I listened closely to this horrible concert, in my reveries surrounded by evil spirits howling in the mountain ravines. The captain was truly out of his mind! Why hadn't he left me one of the escorts with a torch? What was I to do now? How could I find the road back to the village? There was no sign of it, not even a spark from a fire showing anywhere. Was I really to stand there like a sentry until the break of dawn? These vain questions were interrupted by an impatient frisk from my steed. I tried to calm him by stroking him, but this measure, always effective before, did not help now; he frisked, reared, arched his neck, snorted, pawed the earth, and sidestepped one way and then the other. There was no possibility of calming the frenzied Hurricane.

The noise of the surrounding forests and the howl of the wind were deafening, but nevertheless I could hear another noise and another howl. Wishing and fearing to confirm my horrible conjecture, unwillingly and with sinking heart I listened closely. To my inexpressible fright I found out that I was not deceived: the stream was falling into a deep chasm, and on the other side of the precipice something was howling that was not just the wind. My imagination was already sketching for me a pack of hungry wolves ripping at my Hurricane, and I was so preoccupied with this desperate speculation that I forgot a more immediate danger with nothing imaginary about it: the chasm into which the stream was plunging was only two paces away from me, and Hurricane, far from prepared to stand meekly. At last I remembered, and my first impulse was to jump off my horse, but the thought that he would break loose and run after the squadron held me back. Oh, my dear father! How would you feel if you could see your daughter now, on a frenzied steed, beside a chasm, at night, in the midst of forests and ravines, in a raging storm? . . . Doom was staring me in the face. But the providence of Almighty God, our celestial Father, follows his children's every step. A gust of wind ripped off my plume and carried it swiftly across the gorge directly into the shrubbery where I thought I heard the howl of the wolves, those terrible companions of my nocturnal watch. A minute later the howling ceased, and Hurricane stopped frisking. Now I could have dismounted, but my earlier apprehensions of his breaking away held me back once again, and, like an equestrian statue, I stood motionless on the cliff over the abyss into which the stream fell noisily.

The rain had long since stopped, the wind began to die down, the night became lighter, and I could make out distinctly the objects that surrounded me: behind me, right next to Hurricane's hind legs, was the chasm! In all my life I never leapt off a horse so quickly as I did now and at once led him away from that terrible proximity. Uneasily I studied the black depths of the shrubbery across the ravine; I could not yet make anything out, but Hurricane was calm, and so evidently there was nothing there. I would have liked to catch sight of my plume, but nothing white showed anywhere. If it was not at the bottom of the gorge, it had been carried off by the whirlwind God alone knew where. I went on looking over my surroundings and made out a number of roads, lanes, and paths leading off into the mountains, ravines, and forests, but where was the one I should take? None of them showed horses' tracks. While I was trying to spot the slightest sign of them, the fog, harbinger of morning, began spreading around me in a white cloud; it thickened and covered every object in an impenetrable haze. And now once again I didn't dare take a step for fear of breaking my neck or losing my way altogether. Weary and dejected, I lay down on the grass beside a crumbling log. At first I just leaned my elbows on it, but insensibly my head drooped too, my eyes fell shut, and sleep took total possession of me.

Paradise was all around me when I woke. The sun had just risen, and millions of rainbow fires burned in the grass and on the leaves; the chasm, the stream, the forest, the ravines—everything that had seemed so dreadful at night—was now captivating, fresh, shining, green, strewn with flowers. How much shade and grass there was in the ravines! I was indebted to the latter circumstance for the fact that Hurricane had not run away. He was wandering quietly over the dewy grass, eating it with great relish. I went over to him, caught him easily, and mounted.

It was not the first time that I have found that there are instances when animal instinct is more useful to man than his own powers of reason. I could have hit on the road the squadron had taken only by chance, but I gave Hurricane liberty to choose our way, and in a quarter of an hour he came out onto a road on which deep tracks of a large number of shod horses were clearly visible: it was yesterday's route! A verst distant, among the ravines, Baron N.'s village was visible. Yesterday the captain had left me only a few yards from it, and the rumpus kicked up by my damned Hurricane had carried me the rest of the way. I turned him back toward the village, intending to go see whether any of our men were there, but to this Hurricane most resolutely objected: he reared and twisted very picturesquely on his hind legs in the direction the squadron had gone. Hurricane is cleverer than I, it seems; even if uhlans had lagged behind the squadron, how could it be supposed that they would stay in those lodgings until sunrise?

I gave my steed liberty to gallop how and where he wished, and he carried me quite rapidly downhill and uphill and along the flanks of deep precipices. The narrow road turned sharply to the right around a steep cliff overgrown with shrubbery. As I galloped past this spot, I caught sight of something white in the bushes. I jumped off my horse and, leading him by the reins, ran over there, without the least doubt that it was my plume—and I was not mistaken. There it was, lying on branches of shrubbery, brilliantly white. The rain had washed it clean, the wind had dried it, and the object of yesterday's derision was white, fluffy, and beautiful as only a horsehair plume can be. I inserted it into my yellowed helmet and applied myself to the difficult maneuver of remounting my devilish Hurricane. I don't know why I cannot part with this horse; why do I like him? He is so malicious, so impatient and arrogant, that my head is never safe on my shoulders when I am seated on this demon incarnate. For a quarter of an hour my steed and I circled the shrubbery while I, trying to get one foot into the stirrup, hopped about on the other, following his capricious gyrations. At last possessed by rage, I pulled on the reins with all my strength and shouted at him in a terrible voice. The steed quieted down, and I made haste to mount him.

Great God! My fate has condemned me to do strange things! Could that really be me shouting in a savage voice, one that can even pacify a frenzied horse? What would my girl friends from the old days say if they could hear me howling so preposterously? I was angry with myself for this feat of necessity, for the insult my *bogatyr*'s exhortation did to the delicacy of the female organs of speech.

The beauty of the landscape and Hurricane's rapid run cheered me up again. My vexation ended, and now I found the means I had used to pacify the recalcitrant steed at once comical and essential, but Hurricane, it seems, wanted to pay me back for his momentary fright and perhaps, too, he sensed that our quarters were not far off: he began snorting, arching his head, and galloping in spurts. I became rather fearful, knowing that when he got excited, he turned a blind eye to everything and ran at hazard. My hasty and ineffectual efforts to restrain him were unavailing; I began to lose my presence of mind. It is astonishing how quick horses are to sense this and at once take advantage of it. Hurricane took off like an arrow from a bow.

It was without doubt God who preserved me. The furious beast, by now flying with me, left the road altogether. At first I was very frightened, but the impossibility of either restraining him or jumping off restored me to reason. I put my effort into keeping my balance and holding firmly to the stirrups.

There is evidently a turning point to disaster as well as to illness. Far ahead of me I caught sight of a black strip intersecting my route. Horror-struck, I would have leaped off the horse, had not a momentary hesitation robbed me of the time to carry out this ruinous intention. The steed galloped up to a spring welling up within precipitous banks and plunged directly into it. I don't remember how I flew into it with him and still kept my seat, but here Hurricane's frenzy came to an end. The spring was no more than twenty feet across. The chastened horse swam it at an angle, with incredible effort climbed out onto the steep bank, and went on at a walk, by now obedient to the slightest twitch of the reins. When he came out onto the direct road again, although he was quivering perceptibly from impatience to rush to his companions, he walked on and, when I permitted him to step up the pace, galloped smoothly, easily, and obediently all the way to our quarters.

"And where, if you please, have you been voyaging?" the captain asked me derisively. "I thought I assigned you to wait for any men we may have left behind; you were supposed to come back to the squadron with them. Whatever kept you? The men got here long ago."

"I spent a long time standing on one spot, Captain. You didn't give me an escort with a torch, and the night, as you know, was dark as a cellar, so I didn't dare start riding about for fear of falling into the gorge."

"And so you really just stood like a bronze equestrian sculpture on the spot where I left you ?"

"For a few minutes I did, but, of course, I would have ended up trying to find the road back to the Baron's village, if my horse had not gone into a frenzy over something that frightened him. Then I could only worry about him—"

"And couldn't master him," the captain interrupted me.

Vexation flared in my heart at this misplaced and unseemly reproach. I picked up my helmet to leave in a hurry and answered coldly, without looking at the captain. "You are in error! I didn't want to master him; neither the time nor the place permitted it."

However much I would have liked to tell my comrades about the events of that stormy night, I refrained from doing so. What use would it be? To them it all seems either too ordinary or altogether improbable. For example, they would not believe in my wolves and tell me they were dogs—and that might well be the truth. And my valiant leap into the river is such an ordinary matter that they would find it comical to hear me relating it as something of a wonder. It never enters their minds, of course, that everything they find ordinary is quite extraordinary to me.

*Prague.* We stood here until nightfall. The city authorities made difficulties about permitting our corps to pass through the city. At last permission came, and we hurried across without stopping even for a minute; this was strictly enforced. However, Ilinsky, Ruzi, and I stopped in a tavern for an offhand supper and then set out to catch up with the squadron at a full gallop, thundering over the cobblestones. The Germans made way in alarm, and an incessant *Schwerenot* resounded at our heels. The winter here is unusually cold. The Germans ascribe this to the Russian invasion and, huddling in front of their fireplaces, say that if they had been forewarned of the arrival of uninvited guests, they would have laid in more peat.

*Harburg.* [8] Yesterday we made a vain attempt to disrupt the peace and quiet of Harburg. Together with the Mounted Jaegers, we advanced to the fortress walls at midnight and settled down to wait for dawn in order to pound it with cannons. My platoon and I were detached to protect two siege-guns. We were all under the command of one of the leaders of the Hanseatic armies. Dawn came, and we began lobbing bombs into the fortress and went on doing so steadily for two hours. We set two or three houses on fire, but were not found worthy of a response. The Harburg garrison might as well have been deserted; not one shot was fired in return. But I can't understand the goal of our incursion. I thought there would be an assault, but our entire alert ended with our throwing a few dozen bombs into Harburg and returning to quarters. The only harm this expedition did was to me. While we were waiting for dawn, I lay down beside one of the guns on the damp sand and, since it is springtime now, I caught a head cold, I think from the earth's damp exhalations. I was so ill for a week that I was as unrecognizable as if I had been suffering steadily for three years.

*Hamburg.* There is nothing more comical than our rounds of the pickets. The passwords, responses, and slogans are so distorted by our soldiers, especially the infantry recruits, that no one could ever invent on

8. After Napoleon's crushing defeat at Leipzig in October 1813, Russia and her allies continued to pursue him westward across Europe. Bennigsen's troops, Durova's regiment among them, were in the Allied contingent assigned to isolate and contain Napoleon's faithful Marshal Davout and the French confederate, Frederick VI of Denmark, in Schleswig-Holstein. In November, Marshal Davout retired to defenses he had prepared in the Hamburg-Harburg area, where his outmanned troops withstood a five-month siege by Bennigsen's Army of Poland, sixty thousand strong.

purpose names as absurd as those they imagine they hear, because none of them are in Russian. Why this fancy for using a German city as a password for Russian pickets? Furthermore, this is how a recruit asks for the password: "Who goes there? Speak! I'll kill you!" (This is an empty threat; he's afraid to aim his gun for fear that, against all expectations, it might go off.) Then, instead of waiting for an answer, he shouts at the top of his voice, "What's the password? The password's the city of—" and says something or other absurd. He asks and answers himself, and any officer riding up to him can only try not to laugh. There is a good side to everything, however: if the blockhead of a soldier who cannot be made to understand that he should ask for the password rather than tell it were to pronounce it correctly, the enemy picket, which is quite close to ours, might hear it and use it to our detriment. But since what the enemy hears is impossible either to understand or pronounce, he remains tranquilly at his post.

Last night our colonel nearly broke his neck, and while that event in itself was not at all comical, the incident that occasioned it was so amusing that the colonel himself laughed as he told us about it. Wishing to verify the reliability of his pickets, he went out alone to inspect them. The colonel rode around for a while, and, when he saw no sentries at the spots where they should have been posted, he was greatly vexed at the carelessness of the picket officer. The colonel thought that no pickets had been posted and was disabused of the idea in a very comical way that nearly cost him his life. The sentries were all at their posts, but since the night was as dark as black cloth, they held their breath instead of challenging when they heard someone ride past them. To our colonel's woe, one of them had fallen asleep sitting against a stump. The snuffling of the horse woke him, and he jumped up precipitately, crying out wildly in alarm, "What's the password? The slogan's Gavrilo!"—the archangel Gabriel, that is. The horse leaped aside and fell with his rider into a pit. By the grace of God, the colonel escaped with light bruises.

# Chapter Eleven

## 1814

The news of the surrender of Paris brought Davout to surrender. The French left Hamburg, and military action ended. We were now the peaceful guests of the Danish king.[1] I want to take advantage of this circumstance to tour beautiful Holstein alone in a cabriolet to which I will harness my saddle horse.

Ilinsky volunteered to go with me. We took a week's leave and set out first for Pinneberg. We wanted to walk for a while along the beautiful, shady avenue that leads from Ütersen to Pinneberg, and so both of us got out of our cabriolet. I wrapped the reins around a little bronze cone on the front of it and, placing my hopes on the old steed's meekness, let him walk down the road alone. We did not notice when the horse, feeling the reduced weight of the carriage, began to step up his pace. But at last I saw that he had gotten far ahead and ran to stop him, but all this accomplished was to set the horse running too, ever more smartly, into a gallop, and at last into an impetuous run. Ilinsky, summoning all his strength, came close to catching up and grabbing the shaft, but the horse knocked him down, ran the wheel over his chest, and galloped on toward Pinneberg at full speed.

Ilinsky jumped up and, rubbing his chest, began running again after the horse as he disappeared from sight. I think it was because our valise was lying on the front of the cabriolet, and in it were the silver pieces from our uniforms and five hundred rubles in gold. Neither of us wanted to lose all that, but there was no way we could run all the way to Pinneberg. Despite this, Ilinsky and the horse vanished from my sight. I also walked on at my fastest pace and caught up with my comrade and my steed at the gates of Pinneberg. They were surrounded by a crowd of Germans, but the valise was no longer there.

"What do we do now?" Ilinsky asked me.

"They have their own authorities," I said. "You speak German well; go see them and tell them exactly what things we had in the valise. They'll surely find them. . . . "

Ilinsky set off on foot, and I got into the cabriolet and rode off to rent quarters. There I handed the horse over to a German worker to look after

---

1. Napoleon surrendered to the allies in April 1814. Davout, however, continued to defend the besieged city in the name of Louis XVIII until late May. Durova's regiment was stationed in Ütersen, thirty kilometers west of Hamburg.

and went to see the town governor. Ilinsky was already there. For some reason or other the German did not want to investigate our loss; he said that the affair was an impossible one: "Your horse ran through the forest alone. How can anyone guess what became of your belongings?"

Vexed by such composure toward our adversity, Ilinsky said that if this had happened in Peterburg our lost things would be found within twenty-four hours, even if thousands of men were involved; there were no police in the world that could match the Russians for energy, perspicacity, and the clever measures they employed to investigate and uncover the subtlest forms of knavery. These words maddened the composed German; he lost his head and, with glittering eyes, seething in vexation, rushed out of the room. We saw no reason to await his return and went to our quarters.

We didn't have the means to go farther. We had lost all our money, our belongings, and even our uniforms; both of us were left with only the frock-coats we were wearing. We didn't take tea that day, we had no supper, and a sad lot awaited us in the morning: no coffee to drink, no breakfast, and a thirty-verst return trip on empty stomachs. I had two marks left, but they were to be spent on the horse. Ilinsky found this unjust and protested fiercely against what he called my partiality for the stubborn animal: "That worthless brute is lucky that the money is in your pocket; if I had it, then, excuse me, Aleksandrov, but your donkey would have to fast all the way to Ütersen."

"But now we are the ones who fast, my dear comrade," I replied. "And why should that bother you? Imagine that you are on bivouac, on the march, that it's wartime again, 1812, that our rusks and provisions fell in the water, Cossacks relieved our orderlies of liquor, roast meat, and bread, or the rascals ate it all themselves and put the blame on the Cossacks; in short, imagine yourself in one of those situations, and you'll be consoled."

"I thank you! You console yourself alone with all that," said the hungry Ilinsky crossly and hid in the cupboard. I don't know what else to call the ingenious Germans' beds; they are exactly cupboards: opening both panels of the door, you find inside a rectangular coffer filled with feather-beds and pillows instead of blankets. If you want to sleep there, you just crawl into the middle of them—and that's an end to it.

When I saw that Ilinsky had gone into the cupboard with no intention of coming out again until morning, I went to persuade our hostess to light a free candle for me. She fulfilled my request, patting my cheek and calling me a nice young man, I don't know why. I wrote a page or two and then dragged out all the featherbeds and pillows to be found in the second cupboard and went to sleep on the floor.

At three in the morning I was stroking and kissing my good steed who, oblivious to these attentions, was eating the oats I had bought with my last two marks. Ilinsky was sleeping. The worker was greasing the wheels of our cabriolet, and from the window our hostess asked me, "Herr

Offizier, wohlen Sie Kaffee?"[2] All these activities were interrupted by the hurried arrival of the irate town governor. "Where is your comrade?" he asked curtly. He was carrying our valise. Overjoyed at seeing again the treasure we had come so close to losing, I ran to rouse my *Kamerad.*

"Get up, Ilinsky," I shouted, approaching the doors of his cupboard to open it, "Get up! They've brought our valise."

"Leave me alone, for God's sake; you're carrying the joke too far," grumbled Ilinsky indistinctly. "Let me sleep."

"I'm not joking, Vasily! The governor of Pinneberg is here with our valise."

"Well then, take it from him."

"But that's not so easily done. Evidently he wants to hand it over only to you—it's my guess, along with some eloquent retort to the doubts you cast yesterday on the efficiency of their police."

"Well then, brother, at least ask him to step into our hostess's parlor while I get up."

Five minutes later Ilinsky joined us. The town governor, who in the meantime had been silent, got up swiftly from his chair and went over to Ilinsky: "Here are your things, all of them down to the last item, and all the money, still exactly in the same coin. Don't think that our police are in any way inferior to your Peterburgers. Here are your things, and there is the thief," he said triumphantly, pointing out the window at an eighteen-year-old youth who was standing in the courtyard. "Yesterday he caught sight of your horse near Pinneberg, snatched the valise from the cabriolet, threw it into a ditch behind some bushes, and led the horse into the city. Now, are you satisfied? We'll hang the thief immediately, does that suit you?"

At this horrible question, which he asked with all German pomposity, Ilinsky turned pale, I began trembling, and my desire to laugh at the Pinneberger's comic anger was transformed into a painful emotion of fear and pity. "Oh, what are you saying?" we both cried out suddenly. "How could we want that? No, no, for God's sake, release him. . . ."

"I see now that I was mistaken about your police. Forgive it as due to my ignorance," added Ilinsky in the most courteous possible tone. The appeased German released the unhappy boy who stood before our window, trembling all over and as white as a sheet. When he heard that he was pardoned, he clasped his hands with such an expression of joy and knelt so humbly before our window that I was moved to the depths of my soul, and even the Pinneberg governor sighed deeply. At last he wished us a pleasant journey around Holstein and left.

Now we boldly demanded coffee, cream, rusks, and cold game for the road.

"Oh, what a happy character you have, Aleksandrov," Ilinsky said to

2. "Would you like coffee, sir?" (German)

me when we were back in the capriolet again. "You didn't grieve at all over the loss of your property."

"Why this great word, *property*, Ilinsky? Are a uniform, pouch, and forty gold pieces really property?"

"But it was all you had. . . ."

"Well, so be it. But I found your sorrow very comical."

"Why?"

Because you should be used to being penniless; whenever you have a gold piece to spend, you immediately stake it on a card and lose."

"Sometimes I win."

"Never! At least I've never seen you come out ahead. You're as unskillful a gambler as I am unlucky."

"That's not true! You have no way of judging my skill. You don't understand anything about gambling," said Ilinsky in vexation. He was silent the rest of the way.

We made our peace over dinner. We spent the night in Itzehoe and went on the next day to Glückstadt. The sad appearance of the Elbe there, flowing on the level between swampy banks, and the flocks of ravens with their sinister cries put us in a bored and melancholy mood. . . . We hastened to get away from it and, turning off the highway, took to country lanes. In one new inn, as it then appeared to us, we were agreeably surprised by our courteous reception and the good table. From outside, the house promised nothing better than potatoes for dinner and straw for a bed, and we came in and asked for dinner the way one usually does in taverns, without paying any attention to our host. But a delicate tablecloth, china dishes, silver spoons and saltcellars, and crystal glasses aroused both our attention and our surprise. There was more to come: the host put the food on the table, asked us to be seated, and sat down with us. Ilinsky, who cannot bear liberties from anyone, asked me, "What's the meaning of this? Why did this peasant sit down with us?"

"For God's sake, keep quiet," I replied. "Perhaps this will be something out of *A Thousand and One Nights*. Who knows what our host might not turn into?"

During this conversation the host's brother came in and sat down at the table, too. I did not dare to start talking. Ilinsky's discontented appearance and the carefree joviality of the two peasants were extremely comical to me. To keep from offending our good-natured hosts with unseemly laughter, I tried to avoid looking at Ilinsky. After dinner they served us coffee in a silver pot on a handsome tray and cream in a pitcher of finely worked silver, with a spoon shaped like a soup ladle, also of silver brightly gilded on the inside. All this they put on the table. Our two hosts invited us to pour our own coffee to our taste and sat down to drink it with us.

"What's the meaning of this?" repeated Ilinsky. "A simple tavern, naked walls, wooden chairs, simply dressed men, and a fine dinner, excellent coffee, china, silver, gilt, an appearance of wealth of some sort and taste combined with rural simplicity! What do you think, Aleksandrov? What can it all mean?"

"I don't know anything about it, but what I think is that we will find it impossible to pay here."

"Why? I think it's the opposite, that we'll pay ten times more than at the other places."

We went out for a stroll through surroundings that were beautiful in the way that only an even, flat land like Holstein can be. On the way back I asked Ilinsky to take charge of everything himself, ordering and paying; I said that I was in dread and expectation of some sort of miraculous phenomenon. They served us tea with the same kindness, good nature, and richness of tableware and taste. At last it was time to go. Our horse had been perfectly groomed, the cabriolet washed, and our host's brother was at the porch, holding our steed by the bridle. I saw that Ilinsky was twiddling two marks in his hands. "What do you mean to do? Are you really going to try paying two marks for such zeal and kindness, and a table set with all the fruits of the earth? Do me a favor, don't pay anything. Believe me, they won't take it."

"We'll see about that," replied Ilinsky, and with this he handed our host the two marks and asked him whether that was sufficient.

"We aren't selling anything; this isn't a tavern," replied our host quietly.

Ilinsky was rather embarrassed. He put away his marks and said in a softer voice, "But you've spent so much on us."

"On you? No. I'm very glad that you stopped at my house, but I shared with you only that which my family and I always use."

"We took you for peasants," said Ilinsky, spurred on by curiosity and the expectation of some extraordinary revelation. His hopes were instantly dashed.

"And you are not mistaken, we are peasants."

At last, after some questions and answers, we found out that these good people had received an inheritance from a distant relative, a rich Jamburg merchant, and that they built the house less than six months ago. They frequently meet with errors like ours; we are not the first to mistake their house for a tavern.

"And you offer them all the same cordial hospitality without disabusing them of their delusion?"

"No, you are the first."

"And why is that?"

"You are Russian officers. Our king has ordered us to treat Russians well."

"But nevertheless, good people, it would be pleasant for the Russian officers if you would not let them go on thinking for such a long time that they were in a tavern. We ordered everything so imperiously, the way one orders only where one expects to pay."

"You should have guessed there was nothing to pay, because we dined with you."

At these words Ilinsky blushed. Neither of us said anything more, but we bowed to our kind host and drove away.

Late autumn has come. Dark nights, mud, drizzle, and a cold wind force us to gather around the fireplace of one or another of our comrades in the regiment. Some of them are excellent musicians. Our evenings fly by quickly and merrily to the enchanting sounds of their flutes and guitars.

## The March Back to Russia

There is not one of us who is happy to be leaving Holstein. We are all bidding farewell to this beautiful land and its good-natured inhabitants with the deepest regret. We have been ordered to march to Russia. Holstein, hospitable region, beautiful land! I will never forget your gardens and flower beds, your light, airy parlors, the honesty and good nature of your inhabitants! Oh, the time I have spent in this blooming garden has been one of the happiest of my life!

I went to tell Lopatin that the regiment was ready to move out. The colonel was standing pensively before the mirror brushing his hair, apparently without even noticing it.

"Tell the regiment to go. I'm staying here for half an hour," he said, sighing heavily.

"Why do you sigh, Colonel? Aren't you eager to return to our native land?" I asked.

Instead of replying, the colonel sighed again. On my way out I saw the younger baroness, one of our colonel's hostesses, a lovely young woman twenty-four years old, dissolved in tears. Now I understand why the colonel does not want to leave. Yes, at times like that one's *native land* doesn't count for much.

And so, reluctantly and mournfully, we parted with Holstein, and, of course, already forever. There we were loved, although not all of us, it's true—but where is everyone loved? They loved us in many respects: as allies, as staunch defenders, as Russians, as good lodgers, and, finally, as gallant lads. The last is confirmed by the fact that three or four amazons are following the squadron, all of them fully expecting to marry the men they follow. But disillusion is nearer than they imagine. One of them was brought along by Pel., a forty-year-old, married scatterbrain. He keeps trying to assure us all that his Phillida is following him under the spell of an inconquerable love for him. We listen and can hardly restrain our laughter. An inconquerable love for Pel., a balding scarecrow, comical and stupid! Perhaps it is some kind of enchantment—*nothing could be more handsome than his froggy eyes!*

What kind of strange reckoning is it that chooses the very worst weather for a march? It is late autumn now, muddy, dark, and rainy. Our only diversion is the comical scenes between our pairs of lovers. Yesterday evening Tornesi told me that he had been to see Pel.; *son objet* was sitting there also, all in black and deeply pensive. Pel. looked at her with a compassion which in him was extremely comical and unseemly. "This is the consequence of love," he said with a sigh. "She languishes and grieves, she cannot live without me! What a fatal passion love is!"

Tornesi almost choked in the effort to keep from bursting out laughing. "But you're with her, after all; why should she grieve?"

"She is always doubting my love; she despairs of keeping me with her always."

"Of course. You're married, after all. I don't understand why you brought her along."

"What else could I do? She wanted to drown herself!"

"I really don't know," Tornesi said to me, "where she could have drowned herself. I don't think there's a river anywhere near Ütersen. Pel. went on talking nonsense in this manner for a while longer, but just listen to the outcome of it all, and how Pel. had the honor of knowing and seeing it: I went to order them to bring around my horse. On my way back I met the melancholy beauty in the hallway. She threw herself on my neck, pressed her face to mine, and began weeping: 'Cher officier! Sauvez moi de ce misérable! Je le déteste, je ne l'ai jamais aimé, il m'a trompé!'[3] That was all she had time to say before Pel. opened the door from his room. He's so sure of the power of his good looks and virtues that he was not in the least disturbed at seeing us together. Damned buffoon!"

*Poznan.* Here fate decreed the dissolution of all the bonds of love. I found out about it by chance. I had to go to the regimental office to see Ja., who is presently serving as adjutant, because our poor Tyzin can no longer either fill the post or even follow the regiment; he remained behind in a German town with his sorrowing young wife. Ja.'s quarters consisted of four rooms, two for offices and two in which he lived with his little page, whom we all called "the handsome baron." When I learned that the adjutant was not at home, I went to his rooms to see the baron. I

---

3. "Dear officer! Save me from that scoundrel! I hate him, I never loved him, he deceived me!" (French)

opened the door and stopped in perplexity, not sure whether to enter or retreat. A young lady was walking around the parlor in great sorrow, weeping and wringing her hands. I glanced around the room and, when I did not see the handsome baron, took a closer look at the face of the weeping beauty and recognized her for Ja.'s page. "Oh, Dieu! à quoi bon cette métamorphose, et de quoi vous pleurez si amèrement?"[4]

She answered me in German that she was very unhappy; Ja. was sending her back to Hamburg, and now she did not know how to show herself in her own land. I went away feeling genuinely sorry for her.

The next day, on the march, I no longer saw any of our amazons behind the squadron and asked Tornesi what fate had overtaken them.

"The most ordinary and inevitable," he replied. "They got tired of them and sent them back."

A chorus usually rides ahead of the squadron and sings almost continuously throughout the march. I wouldn't think that they find this very enjoyable; it would be boring to sing all day even of one's own volition, and all the more so against it. Today I witnessed an amusing method of arousing enthusiasm for singing. Sergeant Verusha is our chorus leader, and the most unfortunate choice possible for the post. He starts every song in a nasal voice more repulsive than any I have ever heard; Tornesi and I always take off at a breakneck gallop to get away from it. Now for some reason or other Verusha was in a bad mood or perhaps ill, and he sang badly as usual but unusually softly. Rszęsnicki noticed it: "Well, well, what's the meaning of that sickly voice? Sing the way you should!" Verusha went on singing the same way. "Ah, then I'll put some spirit into you!" and with these words Rszęsnicki began using his whip to beat time on Verusha's back as he sang.

I caught sight of this tragicomedy from a distance. I galloped up to Rszęsnicki and seized his arm: "That's enough, Captain, please. What's come over you? How can he think about songs with a whip at his back?"

I have a certain authority over Rszęsnicki's mind. He listened to me and stopped encouraging Verusha with his whip, leaving him at liberty to twang away as he chose.

*Vitebsk.* Here we are, back on our native soil again. I'm not at all pleased; I can't forget Holstein. There we were guests, and for some reason I like being a guest better than a stay-at-home.

Our regiment has been assigned to quarters in Janovichi, the muddiest little town in the world. I found my brother here. He has been promoted to officer's rank and, at his own request, transferred to our Lithuanian

---

4. "Oh, my God! To what do we owe this transformation, and why are you weeping so bitterly?" (French)

regiment. Honestly, I can't understand why both of us are always short of money. Papa gives money to him and the emperor to me, and we are perpetually short! My brother tells me that if we were to march out of Janovichi, the Jews would cling to the tail of his horse; there is no more forceful way to express how much he owes them.

"What's to be done, Vasily? My only advantage over you is that I'm not in debt, but I have no money either."

"You will have. The emperor will send it to you."

"And Father to you; and Father will give you all that he has."

"That's true, too. Perhaps I should write to Papa?"

"You haven't done it yet?"

"No."

"Write then, write by this very post."

While we wait for spring to set in, we are both staying at headquarters, because there is absolutely nothing to do in the squadrons. My brother and I obtained a sort of tea which is beyond belief both for cheapness and quality. I paid three silver rubles for it, and no matter how much water we pour into the teapot, the tea remains just as strong. We drink it most contentedly and don't worry about the reason for this singularity.

*Janovichi.* The time for exercises, for drill on foot and horse, has come; spring is here. The squadron commander insists that I return to the squadron.

Comical news! K. is in love! He came to Janovichi to take me with him to the squadron. On the way he told me that he had become acquainted with the landowner P., and that young P., her daughter, is never out of his mind; and, finally, that he sleeps all the time from love and sorrow. He confirmed the truth of these words with action: he immediately fell asleep. I found all this extremely comical, but since I was alone, I somehow was able to keep from laughing and tranquilly studied the charms of a nature once again in bloom. However, it is evident that K.'s love is no joking matter. As soon as he and I arrived in the squadron, he woke up as if by instinct, sent at once for the sergeant-major, gave him a few quick instructions, and ordered new horses harnessed. "Come with me, Aleksandrov, I'll introduce you."

"To whom, Major?"

"To my neighbor ladies."

"Undoubtedly to your P.?"

"Well, yes."

"Let's go then. I shall be very happy to see our major's future wife."

"May it only be so, my dear fellow! Somehow I keep thinking about her day and night."

"Well, let's hurry then."

I thought that on the road there would be no end to K.'s talk of the beauty, virtues, talents, and all possible bodily and spiritual perfections of the divine P., but my apprehensions were very pleasantly deceived. K. got into the *bryczka* without even saying, "Make it quick," and, as if he were going not to see a sweet, lovely, and amiable young lady, but to a drill or review, began discussing formations, horses, lances, uhlans, and pennons—in short, everything good and bad except the subject which I thought must be engaging his mind and heart. What an odd person! After talking for half an hour, as if to order, about every aspect of our life in the ranks, at last he sighed and said, "It's a long way yet," muffled his head in his greatcoat, leaned back in the corner of the *bryczka*, and fell asleep. I was delighted that he did. K. is a kind man and a reliable officer, but he has neither the education nor the breadth of knowledge nor even the sort of wit that makes companionship and conversation agreeable. I was glad to be left free to think about and look at whatever I wished.

Everything about this odd lover is comical! How can he wake up exactly when it is necessary? Right at the portal he opened his eyes, looking as if he had not slept for a minute. We got out of our carriage. As we climbed the stairs, I told K. that he should present me to the ladies. "Don't worry. I'll know how to do that!" This comical answer made me fear some strange recommendation, but he managed the business better than I expected. K. pointed at me and said simply, "An officer from my squadron, Aleksandrov."

The young woman who has subdued K.'s martial heart is eighteen or so, white-skinned, blonde, tall, slender, with long, shining hair, large, dark gray eyes, a large mouth, white teeth, and the bold mien of a grenadier, all of which pleased me greatly. If I were K., I too would choose her for my life's partner and love her just the way he does: I would come to see her without hurrying to arrive, sleep the entire way, and wake up at the front door. I immediately set about becoming acquainted, and in half an hour we had become fast friends. But it was her mother who amazed, dumbfounded, and captivated me. She is a truly beautiful woman, a real Venus, if Venus could show signs of being forty years old. That enchanting face combines every possible lovely charm: sparkling black eyes, thin black brows, coral lips, a complexion beyond description! I couldn't stop looking at her. At last, since I only know how to say what I think, I told her bluntly that I couldn't take my eyes off her face and found it hard to imagine what a ravishing creature she must have been in youth.

"Yes, young man, you are not mistaken. I was a Venus. There was no other name or comparison for me. Yes, I was a beauty in the full sense of the word!"

Despite the fact that she says this about herself, I find her still very modest. She says, "I was a beauty," but she is now, this minute, extraordinarily beautiful. Does she really not see it?

K. has asked for P.'s hand! The wedding is next week, and I am very glad. The young woman is rather well educated, cheerful in disposition, and free and unconstrained in manner. I hope to have a good time at their house when she becomes our regimental lady. Oh, how I dislike those unapproachable she-bears who try to maintain a high tone and fail to remark that they have all the outward appearance not of distinguished ladies but rather of sulky merchants' wives. Silly women!

Yesterday we were invited to a ball. I went with the K.s. The bride-groom followed his previous habit and fell asleep, and, since the journey was about ten versts, I had ample time to talk to the major's young wife. We told each other stories and comical incidents and laughed up-roariously with no fear of rousing the happy husband. At last our conversation took on a new tenor; we talked of the heart, love, ineffable emotions, constancy, happiness, unhappiness, intellect—God knows what all we talked about. I noticed in my companion a turn of mind that made me wonder why she had married K. and asked her about it. "I am poor," she replied, "and, as you see, no beauty. My heart was free, Mama found K. an advantageous suitor for me, and I saw no great hardship in obeying her will."

"That's all very well, but do you love him?"

"I love him," she said, after a moment's silence. "I love him, of course, without passion or ardor, but I love him as a good husband and a good man. He has an excellent disposition; his kind heart makes up for all his shortcomings."

Our army ball was just like any other: very merry in fact and very dull in the telling.

Now I must describe an action of which I have been feeling ashamed from morning to night for several days. Let this be a form of con-fession and my punishment.

I wanted to make an excursion to the beautiful woods around Polotsk, so I asked for a week's leave and, taking R. as my companion, drove with him to his father's estate. We were given horses that were not only half dead, but quite prepared to finish the process, and we rode in a simple cart down a muddy road, dragging or jolting, depending on the horses we had. There were no adventures to speak of, unless one considers it an adventure that the yawning coachman, passing a crowd of oncoming peasants, brushed one man with the shaft, knocked him down, and rode over him; and that the outraged *muzhiks* followed us with clubs for over half a verst, calling us—namely us, and not our coachman—*dogs* and *hotheads*.

At last we arrived at the river across which lay R.'s estate. While they prepared the ferry, my comrade went into the hut to smoke a pipe, and I stayed on the bank to admire the sunset. Just then an old man about ninety years old approached me, as I thought, to ask for alms. At the sight of his white hair, stooped body, trembling hands, and dim eyes, his dreadful gaunt body and ancient rags, compassion, a heartfelt compassion, overwhelmed me! But how this divine emotion could become confounded with a devilish one, I swear I don't understand. I took out my purse to give the poor man some substantial aid. The money in it was eight gold pieces and a paper bill worth ten rubles. At more than one station they had refused to accept this miserable bill, considering it dubious, and I was shameless enough to give it to that poor old man.

"I don't know, my friend," I said to the overjoyed beggar, "whether anyone will give you the full amount for it, but in case they don't, take it to the Catholic rector, and tell him that I was the one who gave you the bill. Then you'll receive ten rubles from him, and he will return this piece of paper to me. Goodbye, my friend!"

I ran down to the ferry. We crossed the river, and an hour later we were under *pan* R.'s hospitable roof. I spent four days there, roaming the dark groves, reading, drinking coffee, bathing, and hardly ever coming face to face with R.'s family or even with R. himself.

"Our guest is not very sociable," said his sister to R. "He goes off into the forest in the morning and returns for dinner, and then we don't catch sight of him again until evening. Does he behave that way in the regiment, too? Does he have his wits?"

"I don't know. The rector praises him."

"Well, the rector's praise doesn't mean a thing. He loves him madly ever since he gave ten rubles to old Józef."

"Why?"

"Why? Why does one give to all those who beg alms in Christ's name?"

"What! Old Józef actually goes out to beg, and his owner permits it? At his age?"

"Yes, at his age. His owner not only permits it; he orders anyone from his village who cannot work for any reason, be it old age, weakness, illness, youth, or slow wits, driven out to ply that trade. Oh, a pretty detachment scatters from his town over the neighborhood each morning!"

"What a horrible man! I didn't know, however, that my comrade is so soft-hearted to the poor."

"Your comrade is unsociable, and all unsociable people have some eccentricity or other."

"Do you really consider compassion an eccentricity?"

"Certainly, when it's carried to extremes. Why give ten rubles to one man? Is he really so rich?"

"I don't think so; I don't know him very well yet, though."

I was forced to listen to this conversation between brother and sister against my will. I had returned an hour earlier than usual from my outing, and, since I took no great pleasure in the chat of old R. and his high-minded daughter, I took a book out to a summerhouse at the far end of the garden. The young R.s arrived at the same spot and sat down on a turf couch five paces away from me. The obliging R. girl kept on talking about me for a while longer and kept on calling me unsociable and the rector's pet.

At last her brother lost his patience. "Do me a favor, quit it now! You're boring me to tears; that's enough about him. I wanted to speak to you about convincing Father to give me some money. We have no stepmother now, there's no one to prevent it."

"But there is someone."

"For instance? Do you advise against it?"

"It's a sin for you to talk like that. I love you, and although I know that all money passes straight from your hands onto a card, I would even be prepared to give you my inheritance, if it were in my power. No, dear Adolf. It is not I who will prevent Father from giving you money, but his own resolve, a firm, irrevocable determination not to give you so much as a *kopeck.* . . ."

I heard nothing more, but when I got to the door of the summerhouse, I saw the brother and sister running toward the house. Evidently the R. girl's last words had driven her brother into a rage. He rushed off to see his father, and she followed him. I hurried there, too.

Old R. has astonishing willpower. I found them all together in the drawing-room. The girl was pale and trembling. Her brother sat on the windowsill, clutching convulsively at the spine of an armchair and trying futilely to appear composed. His eyes burned and his lips quivered. But the old man received me very kindly and asked me calmly and jocularly, "Do you really intend to become a hermit in my woods? I would like to know in advance so I can prepare you a nice little cave, moss, dry leaves, and all the necessities of the reclusive life."

I don't know how the business between father and son ended, but their parting was amicable. The capricious Adolf embarrassed his sister dreadfully and me somewhat, by insisting that she and I look very much alike and that, since his sister is his portrait to the life, all three of us are identical. How flattering! Young R. and the devil are as alike as two drops of water. . . .

At last we clambered back into the cart and left. At the first post-station I had to pay for horses, and, when I took out my purse to get the money, I was astonished to find that I was short two of my eight gold pieces. I tried to recollect whether I had left the purse on the table or on the bed when I went for my outings, but no, it seems that it was always with me. At last I remembered and rejoiced wholeheartedly: the gold pieces had undoubtedly fallen into the bill which lay with them in the purse, folded into eighths in order to fit. I pulled it out and gave it to the beggar at the ferry without unfolding it. And thus he received by God's providence the aid which I intended for him but nearly ruined by my satanic reckoning. Only a monster, however, would be capable of giving a poor man help which he can't be sure is valid. No, when I handed over the bill, I thought only that it would be redeemed for a much lower sum than it was worth, and at the stations they refused it because they saw that I had gold, and the Poles can't bear any currency except jingling coin.

*Vitebsk.* I am living at the house of commission-agent S. My leave is not yet over, and I will enjoy myself more here than in the squadron. His Royal Highness, Prince Württemberg, likes to have army officers gather at his house in the evenings, and I join them there.[5] We dance and play various games, and the prince himself sometimes joins in our diversions.

## A Duel

Today, at about ten o'clock in the morning, R. came to tell me that he quarreled with Prince K. and the prince called him a scoundrel.

"I congratulate you! And what did you do?"

"Nothing. I said that he was a villain, but apparently he didn't hear it."

"That's a fine thing! And you've come to boast that you were called a scoundrel? That's the first time in my life I've ever heard of anyone calling a nobleman that and getting away without being slapped."

We were both standing by an open window as we talked, and I had no sooner finished speaking when, as ill luck would have it, Prince K. walked past. R. called him over. I think K. must have mistaken R.'s voice for mine, because he bowed politely and at once headed for my room; but he was as greatly astonished as my host, two other officers, and I were when R. met him at the door with a question ("Was it me you called a scoundrel?") and a sudden slap.

S. asked us all to get out of his house. "Fight wherever you wish, gentlemen, but not here!"

We all left the town. A duel was inevitable, of course, but what a duel! I could never have imagined anything so comical as that which I now saw. It began with conditions: to avoid headwounds, and to fight until first blood. R. made difficulties over finding someone to act as second and a sharp saber. I immediately volunteered to be his second and handed him my saber, quite sure that we were in for nothing more than a good laugh.

5. Prince Alexander Württemberg (1771–1833), Alexander I's maternal uncle, was appointed governor of Belorussia in 1811.

At last the two scatterbrains joined combat. There was no way I could continue to look serious, and no reason to; from start to finish of this parody of a duel, I wore an involuntary wry smile. In order to observe the condition against head wounds and obviously in mortal fear of their own sabers, the two adversaries bowed down almost to the ground. Each stretched the saber-equipped arm as far out in front as he could and aimlessly waved it right and left. Furthermore, they avoided seeing the dreadful gleam of steel by not looking—and it seems to me that they could not have looked, because both men were bent almost double. The consequence of these measures and precautions to keep the first condition was exactly its breach. R., who could not see where and how he was waving his saber, struck the prince on the ear and cut him slightly. The adversaries were overjoyed that this made it possible to end hostilities. The prince, however, was inclined to make a fuss about the cut on his ear as a violation of the pact, but I quieted him by submitting that the only way to correct the error was to fight again. The two eccentric fellows went to the tavern, and I headed back to S.'s house.

"Well, what happened? How did it turn out?"

I told him.

"You're a mad fellow, Aleksandrov! What got into you, goading R. that way? On his own he would never have dreamed of challenging anyone to a duel, much less slapping anyone." (It had really not occurred to me that I was goading him into an illegal action, and only now do I see that S. was right.) Remembering the scene at the door, S. burst out laughing.

I have to bid farewell to Prince Württemberg's drawing-room! I must leave Vitebsk and return to muddy Janovichi. The squadron commanders are howling for the return of the officers to their posts. There's nothing to be done; tomorrow I will go.

*Janovichi*. The mud here seems to be muddier than anywhere else in the world. The only way to get across the square to see a comrade is on horseback. True, it might be possible on foot, but only by sticking to the Jews' houses and making one's way along earth embankments, pressing right up against walls, windows, and doors, from which the voyager from different stock is deluged with steam and smells like vodka, beer, goosefat, goat's milk, mutton, and so on. After making this repulsive detour, one can be sure of a cold in the head.

*Vitebsk*. When I arrived this time, old S., who had been alarmed by our rowdy scene, would not let me take quarters with him, and I was assigned to the house of a merchant's young and lovely wife. I had no sooner made myself at home there when Kherov, a friend of my brother's, came to see me. "Hello, Aleksandrov! Have you been here long?"

"I just got here."

"And your brother?"

"He's with the squadron."

"Where are you dining, at the prince's?"

"I don't know. I'll report to the prince. If he invites me, I'll dine there."

"Look what famous spurs I bought."

"Silver?"

"Yes."

We were both standing by the table, and I rested my elbows on it in order to take a closer look at the spurs. Just then Kherov trod lightly on my foot. I glanced around. My hostess was standing right next to me. "Aren't you ashamed, gentlemen, to use such words in a house where only women are living?"

This was novel! I assured my hostess that our words could have been spoken in the presence of angels, let alone women.

"No, no! You can't convince me; I know what I heard."

"It can't be. You heard wrong, sweet hostess."

"I ask you not to call me *sweet* and to conduct yourself better in my home." And with this she went off grandly to her own rooms, leaving us to think whatever we wished of her sally.

As Kherov was picking up his shako to go, his eyes fell by chance on my purse. He saw the glitter of gold in it and stopped. "Your brother owes me money, Aleksandrov. Won't you pay it for him?"

"Gladly! How much does he owe you?"

"Two gold pieces."

"Take them, please."

"What a capital fellow you are, Aleksandrov! For that I'll make you a gift of my silver spurs."

Kherov left, and I ordered the new spurs screwed onto my boots at once, put them on, and went to report to the prince.

I returned to my quarters at one in the morning. A bed had been made for me on the floor of my little room. The house was already quiet, and only in my hostess's chamber was there a light still burning. Supposing myself in complete seclusion and full mistress of my room, I undressed without the least misgiving. True, I would have liked to lock the door, but since there was no hook, I merely shut it and went to bed, and I must have fallen asleep. At least I didn't hear the door to my chamber opening. I woke to the sound of shuffling feet as someone moved around my room. My first impulse was to cover my head with the blanket. I was afraid that the wandering creature would strike my face with its foot. I don't know why, but I didn't want to ask who was walking around, and that was for the best; suddenly I heard a voice, asking not at all loudly, "Where are you?" It was my hostess; she repeated impatiently, "*Where are you?"* and went on shuffling across the floor, saying, *"Where are you, anyway?* Come and see what I have in my ears instead of earrings; something wicked. It seems there's a wicked thing hanging in each ear— a devil, that is. A devil in each!" And with this she laughed, a wild sort of laughter, but still quite soft.

I was horrified. There was no doubt that my hostess was mad, that she had crept away from her maids' supervision and come to see me, namely me, and that she would very quickly find me in a room that was barely ten feet on a side. What would she do with me then? God knows what turn her thoughts might take. Perhaps she would take me for one of the demons she thought were hanging in her ears instead of earrings. I have heard that crazy people are very strong and so, if she were to attack me, I had little hope of coming out of the ludicrous single combat with honor. Thinking about all this, I held my breath, afraid to stir, but I found lying with my head muffled unbearably stuffy. I tried to throw back the blanket a little, and with this motion I touched the candlestick. It fell with a thump. A joyful cry from the madwoman froze my blood! But fortunately that same cry roused her women, and, just as she, exclaiming, threw herself on me, they ran in and seized her already falling on me with outstretched arms.

Nature has given me a strange and disturbing trait of character: I like and get accustomed and wholeheartedly attached to the quarters where I live, the horse I ride, the dog I take in out of pity, and even the duck and the chicken I buy for my table: I immediately become sorry to use them for the purpose for which they were bought, and they live with me until they vanish somewhere by chance. Knowing that I have this comical weakness, I thought that I would regret muddy Janovichi when I was forced to part with it. However, thank God, no! We are off on the march, and I am extremely glad to be leaving this perpetual, never-drying swamp. It is the one place on the earthly globe to which I never want to return.

*Polotsk.* This morning as I left the Catholic church I caught sight of R. He was walking very fast and seemed to be worried about something. I'm always very amused by tales of his victories: he is the perpetual hero of some incident or other and comes out of each crowned with myrtle or laurel. In hopes that I might hear something of the sort now, I ran after him, caught up with him, came up beside him, and took his arm to stop him. "What are you so worried about, comrade? Do you need a second again? I'm at your service." My appearance seemed to make a disagreeable impression on R. This surprised me. "What's wrong with you? Where are you going in such a hurry?"

"Nowhere! I'm just walking. Papa sends you his greetings. . . . Forgive me, brother, I owe you an apology. I gambled away your money."

"What money?"

"The two gold pieces."

"I don't understand you."

"Didn't you get a letter from the rector?"

"No."

"Well, then you can't in fact know anything about it. The poor old man to whom you gave ten rubles found two gold pieces in the bill and, assuming quite sensibly that you had no intention of giving him such a sum, took them to the rector who praised the poor man's rare honesty and brought the gold pieces to Papa. I was there at the time. The rector recounted the story of the gold pieces and asked us to send them back to you. I undertook the commission, but, unfortunately, before we saw each other, I encountered a tempting chance to try my luck. I staked them on a card and—was left your debtor."

"My pleasure! Be so as long as you like. But why did your papa deal with the matter so misanthropically? The money should have been left to the person Providence designated to have it."

"Well, well, aren't you the philosopher! I could argue the opposite case, but God be with you, I haven't the time just now. I'm on my way to borrow a cordon and epaulets from the officers' supply. Goodbye!"

The scatterbrain ran off, and I went for a walk. I always walk very fast, surrendering myself totally to alluring dreams. Now I began thinking of the beauties of nature and of the many joys this world has to offer mankind! I also thought about the enigmatic paths which direct us toward some chance or other in life. I thought that the very best way to maintain our spiritual peace is by following humbly the Right Hand which leads us in those paths, without seeking to understand why this or that happens one way rather than another. My thoughts were now grand, now pious, now sad, now cheerful, and at last even cheerfully scatterbrained. The joyful supposition that someday I will have a fine house where I can accommodate my old father, furnishing his rooms with all the comforts and all the splendor of luxury; of buying him a calm saddlehorse; of seeing that he has a carriage, musicians, and a first-rate cook—this supposition so enraptured me that I began capering on the spot like a wild goat. Now I see how true to life Perrette is: the strong bodily motion dissipated my daydreams.[6] Once again I found myself an uhlan officer who wears all his silver and has none put aside. To make my dream come true will take miracles at the very least, and without them it is not to be. Having once more become an uhlan lieutenant, in that capacity I had to rush back to the squadron in order not to miss the time fixed to march. Lateness is sometimes harshly penalized.

6. Durova is referring to the Fontaine fable, "La Laitière & le Pot au lait," in which the milkmaid Perrette is so excited by dreams of multiplying profits that her capers spill the milk she is carrying to market.

# Chapter Twelve

## 1815

There is nothing remarkable about this march of ours except the reason for it: Napoleon somehow disappeared from the island which the allied monarchs deemed fit to hold, along with the man himself, his plans, objectives, and dreams, his talents as a great military leader, and his wide-ranging genius.[1] Now all of that has again broken free, and once more there is movement throughout Europe. Troops are on the march. Once more our pennons flutter in the air, our lances gleam, our good steeds frisk! There bayonets glitter, and the drum is heard. The menacing sound of cavalry trumpets solemnly wakes the still drowsy sunrise. Everywhere life is ebullient and movement never ceases. Here the cuirassiers advance in imposing ranks, there the hussars sweep past, beyond them the uhlans fly, and now here comes our fine, disciplined, menacing infantry and the main defense, the powerful bulwark of our native land—the invincible musketeers! Although I love the cavalry madly, although I am a horse soldier from my cradle, every time I watch the infantry advancing at a sure, firm pace, with fixed bayonets and menacing drum-roll, I feel an emotion which has something of both reverence and dread, I don't know how to express it. All that comes to mind at the sight of a formation of hussars or uhlans flying past is the thought of what gallant lads they are, how well they ride, how dashingly they cross sabers! Woe to the enemy, and this woe usually consists of more or less dangerous wounds or captivity, and nothing more. But when columns of infantry rush toward the enemy with their rapid, smooth, disciplined motion, there are no more gallant lads, that's all over: these are heroes who bear inevitable death or go to inevitable death themselves—there is no middle ground. The cavalryman gallops up, gallops away, wounds, rushes past, turns back again, and sometimes kills, but his every motion is eloquent of mercy for the enemy: all this is merely the harbinger of death. But the infantry formation is death itself, dreadful, inevitable death.

*Kovno.* With no further adventures we arrived at the border and settled down in quarters in the vicinity of this small town. Sometimes one gets into devastating positions quite unexpectedly. Yesterday a most comical misfortune befell me. My brother and I went to dinner with a Kovno

---

1. Napoleon left the island of Elba on February 15/27, 1815 to raise an army and reclaim his empire.

201

squire, pan St-la, a hospitable Pole of the old school. Despite his sixty years, St-la is still a handsome, gallant fellow, one of those rare people who live long and never age until the day they die. He seems no more than forty. His sister and his niece, an ordinary looking girl of eighteen or so, live with him. It must be assumed that pan St-la took a liking to my brother and me, because he spared nothing to make our visit agreeable. After a sumptuous meal, delicacies of all sorts, coffee, ices—in short, everything to satiate us—he decided to crown his hospitality with what he considered the most elegant treat of all, his niece's singing: "Zaśpiewaj że, moja kochana, dla tych wałęcznych żołnierzów."[2]

In vain the poor girl tried to persuade him that she could not sing, that she had a head cold and a sore throat. Her despotic uncle would hear none of it and persisted in his demand that she sing that very minute. She had to submit and start singing for the two young uhlans. She started singing! . . . A voice like that can never be forgotten! I haven't the heart either to describe it or draw a comparison. The girl was right to resist this fatal singing with all her might. As I heard the first sounds of her voice, I felt a shudder running through my body. I wished I could drop through the floor or be a hundred versts away from the singer, but instead I was on the sofa directly opposite her, and, to my misfortune, the spirit of temptation made me glance at my brother. He didn't dare to raise his eyes and was glowing as red as fire. I didn't know what to do with myself, I didn't know how to keep from laughing out loud, and at last I realized that my efforts were bound to fail and gave up trying. As the saying goes, I split my sides with laughter. The singer fell silent. And I, who had made an utter fool of myself in her eyes, sought in vain for some way to excuse that damnable laugh. Fortunately for me, she was singing a Russian song. In it there was some mention of a butterfly, a *babochka*, and the girl, being Polish and not knowing the correct pronunciation, called it a *babushka*. I put all the blame on this word and they all pretended to believe me, but nobody asked for the singing to continue. Having so well recompensed pan St-la for his hospitality and consideration, we rode back to Vilna, where our headquarters is located and where we will be stationed—until further orders.

K.'s squadron is stationed on the estate of Prince Bishop G. where his sister lives. There is nothing on earth she resembles less than what she is—that is, Princess G.

Yesterday I saw our major's young wife for the first time since her marriage. She has changed beyond all recognition; she has gotten taller

2. "Give us a song, my dear, for these gallant soldiers." (Polish)

and stouter. Looking at her, I couldn't believe my eyes. How could she, in such a short time, have become such a real *bogatyr Dobrynia?* I call her that, because K., enraptured by her height and weight, tells everyone who will listen to him, "My Sasha has gotten *nicely* stout."[3]

At midnight today, as I was returning from headquarters and riding past fields sown with oats, I saw something white flitting among the heads of grain. I rode over and asked, "Who's there?"

At this question the white object straightened up and answered loudly, "It's me, your honor, an uhlan from the fourth platoon."

"What on earth are you doing here?"

"I'm trying, your honor!"

I ordered him to go to his quarters and never "try" again. These cutthroats have found an amusing way of fattening their horses. They take bags into the middle of the fields and spend all night tugging up oats; this is what they call "trying."

It rained for three days straight, but today the sun finally came out. I took my platoon into the green meadows and flew around with it for two hours—that is, we practiced platoon drill. After that I sent the men home and went for a ride. I dropped in on V. and saw his *divinité,* who now wears woman's dress and looks astonishingly like a peg-top. From there I returned to my hamlet. As I rode up to my quarters, I thought I heard a whacking noise. At last I made out voices begging for mercy. *Oh, God, that's at my place, someone's punishing the men with rods! Who on earth would dare?*

I pushed my horse to a gallop, and, just as I raced into the yard, K. ordered the men to quit and came to meet me: "Excuse me, Aleksandrov. I was taking care of some domestic business for you. Your uhlans stole eighteen jugs of vodka from a Jew and hid them in the straw in your stable. They wouldn't let the Jew in to see you, so he came to me, and I've been sorting it out and punishing them. Don't be angry, brother; it was the only way."

"Why should I be angry? On the contrary, I'm very grateful to you." But vexation seethed in my heart. What damnable folk these uhlans are! Who would willingly be their commander when others come and beat them before my very eyes?

Our entire life here on the border passes to no purpose: some of us smoke tobacco, some play cards, shoot at targets, break horses, and jump

---

3. Dobrynia is one of the heroes [*bogatyri*] of Russian epic songs; Durova is making a pun on the root *dobr-* [good, nice] in that name and in the verb *razdobret'* [to put on weight].

ditches or obstacles. But what I find most comical are our evening gatherings at the quarters of one or the other of our officers. Of course, there are no ladies at these gatherings, but despite that, music blares and we dance by ourselves. Everybody dances, young and old—mazurkas, quadrilles, ecossaises. I find it all most amusing. What pleasure can they, especially the older men, get from dancing without ladies? I always take the lady's part.

We are returning to Russia through Vilna.[4] Day after day passes repetitiously, monotonously. One day is just like the next: dawn breaks, and the general-march is played; we saddle up, lead out the horses, mount, and ride out—and off we go, pace by pace, to our evening quarters. Nothing disrupts the tranquillity of our peaceful marches. Not only does nothing ever happen, there is never even any rain or wind or storm—nothing that could rouse our sleeping march! We go, go, go—and get there. That's all there is to it.

This morning I was overjoyed! I should be ashamed of feeling it and ashamed to write it—but I was truly overjoyed to hear a plaintive wail somewhere near the major's quarters. At least it gave me a reason to spur my horse, gallop over, ask with concern, investigate. I took off at a full run to K.'s quarters and saw a scene at once comical and pitiful. I hastened to jump off my horse and stop the tragicomedy: the major was punishing the uhlan Bozier (whose comrades call him *Bozja*). At the first stroke the poor fellow set up a pitiful howl, stretching his arms to the heavens, "O mon Dieu, mon Dieu!"

"I'll give you *med'ju, med'ju,* you rascal!" said K., trying to look angry, an expression which was completely at odds with his comical face, however. But he really was quite vexed, and the poor Frenchman would have been forced to exclaim, "O mon Dieu, mon Dieu!" ten more times, and the honorable K. to repeat as often his, "I'll give you *med'ju, med'ju,*" if I had not persuaded him to quit. "Well, you shirker, thank this officer, or I would have given you thirty strokes instead of three."

"What did he do, Major?"

"He won't obey anybody, brother! The sergeant ordered him to clean his saddle and equipment and get ready to serve as courier to the colonel, and he didn't do any of it."

"But did he understand the sergeant's instructions?"

"That's a fine thing! Did he understand? It's his duty to understand!"

It would have been useless to try to reason with K.; I simply asked him

---

4. The regiments' westward movement was cut short by Napoleon's final defeat by the English and Prussians at Waterloo in June 1815.

to transfer poor Bozier to my platoon, and he readily agreed, saying, "Take him, take him, brother. I'm sick to death of that *German*."[5]

*Velikie luki.* We have arrived. We are at our post. These are our quarters, and it's all over! The enchanting scenes of foreign lands and foreign customs have vanished. The greeting of good-natured, honest Teutons will be heard no longer. There will be no more of those delightful, charming Polish evenings. Here everything is so pompous, so cold. Just try asking a peasant for a glass of water. It takes him a minute to stir from the spot, he goes lazily, barely moving; at last he gives you the water, and you've no sooner drunk it than it's: "Two kopecks for my trouble, sir!" Damn them all.

Our squadron is quartered in a place called Vjazovshchina. What a melodious name! A rhyme, and a very suitable one at that, leaps to mind.[6] Honestly, I have become so bad-tempered from boring quarters, smoky cottages, mud, rain, and cold autumn weather that I am vexed with everything: the dirty peasants for being dirty, their women for being ugly, for dressing repulsively and talking even more repulsively—for example, "*svetsa*," "*na petse*," "*sotsyla*." Damnable woman! Who could guess what she was doing when she "*sotsyla*"? Not what you might think: she was looking for something.[7]

It is living death to be stationed in this Vjazovshchina, with no books and no company, lying all day on planks beneath clouds of acrid smoke, listening to fine autumn rain lashing at windows covered with isinglass or, what is even more vile, bladder. Oh, nothing could be baser. . . . No, God be with them, all the agreeable features of such quarters! I am going back to headquarters.

*Velikie luki.* At least here the smoke does not sting my eyes, and I can look at God's world through clean glass. Every day G. comes to visit me and reminisce about the happy days we spent in Hamburg. He tells me for the hundredth time about the unforgettable *Josephine* and the enchanting evening when she took from him a gift of one thousand *louis-d'or* he had won gambling and found him quite amiable for an entire week. But afterwards she locked her door against him forever, and he, like a

5. In Russian, the word is *nemets.* Its root meaning is "mute" and in popular speech it was applied indiscriminately to all foreigners. In the next paragraph, where Durova has "Germanets" I use "Teuton."

6. The rhyme would be with the word for mud, *grjaz'.*

7. *Iskala.* The words are typical of northern and western Belorussian dialects. The Russian equivalents of the other words are *svecha* [candle] and *na peche* [on the stove].

lovelorn Spaniard, would bring his guitar before the house where this jewel lived. After a few romances, sighs, and other such tomfooleries, he would stretch his arms to the mute stone pile and exclaim like Abelard, "Retreat of Godfearing, honest maidens!" And he tells me all this completely seriously, with heartfelt sighs and tears welling up in his eyes. Oh, crazy, crazy G. . . .

## 1816. Two Weeks on Leave.

"Otto Ottovich! Give me leave to go to Peterburg for a week or two."

Stackelberg replied that it was impossible just now. The season for leaves was over, and, furthermore, His Majesty was in Peterburg. "But you could go on a commission, however," he said, after thinking it over for a minute.

"What commission, Colonel? If it's not something beyond my grasp, do me a favor and give it to me."

"The regiment has not managed to get from the Commissariat canvas, boots, scrap-iron, some kinds of weapons and harness, and about thirteen thousand in cash besides. If you undertake to receive it all and bring it back to the regiment, you can go. I'll give you authorization."

"Can I manage a commission like that, Colonel? After all, I don't understand anything about such things."

"There's nothing to understand. I'll give you an experienced sergeant and soldiers, they'll do everything. All you have to do is pick up the thirteen thousand from the Supply Depot. But to avoid misunderstandings, consult with Burogo. He's the paymaster—it's his department."

"Very good, Colonel. I'll go see Burogo right now and ask him. And if the duties of the commission are not beyond my grasp, then with your permission I'll leave for Peterburg tomorrow."

I couldn't get anything sensible from Burogo. When I asked him what I would have to do if I were sent to receive the supplies, he replied, "Observe the strictest honesty."

"How's that? Explain it to me."

"No explanations are necessary. Be honest! That's all there is to it. There's no other advice or directions I can give you, and no point in doing so."

"And those are of no use to me! I don't need your advice or directions in order to be honest."

"Don't bluster, brother. You're young yet, and there are situations you haven't met with in life. I know what I'm saying: be honest!"

Burogo is stubborn. I knew that once he started harping on the theme of honesty, he wouldn't have anything else to say. Well, God be with him! After all, Stackelberg said that he would send me an experienced sergeant. I'll risk it.

*Peterburg.* I went directly to my uncle's apartment. He is still in the same place and as happy with it as ever. His tastes are droll. His apartment is on Haymarket Square, and he says that he always has the most lively and varied scenes before his eyes. Yesterday he led me over to the window, "Look, Aleksandr, isn't this a truly picturesque spectacle?"

Thank God my uncle did not call it beautiful. Then I could not have agreed without lying, but now my conscience is clear. I replied, "Yes, it's just like a picture," adding mentally, *but it's a picture from the Flemish school.* I can't understand how anything so disagreeable to the eyes can be considered nice. What is there diverting about watching a crowd of clumsy, coarse, badly dressed peasants surrounded by carts, tar, bast mats, and other such vile stuff? That is the lively picture in all its diversity that my uncle has been admiring for ten years now.

Today there is a concert at Philharmonic Hall. I will most certainly go. I think it will be enchanting: they say that the orchestra is made up of first-rate musicians. It's true that I don't know much about music, but I love it more than anything. It has an ineffable effect on me: as soon as I hear those sounds whose power I can neither understand nor explain, I feel that there is no virtue or great feat of which I am not capable.

I sat along the wall below the orchestra, facing the assembly. A dignified, noble-looking, middle-aged man wearing a black frock-coat was sitting next to me.

The hall was teeming with ladies. They all seemed to me beautiful and beautifully attired. I always enjoy looking at women's costumes, although I would not wear them myself at any price. Their batiste, satin, velvet, flowers, feathers, and diamonds are seductively beautiful, but *my uhlan jacket is better!* At least it becomes me better and, after all, they say that one mark of good taste is to dress becomingly.

The ladies continued to arrive, and the rows of chairs kept moving closer to my neighbor and me.

"Look how close they are," I said, "Won't we have to give up our seats to them?"

"I don't think so," he said with a sardonic smile. "Our seats would be uncomfortable for them."

"Now they've added another row! One more, and they'll be right in our laps."

"Would that be so terrible?"

I said nothing and once again began studying the costumes of the new arrivals. A lady in a pink beret and dress was sitting directly opposite me. She was gaunt and swarthy, but her face was pleasant and her features intelligent. She appeared to be at least thirty. General Khrapovitsky was standing beside her armchair. Could she be his wife? I stared fixedly at her. Her appearance seemed to suggest something out of the ordinary.

At last I turned to my neighbor, "Permit me to ask, who is the lady in pink, directly opposite us?"

"Khrapovitskaja, the wife of the general who is standing beside her armchair."

"I heard something—"

My neighbor gave me no chance to finish. "Yes, yes, we haven't many heroines like that one!"[8]

This comment pricked my self-esteem. "It seems there was one—"

Again I was interrupted. "Yes, there was, but not any more. She died; she couldn't take it."

This was a novelty! I have had occasion to hear my own story many times with all possible additions and emendations, often absurd ones; but no one has ever before told me to my face that I am dead. Where did he get that? How can the rumor of my death be spreading when I am alive and known personally to the tsar? However, let them think so; perhaps it is for the best. . . . While these thoughts were flying through my head, I was looking at my neighbor—without seeing him, of course—but he was also looking at me and seemed to read my thoughts from my eyes. "You don't believe it? I heard it from people who are related to her."

I didn't reply. This sepulchral conversation alarmed me, and, furthermore, I was afraid that he might notice how personally I was taking it. I didn't say another word to him until the end of the concert.

Today marks a week since my arrival in Peterburg, and today I had to get down to business. I went to report to the colonel on duty, Dobrovo. The name suits him very well: he has a pleasant, good-natured face.[9]

"When did you get here?" he asked, as soon as I had finished the usual routine patter by which we inform our commanders who we are, where from, and for what purpose.

8. Sof'ja (born Dedeneva) Khrapovitskaja was one of the other "amazons" of the Napoleonic era. Dressed as a page, she accompanied her husband, Matvej Khrapovitskij, throughout the 1812 campaign and received a medal "For the Taking of Paris" in 1814 (For Khrapovitskij, see [fon-]Frejman, O. P., Pazhi za 183 goda (1711–1894), part 1 [Friedrichshamn, 1894], 99–101; his wife's exploits are mentioned in a memoir by M. M. Muromtsev, "Vospominanija," Russkij arkhiv [1890], 1:68). A woman calling herself "Saltan" was arrested in Orlov in April 1815 passing for an uhlan lieutenant (Istoricheskij vestnik [1894], 11:592–93). Yet a third amazon of the period was Vasilisa Kozhina, a peasant who organized a partisan brigade of boys and women in the Smolensk region in 1812 (Bol'shaja Sovetskaja Entsiklopedia, 2d ed., 21 [1953], 537).
9. This is another pun on the dobr- [good, nice] root.

I said I had been in Peterburg for a week.

"And you're just reporting? You deserve a good dressing down for that. Have you reported to the prince?"

"Not yet."

"I've never heard the like! Come here at eight o'clock in the morning, and I'll take you to see the prince."

From Dobrovo I went to the Commissariat. Dolinsky, the manager, thought I was fresh from the cadet academy and was astonished when I said I had been in the army for ten years.

My uhlans are master thieves. I am not exaggerating in the least. Every day they tell me, "Your honor, today we made such and such *economies.* At first I didn't understand, but now I know: they take canvas to measure and steal it on the spot. What a queer fellow Burogo is! That must be what he meant when he kept on telling me to be honest. How amusing! What can I do about it? Am I really supposed to preach honesty to men who, like the Spartans, consider adroit theft a proof of gallantry? We tell an uhlan, "*Try* to see that your horse has enough to eat." He interprets the order his own way by *trying* to steal oats from the fields. No, no, I really have no intention of bothering with all this nonsense; let them steal! Who told Stackelberg to give me a commission which is so totally beyond my grasp? He said he would give me an experienced sergeant. A great help that is! The pilfering has gone much more smoothly since the experienced sergeant arrived. Now they tell me that they will be able to *economize* enough canvas for the entire infirmary. I heard this as I walked past while they were tying up bales. Damn them anyway, with their canvas and their bales! All these unaccustomed pursuits—standing, watching, counting, and making reports—have given me a headache.

Today I was at my tedious duty by eleven o'clock, and, since I saw no great need for standing exactly where they were receiving things, I strolled through the passageways, sometimes stopping to rest my elbows on the railings, carried away in thought to places that bore not the slightest resemblance to the Commissariat. On one of these stops, a peremptory challenge rang out near me: "Honorable officer!"

I looked around. Behind me stood a tall, dried-up official with a German face. He was wearing a uniform with tabs on the collar. "What can I do for you?" I asked.

"What is your regiment?" I told him. "You're here to receive supplies, of course?"

"Yes."

"How dared you start taking them without letting me know? How dared you not report to me?"

Dumbfounded by this question from a man who looked to me like a civilian official, I replied that I was obliged to report only to my military superiors.

"I am your superior now! Be so good as to report to me, sir! I am ordering you in the name of the prince. And why aren't you accounting to me for your progress? You are the only men I know nothing about and from whom I get nothing."

"And you are the only man I don't understand at all!"

"What! How's that? You dare to talk to me like that? I'll inform the prince."

"And I will tell you the same thing in the prince's presence: I don't understand you, I don't know who you are, what rights you have to demand accounts and reckonings from me, and why I should report to you."

He quieted down. "I am Counselor P. The prince has entrusted me to see that officers here to receive supplies do not waste their time and that there are no delays in the reception. That is why you should inform me every evening how much you have taken. Now do you understand me, honorable officer?"

"I do."

"And so tomorrow please report to me for instructions. I demand it in the name of the prince."

"I can't. Tomorrow I have to be at Colonel Dobrovo's and go with him to see the prince."

"No, you have to go with me. I will present you to the prince."

"For heaven's sake, what authority do you have to present me? My actual superior, a military man, should do it."

At these words P. went nearly berserk. He shouted and ordered other things in the name of the prince, but I stopped listening and went back to my men. I saw that they were about ready to stop work for the day, and I returned to my uncle's. I told him all about my comical encounter in the passageways.

The next day I went to see Dobrovo, and from there together with him to see the prince. Our corps commander received me like anyone else; he heard who I was, why, and where from. When I was through, he nodded his head slightly and paid me no further attention, leaving me at liberty to do as I wished—stand, sit, walk around, stay there for an hour or two, or go away immediately. I chose the last alternative and went to the Commissariat. There I found my men already at work, once again taking in supplies, measuring, cheating. I don't consider that I have any obligation to try to make sense of it. Why entrust such a commission to a line officer? I am not a paymaster or quartermaster. If I take in things I shouldn't, they have only themselves to blame.

Thus justifying myself to my conscience, I went to see Count Arakcheev. While the adjutant was announcing me, a staff officer entered. My free ways in the count's anteroom clearly made him ill-at-ease; he huffed up and began looking me over, measuring me visually from head to toe. I didn't notice it for five minutes or so, but when I walked over to a table to look at a book lying open there, I happened to glance at him. He could no longer bear such disrespect; his face expressed insulted pride. How dare a mere officer walk around, how dare he pick up a book? In short, how dare he even stir in the presence of a staff-officer? How dare he fail to notice him, when he should be standing still in a respectful posture with his eyes fixed on his superior? All these words were stamped on the officer's countenance as he asked me with a disdainful mien, "Who are you? *What* are you?"

I ascribed this odd question to his inability to ask a better one and replied simply, "An officer of the Lithuanian regiment!" Just then I was called to the count.

They say that the count is a harsh man but, no, to me he showed himself to be kind and even good-natured. He came over to me, took my hand, and said he was very pleased to meet me in person. He reminded me obligingly that he had done everything my letters asked without delay and with pleasure.

I replied that I considered it my duty to come and see him to repeat again in person my gratitude for his gracious attention.

The count bade me farewell with the assurance that he was prepared to do everything he could for me. Such great courtesy seemed to me quite incompatible with the rumor that is spreading everywhere of his mo-roseness—his haughtiness, as some call it. Perhaps the count merely loses his temper at times; there is no great harm in that.[10]

From the count's I went to see the NN family, who love me like one of their own kin. They were about to go to the theater: "Wouldn't you like to come with us? They're giving *Fingal* today; you're a lover of tragedy, I believe?"

I accepted the invitation with delight. At six o'clock two gaunt spinsters, the sisters D., came to see them: "Oh, dear, you must be on the way to the theater!"

"Yes. Wouldn't you like to come too?"

"Won't we crowd you?"

"Not at all!"

At seven o'clock they came to tell us that the carriage was waiting, and

---

10. After the War of 1812, Arakcheev was entrusted by Alexander I to reform the army through the creation of a military caste which could lead self-sufficient lives in permanent settlements on government lands. Arakcheev's zeal brought him the reputa-tion of martinet to which Durova refers.

out we went—I could have said, out we spilled—onto the portal. There were exactly eight of us, and the carriage had room only for two! "How on earth will we all fit?" I asked in amazement.

"I'll manage it," said NN, making haste to seat me in the carriage. "Sit as far back in the corner as you can." I thought that he needn't have bothered with the advice, because the other seven would undoubtedly crush me farther into the corner than I would like. To my woe, I had brought along my raincape, too. I don't know what unfathomable means NN used to seat us all so that we were sitting peacefully without crumpling our costumes or suffocating, even though we were all of a respectable height and weight—that is, there were among us neither dwarfs nor skeletons. *Praise be to your tactics, estimable NN*, I thought.

Two guards officers drove up to the portal of the theater just as we did. One of the ladies of our company was a beauty, and unfortunately she had to be the first to get out the carriage. This circumstance put us in a critical situation. The officers caught sight of the lovely woman, stopped to look, and were the witnesses of a comical spectacle as an endless procession came dragging out of a two-seated carriage, concluding at last with an uhlan muffled in a broad cape.

The evening ended as comically as it had begun: *Fingal* is a first-rate tragedy, but today, toward the end of the last act, an unforeseen incident turned it at once to farce. The actor who usually plays Fingal was ill. His role was given to another, to whom it was still new; he played it tensely and in a rush, but the man who performed Starn was a real Starn! His acting aroused both sympathy and astonishment; it seemed to each of us that we were actually seeing the king and outraged father rather than an actor. It must be assumed that the excellence of his acting embarrassed poor Fingal; he was thrown into confusion! . . . Just as Moina was supposed to run onstage, the flustered Fingal, rushing to seize Oskar's sword, brushed clumsily against Starn somehow and tore off his beard. Instantly the violent wrath of the old tsar died away. The *parterre* burst out laughing, Moina ran on and stopped like a statue, and the curtain came down.[11]

This evening Dolinsky told me that P. had complained to the prince. "Why?" I asked.

"First, because you didn't report to him, and second, because instead of accounts you simply write notes about how much you've taken."

"And what about the prince?"

---

11. Fingal's performance that evening may have been an exploit of A. G. Shchenikov, who was the second juvenile of the Peterburg troupe. P. A. Karatygin noted that Shchenikov's "clumsiness and blundering figure [were] always making the public laugh" (*Zapiski* [Leningrad, 1970], 76).

"It's all right. He didn't say anything."

It could not be otherwise. P.'s complaint is absurd. Apparently no one ever makes out formal accounts of the supplies they have received. And what an odd person he is! How can he fail to understand that he has no right to expect them from an army officer?

I have been ordered to report tomorrow to Staff House at five in the morning.[12] I'll have a fine time trying to get there at night without knowing the way and with nobody to ask. At that hour it is still the dead of night here.

They roused me at four o'clock. I got dressed. "What on earth am I going to do, Uncle? How will I find Staff House? Can't you tell me?"

"Of course I can. Just listen. . . ." And my uncle began telling me in great detail and at length and tried so hard to make the route clear to me that, for exactly that reason, I couldn't understand any of it. I thanked my uncle for his efforts and set out at hazard. Passing the shopping arcades,[13] I decided to cross over and walk under the shelter of the shops, but I no sooner started to step across the rope which stretched their entire length when a dog's dreadful growls stopped me and forced me to jump back into the middle of the street. It would have been quite diverting for me to journey at four in the morning through the empty streets of Peterburg toward a goal I had no idea how to reach, if I were not troubled by the fear of coming late or failing to arrive by the designated hour altogether. From my uncle's entire prolonged narrative, I remembered only that I had to go past the arcades, but after all, they were not endless: where next? I was already approaching the last shop and would have headed directly for the palace, under the assumption that such places as Staff House were surely not far from it and I would be able to find out from a sentry, when the rumble of a *drozhky* made me abandon all such plans at once. It was a cab for hire; I stopped it, and, without waiting for my question, the driver himself asked me, "To Staff House, sir?"

"Yes!"

"If you please, get in. I just took an officer there."

"Go as fast as you can."

And so everything romantic about my voyage in the dead of a December night, through the deserted streets of the vast city, fully armed, trying to find a building to which I didn't know the way—all this instantly vanished, and now I was an ordinary officer rushing in a hired

12. *Ordonans-gauz* [Staff House in German] was the name given the offices of the General Staff, which until the late 1820s were located on the Neva just east of the Hermitage.

13. *Gostinyj dvor.*

*drozhky* to Staff House, the least romantic place in the world, where I would be given some order or other in a dry and peremptory tone of voice.

"Please, make it faster! Is it a long way yet?"

"We're here," said the driver, halting his horse at the portal of a huge building over the doors of which was a black sign with the inscription, *Staff House.* I ran up the stairs and entered an anteroom in which there were quite a few infantry and cavalry officers. An adjutant was sitting at a desk writing something. There was a fire burning in the fireplace, and I sat down beside it to await the outcome. None of the officers were talking to each other; they were all silent, either walking around the anteroom or standing by the fireplace staring pensively at the flames. Suddenly the sleepy scene came to life. Zakrevsky came out.[14] "Gentlemen!" At this word the officers formed ranks. "The cavalry to the front, on the right flank!" At this all four of us—a cuirassier, two dragoons, and one uhlan— went to stand on the right directly facing Zakrevsky. He glanced at me once or twice very attentively while he was giving us his orders: "Report to Arsenev, the commander of the Horse Guards!"

At last it was announced to us in greater detail that in the Horse Guards our soldiers would be outfitted in uniforms with changes of some sort. We listened and left. The cavalrymen went home, and the obedient infantrymen set out directly to see Arsenev. I found this out because at the portal they were agreeing to go there and asked us, "And you gentlemen, are you coming with us?"

"I haven't time today," I replied.

I sent Raczyński to the offices of the Horse Guard to be measured for some sort of new uniform. When he returned, he told me, "Your honor is ordered to report there in person."

"Where?"

"To Major Shaganov, in the tailor shop."

I have had enough of these whims! I had a hard time freeing myself from them. I went to Arsenev's just once and told Shaganov that I would send an uhlan to him, there was no reason at all for me to be present at the time, and I had another commission altogether from my regiment.

And having said this I left.

Tomorrow I am returning to the regiment. My two weeks of leave are over. I spent them tediously: in uniform from morning to night, at attention, saluting, receiving summons to report here and report there. I will never spend a leave like that again!

14. Arsenij Zakrevskij was named Adjutant General of His Majesty's General Staff in 1815.

# Chapter Thirteen

## A Journey to the Izhevsk Munitions Factory

I didn't know how to pass the time of my four-month leave. In provincial towns there are few ways of spending time agreeably, especially during the winter: boston, whist, whist, boston; pie, snacks, snacks, pie—these are the only ways of getting through the idle hour which falls to nearly all of us. None of them suits me: I don't like to play cards, and pies and snacks are good for only half an hour.

I got through a month without boredom, however, while I still had something to tell my father, brother, and sisters and while I still had forest paths to explore, now clambering uphill and now descending into ravines. At last, after I had become familiar with every spot for twenty versts around, talked over everything, the amusing and the scary, the grand and the ridiculous, and even re-read all the horrors of Mrs. Radcliffe, I realized that not just one, but all of my hours were becoming idle. My leave had two more months to run, and to leave before they were over would be odd, and a departure from custom as well. And so I decided to ask Papa to permit me to go somewhere for two weeks or so. At the first mention of it, my indulgent father consented. "You have a good idea there, my friend," said Papa. "There's a munitions factory in the neighborhood.[1] Go there. The commander, General Gren, is a good friend of mine. The society there is excellent, made up of educated, well-bred people. They have their own theater and music, and many of them have choice libraries. Go with my blessing. I'll permit you to stay there over the Christmas and New Year's holiday. When do you want to go?"

"Tomorrow, if you'll permit me."

"Certainly, but can you be ready by then? You'll have to get a sleigh; I have nothing roadworthy."

"Kazantsev has one ready; he just recently finished it. I'll buy it."

"What does he want for it?"

"Three hundred rubles."

"Ask them to bring it around; we'll have to look at it."

I sent for the sleigh. It seemed to Papa and me to be worth much more than the price Kazantsev was asking, and I paid for it on the spot.

The next day after breakfast I embraced and kissed all my family in

---

1. The factory at Izhevsk, fifty kilometers northwest of Sarapul, was founded by Andrej Shuvalov in 1760 to produce iron. It became a munitions factory in 1807 and a military facility in 1809.

turn. With emotion I clasped to my breast the hands of the kindest of fathers and kissed them. I said good-bye to everyone once more and jumped into the sleigh.

The *trojka*, which had long been shivering from cold and impatience, reared and tore from the spot as one. The runners screeched, and the sleigh rushed like a whirlwind down a road smoothed and frozen solid by a thirty-degree frost.

It was eleven o'clock when I approached the gates of Colonel Tseddelman's house.[2] He was an old friend of my father. My inquiry as to whether I could stay with them was greeted by joyous shrieks from his wife's two sisters, young girls to whom I took a great fancy. They both leaped out onto the porch, snatched my greatcoat from my shoulders, tossed it into the man-servant's arms, and rushed me inside. It was a quarter of an hour before Tseddelman had a chance to embrace me, ask after my father's health, and offer his cordial hospitality. Natalia and Maria would not let go of me; either they both talked at once or interrupted one another, so I didn't know which to listen to.

"That's enough now! You'll deafen him," said Tseddelman, laughing and attempting to free me from their hands. "Give me a chance to greet him now. . . ."

At last my friends' joyful enthusiasm quieted somewhat; and since they had been at supper when I arrived, they invited me to join them and sat down at the table again. During the meal they took turns telling me about the everyday round of amusements at the factory, the chief of which was theater.

"But who are your actors?" I asked.

"The general's son and many other officals."

"And the ladies, do they act?"

"Not one of them."

"Then who plays the women's parts?"

"Sometimes apprentices; sometimes they choose someone from the general's office."

"And do they act well?"

"Well, it varies. The men's roles are performed very well indeed, because young Gren, Smirnov, and Davydov are actors such as one rarely sees on the stage, even in the capital."

"What sort of plays do they like to put on?"

"Comedies and operas."

"Operas?"

"Yes, and what operas! Such voices! Such music!"

"Honestly, I can't wait to see them. I'm delighted that I decided to come. Do your players perform often?"

2. At night.

"Twice a week."

"And young Gren, is he married?"

"Yes, and to a beauty."

After supper Natalia and her friend still had much more to tell me about various happenings in their little kingdom, but Tseddelman led them both away, saying, "Tomorrow! Leave it for tomorrow, not all at once. Let him see something for himself. . . . I hope you'll be our guest?"

"Until you tire of me."

"In that case you'll spend the rest of your life with us. This is your room. Sleep well."

I remained at the door until Tseddelman and the two girls had crossed the parlor and disappeared into the room opposite. Then I opened the door of my chamber and, expecting to find warmth and light in it, was astonished to find neither one nor the other: the cold of Greenland blew on me through the aperture, and in the darkness only the windows, covered with frost an inch thick, showed white. My consternation was instantly interrupted by the arrival of my servant with a candle in one hand and a brazier in the other.

"Is there really no warmer room? This one might as well be outdoors."

"What's to be done, sir? It's impossible to heat this room. It's always given to guests, not because they want to freeze them, but because it's the most suitable for them: separated from the owners' bedrooms, next to the parlor, with the best furniture and a separate entry. Its only fault is that on a winter night it's as cold as a dog kennel."

Listening to this nonsense from my man, I entered the room. A bed had been made up for me out of wolf and bear hides. The servant put down the brazier, and on it a small bowl of alcohol, which he at once lit. "Now, sir, you'll be warm for at least half an hour. That's long enough to undress and get into bed, and there you'll even be hot among that great pile of furs. . . ." And in fact the air did begin to warm up at once.

I wanted to take a closer look at my couch of wild skins, and, approaching the bed, I was surprised and delighted to see the sweetest little puppy, six weeks old, in the very middle of a wolfhide. He was sleeping, curled up into a ball. I turned to my servant to ask where the pretty little animal had come from, and, from the silly triumphant grin which I remarked on his face, I guessed immediately that it was he who had arranged this surprise for me. "Where did you get him?" I asked.

"On the street. Some boys had tormented him and abandoned him. He was already beginning to freeze and could hardly crawl when I saw him and at once picked him up. If you don't want him, permit me to keep him in my room."

"No, let him stay here with me."

I sent the servant away, undressed, and got into bed, after picking up the sweet little creature, gentle, defenseless, and endowed by nature with a capacity for love that humans, notwithstanding all the subtleties of their sensations, will never attain.

My servant was right when he said that the furs would make me hot. I slept less than half an hour and was awakened by a yelp from the sweet puppy. He had fallen off the bed. I picked him up and put him back under my fur, but it had become unbearably hot for him as well as for me. He crawled out on top, stretching out on the skins and panting despite the extreme cold in the chamber. He was evidently thirsty, and, besides, the warmth of his natural furcoat and that of the hides made his fever unbearable. He would thrash around on the bed, fall off it, and wander about the floor yelping. Each time I got up, felt around under the bed for him, and lay down again. I ended up not at all happy with my acquisition.

In the morning I got dressed in my Lapland, shivering and hurrying faster than I had ever hurried in my life. In five minutes I was fully attired. I snatched up my little comrade and went to join the Tseddelman family. They were already gathered at the tea table.

"How charming he is!" cried the two girls as they caught sight of my little dog. "Where did you get him?" "Did you really bring him with you?" "Why didn't you tell us yesterday?" "Where has he been?"

"This is a homeless orphan. Yesterday he was condemned to death by your street urchins, but fate decreed otherwise, and so he turned up in my bed in the midst of the half-dozen furs of which it is composed."

"Ah, yes, speaking of furs, were you warm enough?"

"Amid the furs, lying down, of course it was not just warm but even sweltering. But there are no words to tell you how it felt when I had to get up and dress—it has to be experienced."

"What? But we ordered your room heated with an alcohol lamp while you were still in bed."

"Well then, evidently I didn't allow them enough time to carry out your order. I never stay in bed once I wake; I get up and dress at once."

Tseddelman brought our idle talk to an end by asking me whether I wanted to go with him to see the general.

"Most willingly, my dear Colonel, let's go!"

"And in the meantime I will take care of your handsome little fellow," said Maria and took the dog from my arms. "He needs a bath," she said as she carried him away.

A sledge was brought, the kind called here *poshevni*, a rather poor vehicle, disagreeable to the eyes, or at least to mine. On the box sat an angry-looking Tatar. He glanced at us both with an expression of hatred. We got in.

"Why is your coachman so gloomy, is he sick?"

"Oh, no, that's just the usual expression of his countenance. He only looks that way, but actually he's a very kind person. I like the Tatars!

They are better folk than ours in many respects. . . ." Tseddelman was off on his hobby-horse; he has a kind of comical partiality for the Tatars and, once he began praising them, was in no hurry to finish his panegyric. In the meantime, we were riding at a very slow trot.

"That well may be, my esteemed Colonel, but why are we going almost at a walk? It is twenty-five degrees below freezing right now, so why can't we order a whirlwind flight instead of this ceremonial pace?"

"What are you saying? God forbid! Sharyn would be in despair, and he simply wouldn't obey. He loves horses more than anyone else in the world."

I said nothing. It was a long distance yet to the general's quarters, and the frost was unbearable. I decided to incite the horses to a run without the consent of Sharyn and Tseddelman. I started to make clicking and smacking noises, the way one usually does to liven up horses. The remedy worked. The horses stepped up to a fast trot, and the outrunner began arching like a hoop and bobbing up and down.

"What's this? What's this? Hold them, Sharyn! Hold them, I say, brother!"

I quit, but when Sharyn reined in the horses I renewed my tactics and achieved the same result.

"I don't understand what's wrong with my horses today! Why are they in such a rush?" said Tseddelman.

Sharyn was irritated and muttered something about a *shajtan*, not in the least suspecting that I was the demon in question. Neither Sharyn nor Tseddelman could hear me urging on their horses: the former was deaf, and the latter too heavily muffled. At last, clicking and smacking, cursing and marveling, frisking and arching, we flew up to the general's front door.

Old Gren received me with great kindness. He is one of those straightforward, indulgent, and at the same time stern men who render useful service to the state in all respects. They usually carry out their duties conscientiously and punctiliously, and they have broad knowledge of their department because they are indefatigable in penetrating every aspect of it. Their subordinates love them because they correct, punish, and reward them paternally; the government respects them because they serve as the solid support of all its dispositions. Old Gren was such a person, and, in addition, he combined with these virtues the qualities of a cordial host of the old school.[3] "Ah, greetings! Greetings, unprecedented guest," he said, embracing me. "Is your father well? Aren't you ashamed of waiting so long to come and see me? Petja! Petja!" he shouted to his son. "What's on tomorrow at the theater?"

"An opera," replied young Gren.

3. *Khlebosol*, a bread-and-salt host.

"Which one?"

"*Miller.*"[4]

"Have all the roles been taken?"

"Yes, they have."

"Too bad! I would like to see you join our troupe," said Gren, turning to me with a wry smile.

I replied that I would be willing to take a part in a comedy.

"Well, that's fine then! What play are we giving on Sunday?"

His son replied that they were performing *The Minor.*[5]

"Oh, there's a large cast in that one! You have a lot to choose from. . . ."

Young Gren very politely invited me to choose any role I wished. "I will order it copied for you, because it has to be memorized before the rehearsal."

I asked which he usually played.

"Kutejkin."

I could not help laughing as I imagined this handsome, stately young officer in a deacon's robes with his hair clubbed on the nape of his neck. "Well, I'll take Pravdin then." It was Gren's turn to laugh.[6]

When I returned to Tseddelman's house, my first concern was to inquire about my foundling. He had become such a charmer after his bath that I wouldn't have recognized him: his coat was long and soft and gleamed as white as snow, except for the ears, which were dark brown. He had a sharp little muzzle, big black eyes, and the rare charm of dark brows as well. They had just that minute taken him out of the furcoat where he had been sleeping all wrapped up; and since he was hot, he opened his little mouth wide to breathe more freely, and his rosy tongue, together with his black eyes, brows, and nose, made him such an enchanting creation that I could not stop admiring him and carried him around with me all day.

"What are you going to name him?" the two girls asked me.

"Cupid, of course. How could I call such a beauty anything else?"

I spent three weeks at Tseddelman's house, and all that time I was his most reliable stove tender. I slept always in the same cold chamber which, since they found it impossible to heat well, they had ceased heating altogether. Naturally, after getting up and getting dressed in the cold, I could never totally warm up all day, and therefore I spent all day

---

4. The performance was of Aleksandr Ablesimov's popular 1779 operetta *Miller, Sorcerer, Cheat and Matchmaker* with music by M. M. Sokolovsky and E. I. Fomin.

5. Denis Fonvizin's famous 1782 play about a domineering lady landowner and her bratty son.

6. Durova chose the role of an upright government official.

making sure that the stoves were well heated and closed while hot. The latter was strictly forbidden by Tseddelman himself; he always felt too warm, although his house was very cold, and even famous for that quality in all the other homes. The fact that his wife and her two sisters went around from morning to night in warm dressing-gowns proved it. It was amusing to watch Tseddelman going from one stove to the next, putting his hand to the damper, exclaiming, "Oh, my God, they're overheating!" and making haste to close it. I followed him around and opened it again immediately. Every evening he reminded the worker to heat less, and every morning the worker received from me a tip for vodka to heat more and, of course, the request and the money prevailed over the threat and the orders. Tseddelman said that he had no idea how to escape the heat, and he couldn't understand what demon possessed the worker who, no matter how he forbade it, heated his stoves not just for dear life, but to death.

During those three weeks, my pup grew a little and became even prettier. He went everywhere with me, of course, except to the theater and the general's house. Then I would entrust him to one of Tseddelman's maids and ask her not to pet or feed him while I was away. I wanted to be the only person with any claim on my Cupid's love, for that love to belong to me alone. I took my own precautions besides to keep my little dog from needing anyone else's indulgence: before leaving the house, I fed him as much as he could eat, played with him, petted him, and finally put him to bed, leaving him to Anisja's care only after he had fallen asleep.

With the end of the holidays, Christmas games, dances, rehearsals, and performances, the time came for me to return home. I fixed tomorrow for the day of my departure and rode over to spend the day with the general. "Why do you want to leave so soon?" the good-natured Gren asked me.

"Papa will be pining to see me after so long."

"Well then, go with God! I can't argue with that."

When we parted, the general added that he wanted to present something to me that he knew I would find very precious. At his orders a servant brought in a beautifully worked steel hammer. "Here it is, Aleksandrov," said the general, handing it to me. "I present you this hammer. You will agree that I couldn't find a more precious gift for you when you learn that it was made for Emperor Alexander—"

Without letting him finish, I seized the hammer, kissed it, and pressed it to my breast. "There are no words to express my gratitude to you for such a gift."

"Wouldn't you like to know how this object missed its purpose and, made for the mightiest of monarchs, now comes to his *protégé?*"

"Be so good as to explain, please. You are more gracious to me than I deserve, General."

"Well then, listen. His Majesty the Emperor decided to inspect all our factories. On these occasions the exalted visitor is usually shown all aspects of the work and takes a hand in carrying it out. We made the hammer for the emperor to use in striking a few blows to a red-hot bar of iron. Afterwards the hammer is stamped with a notation of the occasion and date, and it is then preserved for all times to come as a souvenir of the visit and the labor of the Most August Father of Russia. But since this hammer did not come out as well as it should have, I ordered a second one made, and so I had this one lying around until it came at last into the hands of a person whose love for our father the tsar is incomparably greater than anyone else's."

I thanked the general once again for the gift, the story, and his cordial hospitality and paternal love for me and bade him farewell—I have to assume, forever.

I found Papa busy dispatching the mail, and, although I knew that he didn't like being bothered just then, I couldn't resist laying the hammer down in front of him. Papa started from the unexpectedness of it and would have lost his temper, but, seeing that it was I, he contented himself by saying merely, "Eh, Uhlan, when will you ever learn? Is startling your old father a proper thing to do?"

"I never thought of that, Papa dear. On the contrary, I wanted to make you happy. Do you know what hammer this is?"

"You'll tell me later. I haven't the time to listen to you now. Go see your sister. . . ." I started out. "And take your hammer with you."

"No, Papa, let it lie there in front of you. It's precious! You'll find that out later."

Papa waved his hand, and I ran off with my Cupid to visit my sister and at once put him in her lap.

"Oh, how charming! What a pretty little dog! It must be a gift for me," said Kleopatra, petting the enchanting Cupid.

"No, sister dear, forgive me! I wouldn't give him up to anyone for anything in the world. He's going back to the regiment with me."

"You can't do that!"

"I can, and I will."

"Well then, take him away. There's no reason to show affection to anything that's not to be mine."

"Yes, and I don't advise it anyway; I'll be jealous."

"From you that's no novelty. You always want exclusive attachments."

"And who doesn't?"

My sister remained silent and a little sulky. I picked up my dog and went to my own room to await the end of Papa's bothersome business.

When he heard the story of the hammer, Papa took it for himself, saying that it was too precious an object for him to permit me to drag it about everywhere; he would keep it. I had to submit. I stroked once more the gleaming, smoothly polished handle which had once had such a lofty destiny, handed it to my father, and told him that I was very pleased to see it in his possession.

I get more attached to Cupid with every passing day. And how could I not love him? Meekness has an unconquerable power over our hearts even in an ugly animal, so how is it when the nicest, most faithful, and best of them looks into your eyes with meek humility, follows your every impulse, exists only for you, cannot be without you for even a minute, and would give his life for you? Even if you are unjust to him, thrash him for nothing, cruelly, even inhumanly, he will lie at your feet, lick them, and without the least resentment of your cruelty, wait only for a kind glance to throw himself into your arms, embrace you with his little paws, lick you, caper. Oh, best and most unhappy of animals! You are the only one who loves the way that we have all been ordained to love, and you are the one who suffers most from the blatant injustices people can inflict. There are actually men who, suspecting that their food has been poisoned, give that food to the dog to eat in order to confirm it. A dog grows old in his master's house, serving him in the way prescribed by nature; he exchanges it for a young one. And what does the man who took it in exchange do? He kills it, of course, for the hide! A *borzoj* is not a good hunter; hang it! And why is all this, why? The miserable lot of the dog has become proverbial, albeit it alone of all animals loves man. That noble beast, the horse, will smash its rider's skull with the greatest indifference; a cat will scratch his eyes out; a bull will never miss a chance to toss him on his horns, no matter how well he has been fed and petted. Only that peerless friend of mankind, the dog, for a stale crust of bread will remain faithful and devoted to the death. There have been occasions when, through some madness I cannot myself understand, I have punished my meek, forgiving Cupid. The poor little thing! How he wound himself around my feet, lying down, crawling, and at last sitting up on his hind legs and fixing his handsome black eyes on me with such an expression of submission and sorrow that I was nearly in tears as I reproached myself for my injustice. I took him in my lap, stroked him, kissed him, and he immediately began playing again. I was never parted from my Cupid even for a minute. No matter where I was, he always either lay beside me on the floor or sat on the windowsill, on a chair, on a sofa, but without fail next to me and without fail on something belonging to me, for example, a handkerchief, gloves, or even my greatcoat. Otherwise he was not at peace.

One day I let him outside at dawn, expecting him to ask to come back in. When a quarter of an hour passed without his returning, I became very uneasy and went looking for him in the yard. He was nowhere to be found; I called him, no answer! Mortally alarmed, I sent a man out looking for him in the streets. A full hour passed in tormenting anticipation and vain searches. At last my little dog came and sat outside the gates. I heard his bark, looked out the window, and could not help laughing when I saw him, howling like a fully grown dog with his little muzzle pointing upward. But how dearly I paid for that laughter! My heart even now suffuses with blood at the memory of that howl. It was a presentiment. . . . I brought my runaway inside and, seeing that he was all damp from the dew, set him down on a pillow and covered him with my *arkhalukh*. 7 He fell asleep at once, but alas! his evil fate was wakeful. An hour later I got dressed and decided to go for my customary walk. Something told me I should go alone. But when do we ever listen to mysterious warnings? They are always so quiet, so gentle. I took the *arkhalukh* off my sleeping dog, "Let's go for a walk, Cupid." Cupid jumped up and began frisking. As we set out, he ran ahead of me.

An hour later I was carrying him, and he was pale and trembling in all his limbs. He was still breathing, but how? The breath was passing through two broad wounds inflicted by the fangs of a monstrous dog. Cupid died in my arms. . . . Since then I have often had occasion to dance all night and to laugh a lot, but there has never been any genuine merriment in my soul; it was buried in the grave of my Cupid. Many will find this odd or perhaps even worse than odd. Be that as it may, the death of my little friend can still force involuntary tears from my eyes amid the merriest of gatherings. I cannot forget him.

I am leaving today. As we parted, Papa said to me, "Isn't it time for you to be quitting the sword? I'm old; I need peace and quiet and someone to take over the household. Think about it."

The suggestion frightened me. I thought that I would never have to quit the sword, and especially not at my age; what will I do at home, condemned so early to the monotony of domestic occupations? But my father wants it that way. His old age! Oh, what else can I do? I will have to bid it all farewell: the gleaming sword and the good steed . . . my friends . . . the merry life . . . drill, parades, mounted formations . . . the full gallop and the clash of swords—all of it will come to an end. It will all fade away as if it had never been, and only unforgettable memories

---

7. A long belted tunic or caftan. The word is of Turkic origin.

will accompany me to the wild banks of the Kama, to the place where I spent my blighted childhood, where I worked out my extraordinary plan. . . .

To past happiness, glory, danger, uproar, glitter, and a life of ebullient activity—*farewell!*

# Documents Relating to Durova's Commission in the Mariupol' Hussars

1. General-of-Infantry Count Buxhöwden's report to Alexander I, dated November 29, 1807, read as follows:

> In fulfillment of the exalted will of Your Imperial Majesty as it was communicated to me by Acting State Counselor Popov, I sent for the recruit Aleksandr Sokolov who is serving in the Polish Horse regiment and dispatched him with Your Majesty's Aide-de-camp Zass. With this I present the official service record which was sent to me from the regiment and most respectfully inform Your Imperial Majesty that the outstanding conduct of Sokolov and the zealous performance of his duties from the day of his enlistment have won for him the complete loyalty and consideration of all his commanders as well as his fellow soldiers. The chief of the regiment himself, Major-General Kachowski, praising his willingness to serve and the diligence and promptness with which he carried out all the tasks at hand while taking part in many battles with the French army, earnestly requests that he be left in the regiment as the kind of noncommissioned officer who gives every hope of becoming with time a very good officer; in addition Sokolov himself has expressed a most decided desire to remain always in the army. [1]

2. When Durova's father received her letter telling him "where I am and what I have become" (chap. 2), he wrote to his brother Nikolaj in Peterburg on August 27, 1807, for help in locating and retrieving her. After relating the details of his wife's death, Durov continued:

> . . . For God's sake, find out about Nadezhda and inform her about it; she will probably come home, let [nezamaj] her be a mother to the children and a friend to me; I love her dearly. That's the news I have for you which has put me in extreme grief; I don't know when I shall be at peace again, but now it's all extremely painful. Time, of course, will bury it all in oblivion, but the memory of her will be eternal. Goodbye, probably you

---

1. The document was reprinted from War Ministry archives in Saks (17).

too will shed a sentimental tear for her. Your brother N.*[sic]* Durov. P. S.
I really would like to know about Nadezhda.

3. On September 28, 1807, Nikolaj Durov submitted a petition asking
Alexander I for aid in locating his niece:

> Collegiate Assessor Durov residing in Vjatka province in the city of
> Sarapul is searching everywhere for his daughter Nadezhda, by marriage
> Chernova, who, due to family dissensions, was compelled to slip away
> from her home and kin, and from whom there was a letter from Grodno
> that she, having enrolled under the name of Aleksandr Vasilev son of
> Sokolov in the mounted Polish regiment, is serving as a recruit and was
> in many battles with the enemy.
>
> Her father and his brother who lives in Saint Petersburg as humble
> subjects request an imperial command ordering the restoration to them
> of this unhappy woman.[2]

4. A month after Alexander I granted Durova her commission, Andrej
Durov wrote to the emperor's counselor Count Lieven in February 1808
as follows:

> My daughter, who spent some time in Peterburg under the name of
> Aleksandr Sokolov, while unfortunately serving as a recruit in the Polish
> Horse Regiment, informs me by letter that I can address myself directly to
> you, which I so do, most humbly begging you, first, to take me and all my
> poor family under your protection and, then, also my unhappy friend
> Sokolov or I don't know what name he is using now.
>
> I beg Your Honor to heed the voice of nature and take pity on an
> unhappy father who served for some twenty years as an officer in the army
> and then has continued in the civil service likewise for more than twenty
> years, who lost his wife or, better, his best friend and [was] putting his
> hopes on Sokolov that at least he would delight my old age and restore
> tranquillity to the bosom of my family; but it all came out otherwise: he
> writes that he is continuing to serve, not explaining in his letter where.
> Can you not be so gracious as to inform me with your most estimable
> information where and in what regiment, and can I hope soon to see her
> at home as the mistress of my household. This favor from you will
> redouble my patience, and I make so bold as to ask you to [let me] write
> to Sokolov sometimes; he assured me that you would furnish him my
> letters. Oh, how grateful I will be to you, my father, for this, and then
> honor me with your gracious answer!

2. Both documents are translated from Murzakevich.

5. Lieven passed this letter from Durova's father to Arakcheev, the newly appointed War Minister, on February 21, 1808:

> Count Aleksej Andreevich! His Majesty the Emperor has deigned to order me to notify Your Excellency, for your information alone, that the daughter of Collegiate Assessor Andrej Durov last year, 1807, concealing her sex, enlisted as a soldier in the Polish Uhlan Regiment under the name of Sokolov and served throughout the last campaign with distinction, for which he was promoted to sergeant and awarded the order of St. George. Her uncle, collegiate counselor Nikolaj Durov, who is here in Peterburg, discovered her secret and asked that she be released from military service; as a result of this, by the emperor's order, she was brought here; but inasmuch as she announced in person to His Majesty her desire to continue to serve, she was placed in the Mariupol' Hussar Regiment as a cornet under the name of Aleksandrov in order to conceal her present situation so that her relatives do not know about this post; she was discharged from the Polish Uhlans.
>
> Upon her departure she asked me to intercede with His Majesty for her father who serves as mayor of the town of Sarapul in Vjatka province.
>
> When I recently received the enclosed letter from him and brought it to the attention of His Majesty, the emperor ordered me to deliver the letter to Your Excellency with the above explanation.[3]

3. This letter and Durov's above were both first printed in: "N. D.," *Golos* (December 31, 1863).

# Hussar Poet Denis Davydov's Recorded Comments on Durova

Davydov read the "Notes of N. A. Durova" in Pushkin's magazine *The Contemporary* and wrote his friend on August 10, 1836:

> . . . I knew Durova, because I served with her in the rear-guard all during our retreat from the Neman to Borodino. The regiment in which she served was always in the rear-guard along with our Akhtyrsk Hussars. I remember that there was talk at the time that Aleksandrov was a woman, but only in passing. She was very solitary and avoided our company as much as one can on bivouac. On one halt I happened to enter a cottage along with an officer named Volkov from the regiment in which Aleksandrov was serving. We wanted to slake our thirst with milk in the cottage (it's clear how bad things were if we had to resort to milk—there was not a drop of liquor to be had). There we found a young uhlan officer who, as soon as he caught a glimpse of me, got up, bowed, picked up his shako, and left in a hurry. Volkov said to me, "That's Aleksandrov who they say is a woman." I rushed out onto the porch—but she had already galloped away. Afterwards I saw her at the front, on vedette, in a word, in all the difficult duties of the time, but I didn't pay much attention to her; there was no time to worry about whether she was of male or female gender. That grammatical category was forgotten about then.

> In her notes there are a few contradictions and oversights. For example: 1) She tells Kutuzov that she was already serving during the Prussian war, distinguished herself, and that Count Buxhöwden noticed her bravery, and in your foreword to her notes you say that she joined the service in 1808. Either the one or the other is incorrect. The Prussian war began in December 1806 and went on until June 8, 1807, but Count Buxhöwden was called away at the beginning of it and would hardly have seen action personally. A corps of his was in action, Dokhturov's corps at Golomin, no more. If Bennigsen noticed her bravery, that's different, but even in this case she would have had to join the service in 1806 and not 1808.

> 2) In the *Notes* it is said that the brigade commander of the Lithuanian Uhlans and Novorossijsk Dragoons was General K[rejts]; that's not true—it was Major-General Count Sievers.

3) She says on page 60: "and I myself went uphill to the walls of the monastery in order to relieve the main vedette." Miss Cornet Aleksandrov can be called a fool for placing a vedette *in the nighttime on a hill.* Nocturnal vedettes stand downhill, keeping the hill in front of them. However dark the sky in the nighttime may be, it is still lighter than the hill itself and any person or horse who goes to the top of it, and therefore the person or horse or whatever would immediately stand out in outline against the background of the lesser darkness. [C'est] l'*a, b, c,* du metier des Cosaques. . . .

On October 13, Davydov again wrote Pushkin. He reported that he had found out more about Durova while he was hunting with an old commander of his, Dmitrij Beketov, in Penza province:

> . . . the subject of Durova came up, and he told me the reason for her chivalry. Beketov was the friend of a lieutenant in the Lithuanian Uhlans, Grigorij Schwartz (whom I knew well and who is now a major-general). This Schwartz previously served on the General Staff and went on a surveying expedition to Kazan' province. Durova fell in love with him, and, when he was transferred to the Don, she ran away from her father's house to follow him. Unfortunately for her, Schwartz was then transferred to the Lithuanian Uhlans, who were then stationed in Volhynia. She galloped off to Volhynia and by the time she got to Berdichev had spent all her money and was faced with death by starvation. At that time the Mariupol' Hussars were recruiting (they were then a recruited regiment) and she put on men's clothing and joined the hussars in order to keep from starving. Only after she had served for a few months as a hussar did she find out the location of the Lithuanian Uhlans and obtain a transfer into it. These were her first adventures. . . .[1]

The Cavalry Maiden had not yet been published in full when Davydov transmitted this gossip to Pushkin and he had no way of knowing how badly it matched Durova's own account and the documented record of her service.

1. A. S. Pushkin, *Perepiska*, vol. 2 (Moscow, 1982), 482–83, 486.

# Selective Bibliography of Works by and about Durova

ABBREVIATIONS USED

Russian journals of the 1830s in which Durova published her works:

BdCh—*Biblioteka dlja chtenija* [The Reader's Library]
OZ—*Otechestvennye zapiski* [Notes of the Fatherland]
LP—*Literaturnye pribavlenija k* Russkomu Invalidu [Literary Supplement to the *Russian Veteran*]
SO—*Syn otechestva* [Son of the Fatherland]
Sov—*Sovremennik* [The Contemporary]
SP—*Severnaja pchela* [The Northern Bee]

Popular pre-revolutionary history journals in which articles about Durova appeared:

IV—*Istoricheskij vestnik* [Historical Herald]
KS—*Kievskaja starina* [Kievan Antiquity]
RA—*Russkij arkhiv* [Russian Archive]
RS—*Russkaja starina* [Russian Antiquity]

Miscellaneous:

PR—*Povesti i rasskazy* [Short Fiction]
PSS—*Polnoe sobranie sochinenij* [Complete Works]
Soch.—*Sochinenija* [Works]

Asterisks indicate items I have been unable to verify.

## WORKS BY DUROVA

In the works Durova published in her lifetime, her pseudonym varied from work to work but always included her tsar-granted male name or the appellation "Cavalry Maiden": "Aleksandrov," "A. Aleksandrov," "Aleksandrov (Devitsa-kavalerist), Al. Andr.," "Aleksandrov (Devitsa-kavalerist)," "Aleksandrov (N. Durova)," "Devitsa-kavalerist," "Kavalerist-devitsa."

"Zapiski" [Notes]. *Sov.* 1836. Vol. 2, 53–132.
about: V. Belinskij. *PSS*. Vol. 2. Moscow, 1953. 236.
       *Russkij invalid.* 1836. No. 274.*

*Kavalerist-devitsa: Proisshestvie v Rossij* [The Cavalry Maiden: It Happened in Russia]. 2 parts. St. Petersburg, 1836.

233

about: A. Pushkin. *Sov.* 1836. Vol. 4, 503.
   *SO.* 1837. Vol. 183, crit., 208–14.

"Elena, T-skaja krasavitsa" [Elena, the Beauty of T.]. *BdCh.* 1837. Vol. 23. bk. 1; also in revised form as "Igra sud'by." *PR.* 1839.

*God zhizni v Peterburge, ili Nevygody tret'ego poseshchenija* [A Year of Life in Peterburg, or The Disadvantages of the Third Visit]. St. Petersburg, 1838; reprinted in *Zapiski* 1960–1979.
about: P. A. Pletnev. *Soch.* St. Petersburg, 1885. Vol. 2, 267–68.
   *SO.* 1838. No. 6, sec. 4, 57–60.
   F. Bulgarin. *SP.* 1838, 10 Nov. 1019.
   *BdCh.* 1838. Vol. 31, sec. 6, 60.

"Nekotorye cherty iz detskikh let" [A Few Traits from Childhood Years]. *LP.* 1838. Nos. 41, 44*; *Zapiski.* 1839. 1–46; reprinted as "Detskie leta moi." In *Izbrannoe.* 1984. 64–104.
about: Belinskij. *PSS.* Vol. 3. Moscow, 1953. 149.

"Graf Mavritsij" [Count Mauritius]. *BdCh.* 1838. Vol. 27.2, 169–92; excerpts differing from the journal text appeared in *Zapiski.* 1839. 103–10.

"Pavil'on." *OZ.* 1839. Vol. 2, sec. 3, 2–138; reprinted in *Izbrannoe.* 1984. Durova printed the frame-tale in expanded form in *Zapiski.* 1839. 213–68; the body of the story appeared as "Ljudgarda" in *PR.* 1839.
about: N. Polevoj. *SO.* 1839. No. 2, sec. 4, 37.
   V. Belinskij. *PSS.* Vol. 3. Moscow, 1953. 149–57.

"Dva slova iz zhitejskogo slovarja: I. Bal; II. Vospominanija" [Two Words from a Dictionary of Everyday Life: I. A Ball; II. Reminiscences]. *OZ.* 1839. Vol. 7, *misc.*, 38–52.

"Sernyj kljuch" [Sulphur Spring]. In *Sto russkikh literatorov* [100 Russian Writers]. St. Petersburg. 1839*; also appeared as "Cheremiska." *PR.* 1839; and in *Zapiski.* 1960–1979.
about: *SO.* 1839. No. 2, sec. 4, 123.

*Zapiski Aleksandrova (Durovoj). Dobavlenie k "Devitse-kavalerist"* [Notes of Aleksandrov-Durova: Addendum to "The Cavalry Maiden"]. Moscow, 1839; reprint: University Microfilms, Ann Arbor, MI (on demand).
about: V. G. Belinskij. *PSS.* Vol. 3. Moscow, 1953. 148–57.
   *LP.* 1839. No. 1, 11.*
   *SO.* 1839. No. 8, sec. 4, 87–89.
   *SP.* 1839, 21 March. 231.
   *OZ.* 1839. Vol. 2, sec. 7, 139–40.

*Gudishki [Hooters].* Novel in 4 pts. St. Petersburg, 1839.
about: *SP.* 1839, 5 Aug.
   *BdCh.* 1839. Vol. 35, "Lit. letopis'," 1–2.
   *OZ.* 1839. Vol. 4, sec. 7, 95–98.
   *SO.* 1839. No. 9, sec. 4, 142–43.

*Povesti i rasskazy* [Short Fiction]. 4 parts. St. Petersburg, 1839:
1. "Nurmeka. Proisshestvie sluchivsheesja v tsarstvovanii Ioanna Vas. Groznogo, vskore posle pokorenija Kazani" [Nurmeka. An Occurrence in the Reign of Ivan the Terrible, Soon After the Conquest of Kazan'].
2. "Igra sud'by, ili Protivuzakonnaja ljubov'. Istinnoe proisshestvie, sluchivsheesja no rodine avtora" [Plaything of Fate, or Illicit Love. A True Occurrence in the Author's Native Land]. (See "Elena..." above.)
3. "Ljudgarda, knjazhna Gota. Rasskaz unter-ofitsera Rudzikogo" [Ljudgarda, Princess of Gotha. A Story Told by Sergeant Rudzikovskij]. (See also "Pavil'on" above.)
4. "Cheremiska. Rasskaz ispravnitsy Lizovetskoj" [The Cheremys Girl. A Story Told by Commissioner's Wife Lizovetskaja]. (See "Sernij Kljuch" above.)
about: OZ. 1839. Vol. 6, sec. 7, 23–26.
SP. 1839, 5 Aug.

*Klad* [Treasure Trove]. St. Petersburg, 1840.
about: V. Belinskij. *PSS*. Vol. 4. Moscow, 1954. 382–83.
P. A. Pletnev. *Soch*. St. Petersburg, 1885. Vol. 2, 303
SO. 1840. No. 5, sec. 6, 253–57.
BdCh. 1840. Vol. 42, sec. 6, 24–27.

*Ugol* [The Nook]. St. Petersburg, 1840.
about: V. Belinskij. *PSS*. Moscow, 1954. Vol. 4, 308–09.
BdCh. 1840. Vol. 42, sec. 6, 24–27.
P. A. Pletnev. *Soch*. St. Petersburg, 1885. Vol. 2, 301–302.

*Jarchuk: Sobaka-dukhovidets* [Jarchuk: The Dog Who Saw Ghosts]. St. Petersburg, 1840.
about: V. Belinskij. Vol. 4. *PSS*. Moscow, 1954. 315–18.
P. A. Pletnev. *Soch*. St. Petersburg, 1885. Vol. 2, 303–304.
BdCh. 1840. Vol. 42, sec. 6, 24–27.
Majak. 1840. No. 12, 199.

Untitled, unpublished article. 1858. In the archive of M. P. Pogodin, Lenin Library; cited by Smirenskii, xxiii. (See Introduction, p. 34.)

*Zapiski kavalerist-devitsy* [Diaries of the Cavalry-Maiden]. St. Petersburg, 1912.*

*Zapiski kavalerist-devitsy*. Kazan', 1960, 1966, 1979. Partial edition of *Kavalerist-devitsa*. 1836, plus "God zhizni . . . ," "Sernyj kljuch," and autobiographical materials.
about 1979 edition: James J. Gebhard, *Slavic and East European Journal*. Spring 1981. 96–98.

*Zapiski kavalerist-devitsy*. Moscow, 1962. Contents the same as the Kazan' editions above.

"Vse, chto ja mog pripomnit': Avtobiografija N. A. Durovoj" [All That I Could Recollect: The Autobiography of N. A. Durova]. *Nedelja*. 1962. No. 26, 7; also in *Izbrannoe*. 1984.

*Izbrannye sochinenija kavalerist-devitsy.* Moscow, 1983. The first reprinting of the complete *The Cavalry Maiden* in the Soviet Union. *

*Izbrannoe.* Moscow, 1984. An edition of the 1960–1979 text of the *The Cavalry Maiden* expanded to include excerpts from her description of the Russian retreat in the summer of 1812; "Pavil'on" (*OZ* text); and "Avtobiografija" ("Vse, chto ja mog pripomnit'", 1962).
about: M. Korallov, *Novyj mir.* 1985. No. 7, 263–64.

Durova, Nadezhda, *Kavalerist-devitsa. Proisshestvie v Rossii.* Leningrad, 1985. 272–502. The complete 1836 text, in a single volume with: Denis Davydov, *Dnevnik partizanskikh dejstvij 1812 g.* [Diary of Partisan Actions in 1812]. Edited, introduced, and annotated by L. I. Emel'janov.

WORKS POSSIBLY BY DUROVA (SEE AFANAS'EV. *IZBRANNOE.* 25–26.)

"Vechera g-zhi Ladinoj." *LP.* 1834. No. 26. *

*Stikhotvorenija.* Moscow, 1859 (published under the name of an otherwise unknown "Aleksandrov"). *

TRANSLATIONS

"My Childhood Years." Translated and with an introduction by Mary Fleming Zirin. In *The Female Autograph (New York Literary Forum 12–13).* 1984. 119–41; Paperback reprint: University of Chicago. 1987.

WORKS ABOUT DUROVA

This bibliography includes every substantive work about Durova I have found listed in standard sources, but it is by no means exhaustive.

*Biographical materials:*

Afanas'ev, V. A. "'Divnyj phenomen nravstennogo mira . . .'" In Durova. *Izbrannoe.* 1984. 5–28.
Bjuler, F. "Zapiska A. S. Pushkina k Kavalerist-devitse N. A. Durovoj." *RA.* 1872. Cols. 199–204.
———— "N. V." "Iz zapisnoj knizhki." *KS.* 1886. No. 2, 398–402.
Blinov, N. "'Kavalerist-devitsa' i Durovy: (Iz Sarapul'skoj khroniki)." *IV.* 1888. No. 2, 414–20.
Broch, Ingvild. "Nadežda Andr. Durova: Forfatterinne og offiser i tsarens haer." *Edda.* 1978. 23–31.
Burnashev-"Bajdarov," V. P. *Kavalerist-devitsa Aleksandrov-Durova.* St. Petersburg, 1887.
"D. K. Z." "K portretu N. A. Durovoj." *IV.* 1901, Sept. 1036–41.
Grossman, L., ed. *Pis'ma zhenshchin k Pushkinu.* Moscow, 1928. 118–28, 242–48.
Heldt, Barbara. "Nadezhda Durova: Russia's Cavalry Maid." *History Today.* 1983, Feb. 24–27.

————. *Terrible Perfection: Women and Russian Literature*. Bloomington: Indiana University Press, 1987.

Judin, P. "K rodoslovnoj devitsy-kavalerista Durovoj." *IV*. 1898. No. 1, 413–14.

Judina, I. "Zhenshchina—voin i pisatel'nitsa: Neizvestnye avtografy *Kavalerist-devitsy* N. A. Durovoj." *Russkaja literatura*. 1963. No. 2, 131–35.

Klimentovskij, V. A. *Russkie pisateli v Tatarskoj ASSR*. Kazan', 1951. 147–69. *

Kutshe, N. I. "Durov-Aleksandrov (Biograficheskaja zametka)." *IV*. 1894. No. 3, 788–93.

————. "K otkrytiju pamjatnika Durovoj-Aleksandrovu." *IV*. 1901. No. 12, 1117–23.

Lashmanov, F. F. "Nadezhda Andreevna Durova: Materialy k ee biografii." *RS*. 1890. No. 9, 657–63.

Men'shov, E. "Vesti iz Elabugi: Moe znakomstvo c devitseju-kavaleristom Nad. Andr. Durovoj -otstavnym shtabs-rotmistrom Aleksandrovym." *Peterburgskij vestnik*. 1861. No. 3, 64–65.

Mordovtsev, D. "Nadezhda Andreevna Durova (Kavalerist-devitsa)." In *Russkie zhenshchiny novogo vremeni: Zhenshchiny devjatnadsatogo veka*. St. Petersburg, 1874. 97–150.

Murzakevich, N. N. "Devitsa-kavalerist." *RA*. 1872. Col. 2043.

"N. D." "K biografii 'Devitsy-kavalerista': Perepiska o vstuplenii ee v voennuju sluzhbu." *Golos*. 1863. No. 346.

Nekrasova, E. "Nadezhda Andreevna Durova (Psevdonimy: Devitsa-Kavalerist, Aleksandrov), 1783–1866." *IV*. 1890. No. 9, 585–612.

Pushkin, A. S., "Zapiski N. A. Durovoj." *Sov*. 1836. Vol. 2, 53–54.

————. "Table-Talk (36): O Durove." 1835, 3 Oct. *PSS*, Moscow-Leningrad, 1937–1959. Vol. 12, 167–68.

————. *Perepiska*. Moscow, 1982. Vol. 2, 482–83, 486, 490–505.

Saks, A. *Kavalerist-devitsa. Shtabs-rotmistr A. A. Aleksandrov (Nadezhda Andreevna Durova)*. St. Petersburg, 1912.

*Sankt-Peterburgskie vedomosti*. 1866, May 10. [Obituary.]

Smirenskij, B. V. "Nadezhda Durova. *Zapiski kavalerist-devitsy*." In *Zapiski kavalerist-devitsy*. Kazan', 1960. iii–xxiv.

————. "Geroinja russkogo naroda." In *Zapiski kavalerist-devitsy*. Moscow, 1962. 5–24.

Veresaev, V. "Nadezhda Andreevna Durova (1793–1866)." *Sputniki Pushkina*. Moscow, 1937. Vol. 2, 322–29.

"Vnuchka I. I. i E. G. Aleksandrovichej." *Storozhenki: Famil'nyj arkhiv*. Vol. 8. Kiev, 1910. 35–38. *

*Encyclopedia and bibliographic sources:*

Cherejskij, L. A. *Pushkin i ego okruzhenie*. Leningrad, 1975. 138.

*Entsiklopedija Brokgauz i Efron*. Vol. 11. St. Petersburg, 1893. 247–48.

Golitsyn, N. N. *Biograficheskij slovar' russkikh pisatel'nits*. St. Petersburg, 1889 (reprint: Leipzig, 1974). 88–89.

*Kratkaja literaturnaja entsiklopedija*, Vol. 2. Moscow, 1964. Cols. 822–23.

Mez'er, A. V. *Russkaja slovesnost' XI po XIX stoletij vkljuchitel'no*. St. Petersburg, 1899. Vol. 2, 12–13 [under "Aleksandrov"].

*Modern Encyclopedia of Russian and Soviet Literatures.* Harry B. Weber, ed. Vol. 6. Gulf Breeze, FL: Academic International Press, 1982. 96–98.

Muratova, Ks. D., ed. *Istorija russkoj literatury XIX v.: Bibliograficheskij ukazatel'.* Moscow-Leningrad, 1962. 320–21.

*Russkij arkhiv.* 1868. No. 12. Cols. 2009–10.

*Russkij biograficheskij slovar'.* Vol. 6. St. Petersburg, 1906. 722–26.

*Voennaja entsiklopedia,* Vol. 9. St. Petersburg, 1912. 243–44.

*Fictional portrayals:*

Bogatyrev, A. *Nadezhda Durova.* 1957 [opera]. *

Borisova, L. and M. Nikol'skaja. *Kamskij najdenysh.* Moscow, 1942.

Churilova-"Charskaja," L. A. *Smelaja zhizn': Podvigi zagadochnogo geroja (Istoricheskaja povest').* Moscow, 1908; 2d ed., 1910.

Dmitriev, D. S. *Kavalerist-devitsa: Istoricheskaja povest'.* Moscow, 1898. *

Glebov, Aleksandr. "Devitsa-voin." *Majak.* 1840. No. 8, 27–28 [poem].

"Kal'ma, N." *Devitsa-Kavalerist.* Moscow, 1942.

Lipskerov, K., and A. Kochetkov. *Nadezhda Durova.* Moscow-Leningrad, 1942 [play].

Mordovtsev, D. *Dvenadtsatyj god.* [n.p.], 1885. *

Osetrov. *Dvenadtsadyj god. Kavalerist-devitsa.* 1887 [play]. *

Rykachev, Ja. *Nadezhda Durova.* Moscow, 1942.

# Index of Historical Persons
# and Places Known to Durova